Political Economy of Development in the Global South Post-COVID-19 Pandemic

Hebatallah Adam · Ravinder Rena
Editors

Political Economy of Development in the Global South Post-COVID-19 Pandemic

Springer

Editors
Hebatallah Adam
Jindal School of International Affairs
O.P. Jindal Global University
Sonipat, Haryana, India

Ravinder Rena
Faculty of Management Sciences
Durban University of Technology
Durban, South Africa

ISBN 978-981-99-4073-8 ISBN 978-981-99-4074-5 (eBook)
https://doi.org/10.1007/978-981-99-4074-5

This Springer imprint is published by the registered company Springer Nature Singapore Pte Ltd.
The registered company address is: 152 Beach Road, #21-01/04 Gateway East, Singapore 189721, Singapore

Preface

The COVID-19 pandemic has had a devastating impact on the Global South, with developing countries bearing the brunt of economic, social, and health-related consequences. Understanding the political economy of development in the Global South is crucial for ensuring equitable and sustainable recovery as the world deals with the economic implications of the pandemic. This book offers a comprehensive analysis of the political economy of development in the Global South post the COVID-19 pandemic. It examines the challenges facing developing countries in terms of economic growth, poverty reduction, and social development, as well as new strategies for promoting economic recovery and development. In addition, it explores the role of international institutions, such as the World Bank and the International Monetary Fund, in providing financial assistance to developing nations.

This book offers an in-depth analysis of the geopolitical, economic, and social developments that are influencing and challenging development in the Global South in the post-COVID-19 pandemic era. It is an invaluable resource for anyone interested in understanding the political economy of development in the Global South. It provides a comprehensive overview of the challenges facing developing countries and offers valuable insights into the potential solutions that can be implemented to foster economic recovery and development. The chapters of this book examine the structural challenges and new challenges Southern countries face on their path to sustainable development. Policy suggestions for economies in the Global South to reach the SDGs and recover from the post-COVID-19 pandemic crisis are also proposed by the contributors. The book's distinctiveness resides in the way it connects theory and praxis with the past, future, and many facets of the political economy of the Global South.

We highly recommend this book to anyone interested in the political economy of development in the Global South post-COVID-19 pandemic. It is an essential resource for policymakers, researchers, and students alike.

Prof. (Dr.) Hebatallah Adam
Associate Professor of Economics
Assistant Dean for Academic Affairs (JSIA)
Founder and Director of Jindal Centre for the Global South, Jindal School of International Affairs (JSIA)
O.P. Jindal Global University
Haryana, India

Prof. (Dr.) Ravinder Rena
Professor of Economics
Durban University of Technology
ML Sultan Campus
Durban, South Africa

Introduction

The Global South is a term used to refer to the countries of the world that are considered to be developing or underdeveloped. These countries are typically located in the Southern Hemisphere and include nations in Africa, Latin America, and Asia. Poverty, inequality, and inadequate access to services are just a few of the many defining features of the Global South. These countries often have limited access to education, healthcare, and other essential services. Many of these nations also suffer from inadequate or lacking infrastructure, making it tough for both firms and individuals to meet their basic needs. The lack of political and economic power is another feature of the Global South. Many of these countries are heavily dependent on foreign aid and investment and often lack the resources to develop their economies. This lack of economic power makes it difficult for these countries to improve their living standards and reduce poverty to meet the 2030 Global Agenda. Lack of access to technology and modern infrastructure is another hallmark of the Global South. They are hampered in their efforts to compete economically on a global scale because they are unable to take advantage of cutting-edge developments in technology.

The COVID-19 pandemic has had a devastating impact on the Global South, with the most vulnerable countries and communities bearing the brunt of economic and social consequences. In the aftermath of the pandemic, it is anticipated that the political economy of development in the Global South will be drastically transformed. Existing economic and social disparities in the global south have been exacerbated by the pandemic, with the most vulnerable countries and people suffering the most. Many of these countries are already facing significant economic and social challenges, such as high levels of poverty, weak healthcare systems, and inadequate infrastructure. The pandemic has exacerbated these issues, leading to a further widening of the gap between the rich and the poor.

The pandemic has also resulted in a decrease in foreign direct investment (FDI) globally and particularly in the Global South, which has led to a decrease in economic growth and job creation, thereby exacerbating economic and social disparities in southern countries. Furthermore, the COVID-19 pandemic has reduced international aid and assistance to the Global South. Numerous nations in the region rely largely on international support and aid to finance their sustainable development projects.

The decline in aid and assistance has further weakened the economies of the Global South, resulting in a decline in economic growth and employment creation.

To address the economic and social disparities in the Global South, the international community must ensure the region's recovery from the pandemic. This includes increasing aid and support to the region and attracting direct foreign investment. It is also crucial that the international community works to enhance the healthcare systems and infrastructure in the region so that the most vulnerable countries have access to the necessary healthcare and other services. Finally, the international community must work to ensure that the political economy of development in the Global South is equitable and sustainable. This involves ensuring that the economic and social imbalances in the region are addressed and that the most disadvantaged countries and communities can access the resources and services they need to prosper and thrive.

This book aims to provide a comprehensive overview of the challenges facing developing countries and offers valuable insights into the potential solutions that can be implemented to foster economic recovery and development post-COVID-19 pandemic. The book covers three parts. First, we discuss the sustainable development challenges in the post-COVID-19 era. Second, several chapters are dedicated to examining the impact of the COVID-19 pandemic on vulnerable groups: women and migrants. Third, several chapters discuss market and development finance challenges post-COVID-19 pandemic.

In Chap. 1, Svitych presents a reflection on progressive alternatives to development in the Global South, advocating for a post-pandemic shift to principles of reciprocity, solidarity, and care. The author reassesses Amartya Sen's development ethic to repoliticize economic growth, engages Karl Polanyi's embeddedness approach to imagine and advance a degrowth-based society, and suggests that post-pandemic development should be grounded in a relational ontology. Drawing on political theory, political economy, and existing degrowth practices, the chapter argues that an emerging alternative world is not only utopian but also real.

In Chap. 2, Thapar discusses technology, economics, and climate change-related challenges in the Global South post-COVID-19 pandemic. He argues that experts and political representatives from all over the world have been debating and discussing the challenges faced by countries of the Global South for decades. Despite the complexity of the issue, the lack of economic resources is a major constraint. The COVID-19 pandemic has only made this worse. If the economic divide and the neglect of the South continue, there is a risk of social unrest and disruption, which could have serious consequences for businesses in the North. To address this, a reformatting of paradigms in both the North and South is necessary.

In Chap. 3, Goyal and Singh examine the relationship between globalization and human development and evaluate whether human development has improved since 1990. They look at the political economy of globalization and human development and evaluate human development in terms of health, education, GDP growth, per capita income, the Gender Inequality Index, the Human Development Index, and the Inequality Adjusted Human Development Index. They found that globalization, because of neo-liberal policies, has led to unequal progress in human development, even in the South Asian region.

In Chap. 4, Kea, Shahriar et al. examine the effects of the COVID-19 pandemic on the ASEAN economies from various perspectives, as well as how the ASEAN member states responded to the pandemic to recover their economies in the post-pandemic era. They explained that the ASEAN Comprehensive Recovery Framework (ACRF) and Implementation Plan were developed and implemented in response to the pandemic; however, external problems such as the US-China rivalry and the Russian-Ukraine war have hindered the smooth implementation of the ACRF.

In Chap. 5, Adam et al. argue that the COVID-19 pandemic has had a disproportionate impact on women in the Global South, leading to job losses and income insecurity and exacerbating existing gender inequalities. They examine the effects of the economic slowdown on the attainment of the Sustainable Development Goals (SDGs) and suggest ways to overcome health and economic challenges. The findings of their study revealed that men and women were affected differently, with single rural women with children being the most impacted. The study promotes the introduction of more inclusive education and encourages academics and researchers to engage in substantial work to promote equality.

In Chap. 6, Pradhan examines the impact of the COVID-19 pandemic on women in the Global South, where gender disparities in public policymaking have been exacerbated. The author highlights the effects of the COVID-19 pandemic and public health response policies on women, particularly in the Asia-Pacific, the Middle East, Sub-Saharan Africa, and Latin America. They also assess the public policy approaches adopted by governments in the Global South to provide protection, healthcare, social security, etc., to empower women. Finally, they evaluate the women-centric government policies in the Global South and suggest alternative policy approaches to achieve women's empowerment in the post-COVID-19 world.

In Chap. 7, Prianto et al. examines the role of Southeast Asian countries in governing migrant workers in the Southeast Asian region during the COVID-19 pandemic and analyse Southeast Asian countries' cooperation to consolidate transnational mitigation strategies to ensure the rights of migrant workers during the COVID-19 pandemic era. They find that in the early days of the pandemic, Southeast Asian countries failed to build solidarity in the region. However, at the end of 2020, the 13th ASEAN Forum on Migrant Labor (AFML) and the ASEAN Comprehensive Recovery Framework (ACRF) were established, providing guidelines and frameworks for transnational mitigation strategies to help the region recover in the post-COVID era.

In Chap. 8, Shahid et al. examines the factors that influence the allocation of multilateral aid from international financial institutions (IFIs) to Pakistan, focusing on the World Bank, the International Monetary Fund, and the Asian Development Bank. The results of their study showed that GDP per capita had a negative impact on the IFIs' lending decisions, while political instability had a positive and significant impact. Bureaucratic interests were also found to be a major factor in the allocation of funds, as the Pakistani executives' directors' voting authority increased the funds' allocation by the IFIs. Additionally, the COVID-19 pandemic had a significant impact on IFI lending to Pakistan, with the World Bank approving a $1 billion loan and the IMF approving a $6 billion loan to support Pakistan's response to the pandemic.

In Chap. 9, Trivedi et al. examines the interdependency, presence of leverage effect, and associated value-at-risk (VaR) models of ten commodity indices from 2000-01-03 to 2022-01-07. The data were partitioned into three phases: before, during, and after the COVID-19 pandemic. The results showed that volatility is persistent, volatility shocks retain a long timeline, and exponential changes in volatility occur during a global pandemic.

In Chap. 10, Khan and Surisetti suggest a transdisciplinary, conceptual model as a fresh lens for research and practice in the Global South and argue that financial literacy (FL) is an essential tool of human capital development and empowerment that is still under-explored. They explained that in the post-COVID-19 era, FL research needs to expand and explore the lived experiences of people in the Global South, capture the praxis of FL outside financialized decisions, articulate the value metrics of social capital, and explore possible models for market information and financial advice.

Summary and Way Forward

This book provides a comprehensive overview of the challenges facing developing countries post-COVID-19 pandemic and offers valuable insights into potential solutions that can be implemented to foster economic recovery and development. The book is divided into three parts. Part I discusses sustainable development challenges in the post-COVID-19 era. Part II examines the impact of the pandemic on vulnerable groups such as women and migrants. Part III focuses on market and development finance challenges post-COVID-19 pandemic.

The chapters in the book cover a range of topics, from progressive alternatives to development in the Global South, to technology, economics, and climate change-related challenges, to the relationship between globalization and human development, to the effects of the pandemic on the ASEAN economies, to the disproportionate impact of the pandemic on women in the Global South, to the impact of the pandemic on migrant workers, to the factors that influence the allocation of multilateral aid from international financial institutions to Pakistan, to the interdependency of commodity indices, to the need for financial literacy in the Global South.

The book contributors argue that the economic divide and the neglect of the South must be addressed, and that a reformatting of paradigms in both the North and South is necessary. They also suggest that more inclusive education should be introduced, and that academics and researchers should engage in substantial work to promote equality. Additionally, they suggest that transnational mitigation strategies should be implemented to ensure the rights of migrant workers, and that financial literacy should be explored as an essential tool of human capital development and empowerment.

Overall, the book presents an in-depth analysis of the challenges developing nations confront in the post-COVID-19 era and interesting thoughts on potential remedies. It is an excellent resource for academics, researchers, and policymakers interested in understanding the political economy of development in the Global South and the problems posed by the COVID-19 pandemic.

Prof. (Dr.) Hebatallah Adam
Associate Professor of Economics
Assistant Dean for Academic Affairs (JSIA)
Founder and Director of Jindal Centre for
the Global South, Jindal School of International
Affairs (JSIA)
O.P. Jindal Global University
Haryana, India

Prof. (Dr.) Ravinder Rena
Professor of Economics
Durban University of Technology
ML Sultan Campus
Durban, South Africa

Contents

About the Editors

Prof. (Dr.) Hebatallah Adam is an academician, editor, and scholar with over 19 years of teaching and research experience in International Economic Development and Global South Studies. She is the Founder and Director of Jindal Centre for the Global South. She is currently working as Associate Professor of Economics, Assistant Dean for Academic Affairs of Jindal School of International Affairs (JSIA) at O. P. Jindal Global University, Haryana—India. She is affiliated as well to the Department of Economics, Faculty of Business, Ain Shams University, Cairo-Egypt. Dr. Adam's research interests include development finance, international economics development, green economy, and financial inclusion.

Prof. (Dr.) Ravinder Rena is a profound academician and distinguished scholar in economics, writer, editor, adviser, motivational speaker, and public intellectual with over 29 years of teaching and research experience in Asia-Pacific, Africa, and European continents. He has been an independent consultant and training expert. Professor Rena is currently working as Professor of Economics, Durban University of Technology, Faculty of Management Sciences, South Africa. He serves as the Honorary Country Director—South Africa for the International Internship University (IIU). He also serves as an Adjunct Professor of Economics for Master's and Doctorate Programmes at Monarch Business School, Monarch University, Hagendorn, Zug, Switzerland.

Part I
Sustainable Development Challenges in the Post-COVID-19 Era

Chapter 1
Beyond the Pandemic: The Promise of Degrowth in the Global South

Oleksandr Svitych

Abstract This chapter is an invitation to reflect on progressive alternatives to development in the Global South. It advocates a post-pandemic turn to the principles of reciprocity, solidarity, and care as expressed in the politics of degrowth. To this aim, it first reassesses Amartya Sen's development ethic to repoliticize economic growth. It further engages Karl Polanyi's embeddedness approach to imagine and advance a degrowth-based society. Finally, it suggests that post-pandemic development needs to be grounded in a relational ontology. By drawing both on political theory and political economy, as well as on existing degrowth practices, the chapter shows that an emerging alternative world is not only utopian but real.

Keywords Degrowth · Post-development · Capabilities approach · Embeddedness · Global south

1.1 Introduction

This chapter is about the possibilities for radical change. An unprecedented public health crisis caused by the novel COVID-19 virus in 2020 brought into sharp relief the damage to institutions of social reproduction, the entrenched precariousness of labour, and the systemic disparities of wealth produced by the mainstream capitalist

---

"The slogan of 'degrowth' is primarily designed to make it perfectly clear that we must abandon the goal of exponential growth, as that goal is promoted by nothing other than a quest for profits on the part of the owners of capital and has disastrous implications for the environment, and therefore for humanity. It is not just that society is reduced to being nothing more than an instrument or a means to be used by the productive mechanism; human beings themselves are becoming the waste products of a system that would like to make them useless and do without them."—Serge Latouche, *Farewell to Growth* (2009: 7–8) [1]

O. Svitych (✉)
Jindal Global University, Haryana-131001, Sonipat, India
e-mail: osvitych@jgu.edu.in

H. Adam and R. Rena (eds.), *Political Economy of Development in the Global South Post-COVID-19 Pandemic*,
https://doi.org/10.1007/978-981-99-4074-5_1

development model. It also demonstrated, quite tragically, that the objective of societies to defeat the virus—the "imperative of life-making"—is at odds with the market imperatives of profit-making [2].

The coronavirus crisis has had severe repercussions on people's economic and mental well-being, leading to unemployment, "lockdowns," and inequalities. It has especially affected precariously employed citizens [3]—those on temporary contracts, informally or self-employed—exposing the fallacy of "flexible" labour market practices. Furthermore, social reproduction capacities such as care, health, and education were severely undermined [4]. In a vicious cycle, the most marginal layers of society became even more insecure during the pandemic, as job insecurity was intertwined with physical vulnerability [5]. COVID-19 has also disclosed that care and health are indispensable for dealing with global health shocks. It has called into question the state's preparedness for such shocks, especially in light of their deregulated healthcare systems. Several nations failed to provide adequate health infrastructure, including treatment, equipment, and large-scale testing for their citizens. In the meantime, governments emphasized individual responsibility to "stay home," quite in line with the neoliberal logic of responsibilization, as the state continued to abandon public health in a push for vaccine development through private pharmaceutical companies.

The effects of the pandemic, of course, were not spread evenly across the globe. Unsurprisingly, developing nations of the Global South took the hardest hit due to informal economies, the lack of robust welfare support, weak healthcare systems, and minimal protection of workers. As the Global North shifted to a remote work mode, the cities in the Global South shut down, leaving people stranded without means of subsistence. Some of the most evocative images had come from India as millions of migrant workers walked across the country back to their home villages. Urban, foreign migrant workers and indigenous people were affected the most [6].

In the meantime, "cleanliness" in the workplace came as a substitute for real worker protections, while the costs of medicines increased, and the wealth of billionaires ballooned. Tellingly, governments began to take the idea of universal basic income more seriously. However, these are piecemeal measures that leave the underlying architecture of development intact, even though the market has failed as an efficient distribution mechanism, as envisaged by Karl Polanyi [7]. On the other hand, we also witnessed an outburst of welfare "from below," with workers leading strikes to demand protective equipment and ordinary people setting up mutual aid networks. Mutual aid initiatives mushroomed, and the world saw a myriad of unprecedented acts of resistance, solidarity, and care.

As death tolls and unemployment numbers surged, so did populist nationalism. The neoliberal populist elites—from Donald Trump in the US to Jair Bolsonaro in Brazil to Narendra Modi in India—resorted to aggressive nationalism to divert attention away from the structural causes of the hardships engendered by the pandemic. While there has been a heterogeneity of government responses to the pandemic crisis, there are common drivers and tendencies that can be teased out from the relationship between the state and the capital [2].

In this chapter, I argue that other worlds are possible. In so doing, I join a rich canopy of critical traditions united by the ethos of questioning mainstream development and charting routes to a more just post-pandemic society. Political philosopher Adam Swift reminds us that the pandemic has starkly exposed what we already knew: "we live in societies where people are subject to unjust laws made in unjust ways" [8]. COVID-19 has raised a set of political philosophical and political-economic issues, calling for more critical engagement with the concepts of growth, capitalism, and development. Simultaneously, it has brought a unique opportunity for scholars, policymakers, and activists to imagine alternatives to the current socioeconomic order. While it is a triviality that crisis and opportunity often go together, it is imperative that the current logic of capitalist development is rethought, while emerging imaginaries, alternatives, and struggles are brought from the margins to the centre.

"Development" is a highly contested term that is open to multiple interpretations. For example, it can mean economic growth, satisfaction of needs, or environmental sustainability. It can be broadly conceived around the notion of "progress," for instance, as "progressive social, economic and political change" [9], or around the notion of well-being, for example, as "improving the well-being of people in less or least developed contexts" [10]. Development, then, is an empty signifier and a "plastic" concept" [11]. What is important, however, is that development has been mostly associated with the Western hegemonic ideas of linear progress, economic growth, expansion of capitalist markets, and neoliberal governance and rationality. This is a sort of development that can be "managed" by experts in a technocratic top-down fashion and "measured" through prescribed indicators, however inadequate they may be, most often through the Gross Domestic Product (GDP).

Against this narrow notion of development, the counterterm "post-development" points to an emerging alternative or rather a "pluriverse" of alternatives [12]. A vast post-development literature has sketched the contours of alternative imaginaries united by the themes of the public good and conviviality, reciprocity and solidarity, human flourishing and respect for the environment. As the subsequent sections will elaborate, post-development strives for a better, more just, and more sustainable society. As such, the post-development ethos is essentially anti-capitalist in nature.

This chapter departs from the premise that post-capitalist development—and the politics of degrowth, in particular—is politically necessary, socially desirable, and economically feasible in the Global South. In this contribution, I discuss the need for such reflexivity and possible action. My rationale is twofold: provide a critique of the neoliberal development model; and move the debate towards rethinking development, growth, and well-being. More specifically, I advance the vision of a degrowth-based social transformation for the Global South by combining Amartya Sen's capabilities approach with Karl Polanyi's embeddedness account. In this manner, I justify degrowth on both ethical and empirical grounds, using the toolkits of political theory and political economy, respectively.

The chapter makes three basic moves. First, theoretically, I take inspiration from Amartya Sen's work and outline a capabilities-based normative strategy to justify degrowth. On a deeper political philosophical level, this implies an intersubjective ontology of relationality and interdependence. Second, I draw on Karl Polanyi's political-economic legacy to argue that degrowth can be understood as a societal "countermovement," to use Polanyi's famous term, against commodification and the neoliberal development model. I also show that Sen's capability approach resonates with Polanyi's notion of embeddedness. Third, I apply this combined framework to the Global South. Here, I put forward and defend two interrelated claims: that degrowth is a logical and natural application of Sen's and Polanyi's ideas; and that developing nations are especially suited to embrace degrowth-based politics and policies. Finally, I suggest several concrete post-pandemic degrowth policies to illustrate the applicability of prior theoretical propositions.

The rest of the chapter is structured in five main sections. In this section, I problematize the neoliberal development model and sketch some major contributions from the post-development literature. In the second and third sections, I build the normative foundations of my degrowth argument. I begin by reassessing Amartya Sen's capabilities approach with respect to development and then extend this emerging framework by engaging Karl Polanyi's intellectual arsenal of embeddedness, commodification, and countermovement. The fourth section introduces and evaluates degrowth with special reference to the Global South. Here, I develop the empirical foundations of the argument through the lens of political economy, survey the existing degrowth literature and praxis, and formulate a degrowth policy kit. The last section concludes the chapter.

1.1.1 Deconstructing Development

The COVID-19 pandemic has revealed the weaknesses of the neoliberal development paradigm. Neoliberalism can be understood as the advancement of human well-being through "liberating individual entrepreneurial freedoms and skills" within a framework of private property, free market, and free trade [13]. At the same time, neoliberalism can be seen as a form of governmentality that produces autonomous, calculating, entrepreneurial subjects through the discourse of "human capital" [14]. Applied to development, neoliberalism entails economic growth, capital accumulation, consumption, and commodification of everything [15].

The adverse effects produced by the pandemic have been well documented: deteriorated global health and loss of lives; increased unemployment and economic insecurity; businesses struggling without state support; growing inequalities; and intensified authoritarianism, among others [9, 15, 16]. A growing body of literature finds the root cause of these impacts—both in the Global North and the Global South—with the dominant neoliberal model of development trajectory that equates well-being to economic growth and profit. It is notable that, despite a recent shift in development discourse and practice towards the notions of equity, inclusiveness, and sustainability [17], hegemonic capitalist templates have prevailed. At the same time, scholars, activists, and practitioners have proposed alternatives that seek to move away from the imperatives of aggregate growth, economic progress, market efficiency, and profit-making towards frameworks based on reciprocity, redistribution, and care.

While the pandemic did not cause these communicative and activist acts of resistance, it certainly amplified them. Old neoclassical economic assumptions have been challenged; new trajectories based on inclusivity and solidarity have been developed; multiple reciprocity-based grassroots initiatives have been implemented; and "key" workers in the sectors of healthcare, social and elderly care, food production and distribution have been appreciated. More profoundly, as the next sections demonstrate, non-Western worldviews and nonmarket motivations have been pushed forward. These efforts have contributed to confronting the neoliberal state and overcoming capitalism—understood both as an economic system of "competitive production of profit" and a broader social order that enables and is fed by this system [18].

Although development is a catch-all term, three distinct meanings can be discerned. The first equates development to economic growth. The second interpretation of development—a variation of the first—is "inclusive growth" or social policy. The third and latest one revolves around the idea of "empowerment," especially women's empowerment [19]. Undergirding all three conceptions is the idea of "progress", usually couched in narrow economistic terms and promoted both by international financial institutions such as the World Bank or the International Monetary Fund (IMF) and by United Nations agencies such as the United Nations Development Programme (UNDP) or the United Nations Environment Programme (UNEP), including through the Sustainable Development Goals [20]. Often, development institutions and corporations have been driven by opportunities to access new markets rather than fight world problems such as inequality or poverty.

1.1.2 Post-Development as a Counter Paradigm

In view of the above, the counter term "post-development" has been coined and understood as a multiplicity of critiques and alternative ways of living and being [11, 21, 22]. This "pluriverse" of radical views, practices, and worldviews encompasses degrowth, eco-anarchism, eco-feminism, eco-socialism, social solidarity and gift economies, indigenous knowledge, ancient philosophies, religious traditions, *buen vivir*, *swaraj*, and other multiple visions from the Global South, to name a few. Despite their diversity, the common themes are detaching humanity from capitalist development as the central organizing principle, seeking social justice and sustainability, and rejecting mainstream development solutions. Furthermore, these diverse transformative initiatives and movements are grounded in relational ontologies of mutual connectedness and interdependence which challenge the Western-centric universalism and individualist worldview. As Ashish Kothari and coauthors explain, pluriverse refers to "a compendium of worldviews and practices, old and new, local and global, emerging from indigenous, peasant and pastoral communities, urban neighbourhoods, environmental, feminist, and spiritual movements" [23].

One such vision is degrowth, a societal project that calls for prosperity without economic growth to attain well-being, social justice, and environmental sustainability, and invokes the ethos of sharing, conviviality, reciprocity, and care [21, 24]. In other words, degrowth is a theory of societal change and a radical emancipatory alternative that strives away from the market society and repoliticizes the commons and the public good, "re-embedding" the economy in society [7]. Similar to other post-development alternatives, degrowth aims to transcend or erode the capitalist system, in the vocabulary of Erik Olin Wright [25], rather than tame or reform it through market-friendly solutions such as "sustainable development," "inclusive growth," or "green growth." This incremental change, however, is what makes systemic change possible.

While the terms "post-growth," "a-growth," and "degrowth" are interrelated, they convey different nuances of meaning. Postgrowth refers to a broader set of approaches and alternatives that aim to move beyond the current Western development models based on growth and market exchange towards more egalitarian and sustainable societies [26]. Postgrowth encompasses many forms, including a-growth and degrowth, among others. A-growth is indifferent to economic growth; it is a rational approach to policy and decision-making that seeks to eliminate the constraint of GDP measurements [27]. In turn, degrowth is a more ambiguous concept. At its core is a vision of society opposing the capitalist growth imperative and advancing a radical social-ecological transformation both in the Global North and the Global South [28]. As Nathan Barlow highlights, degrowth aspires to "an alternative way to organize society, structure the economy, and re-embed human activities within ecological boundaries in a convivial and equitable way" [29]. The ideas of life-making, ecological sustainability, and social justice are central to this vision.

1.2 Normative Justification: Amartya Sen's Capabilities Approach

The disruption of "business as usual" is an opportunity to reflect upon and critically assess the current predicament, as well as formulate and take drastic steps towards a better world. As Fay Niker and Aveek Bhattacharya suggest, "By exposing our vulnerabilities and highlighting deep social problems (often through exacerbating them), they [crises] summon us to consider how to redress, repair and rebuild our societies" [30]. For this purpose, I approach the topic of post-COVID-19 development from a conjoined perspective of political theory and political economy. Both normative theorizing and political-economic analysis matter. The questions of social justice and emancipation from economic precarity are mutually intertwined. In this section, then, I deploy Amartya Sen's capability approach to provide a normative justification for degrowth. Combining it with Karl Polanyi's account of social embeddedness in the next section will generate a reasonable defence of degrowth in the Global South while avoiding the pitfalls of "ontological blindness" and "epistemological violence" [31].

More fundamentally, we need to rethink the ontological foundations of mainstream development. Ultimately, ontology underpins every policy [32]. It is necessary to reflect upon what a shift from a neoliberal social ontology to an ontology based on mutual interdependence and recognition means for post-pandemic development. The COVID-19 crisis calls for replacing an atomist ontology with an intersubjective one that recognizes mutual interconnectedness and recognition [33]. An intersubjective-based approach to social justice implies the ethics of public care rather than the market—a position also highlighted by critical feminist scholars [34–38]. In this regard, I argue that a *Polanyian capabilitarian* perspective carries a radical emancipatory potential to imagine alternative development grounded in an intersubjective ethos.

1.2.1 Misguided Political Theory

Before outlining the contours of a post-development perspective from a capabilitarian-Polanyian framework, it is worthwhile to note that the mainstream development practice and discourse have been based on dubious political theoretic assumptions. These assumptions form an eclectic mix of utilitarianism, liberalism, cultural chauvinism, and a co-opted capabilities approach.

Utilitarianism has been commonly linked to capitalism as its hegemonic culture. Milner describes utilitarianism as

> a view of the social world as consisting, ideally or factually, of a plurality of discrete, separate, rational individuals, each of whom is motivated, to all intents and purposes exclusively, by the pursuit of pleasure (or utility) and the avoidance of pain [39].

Utilitarian logic underlies many of the mainstream economics' assumptions, producing a rational *homo economicus* and a possessive individual [40]. Since mainstream development theory has been equated with economic growth and investment opportunities, it has adopted a utilitarian logic by trying to create possessive individuals [19]. Referring to women's empowerment, for instance, Uma Narayan talks about "insane utilitarianism":

> If the education of poor women and girls is valued because it is a counterterrorism device that might work better than the dropping of bombs, and the empowerment of women is important because it might disempower terrorists, then the protection of the basic rights of poor women in poor countries is clearly in the grips of an insane utilitarianism with a giddying roster of greater goods that women's empowerment will allegedly bring about [41].

Development agencies, private subcontractors, and international financial institutions thus approach the recipients of development aid according to utilitarian notions of efficiency, profitability, and economic outcomes rather than treat them as human subjects with dignity and social rights. Poverty reduction, increased literacy, women's empowerment, and other development objectives, then, are not considered worthwhile goals in and of themselves [42].

Other political philosophical foundations of development theory include a distorted capabilities approach (a topic of the next sections) and oppressive cultural chauvinism. Escobar refers to development as "top-down, ethnocentric, and technocratic" [42, 43] because development experts impose their narratives, programme objectives, and economic models onto people instead of listening to them. This move recalls one of the "five faces of oppression" outlined by political theorist Iris Marion Young, who pointed to cultural imperialism as "the universalization of a dominant group's experience and culture, and its establishment as the norm" [43, 44]. In a rather twisted logic, development technocrats assume that the free market and democratic governance are the goods that people require, including in the Global South, while disregarding the local context, culture, and institutions. If cultural imperialism is "to experience how the dominant meanings of a society render the particular perspective of one's group invisible" [45], then mainstream development theory, discourse and practice are that.

A final political theoretic critique of development can be tied to the broader critique of liberalism. As anthropologist Jason Hickel observes, the development industry seeks to produce an abstract possessive individual devoid of stifling societal constraints and social norms. However, the assumption that individuals can exist outside of culture and power relations has been debunked both by social theory [34, 46] and communitarian political philosophy [47, 48]. As Charles Taylor has put it, a crucial feature of human agency is that we need some orientation to the conception of the good rather than be free from all conceptions [49].

1.2.2 Capabilities Approach

In this section, I ground a justification of post-development in Amartya Sen's capabilities approach. Unlike other perspectives, this normative framework appeals to a conception of justice rooted in the importance of capabilities rather than liberty or equality. On the other hand, I will engage Karl Polanyi's critical political economy to identify socioeconomic injustices that can be alleviated through the politics of degrowth. In this manner, I develop the case for degrowth in the Global South from a conjoint normative (ontological) and empirical (advocacy) perspective.[1]

The capabilities approach to justice and development was pioneered by Amartya Sen [51, 52] and developed later by Martha Nussbaum [53] as an alternative to the utilitarian interpretation of development as economic growth. It states that people's potential capabilities to function—their "beings and doings"—should guide social policies and institutions. Such functionings can be grouped into those relevant to

[1] As Charles Taylor reminds us: "Taking an ontological position does not amount to advocating something; but at the same time, the ontological does help to define the options which it is meaningful to support by advocacy" [50].

distributive justice, such as being healthy, well-educated, safe, or economically secure, and those more relevant to recognition, such as being politically active, being respected, or being part of a community [54]. Against John Rawls's primary goods and Ronald Dworkin's equality of resources, Sen's capability approach focuses on the diversity of humans and what these goods enable them to do.

Today, the traction of the capabilities approach can be witnessed in the Human Development Index (in contrast to economic measures of development such as GDP) and the UN's Sustainable Development Goals (which succeeded the Millennium Development Goals). Ironically, however, this approach has been mainstreamed in development discourse according to the utilitarian criterion of "efficiency" [19] and as the "capability to function within the market sphere" [55]. Sen's original understanding of development as the expansion of peoples' capabilities to enjoy full and meaningful lives has been side-lined. Although development agencies such as the World Bank use the capabilities approach in their justifications of development policies, they focus on individual capabilities only, circumscribing the relational foundations of the approach. Stripping the capabilities approach of relational goods, they reproduce a liberal individualist ontology that Sen challenged. This mistake is the result of the analytic error that Ingrid Robeyns warned against:

> Some applications of Sen's capability approach in mainstream economics tend to be quite uncritical and reduce the capability approach to its material dimensions only, thereby eliminating its potential to integrate concerns of distribution with those of recognition. However, given Sen's wider work, … the capability approach needs to be used in a critical-feminist-liberal fashion, and not in an androcentric libertarian fashion or only for applications that reduce capabilities to those that are measurable [56].

In contrast, the capabilities approach is based on a relational ontology that incorporates both individual and social components [57]. While Sen admitted that modern economics assumes individual self-interest as the primary motivation, he questioned this narrow assumption, claiming that "economics is supposed to be concerned with real people" [58]. Sen aspired to combine economics with ethics [59], which places him firmly in the tradition of other moral economists, including Karl Polanyi, who seek to enhance human flourishing in the Aristotelian sense. Neither pleasure (utility) nor self-interest alone affects economic decisions; other nonmarket values, such as political or civil freedoms, are important in and of themselves [60]. This means that the "economy is in service of human, societal benefit and not vice versa" [61]. In the Polanyian language, the economy is embedded in society.

1.3 The Political Economy of Karl Polanyi

At this point, it is useful to combine Amartya Sen's capabilities approach with Karl Polanyi's critical political economy. As Ingrid Robeyns writes, "the most urgent issues of justice do not require theories of justice, but rather a political and economic analysis of unjust structures" [62]. In this section, I argue that Karl Polanyi's intellectual legacy is helpful to imagine how the economy can be "re-embedded," especially in the wake of COVID-19. While Polanyi's theory of "double movement"—the dynamic of market expansion and simultaneous societal protection against it—helps understand key political-economic developments in the Global South, it also carries a radical transformative potential to rethink mainstream productivist development. I begin by briefly reviewing Polanyi's key messages from his major work *The Great Transformation* and by outlining his substantive view of the economy. Next, I draw parallels with Amartya Sen's capabilities approach. In the section that follows, I apply this combined Polanyian capabilitarian position to defend the politics of degrowth in the Global South.

1.3.1 Karl Polanyi and Social Embeddedness

To summarize the argument thus far, Amartya Sen's capabilities approach highlights social connectedness and the inadequacy of neoliberal and utilitarian frameworks that stress self-interest and profit maximization. It is intriguing how this is similar to Karl Polanyi's concept of "embeddedness" and his substantive view of the economy [7, 63]. Challenging the assumptions of autonomous rational choice and individual gain associated with the "formalistic" perspective on the economy [64], Polanyi advanced the view that human motivations are complex and cannot be reduced to material interest: "man was never as selfish as the theory demanded" [65].

In other words, the human economy and motivations are enmeshed in both economic and social institutions. Methodologically, this means that "the economy cannot be separated from the analysis of the social totality" [66]. Embeddedness, according to Polanyi, is thus both ontological—departing from individualism—and methodological—taking society as the starting point of analysis [67]. Furthermore, since the formalistic perspective on the economy is far from being natural, there is space for imagining alternatives to the hegemonic socioeconomic order.

Peadar Kirby writes: "The Polanyian moment has arrived" [68]. Karl Polanyi's critical political-economic arsenal laid out in *The Great Transformation* is key to reimagining the neoliberal economy and development, especially in the post-pandemic era [69]. In this regard, Polanyi's concepts of embeddedness and disembeddedness (coconstitution and separation, respectively, of the economy and society), fictitious commodities (land, labour, and money), and double movement (protective countermovements to restore constraints over the market) form an important background for the defence of post-development, more generally, and the politics of degrowth, in particular. From a Polanyian viewpoint, such radical alternatives advance decommodification, that is, removing labour, land, and money from the market [70, 71].[2] Decommodification is important because it "offers people a secure sense of belonging within flourishing local communities" [73]. Not only can decommodification relieve people from taking precarious jobs [3] and reduce economic insecurity [18], but it can also, in Polanyi's terms, re-embed the economy into society by prioritizing *homo socius* over *homo economicus*, that is, public welfare over private gain; livelihood over market exchange; communal embeddedness over narrow utilitarianism; and solidarity over reactionary nostalgia about the past.

Overall, Polanyi's political economy of social embeddedness makes us reconsider the assumptions underpinning the dominant model of neoliberal development. COVID-19 accentuated this task, highlighting the tensions between the economy and society or, in Polanyi's words, between "improvement"—economic growth and progress—and "habitation"—security of livelihoods [74]. The "market society" Polanyi described meant that "instead of economy being embedded in social relations, social relations are embedded in the economic system" [75]. In turn, the expansion of the market would be checked by a countermovement—"the principle of self-protection aiming at the conservation of man and nature as well as a productive organization" [76]. It is notable that, according to Polanyi, market exchange was only one mechanism to organize the economy and society, the others being reciprocity, redistribution, and household [77].

Polanyi's comprehensive critique of economism, market society, and commodification also suggests that COVID-19 was not an accidental phenomenon but an inevitable outcome of capitalist development [78]. At the same time, his ideas of substantive economy and embeddedness provide a radical alternative to the status quo. I am with Duzgun [70] and Kirby [68] that, unlike the conventional social democratic interpretation of Polanyi's solutions [79], the post-pandemic vision that we can derive from his work is much more transformative and anti-capitalist. For Polanyi, the embedded economy had more to do with a post-capitalist social order than with regulated capitalism. Unless labour, land, and money are removed from the market, no "green capitalism" or "embedded liberalism" would push the market-protection pendulum towards the latter. Polanyi writes: "Nothing obscures our social vision as effectively as the economistic prejudice" [80]. Degrowth is a key part of this new nonmarket story beyond neoliberalism.

Although degrowth can be interpreted in strict economic terms as decreasing economic output accompanied by increasing welfare, more importantly, it is a social imagery that advocates for human well-being outside the economic development straitjacket [24]. Unsurprisingly, degrowth gained extra momentum during the COVID-19 pandemic as the fallacy of unrestrained economic growth had been exposed. This resonates with Polanyi's observation on the tension between habitation and improvement: "It should need no elaboration that a process of undirected change, the pace of which is deemed too fast, should be *slowed down*, if possible, to safeguard the welfare of the community" [81]. According to Polanyi, this transformed world

[2] In *The Great Transformation*, Polanyi identified such decommodification in Britain's 1795 Speenhamland minimum income scheme, the abolition of which in 1834 set the "satanic mill" of the free market in motion [72].

would serve "the general interests of the community" [82] instead of private interests that drove humanity to the verge of social and ecological catastrophe. Although degrowth and other alternatives operate on the margins of capitalist society, they have the potential to lead to a decisive break with the system since they target the very operational logic of capitalism rather than stabilizing and relegitimizing it [83].

1.3.2 Polanyi, Sen, and Ontology

In view of the discussion above, Polanyi's insights into the embedded nature of economic institutions and Sen's capabilities approach display several affinities: (1) from a normative perspective, the view of society that ought to enhance human capacities and development; (2) from an economic perspective, the substantive view that rejects simplistic foundations of individual autonomy, rationality, and material gain; and (3) from an ontological perspective, a communitarian and relational social ethos. Similar to "communitarian" critics of liberalism [47, 48, 84], they both located the obstacles to developing human capabilities in the disembedded market.[3]

To gain a reasonable purchase on post-development and degrowth, it is necessary to develop normative accounts that accommodate both individuality and connectedness with nature and one another. Margaret Stout and Eric Hartman call this "the differentiated relational ontological position," in which "we are a dynamic, mutually influencing multitude of unique but related individual parts cocreating a whole" [86]. As I have argued in this chapter, the political-economic philosophies of Karl Polanyi and Amartya Sen, both sharing a communitarian ethos, are embedded in such a relational ontological position. From this perspective, degrowth is morally justified not simply because individuals have the right to pursue their conceptions of a good life, but also because it provides a more inclusive vision of society.

Amartya Sen's capabilities approach sees human well-being as substantive freedoms and opportunities to be and to do what people have. In a similar vein, Karl Polanyi's account of embeddedness brings the substantive view of the economy into the foreground. Both thinkers rejected the orthodox ontological and epistemic preference for individual wants which revolve around commodities and utilities. Both refused to reduce society to individuals, recognizing their embeddedness in social structures. And both deployed ontologies that incorporated relationality and connectedness [cf. 57, 87, 88]. Polanyi and Sen undoubtedly related their analyses to individualized subjects. At the same time, however, they saw individuals as citizens embedded in relations with others rather than disembedded consumers. As Robeyns has argued with regard to Sen's capabilities approach—an observation that

[3] These communitarian philosophers adopted an Aristotelian perspective in conceiving human life as unified and rejecting a social ontology of "unencumbered selves" [84] without any value orientation. Both Sen and Polanyi, then, can be placed on the communitarian side of the liberal-communitarian debates [cf. 85].

equally extends to Karl Polanyi—it is ethically individualistic but not ontologically individualistic [89].

This discussion suggests that it is important to recognize the question of ontology as the basis for public ethics and governance [48]. Mainstream development has been driven by Western individualist ontologies centred on the atomistic, rational and materially interested self. This creates an opportunity, in Stout and Hartman's words, to "move beyond unwitting ontological domination and perhaps even discover the potential of alternative ontologies as better foundations for governance" [90]. This call has also been voiced by scholars of post-development [31, 43, 91] and coloniality critique [92–94]. To simplify, the former camp highlights how mainstream development theory and practice overlook diverse ontologies of the "non-developed" world, objectify those who need development, and produce "epistemological violence" through unequal relations of power. The latter group interrogates "Western hegemonic rationalities" embedded in prescriptions from the Global North, pointing to the diversity of worldviews and indigenous systems of knowledge. All this raises important ontological and epistemic questions on development in the Global South.

To conclude, Karl Polanyi and Amartya Sen share several important affinities. They developed their views in opposition to orthodox economics. They sought to reconcile the interests of the individual with those of the community through socially embedded autonomy, as well as to ensure secure livelihoods and flourishing communities. Finally, they advanced understandings of freedom different from its narrow market-based interpretation as individual choice. Polanyi linked freedom to social responsibility, whereas Sen connected it to capability expansion and real choices, such as the choice to enter and exit the labour market voluntarily, for instance. In this, they both carry a much more radical and emancipatory potential than what has usually been ascribed to them. What is at stake, according to Sen and Polanyi, is a vision of social justice decoupled from the productivist ethos of development and geared towards decommodification and emancipation.[4]

1.4 The Promise of Degrowth in the Global South

In this section, I examine development tendencies in the Global South from a critical political-economic perspective, followed by the assessment of degrowth prospects in the region. While I focus mostly on India, a major developing nation and an important regional power in South Asia, the implications travel well beyond its borders. Exploring post-development alternatives is even more relevant for the Global South, as it saw less decommodification prior to marketization than the Global North [96]. In many respects, the nations of the Global South exemplify many of the tensions

[4] This dovetails with Albena Azmanova's vision of "securing every citizen a place in the productive economy yet decoupling sources of livelihood from one's entrapment in the process of economic production" [95].

identified by Polanyi in his classic account of marketization and protective movements against it [97–100]. The processes of neoliberal development and ensuing social and ecological dislocations—multiplied by the COVID-19 pandemic—make the region especially prone to the critique of unregulated markets and the need to recover livelihood security and social justice.

1.4.1 The Political-Economic Context

Even before the pandemic, the political economies of the Global South produced multiple forms of precarity, injustice, inequality, poverty, and social and environmental dislocations. These were the results of the neoliberal models of development promoted by international financial institutions and development agencies and embraced by local governments since the 1990s [101]. These effects were exacerbated by informal economies, weak welfare states, poor health systems, and a lack of social security. This is not to say that the unprecedented growth since the 1990s did not benefit anyone. As developing countries became more integrated into global production networks, new jobs appeared, new businesses opened up, new professions and opportunities emerged, and further avenues for social mobility materialized. At the same time, economic globalization did not benefit the most vulnerable and poor strata of society who were already invisible to their respective welfare states, even before COVID-19 [102]. Insecurity became universalized both within and across nations [103]. Moreover, in the Global South, unequal capitalist development remains linked to the legacies of colonialism, imperialism, slavery, and a marginalized position in the capitalist world system [104, 105].

For example, India—one of the largest economies in the Global South and the world—achieved remarkable growth and modernization accompanied by poverty and uneven development [106]. From a political-economic perspective, it exemplified a variation of the "developmental state" [107, 108] spearheaded by Jawaharlal Nehru, considered the architect of modern India. The Indian developmental state actively intervened in the economy and promoted the welfare of its citizens, assuming the roles of "protector" and "modernizer" [109]. Market reforms introduced in 1991, however, marked a break with the developmentalist, secular, and pluralist politics of the post-independence era. While the reforms increased economic growth and generated wealth in the country, they also increased the commodification of labour and land [98, 99], affecting the lives of the poor and triggering multiple societal protective movements—just as Karl Polanyi would predict. The myriad grassroots countermovements that followed were rooted in anti-colonialism and ranged from farmers' protests to trade union movements to radical feminist groups [110]). Marketization also led to stark inequality, as "the rising tide produced by economic liberalization appears to have lifted many boats, but not all" [111]. These processes were exacerbated by the oppressive social structures of caste, gender, and religion. As Harriss-White and Heyer note, "in India, these institutions constitute a structure of discrimination as well as of reproduction essential to [capitalist] accumulation" [112].

The COVID-19 pandemic and lockdowns have been more devastating to the countries of the Global South than to those of the North. The crisis exacerbated the already unjust, unsafe, and insecure living conditions of the informal sector, "gig" workers and urban poor communities, as Sandya Hewamanne and Smytta Yadav [113] vividly documented in their recent edited volume (cf. also [114, 115]). For example, similar to the Indian case, the dynamics of informal economies, poverty, and precarity have been observed in the neighbouring countries of Bangladesh and Sri Lanka. Thus, Chowdhuri et al. [116] and Rahman [117] analyse the Bangladeshi garment industry and how it was affected by the pandemic, exposing the vulnerability of workers employed in the industry. Hewamanne [118], in turn, shows how women workers in Sri Lanka lost their labour rights in the wake of the pandemic, exposing the fallacy of the neoliberal development model. In another example across the Atlantic, Lemos [119] demonstrates how COVID-19 exacerbated the already precarious conditions of supermarket workers in Brazil. This predicament calls for a drastic rethinking of the current neoliberal development model in the Global South in terms of nonmarket foundations such as reciprocity and redistribution.

Joseph Wong argues that the welfare state in the developing world was not intended to protect informal workers and poor people [102]. Unlike the Global North, where the capitalist welfare state was born as a product of political-economic compromise between capital and formal labour, the labour market is much more informal in the Global South. This means that informal workers are excluded by design from welfare state benefits such as stable and decent wages, unemployment and health security, or membership in trade unions. Informality, invisibility to the state, and precarity are the defining features of developing economies. Wong writes, "To be informal in the developing world is to live in the blind spot of the welfare state—it is to be invisible economically, administratively, politically and even physically" [120]. These unjust institutional arrangements became especially visible as COVID-19 raged in the Global South, and precarious workers experienced the hardships of lockdowns and economic devastation. From seasonal migrant workers to construction workers, to women, to "volunteer" health and child development workers, to garment industry workers, and to other "contract workers" in India, Bangladesh, or Sri Lanka, the pandemic exposed common vulnerabilities of economic insecurity and precarity [113]. What is urgently needed, then, is "an alternative economic imagination … which is more mindful of how our health futures are globally connected and thus cannot be secured without global social, economic justice" [121].

1.4.2 Degrowth in the Global South

The analysis thus far suggests that it is time to rethink development from more radical and egalitarian perspectives. As argued earlier, degrowth presents one such transformative post-development avenue, grounded both in the capabilities approach and in critical political economy. Exploring the possibilities for degrowth is particularly important in the Global South due to a larger degree of the informal economy, precarity, and inequality in the region. However, isn't the degrowth debate another attempt to transpose a Western paradigm into the developing world? While such a critique is warranted, the answer is a resounding "No." There are several reasons why degrowth—as a political project, a movement, and a field of study [122]—is both ethically desirable and politically feasible in the Global South.

To recall the theoretical discussion in the chapter, I interpret degrowth as a natural outcome of both Amartya Sen's capability approach to well-being and Karl Polanyi's ideas of embeddedness and decommodification. I argue that the politics of degrowth are especially promising for post-pandemic development in the Global South for three reasons: historical, intellectual, and practical. All three rationales overlap with the fourth reason discussed above—the political-economic context of higher precarity and uneven development in comparison with the Global North.

First, the roots of degrowth can be found in the Global South, even though they may have been forgotten or ignored. Julien-François Gerber and Rajeswari Raina argue that degrowth thinking was not invented by the Global North. For example, some of the sources of post-growth thinking in India include Gandhi's critique of modern civilization and his idea of *swaraj* or self-rule; a socioecological critique of modernization and the continuous pursuit of wealth by the Bengali philosopher and writer Rabindranath Tagore; and the ideas of renowned Indian economists Radhakamal Mukerjee and J.C. Kumarappa [123–125]. At the beginning of the twentieth century, Mukerjee wrote eloquently against market fundamentalism:

> India stands for living humanity as against inert matter; for more equitable distribution of wealth; for less luxury and more brotherhood; for less industrial conflict and more cooperation; for wealth as means as against wealth as an end; and for finding happiness not in restless self-serving but in the consecration of life to the welfare of Society and Humanity [126].

This quote conveys an ethos and vision that are remarkably similar to Karl Polanyi's ideas of substantive economy and embeddedness, as well as to Amartya Sen's people-centred capabilities approach and heterodox economics. Other non-Western sources of the critique of growth include Buddhist economics, alternative ways of measuring development beyond GDP, and broader post-development scholarship and activism.

The intellectual support for the politics of degrowth in the Global South constitutes the second pillar of this vision, and the rich tradition of activism constitutes the third pillar. While the former defends degrowth on the premise of desirability, the latter shows that this paradigm of organizing economy and society is not only meaningful but possible.

In this regard, Matthias Schmelzer [125] provides a comprehensive historical overview and a taxonomy of the critiques of growth, including ecological, socioeconomic, feminist, South-North, cultural, and reactionary approaches, as well as broader critiques of capitalism and industrialism. The first four of these also contain a narrower critique of GDP as a measure of growth. The socioeconomic critique, for instance, debunks the association between growth and well-being, while the South-North critique points to the relations of domination and exploitation between the "developed world" and the "rest." The broader literature on post-development [11, 43, 127, 128] has highlighted the need for radical practices and worldviews as transformative alternatives to development. The vast canvas or "pluriverse" of these ideas that deconstruct development—such as *buen vivir*, *ubuntu*, or *eco-swaraj*—has often been associated with the imaginaries of postcapitalism, degrowth, and postpatriarchy [21, 129]. In many ways, then, avenues of convergence between post-development and degrowth frameworks emerged despite distinct intellectual traditions, as both challenged the core assumptions of growth and economism in favour of ecological integrity and social justice [22]. Other scholars have demonstrated that degrowth practices can coexist with the hegemonic capitalist development paradigm, such as in the Indian state of Kerala [130]; attempted to "decolonize" degrowth by turning attention to indigenous movements, such as Zapatista in Mexico and Adivasi communities in Southern India [131]; and highlighted the linkages between degrowth and environmental justice movements [132].

Finally, the myriad examples of local activism and social movements in the Global South illustrate the effectiveness of degrowth. One such vivid case is the conflict between indigenous communities and a mining conglomerate over bauxite extraction in the Niyamgiri hills of the Indian state of Odisha. Whereas the company regarded the hills as a source of profit, the community viewed them as sacred and vital for their well-being, thus resisting pro-growth thinking and development. Commenting on this and other cases of indigenous resistance, Ashish Kothari writes, expressing the ethos of degrowth:

> These initiatives are a complex mix of fundamentally challenging the system, creating further systems within the existing system, retaining or regaining the best parts of tradition while discarding its worst, and synergizing old and new forms of knowledge. Most of these initiatives point to a different set of values and principles that the ones on which the currently dominant economic and political structures are based [133].

It is notable that change happens, as Ashish Kothari highlights, within the existing system and through grassroots action. To engage once again the work of Erik Olin Wright [25], it reflects a bottom-up interstitial strategy of eroding capitalism from within, rather than taming it from above or overthrowing it altogether. I am with Chertkovskaya, however, that degrowth must involve the whole spectrum of modes of transformation and strategic logics, "with interstitial transformation at the core of degrowth practice, symbiotic transformation helping to expand the horizons for radical possibilities, and temporal and localized ruptures enabling radical change by taking power" [134].[5]

---

[5] Erik Olin Wright reminds us of three logics of resisting capitalism: *smashing*, *taming*, and *eroding*. Much of grassroots resistance during the pandemic has followed the last strategy, that is nurturing new relations "in the spaces and cracks" of the capitalist system and trying to expand them beyond it. Wright's taxonomy also resonates with Nancy Fraser's two distinct yet interrelated strategies: *affirmative* (within a structure) and *transformative* (changing the structure) [135].

1.4.3 From "Real Utopia" to Real Policies

The analysis suggests that it is time to rethink development from more radical and egalitarian perspectives. As argued earlier, degrowth presents one such transformative approach.

Which policies does degrowth entail in the Global South? Within the logic outlined thus far, a Polanyian capabilitarian approach forms the general framework for policymaking. As discussed in the preceding sections, the dominant interpretation of the capabilities approach is the one that meets the demands of the market through the narrative of "inclusive growth" (cf. [136]). However, Amartya Sen defied economic growth as the yardstick for progress and well-being in society. In other words, while he conceived the approach to challenge the system, it was reappropriated to stabilize it through the discourses of "inclusiveness," "innovation," "empowerment," "investment," and "human capital" (cf. [19, 130]). To illustrate what an alternative capabilities approach entails, I focus on three areas of policymaking: employment, education, and welfare support.

The capabilities approach has been used to justify full employment. I am with Laruffa, however, that the "employment-focused" paradigm [137], based on the assumption that inclusion in the labour market expands individual autonomy, contradicts the original ethos of the approach aimed at decoupling the expansion of capabilities from economic growth. People's choices cannot be limited to formal employment. Other non-paid activities can be as fulfilling and meaningful, such as care work, civic engagement, or political participation. A capability-informed and degrowth-oriented social policy would advance these options alongside employment. Another way it can provide real choices to people is to ensure an option for voluntary entry into and exit from the labour market. This could take the form, for example, of a universal basic income or other unconditional forms of assistance. Even more radically, the meaning of work itself may be rethought through the lens of "care," as insisted upon by theorists of care ethics and critical feminist scholars (cf. [34, 38, 135]).

Similarly, from a capabilities perspective, education cannot be restricted to including individuals in the labour market by enhancing their skills and training. Such an instrumental view of education echoes Michel Foucalt's discussion of "human capital" as a manifestation of neoliberal governmentality [14]. In the context of education, we might add that the capabilities approach emphasizes other roles of education, such as the intrinsic value of learning, improving one's life chances, contributing collectively to the economy, gaining vital information, for example, related to one's health, and internalizing respect for others and the world [138]. As Laruffa succinctly summarizes, "the functions of education … that are neglected in the employment-focused paradigm but that should be central for a capability-oriented social policy consist in nourishing individual and collective autonomy" [139]. In other words, education and employment are valuable only if they promote human flourishing.

Finally, as indicated earlier in the chapter, the welfare state—especially in the Global South—may be inadequate to cope with modern risks such as economic insecurity, pandemics, and lack of social protection. From a capabilities perspective, reinforcing safety nets, such as through unemployment assistance, for instance, may not be enough, as it perpetuates the economistic paradigm of social insurance (cf. [12]) rather than advancing the flourishing of individuals and communities. Universal basic income, once again, appears as a candidate for an alternative solidarity-based regime (cf. [140]).

Applying Karl Polanyi's insights to the discussed examples of employment, education, and welfare, a degrowth-driven public policy would entail the decommodification of labour, education, healthcare, and life-making activities in the spirit of "public good over private gain, personal and communal embeddedness in land and nature, the localization of economies, secure belonging to communities providing livelihoods but also respect" [141]. In sum, the reformist policies of "inclusive growth" and employment-focused paradigm sideline and politicize more radical forms of empowerment as prescribed both by Amartya Sen's capabilities and Karl Polanyi's embeddedness approaches.

1.5 Conclusion

This chapter is a contribution to the debate on the possibilities of a decisive break from the paradigm of capitalist and growth-centric development. The need for radical measures and emancipation has been punctuated by COVID-19, which exposed and exacerbated already existing vulnerabilities and injustices. I have defended one such radical socioecological transformative path for the Global South—the politics of degrowth as a longer-term social transformation rather than a short-term technocratic fix. To that effect, I have proposed a framework that combines Amartya Sen's capabilities approach with Karl Polanyi's account of social embeddedness, incorporating both normative and political-economic concerns. Both social theorists took a holistic approach to study economy and society, grounding their analyses in a relational ontology. In presenting the argument, I followed the call of Hewamanne & Yadav [142] that the COVID-19 pandemic presents "an opportunity to rethink neoliberal development models and to put forwards alternative economic paths that are contextually conducive and meaningful."

Three common objections to degrowth are worth considering in conclusion. One is conceptual, another one is empirical, and the last one is normative. The first objection—or rather a misconception—equates degrowth to negative growth or economic recession. However, proponents of degrowth make clear that the movement does not call for recession or stagnation. As Federico Demaria and Serge Latouche argue, for instance, "a degrowth transition is not a sustained trajectory of descent, but a transition to convivial societies living simply and in common" [143]. Similarly, Giorgos Kallis emphasizes the following:

> In economic terms, degrowth refers to a trajectory where the "throughput" (energy, materials and waste flows) of an economy decreases while welfare, or well-being, improves. The hypothesis is that degrowing throughput will in all likelihood come with degrowing output and that these can only be outcomes of a social transformation in an egalitarian direction [144].

On this account, the drastic reduction in economic and social activities due to COVID-19 is not degrowth, although the pandemic has demonstrated the need for degrowth as an alternative social imaginary focused on human development and well-being rather than on brute economic growth.

The second and related objection is that growth is necessary to ensure employment and overcome poverty, which are prerequisites for economic and social stability. However, these two interrelated statements are rather debatable. On the one hand, both neoclassical and Keynesian economic models show that there is no direct causal relationship between the free market and growth; change does not always come from growth; and full employment is not incompatible with negative or zero growth (cf. 147, 148]). As Lange [146] argues, economies and employment can be stabilized through the recalibration of monetary, fiscal, labour, and welfare institutions, such as via reduction of working hours, new investments, redirection of technological change, and redistribution of wealth. The last point also echoes debates on poverty and whether "a rising tide lifts all boats." As growth has often benefited the rich more than the poor, including in the Global South, human needs can be better satisfied by proper redistribution of wealth and resources rather than increased growth. In essence, this is what degrowth implies—a strategy of radical and equitable redistribution.

The third and related objection to degrowth is its normative and utopian thrust. Two rebuttals are in order here. First, all political debates and policies are structured by moral values. On this account, degrowth-related research and activism do not differ from mainstream economic approaches that take for granted the desirability of growth and development. Kallis et al. [147] summarized this succinctly: "Degrowth is a normative concept with analytical and practical applications." Second, while degrowth may sound utopian to an extent, the elements of this radical social vision already exist in real societies, as documented by abundant anthropological and sociological research. Thus, degrowth is an example of what Wright [25] calls a "real utopia". A degrowth utopia is real because it is an emancipatory alternative that combines the deepest human aspirations with already emerging institutions, proposals, and strategies.

I conclude the chapter with two final observations. This first is more abstract and relates to ontology. The second is more practical and concerns strategy. First, as critical development scholars remind us, we need to be aware of ontological diversity to avoid endorsing "Western hegemonic rationalities" [148]. Degrowth—as justified by the framework developed in this chapter—meets this condition. A degrowth-based vision also suggests that ethical relations cannot be reduced to relations between individuals. At the same time, the idea that autonomous individuals are a misleading unit of analysis, highlighted both by Amartya Sen and Karl Polanyi, travels well beyond the Global South. Development needs to move beyond frameworks that continue to perpetuate disembedded individualism.

Second, while interstitial transformations ("escaping" capitalism), in the language of Erik Olin Wright, form the basis of anti-capitalist and bottom-up politics of degrowth, symbiotic modes matter as well. Although the former is the most radical one ("smashing" capitalism), it may be useful as a temporary strategy of resistance, as highlighted by multiple indigenous movements. In turn, symbiotic transformations ("taming" capitalism) conducted by and through the state can also be pursued in line with degrowth, as illustrated, for example, by the state enactment of the National Rural Employment Guarantee Act (NREGA) and the National Food Security Act (FSA) in India. These approaches are not contradictory and can be combined creatively to advance systemic change. Then development can be reimagined both intellectually and politically.

References

1. Latouche S (2009) Farewell to growth. Polity, p. 7–8
2. Bhattacharya T, Dale G (2020, April 23) Covid capitalism: General tendencies, possible "leaps." Spectre. https://spectrejournal.com/covid-capitalism
3. Standing G (2011) The precariat: The dangerous new class. Bloomsbury Academic
4. Jaffe S (2020, April 2) Social reproduction and the pandemic, with Tithi Bhattacharya. Dissent. https://www.dissentmagazine.org/online_articles/social-reproduction-and-the-pandemic-with-tithi-bhattacharya
5. Apostolidis P, Azmanova A (2020, April 16) In a pandemic, we're more precarious than ever. Jacobin. https://jacobinmag.com/2020/4/coronavirus-pandemic-precarity-risk-vulnerability
6. Nanda S (2021) Inequalities and Covid-19. In: Ryan JM (ed) COVID-19: Volume II: Social consequences and cultural adaptations. Routledge, pp 109–123
7. Polanyi K (2001) ([1944]. The political and economic origins of our time. Beacon Press, The great transformation
8. Swift A (2021) COVID-19 as a kind of natural experiment. In Nyker F, Bhattacharya A, (Eds), Political philosophy in a pandemic: routes to a more just future, (pp 257–266). Bloomsbury Academic, p 258
9. Leach M, MacGregor H, Scoones I, Wilkinson A (2021) Postpandemic transformations: How and why COVID-19 requires us to rethink development. World Dev 138:105233
10. Kingsbury D (Ed) (2013) Critical reflections on development. Palgrave Macmillan, p 7
11. Kothari A, Salleh A, Escobar A, Demaria D, Acosta A (Eds) (2019) Pluriverse: A postdevelopment dictionary. Tulika Books, p xiii
12. Ibid
13. Harvey D (2007) A brief history of neoliberalism. Oxford University Press, p 2
14. Foucault M (2008). The birth of biopolitics: Lectures at the College de France, 1978–1979. Palgrave, pp 226–232
15. Büscher B, Feola G, Fischer A, Fletcher R, Gerber JF, Harcourt W, Wiskerke H (2021) Planning for a world beyond COVID-19: Five pillars for postneoliberal development. World Dev 140:105357
16. Córdoba D, Peredo AM, Chaves P (2021) Shaping alternatives to development: Solidarity and reciprocity in the Andes during Covid-19. World Dev 139:105323
17. Hasmath R (ed) (2015) Inclusive Growth, development and welfare policy. Routledge, Abingdon
18. Azmanova A (2020) Capitalism on edge. Columbia University Press, In Capitalism on Edge
19. Hickel, J. (2014). The "girl effect": Liberalism, empowerment and the contradictions of development. Third world quarterly, 35(8), 1355–1373

20. See Ref. 11, p xiv
21. Demaria F, Kothari A (2017) The postdevelopment dictionary agenda: Paths to the pluriverse. Third World Quarterly 38(12):2588–2599
22. Escobar A (2015) Degrowth, postdevelopment, and transitions: a preliminary conversation. Sustain Sci 10(3):451–462
23. See Ref. 11, p xix
24. D'Alisa G, Federico D, Kallis G (Eds) (2014) Degrowth: A vocabulary for a new era. Routledge
25. Wright EO (2016) How to be an anti-capitalist for the 21st century. J Aust Polit Econ 77:5–22
26. Gerber JF, Raina RS (Eds) (2018b) Postgrowth thinking in India: Towards sustainable egalitarian alternatives. Orient Blackswan, pp 8–9
27. Van den Bergh JC (2011) Environment versus growth—A criticism of "degrowth" and a plea for "a-growth." Ecol Econ 70(5):881–890
28. Barlow N, Regen L, Cadiou N, Chertkovskaya E, Hollweg M, Plank C, Wolf V (2022) Degrowth & strategy: How to bring about social-ecological transformation. Mayfly Books
29. Barlow N (2022) Taking stock: degrowth and strategy thus far. In Barlow N, Regen L, Cadiou N, Chertkovskaya E, Hollweg M, Plank C, Wolf V, (Eds), Degrowth & strategy: How to bring about social-ecological transformation, (pp 72–92). Mayfly Books, pp 72–73
30. Niker F, Bhattacharya A (Eds) (2021) Political philosophy in a pandemic: routes to a more just future. Bloomsbury Academic, p 2
31. Teo T (2010) What is epistemological violence in the empirical social sciences? Soc Pers Psychol Compass 4(5):295–303
32. Stout M, Hartman E (2012) Competing ontologies: A primer for public administration [with Commentary]. Public Adm Rev 72(3):388–400
33. Anderson E (2013) Optional Freedoms. In: Widerquist K, Noguera JA, Vanderborght Y, de Wispelaere J (eds) Basic income: An anthology of contemporary research. Wiley Blackwell, pp 23–25
34. Butler J, Gambetti Z, Sabsay L (eds) (2016) Vulnerability in resistance. Duke University Press, Durham; London
35. Held V (2006) The ethics of care: Personal, political, and global. Oxford University Press
36. Tronto JC (1994) Moral boundaries. Routledge, A political argument for an ethics of care
37. Weeks K (2011) The problem with work: Feminism, marxism, antiwork politics, and postwork imaginaries. Duke University Press
38. Young IM (2000) Inclusion and democracy. Oxford University Press
39. Milner A (1994) Contemporary cultural theory. UCL Press, p 8
40. Macpherson C (1962) The political theory of possessive individualism. Oxford University Press
41. Narayan U (2010) Global gender inequality and the empowerment of women. Perspectives on politics, 8(1), 282–284, p. 283
42. See Ref. 11, p 1362
43. Escobar A (1995) Encountering development: The making and unmaking of the third world. Princeton University Press, p 44
44. Young M (1990) Justice and the politics of difference. Princeton University Press, p 59
45. Ibid
46. Foucault M (1995) Discipline and punish: The birth of the prison. Random House
47. MacIntyre A (1984) After virtue: A Study in moral theory. University of Notre Dame Press
48. Taylor C (1989) Sources of the self: The making of modern identity. Harvard University Press
49. Ibid., p 33
50. Ibid., p 161
51. Sen A (1982) Choice, welfare and measurement. Blackwell Publishing
52. Sen A (1999) Development as freedom. Oxford University Press
53. Nussbaum M, Sen A (2009) Quality of life. Oxford University Press
54. Robeyns I (2003) Is Nancy Fraser's critique of theories of distributive justice justified? Constellations, 10(4), 538–553, p 543

55. Jayasuriya K (2006) Statecraft, welfare, and the politics of inclusion. Palgrave, p 54
56. See Ref. 55, p 553
57. Smith ML, Seward C (2009) The relational ontology of Amartya Sen's capability approach: Incorporating social and individual causes. J Hum Dev Capab 10(2):213–235
58. Sen A (1991) On ethics and economics. Blackwell Publishing, p 1
59. Harvie T (2013) Thomas Aquinas, Amartya Sen, and a critical economic discourse. Philosophy, Culture, and Traditions 9:73–86
60. See Ref. 59, p 16
61. See Ref. 60, p 82
62. Robeyns I (2017) Wellbeing, freedom and social justice: The capability approach re-examined. Open Book Publishers, p 194
63. Polanyi K (1992) The economy as instituted process. In: Granovetter M, Swedberg R (eds)), The sociology of economic life. Westview Press, pp 29–52
64. Rodrigues J (2004) Endogenous preferences and embeddedness: A reappraisal of Karl Polanyi. J Econ Issues, 38(1), 189–200, p 191
65. Polanyi K (1947) Our obsolete market mentality. Commentary, 3(2), 109–117, p 114
66. See Ref. 65, p 192
67. Gemici K (2008) Karl Polanyi and the antinomies of embeddedness. Soc Econ Rev 6:5–33
68. Kirby P (2021) Karl Polanyi and the contemporary political crisis: Transforming market society in the era of climate change. Bloomsbury Academic, p 111
69. Goodwin J (2022) Double movements and disembedded economies: A response to Richard Sandbrook. Dev Chang 53(3):676–702
70. Duzgun E (2021) Ecology, democracy, and COVID-19: Rereading and radicalizing Karl Polanyi. In: Ryan JM (ed)), COVID-19: Volume I: Global pandemic, societal responses, ideological solutions. Routledge, pp 54–67
71. See Ref. 69, chs. 5–7
72. See Ref. 7, pp 81–89
73. See Ref. 69, p 72
74. Holmes C (2018) Polanyi in times of populism: vision and contradiction in the history of economic ideas. Routledge, p 26
75. See Ref. 7, p 60
76. Ibid., p 138
77. Ibid., p 50
78. See Ref. 71, p 57
79. Block F, Somers M (2014) The power of market fundamentalism: Karl Polanyi's critique. Harvard University Press
80. See Ref. 7, p 166
81. Ibid., p 35, emphasis added
82. Ibid., p 162
83. See Ref. 18, pp 51–55
84. Sandel MJ (1984) The procedural republic and the unencumbered self. Political Theory 12(1):81–96
85. Akturk S (2006) Between Aristotle and the welfare state: The establishment, enforcement, and transformation of the moral economy in Karl Polanyi's "The Great Transformation." Theor: J Soc Polit Theory, 109, 100–122, p 114
86. See Ref. 32, p 395
87. Martins N (2007) Ethics, ontology and capabilities. Rev Polit Econ 19(1):37–53
88. White SC (2017) Relational wellbeing: Recentring the politics of happiness, policy and the self. Policy Polit 45(2):121–136
89. Robeyns I (2005) The capability approach: A theoretical survey. J Hum Dev, 6(1), 93–117, 108
90. See Ref. 32, p 393
91. Ferguson J (1990) The anti-politics machine: "Development", depoliticization, and bureaucratic power in Lesotho. Cambridge University Press

92. Escobar A (2018) Designs for the pluriverse: Radical interdependence, autonomy, and the making of worlds. Duke University Press
93. Quijano A (2000) Coloniality of power, eurocentrism, and Latin America. Nepantla Views South 1(3):533–580
94. Spivak GC (1988) Can the subaltern speak? In: Nelson C, Grossberg L (eds) Marxism and the interpretation of culture. University of Illinois Press, pp 271–313
95. See Ref. 18, p 184
96. Goodwin J (2018) Rethinking the double movement: Expanding the frontiers of Polanyian analysis in the global south. Dev Chang, 49(5), 1268–1290, p 1280
97. Gemici K, Nair M (2019) Against the market: Local communities and Polanyian contention in India and Turkey. J Glob South Stud 36(2):312–340
98. Levien M (2021) Fictitious but not utopian: Land commodification and dispossession in rural India. In Asher Ghertner D, Robert W Lake (Eds), Land fictions: The commodification of land in city and country, (pp 26–43). Cornell University Press
99. Sahoo S (2017) Market liberalism, marginalized citizens and countermovements in India. Asian Stud Rev 41:1–19
100. Udayagiri M, Walton J (2003) Global transformation and local counter movements: The prospects for democracy under neoliberalism. Int J Comp Sociol 44(4):309–343
101. Hewamanne S, Yadav S (2022) Neoliberalism, informality and precarity. In: Hewamanne S, Yadav S (eds) The political economy of post-COVID life and work in the Global South: Pandemic and precarity. Springer Nature, pp 1–16
102. Wong J (2015) Poverty, invisibility and the welfare state in the developing world. In: Hasmath R (ed) Inclusive Growth, development and welfare policy. Routledge, pp 211–228
103. See Ref. 18, p 2
104. MacKay S (2022) The global south, degrowth and The Simpler Way movement: The need for structural solutions at the global level. Globalizations 19(5):828–835
105. Wallerstein (2004) *World-systems analysis*. Duke University Press
106. See Ref. 101, p 317
107. Chatterjee P (1997) Introduction. In: Chatterjee P (ed)), State and politics in India. Oxford University Press, pp 1–39
108. Evans P (1995). Embedded autonomy: States and industrial transformation. Princeton NJ: Princeton University Press
109. Nandy A (2002) Democratic culture and images of the state. In: Nandy A (ed)), *Time warps*. Hurst & Co, pp 36–60
110. See Ref. 101, p 331
111. Varshney A (2007) India's democratic challenge. Foreign Affairs, 86(2), 93–106, pp 99–100
112. Harriss-White B, Heyer J (2015) Introduction. In Harriss-White B, Heyer J, (Eds), Indian capitalism in development, (pp 1–22). Routledge, p 7
113. Hewamanne S, Yadav S (Eds) (2022b). The Political economy of post-COVID life and work in the Global South: Pandemic and precarity. Springer Nature.
114. Hensman R (2020) The COVID-19 lockdown in India: A predictable catastrophe for informal labour. Global Labour Journal, 11(3)
115. Yadav S (2020) Precarity as a coping strategy of the gonds: A study of insecure and long-distance seasonal migration in central India". Indian J Hum Dev 14(1):7–22
116. Chowdhury FS, Choudhury A, Islam F, Shajahan S (2022) Ready Made Garment (RMG) Factories During the Pandemic: Mapping the Effects in Bangladesh. In: Hewamanne S, Yadav S (eds) The political economy of post-COVID life and work in the Global South: Pandemic and precarity. Springer Nature, pp 163–190
117. Rahman S (2022) Demoralizing Impacts of the COVID-19 on the Bangladesh Ready-Made Garment (RMG) Supply Chain. In: Hewamanne S, Yadav S (eds) The political economy of post-COVID life and work in the global south: Pandemic and precarity. Springer Nature, pp 191–216

118. Hewamanne S (2022) Wither labor and human rights? Precarious work and informal economies in the post-COVID-19 Global South. In: Hewamanne S, Yadav S (eds) The political economy of post-COVID life and work in the global south: Pandemic and precarity. Springer Nature, pp 217–242
119. Lemos PR (2022) Supermarket workers: Discovered and uncovered during Covid-19 pandemic. In: Hewamanne S, Yadav S (eds) The political economy of post-COVID life and work in the global south: Pandemic and precarity. Springer Nature, pp 243–262
120. See Ref. 103, p 220
121. See Ref. 102, p 14
122. Asara V (2022) Strategizing within diversity: the challenge of structuring. In Barlow N, Regen L, Cadiou N, Chertkovskaya E, Hollweg M, Plank C, Wolf V (Eds), Degrowth & strategy: How to bring about social-ecological transformation, (pp 93–109). Mayfly Books
123. Gerber JF, Raina RS (2018) Postgrowth in the global south? Some reflections from India and Bhutan. Ecol Econ 150:353–358
124. See Ref. 26, pp 19–21
125. Schmelzer M (2022) From Luddites to limits? Towards a systematization of growth critiques in historical perspective. Globalizations 1–18:9
126. Mukerjee cited in Ref. 26, p 20
127. Rahnema M, Bawtree V (1997) The postdevelopment reader. Zed Books
128. Sachs W (Ed) (1997) The development dictionary: A guide to knowledge as power. Orient Blackswan
129. Kothari A, Demaria D, Acosta A (2014) Buen Vivir, degrowth and ecological swaraj: Alternatives to sustainable development and the green economy. Development 57(3):362–375
130. Pansera M, Owen R (2018) Innovation for degrowth: A case study of counterhegemonic practices from Kerala, India. J Clean Prod 197:1872–1883
131. Nirmal P, Rocheleau D (2019) Decolonizing degrowth in the postdevelopment convergence: Questions, experiences, and proposals from two Indigenous territories. Environ Plan E: Nat Space 2(3):465–492
132. Rodríguez-Labajos B, Yánez I, Bond P, Greyl L, Munguti S, Ojo GU, Overbeek W (2019) Not so natural an alliance? Degrowth and environmental justice movements in the global south. Ecol Econ 157:175–184
133. Kothari A (2018) Radical ecological democracy: An orchestration of alternatives for a post-growth India. In Gerber JF, Raina RS, (Eds), Postgrowth thinking in India: Towards sustainable egalitarian alternatives, (pp 264–286). Orient Blackswan, p 266
134. Chertkovskaya E (2022). A strategic canvas for degrowth: in dialogue with Erik Olin Wright. In Barlow N, Regen Cadiou L, Chertkovskaya E, Hollweg M, Plank C, Wolf V (Eds) Degrowth & strategy: How to bring about social-ecological transformation, (pp 56–71). Mayfly Books, p 61
135. Fraser N, Jaeggi R (2018) Capitalism: A conversation in critical theory. Polity, p 174
136. Laruffa F (2020) What is a capability-enhancing social policy? Individual autonomy, democratic citizenship and the insufficiency of the employment-focused paradigm. J Hum Dev Capab 21(1):1–16
137. Ibid, p 3
138. Robeyns cited in ibid, p 10
139. Herzog, L (2021). Rebuilding social insurance to end economic precarity. In Niker F, Bhattacharya A, (Eds), Political philosophy in a pandemic: routes to a more just future, (pp 85–96). Bloomsbury Academic
140. Popescu D (2021) Pandemic solidarity and universal basic income. In Niker F, Bhattacharya A, (Eds), Political philosophy in a pandemic: routes to a more just future, (pp 87–108) Bloomsbury Academic
141. See Ref. 69, p 138
142. See Ref. 102, p 5
143. Demaria F, Latouche S (2019) Degrowth In Kothari A, Salleh A, Escobar A, Demaria F, Acosta A, (Eds), Pluriverse: A postdevelopment dictionary, (pp 148–151). Tulika Books, p 149

144. Kallis G (2018) Degrowth. Agenda publishing, p 9
145. Fontana G, Sawyer M (2015) The macroeconomics and financial system requirements for a sustainable future. In: Arestis P, Sawyer M (eds), *Finance and the Macroeconomics of Environmental Policies*. Palgrave Macmillan, London, pp 217–242
146. Lange S (2018) Macroeconomics without growth. Sustainable economies in neoclassical, Keynesian and Marxian theories. Marburg: Metropolis Verlag
147. Kallis G, Kostakis V, Lange S, Muraca B, Paulson S, Schmelzer M (2018) Research on degrowth. Annu Rev Environ Resour, 43(1), 291–316, p 293
148. Fouksman E, Klein E (2019) Radical transformation or technological intervention? Two paths for universal basic income. World Dev 122(492–500):494

Chapter 2
Addressing Technology, Economics and Climate Change-Related Challenges in the Global South in the Post-COVID-19 World

Ravi Thapar

Abstract The resolution of the multifarious challenges faced by countries of the Global South has evoked active debate and concern by experts and senior political and multilateral representatives all over the world for the last many decades. A plethora of studies, research and analyses on this theme have already been undertaken, and a review in this regard is ongoing. Given the complexity and extent of the challenges and the bearing that these issues have on the prosperity and well-being of millions in our world, it would be presumptuous to suggest that any single solution or panacea can be effective in this regard. Based on this premise, this paper constitutes yet another attempt to understand the rigours of this issue in light of contemporary economic and political developments. The absence of adequate and optimal allocation of economic resources for addressing the predicament of the Global South has always been a major constraint. Some authors have likened these symptoms to neo-colonialism. COVID-19 has seriously aggravated the severity of such bottlenecks. As the availability of data about the subject continues to be constrained by data-collection capabilities and facilities in the South, this paper relies on a review of diverse academic, multilateral and other commentaries, literature, and documents to simulate overview perspectives in this regard. A key finding that emerges from an analysis of the above is that if problems associated with the mounting economic divide and state of prolonged economic neglect and deprivation in many countries of the South continue unchecked, repudiation and rejection of ongoing economic and political processes in the contemporary World Order cannot be entirely ruled out. In the social media-based and online-connected world today, such rejection could rapidly deteriorate into major social unrest and disturbances that might be even more vigorous and pronounced than those witnessed during the Arab Spring. In such exigencies, the prosperity and fortunes of business entities in the North, which heavily rely on the purchasing power of the populated Global South, will stand compromised. Such trends could also pose existential threats. A reformatting of paradigms, both in

R. Thapar (✉)
Jindal School of International Affairs, O.P. Jindal Global University, Sonipat, Haryana, India
e-mail: rthapar@jgu.edu.in

H. Adam and R. Rena (eds.), *Political Economy of Development in the Global South Post-COVID-19 Pandemic*,
https://doi.org/10.1007/978-981-99-4074-5_2

the North and in the South, is, therefore, both necessary and inevitable. Some of the perspectives that could be urgently considered in this regard—which by no means are the only ones—are what this paper seeks to draw attention to.

Keywords Interconnected · Interdependence · Debt · Technology and digital divide · Global North · Global South · North · South · Climate change · Inequality · Equitable · Repudiation · Disruption · Prosperity · Well-being · Economic divide · South-South cooperation · COVID-19 · Resources · Security

2.1 Introduction

COVID-19 has put the entire world into an unanticipated tailspin [1]. As both developed and developing economies struggle to recalibrate budgets and financial limits, national economic priorities, rather than disbursal of assistance through multilateral or bilateral assistance programmes, take precedence. In addition to the Global South already being, with a mounting Global Economic Divide and stark inequalities in income and wealth in comparison with counterpart nations in the Global North [2], the pandemic has considerably intensified ongoing challenges and difficulties for economically disadvantaged countries. For how else, could the shortfall of US $13 trillion in global revenues, estimated to have been incurred during COVID-19 by UNCTAD, unfold? [3] Before the pandemic, developing countries were already struggling to arrange funds for minimalistic, UNSDG-based initiatives for economic development. Post-COVID, these resources have been curtailed even further. Equally arduous financial constraints confront countries of the South in their mission to adopt green technologies to ensure that global warming should preferably be limited to well below 2 or not more than 1.5 °C higher compared to preindustrial levels [4].

The above exigencies are severe and compelling enough. However, no one in the wildest of his or her dreams could have possibly foreseen that the global economy would face yet another setback—this time because of a man-made crisis in East Europe—precipitating economic sanctions and steep escalation of wheat, fuel and commodity prices triggered off because of a war between Ukraine and Russia, as also identified in the IMF World Economic Outlook Report, 2022 [5]. That the conflict seriously undermines the global peace architecture 75 years after the founding of the United Nations, only exacerbates the uncertainty and despair faced by developing nations in the South [6]. Here, it would also not be out of place to point out that the ongoing trauma and misery of the South would significantly worsen, should a natural calamity or disaster break out in the region in the not-too-distant future.

2.2 Mounting Debt in the South and Deeper Global Economic Divide

The scenario in terms of resources available with disbursed to or shared with the Global South has always been bleak. Post-COVID, this has only deteriorated further, given that in the wake of the pandemic, many countries of the South were compelled to allocate unanticipated expenditure for ensuring vaccination and minimalistic health-care facilities either for tackling COVID or for staving off future pandemics [7]. These burdens have added to their existing liabilities because of previous assistance or loans available to address their developmental aspirations, and developing nations find themselves wallowing in mounting debt with no immediate relief in sight. Reiterating the difficulties posed by the crisis, UN Secretary-General Antonio Guterres, in his Foreword to the "UN Financing for Sustainable Development Report 2022," emphasizes that "most developing countries continue to face increasingly high costs of lending and have had to cut their education and health budgets and other SDG investments, undermining not only their recovery but also their medium and long-term development prospects." The UN Report, after carefully taking into consideration the unprecedented COVID-19-related aftermath, ongoing climate change difficulties and the Ukraine conflict, cautions against donor countries continuing to increase their defence expenditure while curtailing Official Development Assistance and other funds earmarked for climate change. It also emphasizes that without global endorsement and multilateral participation, the inequality between nations will worsen, and chances of forging more inclusive growth and prosperity in the future would be considerably compromised [8].

2.2.1 Fault Lines in the Global Monetary and Trading Architecture

This brings us to more long-term and historical issues—which persist despite all the strenuous initiatives taken after the establishment of the Bretton Woods institutions and during the run-up to the current Global Economic Order. Founded in the wake of World War II with the promise of delivering the South onto a new path of dizzying prosperity and development, the liberal, free-market economies meticulously laid down the foundations and espoused the relevance of the current economic order during the 1950s and in subsequent decades. However, despite all the expertise offered and strategies applied, conducive conditions for economic development continue to mostly elude developing nations. It is only rarely, as in the case of South Korea in late 1997, that an IMF bailout has been able to avert a national financial crisis [9, 10]. To benefit from such a rescue package, a diverse and adequate infrastructure along with tenacious and calibrated measures by the recipient country's government is a prerequisite. However, as most developing countries in the South do not have such infrastructure and processes in place, they are unable to develop enough momentum in the national economy, either for paying off loans and assistance—while implementing stringent conditionalities (IMF) and SAPs (World Bank) prescribed by multilateral financing institutions—or for maintaining inflows of revenues to sustain their economies during challenging, financial times.

Similarly, not all developing nations have been endowed with talented human resources and the political will to swim against the tide. Many leaders in the South, pandering to impatient electorates, resort to short-term options of quickly setting up ostentatious infrastructure or other such facilities through the availability of bilateral or multilateral assistance. Unless, however, they are careful in ensuring the flow of adequate revenues from other economic sectors, they risk falling into unending debt traps with no alternative left but to keep mechanically paying instalments against loans almost on a 'perpetual' basis, without being able to substantially diminish the outstanding liability owed by them against the principal loaned to them by external donors. The recent economic woes confronting Sri Lanka typify the serious consequences of delaying timely action to address ongoing problems of unsustainable debt and adverse balance of payments accounts [11].

Here, it would be relevant to take into consideration the strong scepticism and disagreement voiced by expert and critic author Professor Jason Hickel regarding the efficacy of economic deregulation measures recommended by multilateral lending agencies for facilitating meaningful participation by developing countries in the current global economy [12]. Although theoretically projected as unavoidable for preparing these economies for their launch into world markets, the open interface mandated by multilateral aid disbursal entities such as the IMF and World Bank mostly ends up conferring one-sided access for MNCs and developed-country investors into their economies. Compelled to cede control of key economic and financial processes to foreign agencies, there is little or no scope for governance authorities in these countries to explore economic growth and development as per the specific requirements and preferences of their local constituents [13]. Immensely restrictive and regulatory as the SAPs and conditionalities' regime generally works out to be, young professionals and nascent industries in such economies are strongly disincentivized from venturing into emerging business sectors. Effectively, this curtails any scope for their benefitting from any new opportunities opening in the global economy owing to MNCs sourcing materials and services from different vendors as E-Commerce steadily gains momentum. Over time, such constraints only worsen, making it increasingly difficult for the South to catch up with other countries, given the intense competition and the rapidly evolving quality and innovation benchmarks in world markets. Rather than herald prosperity and economic development, such prescribed measures mostly tend to deepen economic inequalities and disparities [12].

Understandably, the efficacy of such multilateral aid in enabling the empowerment of the South is being questioned by experts. It would be difficult to rebut the evidence cited by them—currency outflows from their financial markets due to tax holidays negotiated by demanding foreign corporations before undertaking FDI; leakages through trade misinvoicing; manipulation of tax liabilities through their subsidiaries in tax havens; payment of royalties against foreign IPR and innovation;

losses sustained due to recovery of minimalistic corporate taxes; low wages; and scant regard to local environmental benchmarks all of which cause considerable leakages in the revenues of developing countries. Indeed, as mentioned by Professor Jason Hickel, according to a report published by the US-based Global Financial Integrity (GFI) and the Centre for Applied Research at the Norwegian School of Economics in 2016, for every dollar of aid that developing countries receive, they lose $24 in net outflows [14].

Some of the other aspects that also merit review in this context are: During robust economic conditions in the South, there is a rapid inflow of funds. However, at the slightest onset of recessionary trends or stagnation, rapid withdrawal of deposits by foreign investors inevitably follows. Easing financial and capital controls, strongly championed by multilateral, and developed country entities, does make markets in developing countries more susceptible to the vagaries of the global economy, given the extensive networking and interdependence of economies in our globalized world today. Foreign institutional investors and other such entities constantly search for better opportunities all over the world. However, at the slightest change of prospects, for example, provoked by raising of interest rates by the US Fed, financial holdings in developing countries could see major outflows at very short notice. These trends are strongly manifested during moments of financial crises, as witnessed in 2008 [15]. The alarm bells sounded by the G20 at the beginning of this millennium on the need to quickly reform the global monetary and financial architecture are best understood in this context. One might recall how the then Brazilian President Luiz Inacio Lula da Silva, on the sidelines of the IBSA Summit held at New Delhi in October 2008, had singled out developed countries for having "transformed the world into a gigantic casino" [16].

In the wake of dissatisfied voices from the South becoming more strident, it is only inevitable that these issues should have at long last, found mention at UN gatherings. However, despite all the noble intentions voiced and enshrined initially, in the Millennium Development Goals and later, in the UN Sustainable Development Goals, the prospects of the Global South being able to substantially resolve its developmental problems seem to be gradually receding. COVID-19 has, of course, decidedly worsened matters. It would be pertinent to recall here that as estimated by UNCTAD, just for investing in basic infrastructure facilities of roads, rail and ports, power stations, water, sanitation, etc., developing countries will need to spend an estimated US$ 3.3 trillion to $4.5 trillion every year. At the prevailing rate of investment in 2014—both public and private—in SDG-related sectors in developing countries, there was an estimated annual shortfall of US$ 2.5 trillion [17]. Today, with added costs because of inflation, this can be expected to be even higher. Given these parameters, with severe dwindling global revenues, the chances of UNSDGs being realized by 2030, as stipulated by the UN, at this point, do not seem too bright.

2.2.2 Lacunae in the WTO and the Global Multilateral Trade Processes

Regarding the scenario on the international trading front, this is not encouraging. This can be easily discerned from the various issues and bottlenecks that currently impede the smooth and efficient functioning of the apex international trading entity—the World Trade Organization [18]. To mention just a few—Inability of the WTO to enforce optimal application and availability of Special and Differential Treatment provisions for all Developing countries—which are guaranteed to them when they enter the WTO [19]; Restrictions applied by developed nations to exports of developing countries through Non-Tariff Measures which require countries of the South to comply with various technical benchmarks which create discriminatory and disadvantageous conditions for international trade by them [20]; unaddressed TRIPS-related concerns which result in developing countries having to pay substantial costs for IPRs and patents for using or acquiring innovative technologies and processes developed in the North; [21] despite the general WTO caveat against provision of subsidies, while developed countries continue to provide subsidies for their agricultural products in order to make their exports competitive, they discourage such subsidies being provided by developing countries for goods and services being exported by them [22]; ongoing imbroglio between various countries owing to state-owned enterprises from some countries—which because of their immense financial strength and turnover—enjoy strong advantage and better negotiating capacity when bidding against private enterprises, including those from developed countries; impasse due to strong reservations by some countries regarding the appointment of members of the Appellate Body of the WTO; failure of this apex world trading body to include new issues pertaining to digital commerce, climate change technologies and other such matters into its agenda [23].

Ironically, in our current era of globalization, economic interdependence and E-Commerce and speedier air and shipping linkages, international trade opportunities, especially for developing countries, should have received a significant boost. Indeed, this was the vision that had been promised at the time of the establishment of this important multilateral trade-regulatory organization on 1 January 1995 [24]. However, despite protracted discussions and negotiations lasting many years, this apex trade body has been unable to deliver a robust and equitable multilateral trading system to world markets even though more than two decades have elapsed since its establishment. Instead, due to a lack of progress in some of the important areas mentioned above, regional trading arrangements have proliferated [25]. In the given exigencies, in the important area of international trade too, which could have at least partially augmented developing country revenues, the interests of the South largely stand compromised.

2.3 Technological and Digital Divide

In mankind's long journey along the path of economic development, the advent of the industrial revolution was indeed a watershed moment. Propelled by colonial powers that had ample access to raw materials and other resources in their affiliated colonies, the movement was quickly emulated in various parts of Europe, North America and other parts of the world [26]. Not only was mechanized manufacturing more efficient and of better quality but it also enabled countries to produce items in large volumes for sales in new markets at immense profits. The critical priority being accorded to the rapid industrialization of their economies by all countries in recent decades is best understood in this light.

In recent years, the outreach of the industrial revolution has received a significant impetus with the arrival of the Internet and the Digital Technologies revolution [27]. Unlike earlier times when technical experts and consultants had to travel across thousands of miles to install or customize their products and services for foreign markets, today, many such services are facilitated through online video conferencing, as amply demonstrated during COVID-19.

While all this has brought about a cascade of opportunities and wealth for the North, the South continues to grapple with classical problems of poverty, absence of physical and human infrastructure, mounting indebtedness, malnutrition, absence of healthcare, vulnerability to natural disasters and calamities and other such exigencies. Add to this lingering corruption and arbitrariness in governance processes in many of these countries, and we have a complete recipe for conjuring up despair, frustration and disillusionment within their masses. Understandably, as things stand, the prospects for the South being able to turn the tide in the not-too-distant future would not appear to be optimal.

COVID-19 has, of course, sharply exacerbated the prevalent conditions of economic deprivation in the South. While business entities in the South either closed down or suffered massive financial losses during the crisis, the large, ICT- and technology-based MNCs and corporations in the North continued to transact extensive business and flourish, even during these troubled times. The consequences are obvious. Not only did COVID-19 widen the glaring inequalities already existing between the North and South [28] but it also significantly deepened the immense technological and digital divide between both regions. For, in comparison with earlier years when digital communications were still in their infancy, the speed and the scale of the gap between the North and the South have increased manifold depending on the extent of availability of such expertise in different economies [29].

2.3.1 Digital Technologies Help Create Better Awareness About the Economic Divide

Although at the current juncture, technology might not have delivered any significant prosperity or economic redemption for many countries in the South, it has nevertheless irrefutably demonstrated the seminal role that the adoption of innovative techniques can play in enabling fruitful participation by the South in the interconnected and interdependent global economy of today. With the proliferation of digital connectivity and social media, communities within these countries can themselves witness online, the facilities and comfortable living conditions that their counterparts in the North have access to. What might have been mere hearsay in the past is now validated information to which they are personally exposed on a sustained basis. Disconcerting although such exposure might initially be, it could also motivate them to intensify their struggle to establish similar facilities in their countries.

2.3.2 The Absence of Digital Capabilities Can Impact Multiple Economic or Other Sectors, Including the Security Infrastructure of Countries

Subject to the availability of online and ICT facilities, not only business processes—barring those that require personal presence at manufacturing sites—but also other essential streams such as imparting education or academic insights, providing medical and healthcare guidance, organizing personal, multilateral, and even global virtual meetings and discussions can be enabled through speedy digital connectivity. The fact that these objectives can be achieved at short notice and relatively economical costs only reinforces the priority that needs to be given to these aspects in any country's economic development initiatives in the future. COVID-19 has substantially reinforced the utility of setting up such online infrastructure for empowering societies [30].

Increasingly, as ICT facilities become integrated into a country's development infrastructure, the induction of technological safeguards for maintaining surveillance on the flow of online data and traffic also assumes priority from the point of view of a country's security processes. This is true not only for developing but also for developed countries—given the menace posed by the dark Web or by hackers gaining access to banking, utility, defence or other strategic systems in a country's governance processes. It is in this context that security authorities in a country often seek selective access to social media platforms such as WhatsApp and Telegram for monitoring exchanges conducted by money launderers, terrorists or other criminal elements on social media [31].

Ironically, the imperatives for accelerating the entry of Southern countries into the world of technology and innovation had been realized more than four decades ago, when in September 1978, senior representatives from as many as 138 countries consensually adopted the Buenos Aires Plan of Action for Promoting and Implementing Technical Cooperation among Developing Countries (TCDC). The wisdom of pursuing the BAPA Plan recommendations, painstakingly crafted for 5 years by a galaxy of international experts, was again recommended at the BAPA + 40 meeting held in Buenos Aires in March 2019 [32, 33].

Having regard to the above, the surging technological and digital divide confronting the South, unless urgently addressed, could increasingly become a principal constraint in these countries realizing their aspirations for kickstarting conditions of development and prosperity in their economies [34].

2.4 Climate Change Trends

This admittedly is one of the most neglected areas, not only by the South but also by the North. Obsessed as the world has been with pillaging the planet for more resources for enhancing creature comforts, Nature's benedictions seem to have been taken for granted. It is now common knowledge that the major polluters in the past have principally been those in the Global North [35]. In the early decades of industrialization, with little awareness about climate change-related consequences, the sole focus of such countries was to quickly enrich and upgrade their economies. It is only now when the repercussions of this intense drive to modernize at any cost are manifesting in unabated carbon emissions, that the devastating threats posed by global warming are being duly acknowledged. Unfortunately, we might already be too late. In 2015, for the first time perhaps, almost all countries formally agreed under the Paris Treaty pursuant to UNFCCC Climate Change deliberations to limit global warming to 1.5 °C in comparison with preindustrial levels [4]. Earlier, at COP 15 during the Copenhagen Summit in December 2009, developed countries agreed to jointly mobilize US$ 100 billion a year by 2020 to address the needs of developing countries [36]. Before this target could be fully implemented, COVID-19 struck, thus possibly reversing by many years, the chances of any progress being made in this regard in future years.

Fortunately, as noted by The Economist [37], there is some forward movement after the COP 27 talks in Egypt in November 2022—in that developed countries have finally acknowledged that there should be funding for environmental loss and damage; that greenwashing will not be accepted and that corporates should not—while claiming to be net zero—continue to expand fossil fuel supplies; in a major departure from past practices, when Food and Farming aspects were excluded from Climate Change discussions, the COP 27 Presidency launched the Food and Agriculture for Sustainable Transformation (FAST) initiative to improve the quantity and quality of climate finance contributions; similarly, initiatives for boosting infrastructural capacity and resilience of communities to address global warming were also initiated during COP 27.

However, more tangible implementation of outstanding commitments and momentum in this regard will need to be ensured. As things stand, given the years of neglect, climate change increasingly threatens to become an existential issue [38]. It would be illogical to make light of the many challenges—which experts have long been cautioning about—pertaining to its adverse impact on agriculture and food cycles; depletion of water tables; melting of glaciers and other related effects; submerging of land territories of small, island countries confronted with rising tides and sea level; distorted working hours and schedules in warmer and tropical countries for persons engaged in agriculture, construction and other outdoor occupations; precipitating unforeseen rains, typhoons or other natural calamities that leave major destruction in their wake and other such adverse effects [1]. Of course, excessive heat can have adverse effects on human anatomy [39].

Here too, the hardest hit would be countries of the South. Living barely in subsistence-level conditions, their ability to bounce back after global warming-induced setbacks is minimal [40]. In any case, with their meagre resources, they would not be able to rebuild any infrastructure or other facilities destroyed either during natural or climate change-based calamities. Developed countries might be able to limit the impact of global warming in some situations, e.g., by warding off personal discomfort through air conditioning; controlling forest fires by dousing them with aerial water sprays or using innovative irrigation methods; implementing soil treatment techniques for curtailing the impact of global warming on agricultural activities, etc. However, as carbon emissions escalate as an increasing number of countries in the South adopt industrial technologies and modernize, the cascading effects of global warming will increasingly become more difficult to contain and eventually can be expected to adversely affect all countries, including those in the North.

2.5 Impact of COVID-19

Here, it would be pertinent to again remind ourselves of the unending economic constraints prevalent in the South despite all the strategies recommended by the Bretton Woods institutions and the transformative vision enshrined first in the Millennium Development Goals and later in the UN Sustainable Development Goals. As mentioned earlier in this paper, the inequitable aspects of the contemporary World Economic Order have already generated copious, critical commentary by author-critics such as Prof. Jason Hickel in 'The Divide'. These were reiterated recently in the comprehensive report compiled by the World Inequality Lab [41]. With no significant improvement in the economic malaise of many countries in the Global South despite the strategies and initiatives implemented at the behest of Northern entities, developing countries can no longer be faulted for being largely hesitant about the efficacy of such options. In the post-COVID era, such scepticism has only deepened.

Given these trends, in the aftermath of COVID-19, redressal of the economic maladies of the South is not going to be easy. Already inadequate even during earlier decades, now, any spare financial resources in the developed economies can be expected to be mainly applied to sustaining their economies. That economic options in most countries today stand severely curtailed because of shrinking domestic and global GDP after long lockdowns and because of steep escalation of food and energy costs pursuant to the Ukraine crisis only complicates matters. Despite these exigencies, it would be unfair and unrealistic to expect the South to postpone its economic redemption processes until salubrious conditions return in the North and the global economy. Not only does this approach contradict the lofty vision of shared prosperity epitomized in the UN and other multilateral developmental cooperation documents, but it is almost tantamount to making light of the ordeals of abject poverty and hunger being suffered by the Global South, made all the more severe, in the aftermath of COVID.

At the same time, the descent of the South into its current economic woes cannot merely be attributed to COVID-19. Historically, the record of disbursal of development assistance by the North to the South has never been robust. It is acknowledged that periodically, there has been spirited theoretical discussion and focus on their plight, as manifested first in the UN Millennium Development Goals in 2000 and later in the Sustainable Development Goals in 2015. However, the results of promises made for ensuring the well-being and welfare of all countries projected at various multilateral fora still have to tangibly unfold. COVID-19 can be expected to considerably delay relief for the South in this regard, as borne by pointed references made in this regard by the UN Secretary-General [1].

2.6 Other Issues

2.6.1 Simmering Unrest and Discontent in the South Might Precipitate Disruptive and Existential Challenges

With regard to all the above technology and economic and climate change-related challenges, unless some radical measures or strategies are explored to redress the expectations of the South, the possibility of large swathes of restless and frustrated communities emerging in the Global South [42] cannot be ruled out. Compelled to embrace oblivion for years, they might wait a little longer for things to improve. However, it cannot be taken for granted that younger generations in affected countries will always be willing to overlook and forgo the comforts and luxuries that their counterparts in developed countries thrive in. Given their sustained online exposure to such facilities—in our current era of 24 × 7 internet connectivity—it cannot be presumed that they will never consider questioning or strongly repudiating the apparent neglect and injustice being meted out to them by the current World Order.

What the world witnessed during the Arab Spring was disturbing. The avalanche of discontentment and unmitigated fury that the post-COVID aftermath and 'decades-old' frustration might trigger off in the South is bound to be far more disruptive [43]. Mob sentiments have always been irrational. In our current era of seamless, 24 ×

7 online connectivity, if such a conflagration spreads—fanned as it could be empathetic NGOs and sympathizing activists in developed countries—the existing world governance, and economic and multilateral processes could face serious, existential challenges.

2.6.2 Interdependence Between Economies

Given the extensive interdependence of economies in our globalized world today, it would seem highly imprudent to keep neglecting the conditions of economic deprivation and discontent festering in the South. Almost four decades ago, the Commission led by former German Chancellor Willy Brandt, in its perceptive reports The North–South (1980) and the Common Crisis (1983), rightly emphasized that there is an integral interdependence between the Global North and the Global South [44]. It is true that through their incessant perseverance, entrepreneurship and research and diligence, countries of the North have made stellar advances in science and technology, medical research and healthcare, transportation, communications, ICT and other varied disciplines. It is also acknowledged that depending on their respective economic strengths and preferences, communities all over the world benefit from innovation and entrepreneurship being regularly churned out by the forward economies of the North. However, a key factor contributing to their prosperity and success is the ability of the multinational business entities in the North to sell their goods and services in the large and populated markets of the South. It would seem difficult to deny that if the South were to continue to wallow in conditions of hunger and poverty, the quantum of profits and wealth that its communities generate for the North will eventually not diminish. Brandt's point and recommendation about the complementarity and interdependence between the North and the South are hence well taken. In fact, with the proliferation of digital communications and e-commerce, the interconnectivity between global markets and the economic interdependence between nations has only deepened further.

In light of these trends, one sincerely hopes that if not for humanitarian reasons, at least on grounds of making better economic choices, the travails of the South will secure more attention and relief in developed country governance and business processes. Again, given the pace at which innovation and new manufacturing processes influence the quality of everyday life, related issues such as the mounting technological and digital divide between countries and the inability of the South to mostly comply with the latest climate change benchmarks without support from the North merit urgent attention while addressing the cause of the Global South. As explained in the foregoing paragraphs of this essay, all such aspects will impact not only the future progress and prosperity of countries in the South but also those in the North.

2.7 Possible Options

2.7.1 Diluting the Technology and Digital Divide

Here, it might be relevant to remind ourselves that the future decades are expected to be strongly influenced and dominated by countries whose populations and economies are proficient in high technology areas such as ICT and digital sciences; biotechnology and pharmaceuticals; telecommunications; environment and green technologies; outer space capabilities; artificial intelligence and other such emerging fields [45]. Unless initiated into these niche disciplines soon, economies in the South will lag considerably behind those in the North in future years and find it exceedingly difficult to get a foothold into global markets, given the array of choices opening up for consumers all over the world and the nexus between innovation, design and competitive pricing and the domestic and global market share of business entities [46].

In these circumstances, it has perhaps become urgently necessary for the South to urgently mull over its various options and devise new strategies for combating the ongoing and upcoming crises it faces. As suggested in the earlier parts of this essay, the important role being played by technological and digital processes in various aspects of the world economy needs to be carefully analysed and reviewed by the South. Technology and innovation are game-changers in our era of seamless online connectivity, and top priority should inevitably be given to this sector by countries in the South to ensure that their communities are skilled and trained in as many critical and emerging technologies as possible [47]. As mentioned earlier, the critical role played by this sector was also emphasized by the Buenos Aires Plan of Action in 1978, which was again endorsed in December 2019 during the BAPA + 40 deliberations.

It cannot be denied that the meagre resources they are endowed with will always be a limitation. However, even if investing in technical prowess involves skimping and saving funds currently being spent on other sectors, the exercise would seem worthwhile because of the tangible impact that technological expertise would have on their future fortunes. Without a doubt, this is going to be arduous, given that many of the countries in the South are incessantly preoccupied with paying up instalments for outstanding loans or assistance taken from various bilateral or multilateral donors and institutions. However, further delay in taking these initiatives will make it even more difficult for the South to catch up with the North, given the speed at which technology and innovation are being incorporated into various sectors of the national and international economy today. Consequently, as a very modest beginning, it might not be imprudent to allocate some budget for providing scholarships to deserving candidates for upgrading their skills or for imparting them training abroad. Similarly, initiatives, even if few, could be taken to install minimal ICT infrastructure facilities in their economies.

It is acknowledged that there can be no immediate shortcut for transforming the economies of the South into centres of economic development, innovation and prosperity [46]. However, the availability of digital expertise and infrastructure enables various segments of their population to quickly connect and interact with experts and entities pursuing excellence in technology and innovation in other countries. Subject to the availability of minimalistic ICT infrastructure, building such awareness would increasingly help more aspirants in the South to be introduced to new knowledge streams. With enhanced exposure to these disciplines, there is a strong likelihood of their becoming motivated to explore opportunities for training themselves and acquiring proficiency for online positions—whether in the field of IT, marketing, business and market analysis, tourism and hospitality and other such areas that might interest foreign employers. Minor although such transformation might be, it would be better than being pessimistic and lamenting about their lot in life. As the positives of this exercise percolate across to the younger echelons of the population in these countries, a burgeoning, professional community—even though modest in size—would be able to salvage some earnings not only to sustain themselves but also their families. Governments, hitherto only focused on repayment of debts and other economic crises, might also be encouraged to step in and foster these initiatives, whether by investing in more infrastructure or sponsoring potential candidates for specialized training in proficient developing or developed countries. As data transmission speeds increase, such online opportunities can only be expected to multiply, given the high wages and salaries that are required to be paid for sourcing similar services from professionals in developed countries.

2.7.2 Opening up Alternate Online Economic and Business Opportunities Through Better Digital Infrastructure

On a similar note, it might be fruitful for developing economies to also consider tapping into other online avenues. Even if present only in small numbers, there might be talented or self-trained artists in these countries—in music, dance or other professional streams. Ordinarily, the chances of their connecting with global audiences would be very slim. However, in the seamlessly connected, globalized world that we live in today, ICT applications such as YouTube or other social media interfaces offer some respite [48]. Going digital could help such candidates find recognition for their proficiency and gradually unravel opportunities for augmenting their incomes and earnings from online sources [48]. In the trying circumstances that confront economies in the South today, no potential avenue or area for engaging their younger population can be neglected. Hence, even though seemingly far-fetched to begin with, it would be useful for the South to stimulate and shepherd the interest of the younger section of their population in such hobbies by establishing more efficient ICT facilities. Needless to point out, any little measure or possibility that inspires meaningful participation in the national drive for upgrading living conditions in their country would have a redeeming effect.

An additional advantage accruing from the establishment of basic digital infrastructure—even though this would take time and require intense efforts and frugal fiscal management—would be that exposure and access to foreign markets would also enable small and medium-level traders and resellers in the South to connect with potential buyers in the North. Possibilities of exporting abroad, even on a small scale, would incentivize them to enhance the quality of their products and ensure better compliance with international benchmarks. The handshake facilitated by an increasing digital interface could, thus, have salutary effects on the social and economic health of the South [48]. It could also be the harbinger of new business alliances and joint ventures and even initiate FDI in some sectors.

Here, it would also not be out of place to keep in mind that owing to multiple product and technology options, consumers today are highly discerning and critical in their choices. The lack of industrial and technological capabilities in the South seriously handicaps their drive to enhance exports of their goods and services to the intensively competitive world markets of today. The absence of technology, therefore, operates as a double whammy. In addition to diminishing the outreach and reputation of developing countries in the global economy, it also blunts their chances of contributing to emerging Global Supply Chains. These lacunae seriously dilute any opportunities available for them to diversify their revenues, which continue to be based on primary occupations and at minimal wages or on the sale of natural or mineral resources at unrewarding prices negotiated with them by exploitative, foreign business houses.

2.7.3 Enhancing South–South Cooperation

This brings us back to the principal and almost insurmountable constraint that always has and continues to thwart economic development in the South—the availability of adequate funds. Given that domestic revenues in these countries will never be adequate and external bilateral and multilateral donors are even more reticent after COVID-19, the South may like to urgently consider renewing enhanced South-South cooperation for partial relief in this regard. Such intra-cooperation in the South would have some immediate advantages. Not only would some prospects open up for garnering development funds at more economical costs, but further, they could be sourced on better and more convenient terms. Thus, in the case of South-South funding, it might be possible for recipient countries to negotiate arrangements that do not require their economies to implement extensive structural adjustment programmes or conditionalities that generally insist on eschewing ongoing or future development initiatives and ceding control of core, domestic, financial processes to external, creditor-guided agencies. Such prospects assume even greater relevance in the wake of COVID-19 [49].

Another advantage accruing from such cooperation would be that experts and technologists from more proficient countries in the South could share expertise and provide training in key disciplines, for example, being provided under the Indian Technical and Economic Cooperation (ITEC) programme [50]. Although no bilateral or regional assistance is without political costs, developing countries would still largely retain their freedom to consider alternate, economic options based on their country's indigenous strengths, talents and preferences. Rather than curbing the drive of aspiring entrepreneurs and talented professionals because of their economies being put into an inexorable, debt-repayment syndrome, their financial authorities would still be able to explore varied avenues for augmenting and diversifying their countries' revenues.

Other positive effects of such South–South cooperation pertain to ease of engaging in overseas trade because of fewer restrictions and benchmarks, closer air and shipping linkages and other such advantages. While the best technologies in consumer goods or other products might not be available, the cost of sourcing imports from counterpart southern countries would be cheaper, (i) because there are minimal or modest licensing fees because of IPR requirements compared to the royalties to be paid for innovations developed in the North and (ii) the goods being imported or sourced are often from a neighbouring country or region.

An interesting offshoot of transacting more trade within the South would also be that it would dilute the current monopoly of Northern suppliers who are active in developing country markets. Confronted with prospects of depleting sales in the South, businesses in the North might consider lowering the prices of their goods and services. Faced with such exigencies, at the time of negotiating joint ventures involving FDI by them, better attention might also be given by Northern corporate entities to the interests of the South—whether in terms of payment of better wages to workers/employees in the South, payment of more taxes, implementing more CSR initiatives, focusing also on indigenous environmental concerns and other such objectives generally neglected by FDI partners venturing into Southern markets.

2.7.4 Climate Change Possibilities

As also suggested earlier, it would be quite counterproductive for all countries to neglect priorities on climate change, given their lasting impact on the living conditions of future generations inhabiting this planet [43]. In this regard, the South is disadvantaged not only because it does not have access to the latest green technologies but also because it still has a long way to catch up with the industrial proficiency and diversity of the North. Although it has been many decades since the North started violating environmental norms, the clamours of the South in this regard have generally been falling on deaf ears.

In this context, deepening intra-South cooperation would also vest the South with better alternatives. Increased coordination of national positions in this regard will imbue the South with enhanced negotiating power at multilateral and other gatherings in this regard. Depending on the extent to which they unitedly pursue their interests in this important area, they could start demanding greater accountability from the North for the damage done to this cause not only during previous years but also at the current juncture.

Responsibility of the North in the context of Climate Change could extend to—payment of penalties for previous pollution caused by them and also for granting carbon credits to those countries in the South that are less or least polluting or that are diluting carbon emissions by maintaining large tracts of rainforests or adopting other green technologies and practices in their countries. As noted above, the decisions made at COP 27 requiring the disbursal of more resources by the North for damage and loss sustained during climate change-induced calamities constitute a welcome step. For, if nothing else works out, at the very minimum, owing to better awareness about these aspects, there would be more pressure on countries of the North to share technologies and funds that enable developing countries to comply with current climate change benchmarks. Coordinated and consultative attention on such issues will help the South to better address its concerns [49] on being able to withstand the adverse effects of global warming, including with regard to the serious threat faced by some of them because their land territories are at permanent risk of becoming submerged by rising ocean waters.

2.8 Concluding Remarks

2.8.1 Empowering Communities in the Global South

Given the complexity and inordinate delay in addressing their aspirations, the challenges faced by the Global South will need the implementation of multipronged solutions and strategies—whether domestic, bilateral, regional or multilateral. As postcolonial decades have slipped past, the initial promises held out by developed country entities to the teeming millions of the South have begun to lose their lustre. All this, coupled with the geo-political challenges in East Europe and the potential, geopolitical fault lines in other regions such as the Indo-Pacific, Middle East, and other regions, seriously worsens the ongoing, varied difficulties faced by countries in the South.

As regaining 'lost' territory is not going to be easy and neither is any windfall imminent, an intense and uphill struggle on the part of the South, for improving its lot, is unavoidable. One also sincerely hopes that the current crises being faced by the South will not overwhelm disenchanted, younger segments of its population. Hence, keeping their hopes alive by initiating small but meaningful changes, e.g., setting aside funds for providing talented candidates scholarships for training abroad, setting up at least minimalistic ICT and technology infrastructure and other such steps, would do a long way in keeping them focused on creative professional interests [48]. With the gradual proliferation of informed and aware communities in the South, some positive effects are likely to also spill over to their governance processes. Indeed, it would no longer be possible for the chosen political representatives in these countries to brush aside or neglect the aspirations of their population to expedite ushering in of prosperity and better living conditions in their economies. With the increasing accountability of the political leadership towards their constituents in these countries [51], governance processes in the South would gradually resonate better with their country's long-term national interests rather than being guided by populist measures based on short-term electoral gains.

Accordingly, the very first step in the direction of redeeming the South would seem to lie in giving urgent priority and minute attention to providing skills and expertise for empowering their masses. Whether this involves salvaging meagre resources from within their economies, engaging in more South-South cooperation or reaching out to benign bilateral or multilateral donors, all channels will have to be kept open. It cannot be denied that while eking out financial resources for creating core-competent clusters and groups within their populations, allocating budgets for critical sectors such as food and hunger, poverty and availability of housing and other facilities cannot be neglected. Understandably, it would be futile to work on the proliferation of innovation and knowledge-based expertise if large sections of their communities do not access basic living conditions. Any policies or initiatives taken in this regard will have to sync with and review prevalent financial and economic trends and constraints in their countries. Cautious and calibrated steps for contributing to global supply chains and tapping into varied opportunities thrown up by the digital and interdependent global economy should, in the long term, find endorsement by their citizens and expedite their chances of recovering lost economic territory.

2.8.2 Formulating Informed and Analytical Insights and Coordinating Positions on Important Multilateral and Global Issues in the South

Some of the above initiatives should give new life and hope to demoralized sections in the Global South. Fortifying them can also be expected to give them more confidence and insights for articulating their concerns more powerfully at global fora, based of course, on greater coordination and resonance of their preferred choices and options. Although minor in comparison with the colossal constraints and difficulties confronting these countries over the years, some of the positives that accrue by implementing some of the above measures would motivate their communities—especially the younger echelons—to stay on course and encourage them to keep empowering themselves. As the extent and scale of their problems are immense and overwhelming, urgently tapping into all available options and avenues—whether domestic, Intra-South, bilateral, regional or multilateral—will need to be pursued.

Without a doubt, a concomitant of enhanced South-South cooperation is that it would foster greater resonance on positions by countries of the South on various global and multilateral issues discussed at international fora such as the UN or at other important multilateral gatherings. Even though this would not immediately impact core processes in UNSC proceedings, coordination of Southern positions on issues of common concern at the UNGA, WTO, IMF and World would go a long way in getting better attention on their concerns during deliberations at such fora [52]. Needless to mention, a lack of unity or understanding of their part in such matters has considerably weakened their bargaining and negotiating position during such discussions.

Here, one should not forget that sharing expertise by leading countries in the South—whether regarding current economic and financial trends, contemporary global issues being reviewed by multilateral fora, or international trade issues under the WTO—would also enhance their awareness for being able to take informed and relevant positions on such matters in accordance with their long-term interests. Needless to mention, having strengthened its role and influence in global affairs, the Global South will be better positioned to espouse its interests at the UN, IMF & World Bank and other leading international entities.

While lobbying for their cause, as more and more of them find their voice in the comity of nations, the chances of getting better focus by the North on their woes would increase. Given the extensively connected and interdependent global economy, we live in today, allowing disruption and repudiation of the prevalent world political and economic order by restless and frustrated youth populations in the South will have cataclysmic effects on the fortunes of MNCs and other business entities that supply goods and services in the South. *These aspects will need to be strongly reiterated by a more 'united' South in its dialogue with the North.*

2.8.3 Reaching Out to NGOs and Other Entities in the North

Here, it would also be relevant to note that some of the NGOs and other entities in developed countries could also help raise modest resources for their critical economic priorities or help them connect with potential private or corporate donors or philanthropic entities. Sensitizing corporate audiences to the need to engage in more substantial corporate social responsibility projects for developmental activities would understandably be very useful. As rightly pointed out by experts, during recent decades, substantial wealth and assets have transitioned from state-owned entities to the private sector [53]. Given that during COVID-19, governments in most countries have had to invest massively in the healthcare sector and support varied initiatives for preventing economic recession, their capacity to contribute to developmental activities is proportionately impaired to that extent.

Another positive effect accruing from such endeavours by the South to win over NGOs and intelligentsia in the North towards its cause would be that such influential stakeholders in developed countries would also be encouraged to, in their several exchanges and dialogues with their leadership on diverse multilateral and global issues, emphasize the desirability of taking positions that resonate with those of the South. As suggested in earlier parts of this essay, from a long-term perspective, ensuring equitable decision-making in these matters would also contribute to more political stability and predictability in global political and security-related trends.

2.8.4 Improved Prospects for Focusing on Climate Change Aspects as Economic Priorities Get Better Addressed in the South

With their economic priorities moving in the right direction, it might not be out of place to surmise that the South might be more willing to accord better attention to long-term challenges such as those posed by climate change. During its interaction with the North, the South might do well to emphasize that facilitating more attention by countries of the South to global warming-related issues will ultimately also impact developed countries positively. While on the one hand, an impoverished South will seriously erode into the profits and revenues of the MNCs from the North—which depend on robust sales of their products and services in the Southern markets—the impact of Climate Change would be far more pervasive and could spell unmitigated and all-round disaster for all countries—including those in the North—now and in the future.

Accordingly, during its dialogue with the North, it would not be out of place for the South to reiterate that (i) countries in the North must urgently operationalize more resources for ensuring the proliferation and greater adoption of green technologies in the South and (ii) there should be more accountability and acknowledgement by the North for the environmental damage, even if caused unknowingly or inadvertently, during their respective industrialization drives undertaken many years ago.

2.8.5 Diverting Valuable Resources Being Spent on the Upgradation of Defence and Security-Related Equipment in the North for Developmental Purposes in the South

The irony, however, is that while palpable neglect of the poor economic conditions in the South continues, countries in the North and some even in the South continue to fritter away valuable resources for the acquisition and modernization of defence and security-related equipment [54]. The Brandt Commission reports had proposed that a stiff tax should be proposed on arms trade so that the fees recovered from the same could be channelled into human development. Very perceptively, it had also expanded the concept of human security "to include hunger, disease, poverty, environmental stress, repression, and terrorism, all of which endanger human security as much as any military provocation" [44].

2.8.6 *Reform of UN Processes to Curtail Security and Terrorism Risks Posed for the South*

Doubtless, the curtailment of conflict and war by strengthening procedural and multilateral checks and balances through a reformed UNSC would provide valuable succour and relief to a beleaguered South. That persisting economic maladies and denial of basic living conditions in the South could easily deteriorate and become fertile grounds for ushering in radical ideologies—including those that foment extremism and global terrorism—is another paramount criticality that merits urgent consideration in this regard.

References

1. The Sustainable Development Goals Report: Foreword (2022). https://unstats.un.org/sdgs/report/2022/The-Sustainable-Development-Goals-Report-2022.pdf
2. Banerjee, Duflo (2022) World inequality report 2022: foreword. World Inequality Lab. https://WIR2022.WID.WORLD
3. United Nations Publications (2022) Trade and development report 2021: from recovery to resilience: the development dimension: overview. United Nations
4. Paris Agreement: Article 1(a) (2015) https://unfccc.int/sites/default/files/english_paris_agreement.pdf. Accessed 5 Nov 2022
5. IMF World Economic Outlook Report: Foreword, xiii (2022). https://www.imf.org/en/Publications/WEO/Issues/2022/10/11/world-economic-outlook-october-2022. Accessed 6 Nov 2022
6. Ocampo JA, Dervis K (2022) Will Ukraine's tragedy spur UN security council reform? Brookings. https://www.brookings.edu/opinions/will-ukraines-tragedy-spur-un-security-council-reform/
7. Financing for Sustainable Development Report 2022: Chapter III.B 3(2) (2022). https://unstats.un.org/sdgs/report/2022/The-Sustainable-Development-Goals-Report-2022.pdf. Accessed 5 Nov 2022
8. Financing for Sustainable Development Report 2022 | United Nations Inter-Agency Task Force on Financing for Development: Foreword (2022). https://developmentfinance.un.org/fsdr2022. Accessed 5 Nov 2022
9. Koo J, Kiser SL (2002) Recovery from a financial crisis: the case of South Korea. https://core.ac.uk/reader/51180488. Accessed 3 Nov 2022
10. Fackler M (2011) South Korea makes a quick economic recovery. The New York Times. https://www.nytimes.com/2011/01/07/world/asia/07seoul.html
11. Sri Lanka Development Update: Executive Summary (2022). https://thedocs.worldbank.org/en/doc/6c87e47ca3f08a4b13e67f79aec8fa3b-0310062022/original/Sri-Lanka-Development-Update-October-2022-final.pdf. Accessed 4 Nov 2022
12. Hickel J (2017) The divide: a brief guide to global inequality and its solutions. William Heinemann
13. Malaluan JC, Guttal S (2003) Poverty reduction strategy papers: a poor package for poverty reduction. http://www.cadtm.org/IMG/pdf/prsp.pdf
14. Hickel J (2021) Aid in reverse: how poor countries develop rich countries. The Guardian. https://www.theguardian.com/global-development-professionals-network/2017/jan/14/aid-in-reverse-how-poor-countries-develop-rich-countries
15. Reforming the international financial architecture: world economic and social survey 2010 (2010) UN. https://www.un.org/en/development/desa/policy/wess/wess_current/2010wess_chapter5.pdf

16. Rich countries 'turned world into casino' (2008). https://mg.co.za/article/2008-10-15-rich-countries-turned-world-into-casino/. Accessed 4 Nov 2022
17. United Nations (2014) World investment report: 2014: investing in the SDGs—an action plan: overview. United Nations (Un)
18. The E15 initiative: strengthening the global trade and investment system in the 21st century: functioning of the WTO: background challenges. (2016). https://www3.weforum.org/docs/E15/WEF_Full_Report_Strengthening_Global_Trade_Investment_System_21st_Century.pdf. Accessed 5 Nov 2022
19. WTO | Doha 4th Ministerial—Ministerial declaration: Para 44 (2001) https://www.wto.org/english/thewto_e/minist_e/min01_e/mindecl_e.htm
20. Asia-pacific trade and investment report 2019: introduction—the rise of non-tariff measures (2019). https://www.unescap.org/sites/default/d8files/APTIR2019_Introduction.pdf
21. Bello (2022) The Global South in the WTO: Time to Go on the Offensive—FPIF. Foreign Policy in Focus. https://fpif.org/the-global-south-in-the-wto-time-to-go-on-the-offensive/. Accessed 1 Nov 2022
22. WTO | Doha 4th Ministerial - Ministerial declaration: Para 13 (2001) https://www.wto.org/english/thewto_e/minist_e/min01_e/mindecl_e.htm
23. Reforming the World Trade Organization (2020) Prospects for transatlantic cooperation and the global trade system. https://www.chathamhouse.org/sites/default/files/publications/research/2020-09-11-reforming-wto-schneider-petsinger.pdf.pdf. Accessed 7 Nov 2022
24. World Trade Organization (2015) The WTO at twenty: challenges and achievements: foreword
25. The E15 Initiative: Strengthening the Global Trade and Investment System in the 21st Century: Regional Trade Agreements—Introduction (2016). https://www3.weforum.org/docs/E15/WEF_Full_Report_Strengthening_Global_Trade_Investment_System_21st_Century.pdf
26. History of Europe | Summary, Wars, Map, Ideas, & Colonialism (2022) Encyclopedia Britannica. https://www.britannica.com/topic/history-of-Europe/A-maturing-industrial-society. Accessed 4 Nov 2022
27. World Economic Forum (2020) The fourth industrial revolution: what it means and how to respond. https://www.weforum.org/agenda/2016/01/the-fourth-industrial-revolution-what-it-means-and-how-to-respond/
28. Oxfam International (2022) Pandemic creates new billionaire every 30 hours—now a million people could fall into extreme poverty at same rate in 2022. https://www.oxfam.org/en/press-releases/pandemic-creates-new-billionaire-every-30-hours-now-million-people-could-fall
29. UNCTAD (2020) The least developed countries report 2020: Overview. https://unctad.org/system/files/official-document/ldcr2020_en.pdf
30. UNESCO (2020) Fighting COVID-19 through digital innovation and transformation. https://en.unesco.org/covid19/communicationinformationresponse/digitalinnovation
31. Interpol National Cybercrime Strategy Guidebook: Section 6.4.4.2 (2021). https://www.interpol.int/en/Search-Page?search=Nationl+Cybercrime+Strategy+Guidebook+April+2021. Accessed 4 Nov 2022
32. Buenos Aires outcome document of the second High-level United Nations Conference on South–South Cooperation: Para 24(h) (2019). https://www.unsouthsouth.org/wp-content/uploads/2019/10/N1911172.pdf. Accessed 1 Nov 2022
33. Buenos Aires outcome document of the second High-level United Nations Conference on South–South Cooperation: Para 30(e) (2019) https://www.unsouthsouth.org/wp-content/uploads/2019/10/N1911172.pdf. Accessed 1 Nov 2022
34. Bridging the technological divide technology adoption by firms in developing countries: foreword (2022) https://openknowledge.worldbank.org/bitstream/handle/10986/37527/9781464818264.pdf?sequence=7&isAllowed=y. Accessed 7 Nov 2022
35. UNCTAD (n.d.) Smallest footprints, largest impacts: least developed countries need a just sustainable transition. https://unctad.org/topic/least-developed-countries/chart-October-2021
36. Paris Agreement: Article 8 (2015) https://unfccc.int/sites/default/files/english_paris_agreement.pdf. Accessed 5 Nov 2022

37. COP27—five key takeaways from the UN climate talks (2022) Economist impact. https://impact.economist.com/sustainability/five-key-takeaways-cop27?gclid=CjwKCAiA-dCcBhBQEiwAeWidtVsOUyxDncZgY-rea7q0kiXpPXLeb-8jMqDQnO4bp01HJQjMrGcJVxoCaEwQAvD_BwE. Accessed 10 Dec 2022
38. Global Risks Report 2022 (n.d.) World economic forum. https://www.weforum.org/reports/global-risks-report-2022/in-full/grr2022-executive-summary/. Accessed 5 Nov 2022
39. Climate Impacts on Human Health | Climate Change Impacts | US EPA (n.d.) https://climatechange.chicago.gov/climate-impacts/climate-impacts-human-health. Accessed 10 Dec 2022
40. UNCTAD (2021) Smallest footprints, largest impacts: Least developed countries need a just sustainable transition. https://unctad.org/topic/least-developed-countries/chart-October-2021. Accessed 31 Oct 2022
41. World Inequality Report 2022: Chapter 10 (2022) https://wir2022.wid.world/www-site/uploads/2022/03/0098-21_WIL_RIM_RAPPORT_A4.pdf
42. Stewart F (2002) Root causes of violent conflict in developing countries commentary: conflict–from causes to prevention? BMJ 324(7333):342–345. https://doi.org/10.1136/bmj.324.7333.342
43. The Global Risks Report 17th Edition, World Economic Forum: Chapter 2 (2022) https://www3.weforum.org/docs/WEF_The_Global_Risks_Report_2022.pdf
44. Quilligan (2002) The brandt equation: 21st century blueprint for the new global economy. https://www.brandt21forum.info/
45. UNESCO (2005) Towards knowledge societies, UNESCO world report: introduction. https://unesdoc.unesco.org/ark:/48223/pf0000141843. Accessed 5 Nov 2022
46. United Nations (2021) The least developed countries report 2020: overview. UN
47. Ben Hassen T (2022) The GCC economies in the wake of COVID-19: toward PostOil sustainable knowledge-based economies? Sustainability 14(18):11251. https://doi.org/10.3390/su141811251
48. Kabanda (2016) Music for development in the digital age. https://thedocs.worldbank.org/en/doc/923101459255847647-0050022016/original/WDR16BPMusicforDevelopmentKabanda.pdf. Accessed 8 Nov 2022
49. State of South Cooperation: Report of the Secretary General. (2021). https://unsouthsouth.org/wp-content/uploads/2021/10/A76403-E.pdf). Accessed 5 Nov 2022
50. Ministry of External Affairs, Government of India (2014) 50 years of ITEC: Indian technical cooperation programme. https://www.mea.gov.in/Uploads/PublicationDocs/24148_REVISED_50_yrs_of_ITEC_brochure.pdf. Accessed 28 Oct 2022
51. OECD (2007) Promoting pro-poor growth, POLICY GUIDANCE FOR DONORS: Chapter 4. https://www.oecd-ilibrary.org/development/promoting-pro-poor-growth_9789264024786-en
52. UNCTAD, South–South cooperation at the time of COVID-19: building solidarity among developing countries
53. World Inequality Report 2022: Executive Summary. (2022). https://wir2022.wid.world/www-site/uploads/2022/03/0098-21_WIL_RIM_RAPPORT_A4.pdf
54. World military expenditure passed $2 trillion for the first time | SIPRI. (2022). https://www.sipri.org/media/press-release/2022/world-military-expenditure-passes-2-trillion-first-time

Chapter 3
Political Economy of Globalization and Human Development: Experience from South Asian Countries

Kamlesh Goyal and Jaskaran Singh

Abstract This study is a thematic attempt to explore the relationship between globalization and human development. It also evaluates whether human development has truly progressed since 1990. The first part of the study describes the genesis of globalization and human development. The second part analyses the political economy of globalization and human development, focusing on how different schools of thought discuss the relationship between both. The last part of the study evaluates human development in terms of health, education, GDP growth, per capita income, the Gender Inequality Index, the Human Development Index, and the Inequality Adjusted Human Development Index specifically in the case of South Asia. This study is based on secondary data sources from 1990 to 2021. The study found that globalization resulted from neo-liberal policies that led to unequal progress in human development in the world as well as in the South Asian region.

Keywords South-Asian countries · Human Development Index · Gender Inequality Index · Inequity Adjusted Human Development Index

3.1 Introduction

Recent years have witnessed an unprecedented debate on globalization. Globalization is a phenomenon which means integrating the national economy with the world economy by removing all sorts of barriers and this phenomenon has been introduced previously in the world. It can be dated back to the era of the Indus Valley civilization when there was a trade relation between Mesopotamian civilization and the Indus Valley civilization. Globalization is a complex process involving the expansion of

K. Goyal (✉)
Centre of Excellence in Teacher Education, Tata Institute of Social Sciences, Mumbai, India
e-mail: kamleshg841@gmail.com

J. Singh
Department of Economics, Ramgarhia College, Phagwara, Punjab, India

H. Adam and R. Rena (eds.), *Political Economy of Development in the Global South Post-COVID-19 Pandemic*,
https://doi.org/10.1007/978-981-99-4074-5_3

global trade, movements of labour, capital, and technology, as well as the exchange of ideas [1, 20, 68].

Globalization is considered the main dominant force in the economic universe. It aims to enlighten the world through economic prosperity and strives for the victory of the market over government and self-interest over altruism. As a dynamic force of change worldwide, it is expected to lead to an unprecedented increase in the wealth of nations, expanding the world's frontier of productive possibilities and redefining the world as a 'global village'. The fear is that it will accelerate the race to the bottom, taking from the poor and giving to the rich, pushing out nations already integrated into the global economy, cutting them off from the scientific advances of the developed world, and widening already existing inequalities in the levels of economic well-being within and between countries to the point where they have become socially, morally and economically unacceptable. Although not in substance but in form, there is a growing fear that developed countries may increasingly use globalization to re-enact colonialism in another way. It is, therefore, not surprising that public support for globalization has declined in both developed and developing countries as a frantic search has been done for a third way out of the morally repulsive system of unrelenting capitalism. At the same time, there is a public demand to restore some of its attractive ambitions to give a 'human face' to the nobler claims of globalization, making the world of business and finance increasingly ungovernable by a global civic ethic [51].

The discourse on human development under globalization is also not a recent phenomenon. It was articulated by various schools of thought specifically, neo-liberal, socialistic and capability approaches. Most recently, it was initiated in the late 1980s during increasing interventions of the International Monetary Fund (IMF), through structural adjustment policies, especially in Latin America, which was caught in the debt trap. This study has tried to evaluate the take of various schools of thought on globalization and human development theoretically and empirically, especially in the context of South Asia.

3.2 Objectives

This study aims to theoretically explore the relationship between globalization and human development and evaluate whether human development has progressed since 1990. The first part of the study describes the genesis of globalization and human development. The second part analyses the political economy of globalization and human development, focusing on how different schools of thought discuss the relationship between both. The last part of the study evaluates the progress of human development in terms of health, education, GDP growth, per capita income, the Gender Inequality Index, the Human Development Index, and the Inequality Adjusted Human Development Index, particularly in the context of South Asian countries.

3.3 Methodology

The study is mainly based on secondary data sources taken from various national and international published reports, published and unpublished work of individual scholars, articles, research papers, and lectures of different authors from multiple journals, books, periodicals, magazines, the World Bank data bank, and the UNDP data bank. The data have been extracted from all the above data sources, analysed using percentage, annual growth rate, combined annual growth rate and other statistical tools, and presented using tables, wherever needed. This study mainly concentrates from 1990s onwards.

3.4 Results and Discussion

3.4.1 Political Economy of Globalization and Human Development

From the review of an extensive literature survey, it has been seen that three different schools of thought are prevailing in the debate on globalization and human development. (1) neo-liberal, (2) socialistic and (3) capability approach. The first school, the neo-liberal school, contends that globalization has removed national borders, which has increased world trade, investment across borders, and innovation in technology, improved production efficiency and produced prosperity through replacing old jobs with new skill-based jobs. It has also argued that globalization has managed to improve the production efficiency in the labour market through its various methods of incentives that increase income returns, which further improves human life [8, 21, 26, 42, 53, 55, 57, 58].

The second school viewed globalization as an offshoot of capitalism. It showed how a new global order architecture has been established with the help of major powers such as industrialized nations and international financial institutions with the primary goal being to promote capital accumulation in the free market economy [5]. This school predicts that due to this there is a worldwide crisis in the standard of living for labour'. This process has led to drastic changes in economic structure from labour-intensive production to capital-technology-based production that has created a growing pool of surplus labour, an industrial reserve army with incomes at or below the level of subsistence [12, 28, 32, 33, 43].

Furthermore, the second school also argued that the present neo-liberal trajectory of global systems has imposed (or we can say enforced) a flexible mode of production that undercuts the redistributive processes advocate and built by Keynesian and social democracy economists [3]. Similarly, Harvey [25] noted that neoliberalism has been ineffective as a catalyst for economic growth but has successfully shifted wealth from weaker to upper classes and from poorer to wealthier nations. Institutions and narratives that were advocating more equitable distributive policies in the previous era had to be dismantled as part of this strategy. Tsai [58] have also noted that the 'market ethos' of globalization is characterized by a fervent pursuit of personal gain that disregards people. Scholte [47] theories that the unfair distribution of benefits favouring the privileged support this claim. Sirgy et al. [52] do not expressly agree with this radical viewpoint, but they do foresee some unfavourable consequences and discover that it has 'double-edged sword' results [4].

The third school of thought, mainly advocated by Haq, Sen, Stewart and Streeten, pointed out that the decade (1980–1990) witnessed many policy changes and the role of the State has drastically changed. They all were trying to think outside of the box. Their basic idea was to create room for state-based development without ignoring market logic. They believe that the state should be involved in areas where market failure is more evident than in producing marketable commodities. Thus, the key was not to nationalize industries and run everything via the State but to retrench from productive activities and concentrate some key activities mainly on education and health; to fashion people-centred policies and pro-poor growth [10, 22, 40, 44, 48, 50].

However, this capability based approach by Haq, Sen and their followers has been widely circulated through the first Human Development Report published by the United Nations Development Programme (UNDP). By stressing and declaring that education, health, and income are fundamental and vital to human development, even the human development reports over the years have made their most notable contribution to the more significant development debate. Accountably, the UNDP has released 27 human development reports over the past three decades. These publications have contributed not being a yearly report but to an agenda for action for governments and NGOs and a catalyst for new ideas in development economics [34].

Moreover, according to the above arguments of all three schools, current liberalization trends had led to the gradual removal of tariffs and non-cost restrictions on goods and services so that they can move freely across national borders and ideally as if national borders did not exist. Since 1948, following the GATT, and then since 1995, due to the WTO, as was previously said, these movements have significantly increased. Both have made an effort, however, with little success to promote 'rule-based' trade and encourage 'market access' in a non-discriminatory, multilateral manner [51]. Contrary to this argument, it has been found that the intervention of the WTO and GATT led to the commodification of health and education by introducing global market-based private players which further led to a decrease in public funding in both sectors. This process has undoubtedly improved many people's lives but has also led to inequality among them.

Indeed, as GATTs and WTO tried to remove the boundaries of nation-states in the interest of capitalistic industrialized economics, they have also fashioned the debate on development discourse. Since then, the countries' development paradigm has shifted from 'growth only' to 'inclusive growth' and then 'growth with sustainable human development'. However, neo-liberalism ultimately aims to liberalize and privatize all the means of production, and everything should be in the hands of big private capitalists that must run through market forces. On the other hand, the socialistic approach emphasizes state ownership of all means of the production process, and the economists of capabilities method are restricted to state intervention in health and education only. These arguments clearly show the sharp contradictions among them and the clear argument that emerged from this debate is that the current capitalistic system submerged by neo-liberal policies has cosmetically articulated human development. It has rejected the argument of both socialistic economists and social capability approach economists through lending all means of production to the hands of big private capitalists. Even GATTs and the WTO have been commodifying education and health services. This pace has started in different forms at different times. Initially, it began as 'development' then 'inclusive development' after that 'sustainable human development' and later 'Millennium Development Goals' and nowadays it is called 'Sustainable Development Goals' [7].

3.4.2 Progress of Human Development Under Globalization

Considering the view of Sen and Haq, the United Nations Development Programme (UNDP) began with a full-fledged project on 'Human Development' in the early 1990s. Accordingly, UNDP came up with its first 'Human Development Report' in 1990, which conceptualized human welfare with the most cited line "people are the real wealth of a nation". According to the first Human Development Report [60] the primary objective of this capability-based human development approach is to create an enabling environment for people to enjoy long healthy and creative lives. Hence, the concept of human development came to the fore with its three essential components: A long and healthy life, knowledge and access to resources needed for a decent standard of living and it mainly focused on people's well-being and freedom. Based on these fundamental arguments Haq and Sen have designed the Human Development Index (HDI). The HDI is a composite index that focuses on three main dimensions of human development: living a long and healthy life, measured by life expectancy at birth; the ability to obtain information in terms of average years of schooling and expected years of schooling; and the ability to achieve a decent standard of living as measured by gross national income per capita (GDP) at purchasing power parity (PPP). Being a simple alternative measure of development towards comparing nations, it has emerged to be an alternative paradigm wherein mutual responsiveness across domains of human development as well as gendered balance alongside inequality adjustment is highlighted. Although, it has been observed that the UNDP has operationalized the overall thoughts of Sen's and Haq's capability approach by quantifying human well-being with a limited number of variables, it has overlooked the many qualitative indicators such as socio-economic-political environment degradation, and so on [11, 22, 27, 59, 60, 66, 67]. Regarding the same Chowdhury [9] contended that the HDI allocates weights to certain components that are rise to trade-offs, when these measurements may not always be equally valuable. According to Sagar and Najam [46], the HDI did not take into account factors such as inequality, poverty and gender inequality. They have raised many questions and argued that a country with a high GDP per capita would mean a developed country, but what if this GDP is achieved by marginalizing certain genders or ethnic groups? What if that GDP is achieved by a small part of the population that is rich and therefore ignores the poor? After these criticisms, the UNDP and many scholars of the capability school of thought came up with many new indexes such as Inequality Adjusted Human Development Index, Multidimensional Poverty Index (MPI), Happiness Index, etc. in order to address above questions. The basic idea of all these indexes was to evaluate human well-being quantitatively using various multiple data sources [18, 39]. The following table shows the progress of human development among all regions of the world since 1990, i.e. under globalization.

Table 3.1 shows the region-wise variations in HDI from 1990 to 2021, from which we can see the improvement in the HDI for the world as a whole and in different regions. In 1990, the HDI of the world was estimated at 0.537, from which the higher level human development was in Europe and Central Asia (0.651), followed by Latin America and the Caribbean (0.625). The lowest level of human development has been seen in Sub-Saharan Africa (0.400) and South Asia (0.437). In 2017, the global HDI was estimated to be 0.728, following the prior pattern among different regions. The highest HDI was in Europe and Central Asia (0.771), followed by Latin America and the Caribbean (0.758), but Sub-Saharan Africa (0.534) was in a low category. The HDI index shows that from 1990 to 2021, all regions and the world registered positive growth in human development, but South Asia (1.16%) and the East Asia Pacific (1.27%) grew more than the world average. This indicates that the South Asia region is progressing more in human development than all other regions. Furthermore, Sub-Saharan Africa (0.96%) has shown slightly more positive growth than Europe and Central Asia (0.59%). Still, the lowest growth has been registered by Latin America and the Caribbean (0.57%). Furthermore, Sub-Saharan Africa is found in development discourse among international forums, and this region is facing many socioeconomic problems, such as extreme poverty, hunger, health problems, and water crisis. There is a need for a particular focus on addressing the issues of this region. Therefore, it is clear from the above table that after the opening of the world economies, HDI has progressed well among all the regions, but it needs to be more consistent in progress. Some regions of the world progressed substantially, and some remained behind.

Table 3.2 indicates the region-wise average annual growth rate of HDI from 1990–2021 in different regions of the world. The world HDI is growing annually from 1990 to 2000 at 0.72%, from which the highest level of annual growth has been registered by East Asia and the Pacific (1.45%), followed by South Asia (1.38%) and Arab states (0.9%), and a very low level of annual growth has been seen in Europe and

Table 3.1 Region-wise variations and comparison of the human development index

Regions	1990	2000	2010	2015	2016	2017	2018	2019	2020	2021	1990–2021 (%)[a]
Arab States	0.553	0.613	0.676	0.687	0.697	0.699	0.711	0.715	0.708	0.708	0.79
East Asia and the Pacific	0.516	0.593	0.686	0.720	0.730	0.733	0.741	0.748	0.748	0.749	1.27
Europe and Central Asia	0.651	0.665	0.731	0.756	0.767	0.771	0.798	0.802	0.793	0.796	0.59
Latin America and the Caribbean	0.625	0.684	0.734	0.751	0.757	0.758	0.766	0.768	0.755	0.754	0.57
South Asia	**0.437**	**0.503**	**0.586**	**0.621**	**0.639**	**0.638**	**0.640**	**0.641**	**0.638**	**0.632**	**1.16**
Sub-Saharan Africa	0.400	0.422	0.499	0.523	0.534	0.534	0.547	0.552	0.549	0.547	0.96
World	**0.537**	**0.641**	**0.697**	**0.717**	**0.726**	**0.728**	**0.736**	**0.739**	**0.735**	**0.732**	**0.64**

Source UNDP data bank, various years. [a]Average Annual Growth Rate

Table 3.2 Region WISESE distribution of average annual growth rate of HDI (in %)

Regions	1990–2000	2000–2010	2010–2021	1990–2021
Arab States	0.95	0.96	0.42	0.79
East Asia and the Pacific	1.45	1.48	0.83	1.27
Europe and Central Asia	0.23	0.94	0.59	0.59
Latin America and the Caribbean	0.92	0.65	0.26	0.57
South Asia	**1.38**	**1.51**	**0.85**	**1.16**
Sub-Saharan Africa	0.57	1.70	0.77	0.96
World	**0.72**	**0.84**	**0.45**	**0.64**

Source UNDP data bank, various years

Central Asia (0.23%). The average annual growth rate of the HDI of the world has been recorded at 0.64per cent during 1990–2021. A shallow level of annual growth has been recorded in Latin America and the Caribbean (0.57%), and a very high level of HDI yearly growth has been registered in East Asia and the Pacific (1.2%). However, if we segregate it and compare it from 2000 to 2010, Sub-Saharan Africa has grown more than all regions, whereas from 1990 to 2021, South Asia grew by 1.16%. Moreover, over the years, Europe and Central Asia grew less than the world's growth rate, which indicates the case of conversion in terms of human development, as this region is highly developed compared to the other areas.

3.4.3 Human Development in South Asia

South Asia, comprising Afghanistan, Bangladesh, Bhutan, India, Maldives, Nepal, Pakistan and Sri Lanka, is ethnically diverse, with over 500 million people and the second poorest region in the world after sub-Saharan Africa. According to the United Nations Multidimensional Poverty Index, just over a quarter of the world's poor live in Africa and whereas half in South Asia [50]. Moreover, South Asia is identified as the largest gender-discriminated region of the world despite its rich resource endowments and high GDP growth rates in recent years [14, 23, 56].

Regional economic cooperation under globalization plays a significant growth engine for developing countries worldwide. The South Asian Association for Regional Cooperation (SAARC) is one such regional integration group established in 1985 with the broader objective of promoting the prosperity of South Asia through regional cooperation. Bangladesh, Bhutan, India, Maldives, Nepal, Pakistan and Sri Lanka have been founding members of the organization since its inception. When Afghanistan joined in 2007, the number of member states was eight. Almost three decades have passed since the SAARC formation, but the concrete result achieved for the advancement and well-being of the region's people has been modest. SAARC is suffering from the region's Indo-centricity concerning human development. New levels of cooperation in the areas of water and energy sharing, labor migration and drug trafficking are being discussed under SAARC. For the first time, simple steps towards opening economies and societies, fueled by a dramatic revolution in information, transportation, and communication, strengthen the prospects for peace in the region. At the same time, there are alarming signs of growing poverty, increased risks of devastating nuclear exchange, growing social tensions, increasing environmental degradation, the spread of ethnic violence and breakdown of political, economic, and civil governance systems [62].

As Table 3.2 shows that South Asia grew at 1.16% from 1990 to 2021 in terms of average annual growth of HDI, Table 3.3 highlights the demographic and economic profile of South Asian countries and indicates that among all eight South Asian countries, India is the most populated county, which is more than the submission of all the remaining seven countries. Indeed, among the mentioned countries, the annual growth rate of the population was high in Afghanistan (2.3%), followed by Pakistan (1.9%) and Nepal (1.8%), and approximately 1 per cent growth has been registered by India, Bangladesh, and Sri Lanka. Among all South Asian countries, the Maldives' population growth was low, i.e., 0.6%. To determine the economic status of any country, the GDP growth rate has been widely used and compared. Among all the South Asian countries, Afghanistan and Bhutan registered a negative growth rate (impact of the COVID-19 pandemic), whereas the Maldives and India registered the highest growth rate in 2020. In the case of GDP per capita (constant 2015, US$) out of the South Asian countries, Maldives ($8,673.80) was observed to be the highest, followed by Sri Lanka ($4157), Bhutan at 2879 dollars, India at 1961 dollars and Afghanistan, Nepal, Bangladesh, and Pakistan's per capita income were found to be very low, i.e., 529.7, 1049, 1715 and 1507 dollars, respectively. The Human Capital Index (HCI) is considered a good indicator to compare the country's human capacity and capability for sustained development. In the case of the HCI of South Asian countries, almost all countries lie in the range of 0.4–0.6. South Asian countries should work to build the capacities of their people to improve the HCI.

Table 3.4 takes the indicators one step further, analyzing how countries perform on the Human Development Index, Gender Inequality Index (GII) and Inequality Adjusted Human Development Index in 2021. Of all South Asian countries, only Sri Lanka and Maldives registered themselves in the high HDI category with a rank of 73 and 90, respectively; the rest, i.e., India 132, Bhutan 127, Bangladesh 129, and Nepal 143, had an HDI in the medium category, and the remaining Pakistan and Afghanistan were registered in the low category of human development with 161 and 180 ranks, respectively, which is the lowest in South Asian countries. In terms of the Inequality Adjusted Human Development Index, the Maldives ranks -9, and Sri Lanka and India only manage to increase their rank positions in IHDI. In terms of the Gender Inequality Index, Sri Lanka, Maldives and Bhutan have less gender inequality than India, Bangladesh and Nepal, and the condition is worse in Afghanistan.

Table 3.3 Demographic and economic profile of South Asia

Country	Population 2021	Population growth (annual %) 2021	Human capital index (HCI) 2020	GDP (constant 2015 US$) (2020 billion)	GDP per capita (constant 2015 US$) (2020)	GDP growth (annual %) 2020
Afghanistan	39,835,428	2.3	0.4	20.6	529.7	−2.4
Bangladesh	166,303,494	1.0	0.5	285.3	1,715.40	6.9
Bhutan	779,900	1.1	0.5	2.2	2,879.60	−10.1
India	1,400,000,000	1.0	0.5	2,733.10	1,961.40	8.9
Nepal	29,674,920	1.8	0.5	31.1	1,049.70	4.2
Maldives	543,620	0.6	–	4.7	8,673.80	31
Sri Lanka	22,156,000	1.1	0.6	92.1	4,157.00	3.7
Pakistan	225,199,929	1.9	0.4	339.4	1,507.10	6

Source World Bank data, various years

Table 3.4 Human development index, inequality index, and inequity-adjusted human development index of South Asian countries

Country	HDI		Gender inequality index		Inequality adjusted HDI		Quality of HDI
	Rank 2021	Value 2021	Rank 2021	Value 2021	Difference from HDI rank 2021	Value 2021	
Sri Lanka	73	0.782	92	0.383	−2	0.676	High
Maldives	90	0.747	83	0.348	−9	0.594	High
India	132	0.633	122	0.490	−2	0.475	Medium
Bhutan	127	0.666	98	0.415	−6	0.471	Medium
Bangladesh	129	0.661	131	0.530	0	0.503	Medium
Nepal	143	0.602	113	0.452	0	0.449	Medium
Pakistan	161	0.544	135	0.534	0	0.380	Low
Afghanistan	180	0.478	167	0.678	–	–	Low

Source UNDP data bank, various years

Table 3.5 compares the Human Development Index of South Asian countries with the world. In 1990, the HDI value of the world was registered at 0.597, and the highest HDI was Sri Lanka (0.636), followed by India (0.434) and Pakistan (0.400). However, the HDI changed drastically in 2021, when the world HDI was 0.732, from which Sri Lanka again had the highest HDI, i.e., 0.782, followed by the Maldives (0.747). In India, the HDI increased to 0.633 in 2021 from 0.496 in 2000 and 0.586 in 2010. The data clearly show that Sri Lanka and Maldives are the only two countries that have been registering HDI up to or even more than the global average.

Similarly, another Table 3.6 shows the average annual growth rate of the HDI of South Asian countries with India and the world. The average annual HDI growth rate of the world from 1990–2000 was 0.71%, from 2000 to 2010 it was 0.78%, from 2010 to 2021 it was 0.45% and from 1990 to 2021 it was 0.64%. Very low average annual growth was registered by Sri Lanka from 1990 to 2021 (0.67%), and the highest growth rate was registered by Afghanistan (1.82%), followed by Bangladesh (1.66%) and Nepal (1.34%). In the case of India, it was 1.22 per cent, which is less than that of Afghanistan and Nepal but higher than that of Sri Lanka (0.67%). This means that similar to the case of regions of the world, the indication of conversion is also found in different countries of South Asia, as low-performing countries have been doing better in HDI growth compared to those that were placed on top previously.

The quality of human development depends on how much the respective government spends on health and education. Table 3.7 provides a brief glimpse of the extent of expenditure on health and education by South Asian countries. Among all eight countries, five countries spend approximately 1% of their GDP on health, except Maldives, Sri Lanka, and Bhutan, where the government spends 6.4% of their GDP on public health, which is the highest among all the mentioned countries. The expenditure on education scenario is equally atrocious, whereas except for Maldives and Bhutan, the countries, despite their poor literacy records, spend just 4–5% of their GDP on providing education for their population. Bangladesh, Sri Lanka and Pakistan

Table 3.5 Comparison of the human development index of South Asian countries

Countries	1990	2000	2010	2015	2016	2017	2018	2019	2020	2021
Afghanistan	0.273	0.335	0.448	0.478	0.494	0.498	0.483	0.488	0.483	0.478
Bangladesh	0.387	0.468	0.545	0.592	0.597	0.608	0.635	0.644	0.655	0.661
Bhutan	–	–	0.566	0.603	0.609	0.612	0.658	0.671	0.668	0.666
India	0.434	0.491	0.575	0.645	0.636	0.640	0.645	0.645	0.642	0.633
Nepal	0.399	0.467	0.543	0.579	0.569	0.574	0.601	0.611	0.604	0.602
Maldives	–	0.603	0.683	0.701	0.712	0.717	0.750	0.755	0.734	0.747
Pakistan	0.400	0.441	0.505	0.534	0.56	0.562	0.545	0.546	0.543	0.544
Sri Lanka	0.636	0.688	0.737	0.764	0.768	0.770	0.776	0.778	0.780	0.782
World	0.597	0.641	0.697	0.717	0.726	0.728	0.736	0.739	0.735	0.732

Source UNDP data bank, various years

Table 3.6 Average annual HDI growth rate of South Asian countries (%)

Countries	1990–2000	2000–2010	2010–2021	1990–2021
Afghanistan	2.07	2.95	0.59	1.82
India	1.24	1.59	0.88	1.22
Maldives	–	0.92	0.75	–
Nepal	1.59	1.52	0.94	1.34
Pakistan	0.98	1.36	0.68	1.00
Sri Lanka	0.79	0.69	0.54	0.67
Bangladesh	2.02	1.32	1.64	1.66
Bhutan	–	–	1.25	–
South Asia	1.24	1.43	0.85	1.16
World	0.71	0.78	0.45	0.64

Source UNDP data bank, various years

spend less than other countries. Life expectancy at birth is considered an important indicator of human development. Countries with life expectancy over 70 years are the Maldives, Sri Lanka, Bangladesh, Nepal, and Bhutan, but all remaining countries with a life expectancy about 70 years or below are similar.

Education is the most important indicator of human development. In the words of Stiglitz, "Improving education and health are not merely means to improve performance, they are ends in themselves." Growth can be undermined when governments reduce budget deficits by cutting critical investments in infrastructure and human capital. Improving education and health are therefore essential measures for growth of GDP [36, 55]. Table 3.8 highlights and compares the brief trends of the Education Index of South Asian countries. Pakistan and Afghanistan have the worst conditions in terms of the Education Index, whereas India and Maldives are doing the same, but Sri Lanka has been at the top since 1990. Afghanistan had a very low EI

Table 3.7 Socio-economic profile of South Asian countries

Country	Public expenditure on health (% of GDP) 2019	Public expenditure on education (% of GDP) 2019	Life expectancy at Birth (Years) 2019
Afghanistan	1.1	3.2	63.21
Bangladesh	0.5	1.3	74.25
Bhutan	2.7	5.7	73.11
India	1.0	4.5	70.79
Nepal	1.1	4.4	70.88
Maldives	6.4	4.1	79.59
Pakistan	1.1	2.5	65.61
Sri Lanka	1.9	1.9	76.87

Source UNDP data bank, various years

(0.122) in 1990, which was the lowest, followed by Pakistan (0.205), Nepal (0.276), India (0.311) and the Maldives (0.354), but they managed to improve it drastically in 2021. Afghanistan grew enormously (0.415) by nearly 200 per cent from 1990 to 2021, followed by Pakistan, Nepal, India, and Sri Lanka. In 2021, however, EI for Afghanistan and Pakistan hit a low of 0.345 and 0.400, respectively, whereas, for India, it remained the same. Other nations, such as Nepal (0.520), Bangladesh (0.532), and Maldives (0.580), showed a positive growth trend.

In all South Asian nations, the poorer segments of the population have substantially worse health deprivation in terms of life expectancy at birth, as seen in Table 3.9. However, there are differences in the degree and intensity of the intra- and inter-country discrepancies. A significant explanation for the high level of human deprivation has been the enormous gap in the health care system [15]. The high level of human deprivation in turn is responsible for both the low value of the HDI and the low ranking of South Asian countries, except Sri Lanka, among all the mentioned countries. The table depicts that in 1990, India's LEI was 0.584 which was lower than Maldives (0.638), Pakistan (0.616), Bangladesh (0.591) and Sri Lanka but higher than Afghanistan (0.459) and Nepal (0.527), had changed drastically and increased to 0.680 in 2021 which was like Afghanistan (0.680) but lower than Maldives (0.592), Nepal (0.780) and Sri Lanka (0.870). The table also indicates that all the mentioned countries show positive growth in terms of LEI; however, it is important to note that among all countries, Bangladesh and Maldives registered a higher growth rate from 1990–2021, followed by Maldives, India, Pakistan and Sri Lanka.

Human deprivation is arguably more pronounced among the poor in various South Asian countries. Inequality is not limited to income, but also prevalent to areas such as health care and education. Table 3.10 highlights the situation and variations in particular and differences in general in the context of SLI among the mentioned countries from 1990 to 2021 and indicates that in the 1990s, India's SLI was 0.432, which was lower than that of the Maldives (0.572), Pakistan (0.523), Sri Lanka (0.543), Bhutan (0.460) and Afghanistan but higher than that of Bangladesh (0.386) and Nepal (0.371), but it has improved to 0.62 in 2021 by growing by more than 45% from 1990 to 2021. Furthermore, from 1990 to 2021, almost all countries registered positive growth except Afghanistan, and the maximum growth rate was registered by India, followed by the Maldives, Sri Lanka, Nepal, and Pakistan. In 2021, the Maldives showed the highest income index, followed by Sri Lanka and Bhutan. The income index for Afghanistan deteriorated over the period and stabilized whereas Bangladesh's income index improved in 2021 to 0.600 from 0.386 in 1990.

Table 3.8 Comparison of education index among South Asian countries

Countries	1990	1995	2000	2005	2010	2015	2016	2017	2018	2019	2020[a]	2021[a]
Afghanistan	0.122	0.179	0.235	0.312	0.371	0.398	0.410	0.415	0.411	0.413	0.339	0.345
Bangladesh	0.252	0.292	0.345	0.386	0.425	0.457	0.490	0.508	0.526	0.529	0.515	0.532
Bhutan	–	–	–	–	0.408	0.452	0.446	0.445	0.495	0.498	0.500	0.500
India	0.311	0.344	0.379	0.429	0.478	0.535	0.556	0.556	0.556	0.556	0.529	0.555
Nepal	0.276	0.299	0.330	0.359	0.443	0.475	0.502	0.502	0.519	0.522	0.467	0.520
Maldives	–	0.354	0.430	0.451	0.495	0.561	0.556	0.556	0.563	0.572	0.545	0.580
Pakistan	0.205	0.232	0.259	0.331	0.363	0.395	0.411	0.411	0.393	0.404	0.330	0.400
Sri Lanka	0.592	0.633	0.679	0.71	0.739	0.752	0.749	0.749	0.739	0.745	0.655	0.720

Source UNDP data bank, various years; [a]author's calculations

Table 3.9 Comparison of the life expectancy index among South Asian countries

Countries	1990	1995	2000	2005	2010	2015	2016	2017	2018	2019	2020[a]	2021[a]
Afghanistan	0.459	0.510	0.540	0.569	0.599	0.626	0.672	0.678	0.685	0.689	0.670	0.680
Bangladesh	0.591	0.644	0.698	0.738	0.770	0.800	0.808	0.812	0.805	0.809	0.800	0.805
Bhutan	0.500	0.560	0.626	0.691	0.737	0.767	0.772	0.778	0.792	0.797	0.790	0.790
India	0.584	0.622	0.656	0.685	0.715	0.743	0.747	0.751	0.760	0.765	0.660	0.680
Nepal	0.527	0.593	0.652	0.700	0.738	0.769	0.773	0.779	0.777	0.782	0.780	0.780
Maldives	0.638	0.701	0.768	0.833	0.864	0.876	0.882	0.887	0.902	0.906	0.900	0.900
Pakistan	0.616	0.638	0.658	0.675	0.695	0.713	0.715	0.717	0.725	0.728	0.680	0.690
Sri Lanka	0.762	0.759	0.785	0.83	0.837	0.847	0.851	0.854	0.874	0.877	0.860	0.870

Source UNDP data bank, various years; [a]author's calculations

Table 3.10 Comparison of income index among South Asian countries

Countries	1990	1995	2000	2005	2010	2015	2016	2017	2018	2019	2020[a]	2021[a]
Afghanistan	0.458	0.373	0.309	0.374	0.422	0.442	0.438	0.439	0.468	0.469	0.340	0.400
Bhutan	0.460	0.485	0.541	0.575	0.622	0.644	0.654	0.663	0.700	0.707	0.700	0.700
Bangladesh	0.386	0.402	0.426	0.455	0.495	0.530	0.537	0.545	0.580	0.590	0.560	0.600
India	0.432	0.455	0.486	0.523	0.570	0.610	0.619	0.627	0.629	0.635	0.580	0.620
Nepal	0.371	0.390	0.412	0.428	0.453	0.476	0.476	0.484	0.527	0.535	0.479	0.510
Maldives	0.527	0.565	0.611	0.641	0.683	0.701	0.732	0.742	0.776	0.779	0.716	0.770
Pakistan	0.523	0.532	0.535	0.562	0.574	0.592	0.596	0.600	0.591	0.591	0.524	0.570
Sri Lanka	0.543	0.574	0.605	0.629	0.671	0.707	0.712	0.714	0.716	0.730	0.712	0.720

Source UNDP data bank, various years; [a]author's calculations

3.5 Conclusions

In summary, it has been observed from the study that the contemporary-globalized-capitalistic system submerged by neo-liberal policies has cosmetically articulated human development. It has rejected the argument of both socialistic economists and social capability economists to make the State intervene in human development. They advocated neo-liberal measures to hand over all means of production to the big private capitalists. Even GATTs and the WTO have been commodifying education and health services. This pace has started in different forms at different times. Initially, it started as 'development' then 'inclusive development' after that 'sustainable human development' later 'Millennium Development Goals' and currently it is called 'Sustainable Development Goals'. Undoubtedly, there is a sharp increase in economic growth in the countries of the world, which in turn has a great impact on the levels of living of people in terms of standard of living, level of education and improvement in health status as well as longevity. However, on the other hand, it has led to a decrease in public expenditure on public services such as public expenditure on health and education through its neo-liberal policies using globalization, which further generated gains for some and losses for others. This pace has tremendously increased in the COVID-19 pandemic phase. The case of South Asian countries is at a crossroads. No doubt globalization has helped in reducing poverty in some of the largest and better-performing economies of South Asia. However, despite some conversion signs in various indicators, some of them are still far behind in terms of human development indicators. Among all the South Asian economies, some have progressed well, and some are lagging.

In summary, the curtailment of public investment, as well as expenditure on the health and education sector due to neo-liberal policies of capitalism following the onset of globalization, has led to unequal progress in human development since 1990 among all South Asian countries. Sustainable human progress and improvement in quality of life cannot rely only on the private sector when a large proportion of the population is living in extreme poverty with high levels of economic inequality. Thus, intensive joint intervention by concerned Government(s), Public Policy Intellectuals, Policy Planners, NGOs, and even the people themselves is the need of the hour to undo inequalities and to improve the quality of life of the people for genuine 'Sustainable and Equitable Human Development'.

Acknowledgements This study is a revised version of 'Globalization and Human Development: An Experience from South-Asian Countries' presented by the author at an International Conference on Globalization, Inequality and Exclusion: Plan for Development or Path to Marginalization, organized by the Department of Economics, Punjabi University, Patiala (June 19, 2020). Mr. Gurjap Singh's support in data processing and Ms. Shreyasi Mitra's help in proofreading are thankfully acknowledged.

References

1. Agarwal M, Ray AS (2007) Globalization and the millennium development goals Negotiating the challenge. Social Science Press, New Delhi
2. Amin S (1974) Accumulating on a world scale: a critique of the theory of underdevelopment. Monthly Review Press, New York
3. Asongu S (2014) Globalization (fighting), corruption and development: how are these phenomena linearly and nonlinearly related in wealth effects? J Econ Stud 41(3):346–369
4. Asongu SA (2012) Globalization and Africa: implications for human development. AGDI Working Paper, No. WP/12/022, African Governance and Development Institute (AGDI), Yaoundé
5. Ayenagbo K, Boukari M (2022) Comparative analysis of the interlinks between globalization, governance and development in African economic communities. J Knowl Econ. https://doi.org/10.1007/s13132-022-01034-6
6. Baran P (1958) The political economy of backwardness. In Aggarwal AN, Singh SP (eds) Economics of underdevelopment. Oxford University Press, New Delhi
7. Baxi U (2017) Post development [Paper presentation]. In: 21st annual conference of the Indian political economy December 8–9. Indian Institute of Technology (IIT) Delhi
8. Bhagwati J (2004) In defense of globalization. Oxford University Press, New Delhi
9. Chowdhury O (1991) Human development index: a critique. Bangladesh Dev Stud 19(3):125–127
10. Desai M (2007) Why India will fail to meet the millennium development goals. In: Agarwal M, Ray AS (eds) Globalization and the millennium development goals: negotiating the challenge. Social Science Press, New Delhi
11. Easterlin RA (2000) The globalization of human development. Ann Am Acad Pol Soc Sci 570:32–48
12. Figueroa A (2014) Economic growth and social progress: lessons from India. J Hum Dev Capab 15(4):424–428
13. Frank AG (1975) On capitalist underdevelopment. Oxford University Press, New Delhi
14. Garden AE (1999) Human development in South Asia. Dhaka, Bangladesh
15. Ghuman RS, Bhullar AS (2010) Economic growth and human development in South Asia: experience of selected countries. Himalayan Res Papers Arch. https://ejournals.unm.edu/index.php/nsc/article/view/635
16. Ghuman RS, Bhullar AS (2010) Economic growth and human development in South Asia: experience of selected countries. https://digitalrepository.unm.edu/nsc_research/39
17. Gill SS, Singh S, Brar JS (2010) Globalization and Indian state education, health and agriculture extension services in Punjab. Aakbar Books, Delhi
18. Goyal K, Singh K (2020) How well is Punjab progressing in human development? district wise analysis. J Sikh Punjab Stud 27(1):117–128
19. Goyal K, Singh K (2016) India in the process of globalization. Polit Econ J Ind 25(3 and 4):69–74
20. Goyal K (2020) Globalization and human development in India with special reference to Punjab. PhD Thesis, Department of Economics, Punjabi University, Patiala
21. Grennes T (2003) Creative destruction and globalization. Cato J 22:543–558
22. Haq MU (1995) Reflections on human development. Oxford University Press, New York
23. Haq K (2000) Human development challenges in South Asia. J Hum Dev 1(1):71–82
24. Haq MU (2003) The human development paradigm. In: Fukuda-Parr S, Kumar AKS (eds) Readings in human development: concepts, measures and policies for a development paradigm. Oxford University Press, New Delhi, pp 17–36
25. Harvey D (2007) Neoliberalism as creative destruction. Ann Am Acad Pol Soc Sci 610:21–44
26. Jolly R (2010) Employment, basic needs and human development: elements for a new international paradigm in response to crisis. J Hum Dev Capab 11(1):11–36
27. Kelley AC (1991) The human development index: 'handle with care.' Popul Dev Rev 17(2):315–324

28. Kellner D (2002) Theorizing globalization. Sociol Theory 20(3):285–305
29. Lall S (2002) Transnational corporations and technology flows. In: Nayyar D (ed) Governing globalization: issues and institutions. Oxford University Press, New Delhi
30. Leibenstein H (1959) Economic backwardness and economic growth. Studies in theory and economic development. John Willy Sons, New York
31. Marcazzo MC (2012) Keynes and the Welfare State. University of Rome, La Sapienza
32. Mehta P (1994) New economic policy, workplace and human development. Econ Pol Wkly 29(22):M75–M82
33. Mehta PS (2001) Globalization and India. http://www.cutscitee.org/pdf/MONOGRAPH01-01.pdf. Accessed 12 October 2016
34. Nayak, P. (2013). Methodological developments in human development literature. North Eastern Hill University, MPRA Paper No. 50608. https://mpra.ub.uni-muenchen.de/50608/
35. Nayyar D (1995) Economic liberalization in Indian economy: analytics, experience and lesson. Orient, Calcutta
36. Nayyar D (2012) Macroeconomics and human development. J Hum Dev Capab 13(1):7–30
37. Nurkse R (1966) Problems of capital formation in underdeveloping countries. Oxford University Press, New York
38. Nussbaum MC (2011) Creating capabilities: the human development approach. The Belknap Press, London
39. Padhi BK, Mishra US (2021) Introspecting human development. Econ Pol Wkly 56(4):29–30
40. Pagrotsky L (2001) Instruments to shape globalization. J Hum Dev 2(1):53–58
41. Patnaik P (2018) Capitalism's discourse on development. Peoples Democr 42(30)
42. Perelman M (2015) The anarchy of globalization local and global, intended and unintended consequences. World Rev Polit Econ 6(3):352–373
43. Petras J, Veltmeyer H (2001) Globalization unmasked: imperialism in the 21st century. Zed Books, London
44. Rabbanee FK, Haque MM, Hasan F (2010) Globalization and human development-realities and reconditions for developing countries. Asian Aff 30(1):33–39
45. Rosenstein-Rodan NP (1943) Problems of industrialization of Eastern and South Eastern Europe. Econ J 53:202–211
46. Sagar DA, Najam A (1998) The human development index: a critical review. Ecol Econ 25(3):250–264
47. Scholte JA (2000) Globalization: a critical introduction. St Martin's Press, New York
48. Sen A (1983) Development: which way now? Econ J 93(372):745–762
49. Sen A (1999) Commodities and capabilities. Oxford University, Press, New Delhi
50. Sen A (2000) A decade of human development. J Hum Dev 1(1):17–23
51. Simplice A (2013) Globalization and Africa: implications for human development. Int J Dev Issues 12(3):213–238
52. Sirgy MJ, Lee DJ, Miller C, Littlefield JE (2004) The impact of globalization on a country's quality of life: toward an integrated model. Soc Indic Res 68:251–298
53. Smart B (2003) Economy, culture and society: a sociological critique of neo-liberalism. Open University Press, Buckingham
54. Stiglitz JE (2002) Globalization and discontents. W.W. Norton Company, New York
55. Stilitz JE (2012) Macroeconomic fluctuations, inequality, and human development. J Hum Dev Capab 13(1):31–58
56. Thas AMK (2008) An empowerment approach to gender equality in the information society: perspectives from East Asia, an empowerment approach to gender equality in the information society: regional analyses from Asia, IT for change, Bangalore, India
57. Trabi G (2015) Foreign direct investment and human development: the law and economics of international investment agreements. J Hum Dev Capab 16(2):316–317
58. Tsai MC (2007) Does globalization affect human well-being? Soc Indic Res 81:103–126
59. Ullaha S, Azim P (2017) Human development in the era of globalization: an Asian perspective. Pak J Soc Issues 8:123–139

60. United Nations Development Programme (1990) Human development report. Oxford University Press, New York. http://hdr.undp.org/sites/default/files/reports/219/hdr_1990_en_complete_nostats.pdf
61. United Nations Development Programme (1995) Human development report. Oxford University Press, New York. http://hdr.undp.org/sites/default/files/reports/256/hdr_1995_en_complete_nostats.pdf
62. United Nations Development Programme (1999) Human development report. Oxford University Press, New York. http://hdr.undp.org/sites/default/files/reports/260/hdr_1999_en_nostats.pdf
63. United Nations Development Programme (2016) Technical notes calculating the human development indices graphical presentation. http://hdr.undp.org/sites/default/files/hdr2016_technicalnotes.pdf accessed on 23/11/2018
64. United Nations Development Programme (2019) Human development report. Oxford University Press, New York. http://hdr.undp.org/sites/default/files/hdr2019.pdf
65. United Nations Development Programme (2022) Human development report. New York. Oxford University Press https://hdr.undp.org/content/human-development-report-2021-22
66. United Nations Development Programme (2014) Human development report. New York: Oxford University Press, Available at http://hdr.undp.org/sites/default/files/hdr14-report-en-1.pdf
67. United Nations Development Programme (2015) Human development report. New York: Oxford University Press, Available at http://hdr.undp.org/sites/default/files/2015_human_development_report_0.pdf
68. Verma AK (2018) Globalization and inequality. Res Discourse 7(25):3–4
69. You J-IL (2002) Then, Bretton Woods institution: evolution, reforms and change. In: Nayyar D (ed) Governing globalization: issues and institutions. Oxford University Press, New Delhi, pp 209–237

Chapter 4
ASEAN Economies in the COVID-19 Post-pandemic Crisis

Sokvibol Kea, Saleh Shahriar, Nazir Muhammad Abdullahi, and Chouna Moa

Abstract The objective of this chapter is to examine the effects of the COVID-19 pandemic on the ASEAN economies from a variety of perspectives along with how the ASEAN member states (*hereafter*, AMS) responded to the pandemic to recover their economies in the post-pandemic era and to address the numerous significant issues affecting ASEAN's post-pandemic strategy. The scope of the current analysis will therefore be confined to the ten AMS. The effects of the COVID-19 pandemic on AMS were examined from numerous perspectives, including food, healthcare, construction, manufacturing, trade and exports, tourism, and real estate, using a range of data sources and the descriptive statistics method. The countries most affected by COVID-19 are Vietnam, Indonesia, and Malaysia, with Indonesia having the highest number of deaths from COVID-19 among all AMS. The "ASEAN Comprehensive Recovery Framework (ACRF)" and "Implementation Plan" were developed and implemented in response to the pandemic. The rising US-China rivalry and the Russian-Ukraine war are external problems that have a substantial impact on preventing the smooth implementation of the ACRF for restoration.

Keywords The Association of Southeast Asian Nations (ASEAN) · COVID-19 pandemic · Regional integration · Great power competition · Russia–Ukraine war · Geopolitics · ASEAN Comprehensive Recovery Framework (ACRF)

S. Kea · C. Moa
Kirirom Institute of Technology, Kampong Speu, Cambodia

S. Shahriar (✉)
North South University, Dhaka, Bangladesh
e-mail: saleh.shahriar@northsouth.edu

N. M. Abdullahi
Kano State Polytechnic, Kano, Nigeria

H. Adam and R. Rena (eds.), *Political Economy of Development in the Global South Post-COVID-19 Pandemic*,
https://doi.org/10.1007/978-981-99-4074-5_4

4.1 Introduction

The Association of Southeast Asian Nations (ASEAN) has contributed significantly to Asian economic integration since its founding in 1967 to foster regional economic, security, and cultural cooperation. The COVID-19 pandemic has had a negative impact, adversely affecting daily life, the economy, and industry around the world, including all ten ASEAN member states (*hereafter*, AMS). Timor Leste which recently joined ASEAN on November 22, 2022, as the 11th AMS did not encompass in this study. The significant COVID-19 pandemic was recognized by the World Health Organization (WHO) on 11 March 2020 as a worldwide pandemic [1]. All facets of our society have been put into jeopardy, leading to enormous health and development crises in the region as well as around the globe that have prompted all AMS governments to apply health and safety measures, including lockdowns, shelter-in-place orders, social isolation, and restricted foreign entry, to protect populations from the infection [2]. By 2021 alone, 4.7 million people in Southeast Asia would be living in abject poverty. According to the Asian Development Bank [3], COVID-19 also resulted in the loss of 9.3 million jobs worldwide. Additionally, it is estimated that the current omics wave will reduce productivity in 2020 to more than 10% below the baseline scenario without the pandemic, and in 2022, it will reduce the region's gross domestic product (GDP) by approximately 0.8% [4, 5].

The COVID-19 pandemic has caused such severe economic damage that it will take a long time for things to return to the way they were before the pandemic. The ASEAN nations' economies are comparable. The third quarter of 2021 saw a downturn because of the continual waves of new COVID variants, but early 2021 showed signs of recovery. As the number of cases continuously decreases, Southeast Asia is returning to the phase of recovery alongside the global economy.

According to the most current economic outlook report from the Asian Development Bank (ADB), the region's GDP would rise by 5.1% this year. This estimate is 3% more than the one from the previous year when enterprises were shut down because of COVID-19-related limitations. The recovery is the consequence of the AMS's well-coordinated efforts. The Hanoi Plan of Action on enhancing ASEAN economic collaboration and supply chain integration was one response to this. Under this strategy, AMS joined forces to increase the ASEAN region's supply chain resilience and expedite the movement of necessities. Against this backdrop, the current chapter is designed to investigate the impact of the COVID-19 pandemic on the ASEAN economic region from numerous aspects and how the AMS has responded to the pandemic to recover its economy in the post-pandemic era. The main focus of the current project is on the ASEAN states for several reasons. First, ASEAN states achieved remarkable economic growth and fast development over the past several decades. The rapid economic transformations of the newly industrializing East Asian countries have since the 1970s daunted observers around the world. Second, the countries have close economic relations with the USA and China. Needless to say,

ASEAN countries have their own internal ethnopolitical and socioeconomic problems, such as uneven economic development among ASEAN member countries, political violence, social instability, ethnic unrest and cross-border insurgencies.

The remainder of the chapter is organized into several segments. The following section provides a short background on the ASEAN economies in connection to the COVID-19 pandemic crisis. It highlights the positions of the AMS in light of COVID-19. Section 4.3 illustrates the data collection strategy and methodology of the project. The results are presented in Sect. 4.3. In several subsections, the underlying factors relating to the issues of COVID-19 as well as the post-pandemic situations are explained and discussed. Finally, concluding observations are presented in Sect. 4.4.

4.2 The ASEAN, COVID-19 and Post-Pandemic Crisis: A Brief Overview

The distribution of COVID-19 cases was different from country to country. Figure 4.1 shows that the people of Vietnam were infected by COVID-19 much more than the other AMS, where the number of COVID-19 cases in Vietnam reached almost 11.4 million cases. Indonesia and Malaysia were the second and third countries with high infected COVID-19 cases in ASEAN.

Figure 4.2 reveals that Indonesia had the most COVID-related deaths among all the AMS, followed by the Philippines and Vietnam. Collaboration across borders is essential for coordinating efforts to halt the spread of COVID-19 infections [6].

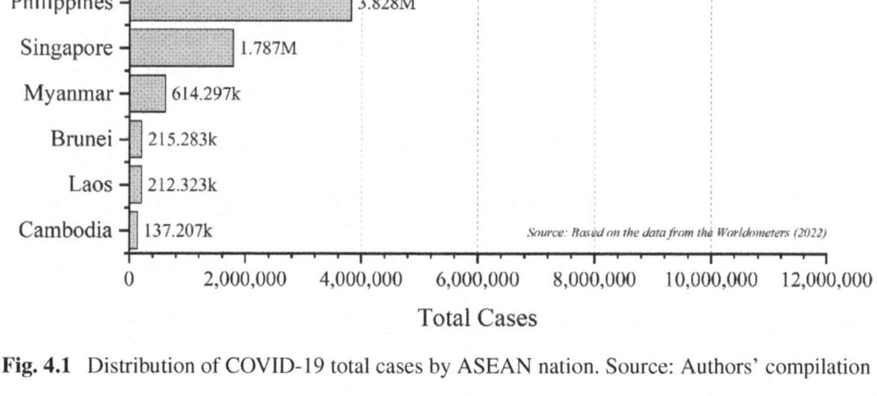

Fig. 4.1 Distribution of COVID-19 total cases by ASEAN nation. Source: Authors' compilation

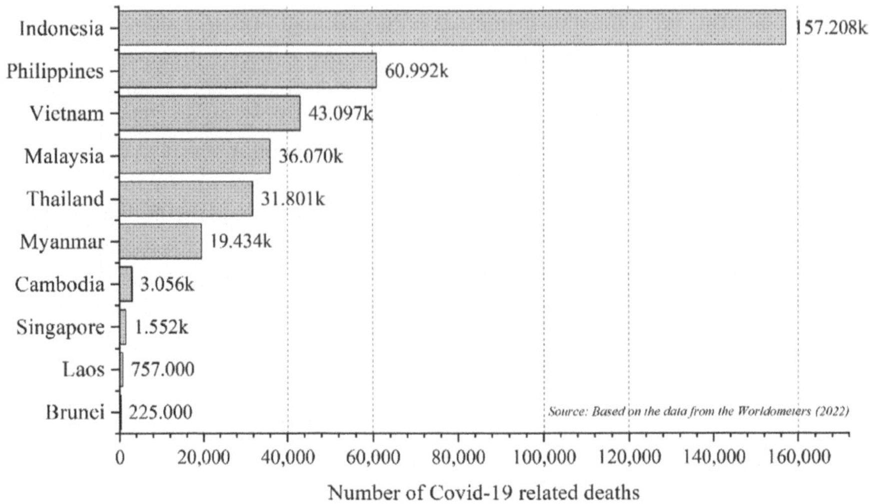

Fig. 4.2 Distribution of COVID-19-related deaths by ASEAN nations

Different AMS responses to COVID-19 have been incredibly variable, ranging from "*stringent lockdown*" conditions in the highly regulated city-state of Singapore to "*business as usual,*" particularly in rural parts of developing nations with sizable informal economies such as Laos and Myanmar. Table 4.1 provides more specific facts about COVID-19's effects on ASEAN. There are still more than 1.3 million active COVID-19 cases in Vietnam. Laos has the lowest number of confirmed deaths. Since the initial COVID-19 pandemic in December 2019, the Laos government has implemented preventative protection measures at the national level following WHO recommendations for the early detection and prevention of COVID-19 outbreaks [7].

4.3 Methodology and Data

Broadly, three pertinent questions guided the data collection methods of the project. First, how has the COVID-19 pandemic affected ASEAN's economy? Next, how did AMS react to the COVID-19 pandemic? Third, how much of a factor in the post-pandemic conditions of the ASEAN economies are external challenges? The Worldometers, the World Development Indicators (WDI) of the World Bank, the United Nations Conference on Trade and Development (UNCTAD), the ASEAN Policy Brief, and the World Development Outlook of the World Bank are the sources from which the project's data were gathered between July and August of 2022. To develop the main points of the study, several prior works on the pertinent topic matter were examined. To support the topic, sources including newspaper stories, op-eds, and reports are analysed.

Table 4.1 Distribution of COVID-19 cases by ASEAN region

AMS	Population	Total tests	Total cases	Total deaths	Total recovery	Active cases
Brunei	374,652	717,784	215,283	225	295,773	9,285
Cambodia	1,206,778	3,030,521	137,207	3,056	133,890	261
Indonesia	279,621,115	105,126,271	6,278,332	157,208	6,067,518	53,606
Laos	7,498,141	1,233,207	212,323	757	N/A	N/A
Malaysia	33,240,253	63,013,524	4,728,168	36,070	4,646,723	45,375
Myanmar	55,178,680	8,601,049	614,297	19,434	593,055	1,808
Philippines	112,655,952	31,820,445	3,827,758	60,992	3,726,442	40,324
Singapore	5,947,333	24,265,502	1,786,643	1,552	1,697,798	87,293
Thailand	70,169,115	17,270,775	4,618,652	31,801	4,565,063	21,788
Vietnam	99,184,865	85,826,548	11,364,355	43,097	10,014,637	1,306,621

Source Authors' compilation using data from the Worldometers (2022). AMS: ASEAN member states

4.4 Results and Discussion

This section analyses the main findings of the present research. The discussion compares the analysis of trade, investments, health, tourism, human security and economic growth in light of the research questions. It also outlines the practical implications of the findings.

4.4.1 Impacts of COVID-19 on ASEAN Economies

The COVID-19 pandemic has taken the world economy completely unawares. Every single nation on earth has been impacted by the COVID-19 pandemic, which has become a global health and economic calamity. Due to the pandemic, the ASEAN region—which has an aggregate population of nearly 650 million people and a GDP of $3.2 trillion in 2019—has also encountered previously unheard-of difficulties and interruptions. Figure 4.3 shows the trends of economic sizes of the ASEAN before the pandemic and two years into the pandemic. According to the World Development Indicators (WDI), Brunei, the Philippines and Thailand are the most hit AMS, with their GDP contracting by nearly 10.87%, 8.16% and 8.03%, respectively.

The COVID-19 pandemic has caused severe contractions in economic activity and trade across the ASEAN region, as well as significant losses in income, employment, and livelihoods. According to the ADB, the ASEAN region's GDP contracted by 4% in 2020, compared with a growth of 4.4% in 2019 [5]. The contraction was driven by sharp declines in domestic demand, tourism, exports, and investment, as well as disruptions in supply chains and production.

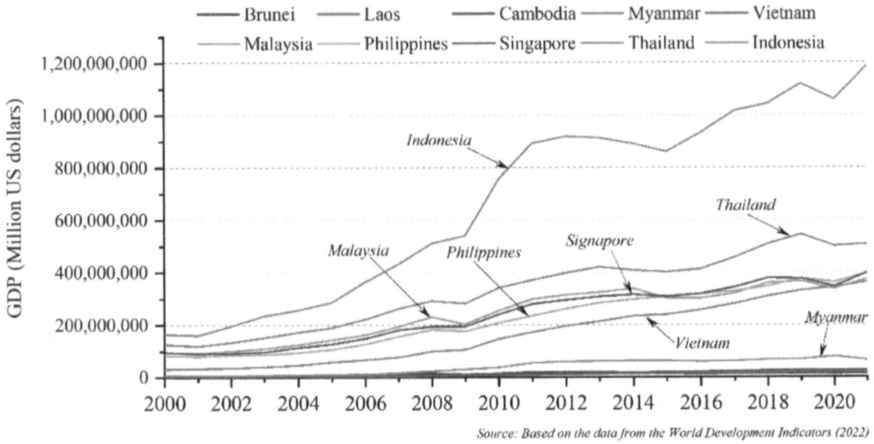

Fig. 4.3 GDP trends of the ASEAN 2000–2021

The consequences of COVID-19 on the AMS varied across from one country to another, depending on their initial conditions, policy responses, and sectoral compositions. Vietnam was the only AMS experienced positive growth in 2020, at 2.9%, due to effective virus containment, strong domestic demand, and resilient exports. Inversely, Thailand and the Philippines, which rely significantly on tourism and services, experienced the greatest reductions, at −6.1% and −9.5%, respectively. Due to lockdowns, movement restrictions, and weak external demand, Indonesia and Malaysia witnessed large GDP reductions of −2% and −5.6%, respectively. Singapore and Brunei Darussalam also experienced recessions, with −5.4% and −1.2%, respectively, owing to their reliance on global commerce and oil prices [8].

The pandemic's unpredictability ultimately provided some insight into problems with supply and demand. Many industrial enterprises were forced to shut down for extended periods as quarantines were put into place [9]. The effects of these closures are still being seen in areas of industry where there is a significant concentration. Food, healthcare, and construction supply shortages are throughout the ASEAN [10]. In some of the largest economies in the area, exports are increasing tremendously as the industrial sector is getting back on track. As of November 2021, Malaysia's exports increased by 30% yearly. This increase is mostly attributable to electrical and electronic products, which together with chemicals and petroleum products accounted for 40% of all exports. Singapore's exports increased by 40%, with the largest increase in ten years. Electronic goods, pharmaceuticals, petrochemicals, and specialist machinery are the key drivers of this growth. The economy has been able to stabilize, thanks to the rising vaccination rates and a decline in hospitalization across several countries.

Figure 4.4 indicates that the export value of the AMS significantly decreases a year into the pandemic, except in the case of Vietnam, where the country's exports increase by 3.66% from the previous year. It is also observable that the largest exporter in the region is Singapore. The country's average export value between 2018 and 2021 was approximately 329.34 trillion US dollars. Although it declined to 296.69 trillion in 2020, which is one year into the pandemic, the country's exports in 2021 increased to 354.64 trillion, remaining as the top exporter in ASEAN. Vietnam, Thailand, and Malaysia are the second, third and fourth top ASEAN exporters, with average export values of 292.81, 227.84 and 227.12 trillion US dollars, respectively, between 2018 and 2021 (see Table 4.2 for further statistics).

From an import perspective, Brunei, Cambodia, Laos, and Vietnam increased their imports in the first year of the pandemic (see Fig. 4.5). The figure indicates that Malaysia and Vietnam are the largest importers in ASEAN, followed by Thailand

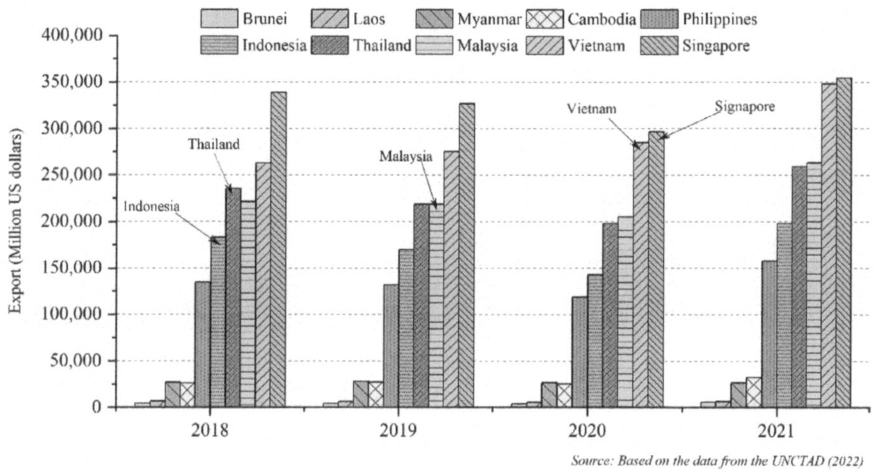

Fig. 4.4 Export value of AMS 2018–2021

Table 4.2 Export value of AMS 2018–2021 (in million US dollars)

AMS	2018	2019	2020	2021	Average
Brunei	4,544.96	4,481.34	4,349.50	6,247.64	4,905.86
Cambodia	26,309.24	27,563.70	25,742.94	32,698.33	28,078.56
Indonesia	183,007.00	170,382.01	142,918.48	198,492.89	173,700.09
Laos	6,952.79	6,743.43	6,049.38	7,004.56	6,687.54
Malaysia	221,275.94	218,612.85	205,190.33	263,391.75	227,117.72
Myanmar	27,096.31	28,290.58	27,102.98	26,894.86	27,346.18
Philippines	134,705.14	131,812.96	118,717.62	157,939.18	135,793.73
Singapore	338,952.00	327,088.98	296,689.02	354,637.53	329,341.89
Thailand	235,542.48	218,745.12	197,973.18	259,110.50	227,842.82
Vietnam	262,582.71	275,065.93	285,141.29	348,455.24	292,811.29

Source Authors' compilation using data from the UNCTAD (2022)

and Singapore, with average import values of 353.04, 350.18, 288.73 and 278.30 trillion US dollars, respectively (Table 4.3). Cambodia is expected to continue to have strong economic growth over the next two years. Several researchers have examined the extent of COVID-19 on the tourism industry in ASEAN countries. International tourism was seriously affected by the COVID-19 outbreak in the ASEAN region [11]. The tourism sector, which relies primarily on gambling and betting services, is also recovering slowly [12].

Figure 4.6 demonstrates the ASEAN total trade value from 2018–2021, while the trade balance is shown in Fig. 4.7. These figures reveal that Cambodia, Myanmar, the Philippines, and Singapore recorded a positive trade balance before and during the

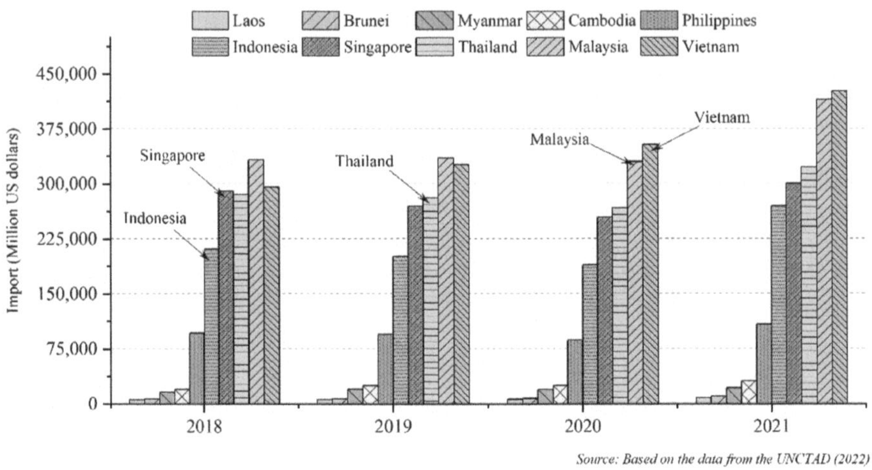

Fig. 4.5 Import value of AMS 2018–2021

Table 4.3 Import value of AMS 2018–2021 (in million US dollars)

AMS	2018	2019	2020	2021	Average
Brunei	6,768.05	7,120.34	7,711.54	10,380.99	7,995.23
Cambodia	20,341.01	24,983.03	25,149.36	31,565.14	25,509.64
Indonesia	211,144.08	200,800.56	189,418.62	269,598.56	217,740.46
Laos	6,058.95	6,018.64	6,678,80	8,527.85	6,821.06
Malaysia	332,706.99	334,887.26	329,702.58	414,872.15	353,042.24
Myanmar	16,444.64	20,088.07	19,711.94	21,841.87	19,521.63
Philippines	96,343.97	94,770.80	87,085.44	108,294.51	96,623.68
Singapore	289,975.54	269,03.52	254,085.94	300,094.16	278,296.54
Thailand	285,369.82	280,386.66	266,910.52	322,256.82	288,730.95
Vietnam	295,506.40	325,979.98	352,955.67	426,282.16	350,181.05

Source Authors' compilation using data from the UNCTAD (2022)

COVID-19 pandemic. However, only Singapore and the Philippines had a positive trade balance above 30 trillion US dollars throughout this period. The performance of Singapore (in comparison to the other ASEAN nations) demonstrates that travel constraints that are too severe may not always be the key to managing a pandemic, as the economic trade-off may be prohibitively expensive [13] (see Tables 4.4 and 4.5 for further statistics).

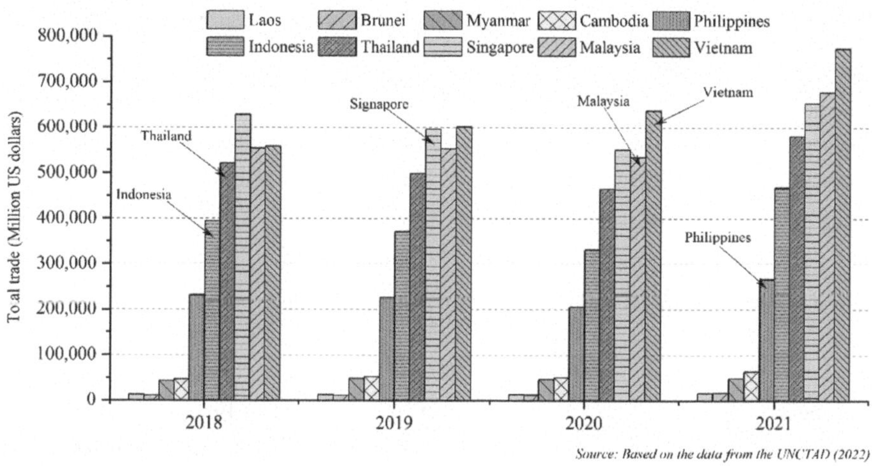

Fig. 4.6 Total trade value of AMS 2018–2021

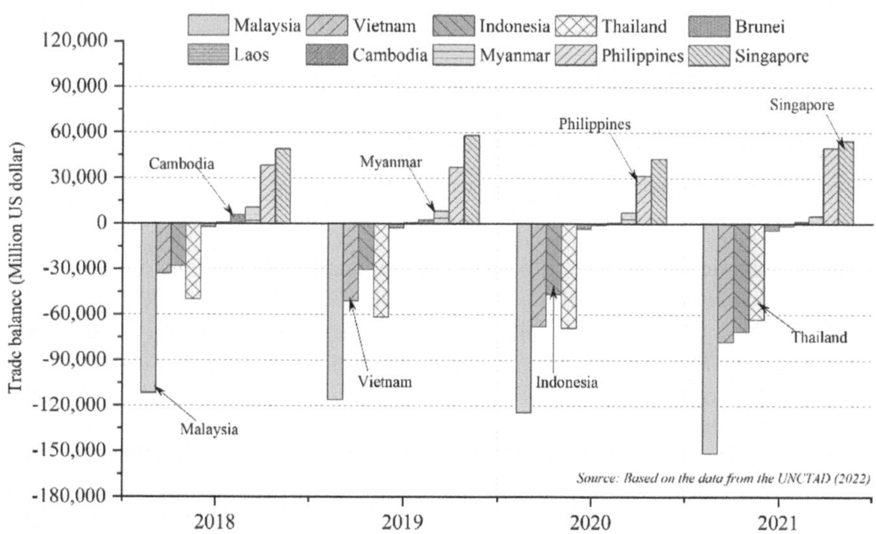

Fig. 4.7 Trade balance of AMS 2018–2021

Table 4.4 Total trade value of AMS 2018–2021 (in million US dollars)

AMS	2018	2019	2020	2021	Average
Brunei	11,313.01	11,601.68	12,061.03	16,628.63	12,901,09
Cambodia	46,650.25	52,546.73	50,892.32	64,263.47	53,588.19
Indonesia	394,151.08	371,182.57	332,337.10	468,091.45	391,440.55
Laos	13,011.73	12,762.07	12,728.20	15,532.41	13,508.60
Malaysia	553,982.93	553,500.12	534,892.90	678,263.90	580,159.96
Myanmar	43,540.94	48,378.65	46,814.92	48,736.72	46,867.81
Philippines	231,049.11	226,583.76	205,803.06	266,233.70	232,417.41
Singapore	628,927.54	596,119.51	550,774.97	654,731.68	607,638.42
Thailand	520,912.30	499,131.78	464,883.70	581,367.32	516,573.77
Vietnam	558,089.11	601,045.91	638,096.95	774,737.41	642,992.35

Source Authors' compilation using data from the UNCTAD (2022)

Table 4.5 Trade balance of AMS 2018–2021 (in million US dollars)

AMS	2018	2019	2020	2021	Average
Brunei	−2,223.09	−2,639.00	−3,362.04	−4,133.36	−3,089.37
Cambodia	5,968.22	2,580.67	593.60	11,33.19	25,68.92
Indonesia	−28,137.09	−30,418.55	−46,500.14	−71,105.67	−44,040.36
Laos	893.83	724.79	−629.42	−1,523.29	−133.52
Malaysia	−111,431.05	−116,274.41	−124,512.25	−151,480.39	−125,924.53
Myanmar	10,651.67	8,202.51	7,391.04	5,052.99	7,824.55
Philippines	38,361.16	37,042,16	31,632.18	49,644.67	39,170.04
Singapore	48,976.47	58,058.47	42,603.08	54,543.37	51,045.35
Thailand	−49,827.34	−61,641.54	−68,937.33	−63,146.31	−60,888.13
Vietnam	−32,923.69	−50,914.04	−67,814.38	−77,826.92	−57,369.76

Source Authors' compilation using data from the UNCTAD (2022)

The pandemic also increased poverty and inequality, as millions of people lost their jobs or incomes, especially in the informal sector and vulnerable groups. The ADB estimates that about 38 million people in Southeast Asia fell into poverty in 2020 due to the pandemic [5]. The COVID-19 pandemic has not discriminated against any sector. This pandemic was predicted to cause a severe decline in global trade [14]. Trade restrictions imposed by many countries have greatly impacted the tourist industry [15]. Tourism is a crucial source of revenue for AMS [3]. Due to COVID-19, one of ASEAN's most important economic sectors has experienced severe losses. The tourism sector is only slowly rebuilding even in 2022 because the region's borders are still closely patrolled. In regard to the efforts to reopen, there has not been much collaboration and cooperation in the area. Growth across sectors is crucial for long-term economic recovery, and no industry should be left behind. Law and Katekaew [3] suggested that a speedy recovery of intra-ASEAN tourism is made possible by the AMS's cooperative efforts, hastening the recovery of the region's economy. Additionally, Chutiphongdech and Zhao [16] suggested that policymakers and tourism entrepreneurs should develop strategies to capture the interest of such a market segment by implementing destination branding or attempting to differentiate attractions in the eyes of foreign tourists because the ASEAN tourism market structure is concentrated but still competitive since foreign tourists visiting AMS are not price sensitive. Because of the price inelasticity of foreign tourists visiting ASEAN, it is suggested that an increase in the price of tourism products will not decrease the number of international tourists but will increase tourism revenue instead. Therefore, it is indeed possible to employ price strategies that increase tourism revenue when tourists recognize the differences between tourist sites. In addition, as these tourist goods are interchangeable across the ASEAN community, AMS will be able to increase their respective tourism profits through collaboration in tourism-linking plans.

The real estate sector was another example of an industry that suffered significantly from the COVID-19-induced slump. Singapore is anticipated to recover from its economic downturn far more quickly than its peers in the region. The housing market in Singapore has held up well despite the pandemic and has increased by 13% annually over the past two years on average. The real estate market in Vietnam is also anticipated to perform better than most of the other ASEAN economies. Foreign investors are also drawn to Vietnam's residential sector. Additionally, the market for industrial real estate and logistics has been doing well. For the other ASEAN economies, things are less rosy. The Philippines, Malaysia, and Thailand will not recover as quickly as their counterparts. Penang, Manila, and Kuala Lumpur residential building prices are all still 3–5% below pre-pandemic levels.

The Regional Comprehensive Economic Partnership (RCEP) Agreement, which is led by ASEAN and entered into force in January 2022, will contribute to greater regional economic integration and give access to a larger market, both of which will foster economic growth and support the post-pandemic recovery of the ASEAN economies. Pushing for digital transformation and investing in cloud computing, cybersecurity, artificial intelligence, and smart manufacturing would significantly help the region's economy recover after the pandemic. The Comprehensive Recovery Framework (ACRF) for ASEAN recognized digital connection as a top need.

It has been able to restore commercial operations in a number of sectors as a result of the plateauing of COVID-19 infections and the rise in immunization rates. The region's largest economies, such as Singapore and Vietnam, are rebounding faster than their counterparts, while those of Malaysia, Indonesia, the Philippines, Thailand, and so on are recovering considerably more slowly than their peers.

4.4.2 Policies and Outcomes of the AMS in Response to the COVID-19 Pandemic

The COVID-19 pandemic has been ongoing for more than two years, and the AMS has made joint efforts to address its effects and continue to address the aftermath of this disaster. Because of the magnitude of the economic harm caused by COVID-19, ASEAN changed its approach to fostering regional economic integration [1, 5]. For instance, the continuing Russia-Ukraine war and the escalating US-China competition require ASEAN to undertake such strategic adjustments. What ASEAN may accomplish in post-pandemic regional economic recovery and resilience is threatened by the geopolitical competitiveness linked with this rivalry and armed conflict [4]. Furthermore, the pandemic inspired AMS to work together to develop and implement a regional economic recovery strategy. As a result, the "ASEAN Comprehensive Recovery Framework (ACRF)" and "Implementation Plan" were approved by the association's members at the 2020 ASEAN summit as a means of avoiding the disastrous effects of COVID-19 [10]. The five broad strategies that make up the ACRF are (1) enhancing human security, (2) expanding intra-ASEAN economic integration, (3) speeding inclusive digital transformation, (4) boosting regional sustainability and (5) boosting regional resilience. Each strategy's exact deliverables, deadlines, and bodies in charge of completing them are listed in the "Implementation Plan".

In addition to the previously mentioned five broad strategies that make up the ACRF, the ADB also highlighted several measures of different sectors that would help put back the ASEAN economy into its pre-pandemic progress. For instance, intensifying marketing activities to reassure passengers that it is safe to go is part of the tourism sector's strategy to strengthen national tourism and rebuild demand. Making a permanent crisis management task team could help make a nation's tourism industry more resilient to future shocks. The ASEAN countries are given the following solutions in the agro-processing sector: improving supply chains' efficiency and transparency. Expanding sales channels, considering changing consumer trends, and addressing new markets, for instance, may minimize delays and compliance costs while also adding significant value to the industry. By focusing on the export of goods with a higher value-added, increasing regional commerce, and mainstreaming the export of goods with competitive potentials, the ASEAN member states can raise the level of product processing [17]. Additionally, the AMS governments and their stakeholders have also adopted a variety of initiatives and policies to lessen the adverse effects of COVID-19 on their economies and society as a whole as well as to aid in the recovery process, such as, fiscal stimulus packages, monetary easing policies, social protection programs, health interventions, regional cooperation initiatives, and digital transformation projects.

Fiscal stimulus offerings: As of December 2020, the ASEAN countries have launched fiscal stimulus packages totaling approximately $695 billion (or 15% of GDP) to assist households, businesses, and sectors affected by the pandemic. Tax relief, salary subsidies, payments in cash, credit assurances, infrastructure development, and health spending are all part of these packages. The size and composition of the packages differ based on the country's fiscal space and demands.

Monetary easing regulations: Since January 2020, ASEAN central banks have decreased policy rates by 25 to 150 basis points to ease financial conditions and promote the expansion of credit. To stabilize financial markets and provide appropriate liquidity, they have also used quantitative easing measures such as bond purchases, liquidity injections, and foreign currency interventions.

Social protection programs: The ASEAN countries have increased their programs for social protection to provide economic support and basic services to the poor and vulnerable groups affected by the global pandemic. These services include cash transfers, food aid, and benefits for unemployment.

Health assessments: The ASEAN governments have developed a variety of health interventions to limit the virus' spread and safeguard the health and well-being of their citizens. Testing, tracing, isolation, quarantine, treatment, immunization, and public health education are examples of interventions. ASEAN governments have also worked together and with outside collaborators to improve their health capacities and capabilities, such as by exchanging medical supplies and devices, distributing best practices and experiences, and collectively procuring and offering vaccinations.

Regional collaboration initiatives: To combat the COVID-19 pandemic and its consequences, ASEAN governments and stakeholders have initiated a number of regional cooperation initiatives. The COVID-19 ASEAN Response Fund, the ASEAN Regional Reserve of Medical Supplies for Public Health Emergencies, the ASEAN Comprehensive Recovery Framework, and the ASEAN Travel Corridor Arrangement Framework are among them. These programs seek to mobilize resources, improve readiness and reaction, aid in recovery and resilience, and allow safe and gradual border reopening.

Digital transformation operations: ASEAN governments and stakeholders have intensified their digital transformation efforts in response to the pandemic's problems and potential. Promoting digital connection and inclusion, improving digital literacy and skills, stimulating digital innovation and entrepreneurship, strengthening digital governance and security, and harnessing digital technology for social and economic development are all part of these activities. The ASEAN Digital Masterplan 2025 provides a strategic framework and action plan for accelerating the region's digital transformation.

The regional recovery and integration effort components are affected by the global pandemic, according to the ACRF. Health and economic issues are intertwined in the minds of AMS. The ACRF therefore strongly emphasizes improving health systems and human security to build workforces within the ASEAN area and achieve regional economic integration. As one of the world's most densely populated areas, ASEAN has made it a priority to secure medical supplies and vaccinations for its population, realizing that these measures would be crucial for the region's economic recovery. Consequently, as of October 20, 2021, 26.4% of the ASEAN population had been fully vaccinated, while 41.4% had received at least one dose [18].

Because of the COVID-19 pandemic, AMS are embracing economic digitalization more rapidly and extensively. In the AMS and throughout the association's efforts at regional economic integration, the pandemic has heightened the role of digital technologies. They have always been a part of regional supply chains and corporate operations (via, for instance, e-commerce and online customs clearances), but today more than ever, they are essential. During the pandemic, teleconferencing and work-from-home arrangements were made possible, thanks to digital technology. Thus, the necessity for increasing economic digitalization in ASEAN countries is captured by the ACRF.

Rapid acceleration in a few industries enhanced the ASEAN economic framework and accordingly supported its ongoing growth strategies. In 2020 and 2021, the industries of science, technology, and innovation (STI) made a significant contribution to the recovery of the AMS as well as the global economy, and they continue to foster growth in a post-pandemic world. For instance, at the peak of the COVID-19 outbreak, the demand for a *yet-to-be-developed* vaccine became painfully obvious. As society became aware of this, the STI community was already advancing research and development (R&D) to generate a safe vaccine. The rapid acceleration of vaccine development opened chances for more employment and income, which helped revive the economy. The Organization for Economic Co-operation and Development [19] indicated that approximately 2 billion US dollars had been committed to global vaccine research by the middle of 2020. Moreover, the utilization of digital technologies/tools, open-access research, and international STI collaboration have all accelerated due to COVID-19 [19]. The need for remote meetings, teaching and learning, communication, and information sharing expanded quickly in response to the rising requirement for social isolation to prevent the viral spread. Digital conferencing software's extensive use serves as an illustration of humanity's capacity for change. Digitalization frameworks must be created as a result of isolation directives to contribute to post-pandemic economic recovery and growth [20].

The labor-intensive textile industry is competitive in several Southeast Asian nations [21]. The first step in reviving this industry is to boost competition to maintain the sector's growth. The ASEAN garment industry can diversify beyond its current markets in the European Union (EU) and the United States while looking into options to pursue product differentiation and produce clothing with a higher value added. Finally, it might also be essential for the sector to embrace more adaptable business and production methods, such as enabling apparel manufacturers to move between manufacturing types to satisfy shifting consumer demand.

The ASEAN nations may act in two directions to address and enhance the competitiveness of the electronics industry post-COVID-19. The first involves modernizing special economic zones (SEZs) by enhancing business clustering to enhance industry links, resulting in more collaboration and resource pooling while fostering competition. SEZs could also be aided by industry-specific regulations, such as those that encourage the export of electronics under free trade agreements, which would help the region's manufacturers. The shift to high-value operations in the electronics supply chain may be facilitated by improved cooperation between the government and business, as well as between domestic players and foreign investors, within the SEZs. To draw foreign direct investment, maintain competitiveness, and move toward producing electronics with high added value, the second sector is aggressively developing human resources.

The ASEAN nations may create an IT Business Process Outsourcing (IT-BPO) roadmap, improve connectivity, assist talent development, encourage micro-small-medium enterprises (MSMEs) to go digital, and reevaluate digital laws to foster an enabling environment for digital trade. For instance, several efforts are required to encourage the development of digital skills to enable MSMEs to go digital. Increased industry participation in curriculum development can ensure that important concepts such as critical thinking, complex problem solving, and English language proficiency are taught. To promote more and better-quality training in the workplace, this needs to be combined with support and financial incentives for companies.

The COVID-19 pandemic's effects on AMS's national economies and economic integration forced them to reconsider their strategy for promoting intra-ASEAN trade, investment, and economic growth. These reforms are part of the association's effort to promote regional economic integration, including highlighting the necessity of strengthening the healthcare system and enhancing human protection [4]. Significant barriers loom in the way of ASEAN's efforts to recover from the pandemic's impacts and fortify its resilience to resist future crises, including the escalating US-China rivalry and the armed confrontation between Russia and Ukraine.

4.4.3 External Challenges Affecting ASEAN's Post-Pandemic Strategy

Three major external problems exist (1) the intensifying US-China rivalry; (2) the global effects of the Russia-Ukraine conflict; and (3) the nature and effects of ASEAN's post-COVID-19 economic recovery and regional integration goals and measures.

The world was considerably more dependent on China from 2010 to 2020 as during this decade China's growth accounted for more than 40% of the increase in global GDP, when the United States and Europe were still recovering from the Great Recession [22]. China is not only the largest investor and trading partner of the ASEAN countries, but also emerging as a worldwide leader in international development financing, with the ability to fill large global development shortages [23]. It provided 6.5% of the total Foreign Direct Investment (FDI) inflows into ASEAN in 2018 and 17.1% of the region's total trade. The Beijing government frequently refers to this region as its "*periphery*," and it is expanding its military presence there while also launching a number of infrastructure projects in Southeast Asia as part of its Belt and Road Initiative (BRI) [24]. China's rise as a great power generates concerns in several AMS about how it may use its growing military capabilities. A scholar argues that China's defensive posture supports its current grand strategy of reassuring its neighbors about its rising power and preventing the creation of counter-balancing coalitions or alignments, especially on its borders, where combined regional forces facing China are significant [25]. Since the Asian Financial Crisis, manufacturing trade between China and ASEAN economies has steadily expanded [26]. ASEAN's supply chains are deeply entwined with China's manufacturing industry, and the massive flood of Chinese tourists is advantageous for the region's tourism industry. The ASEAN-4 nations—Malaysia, the Philippines, Singapore, and Thailand—dominate ASEAN trade in manufactured goods with China [26]. The COVID-19 outbreak has raised awareness of the importance of an ASEAN-China community for a shared future [27]. The pandemic might create chances to advance ASEAN-China regional economic integration, encourage post-pandemic recovery, and foster further growth by improving policy cooperation, fostering an environment that is open and transparent for trade, and guaranteeing the stability of industry and supply chains. However, the US and the Eurozone Countries, two of the outbreak's other major victims along with China, are among ASEAN's biggest trading and investment partners, and the AMS are also directly impacted by the outbreak. In 2020, the WTO predicts that global commerce will shrink by 13% to 32%, topping the decline caused by the Global Financial Crisis. As a result, the overall impact on ASEAN would probably be significant and wide-ranging; however, it could differ depending on the region [1].

US-China power competition is currently playing out on an increasingly global scale. Trade between the US and China is impacted by the tech war. There has been a dramatic decline in trade in both directions for high-tech goods such as telecommunications equipment, semiconductors, and computer accessories. According to a study, Vietnam's exports to the US increased significantly in the sensitive categories between 2018 and 2021, and altogether, they more than doubled [28]. President Joe Biden has maintained the previous administration's $350 billion worth of Chinese goods subject to US tariffs. By encouraging businesses to move from China to Southeast Asia to benefit from cheaper operating costs, these trade barriers have disrupted supply chains. Such supply-chain reconfiguration is having an immediate positive impact on the economies of AMS; however, the US-China trade war will have a negative long-term impact on them in numerous ways. The US-China trade war has discouraged foreign investment by creating uncertainty throughout the global economy [4]. This uneasy environment frequently encourages investors to take a wait-and-see approach and postpone new investments. Although the Regional Comprehensive Economic Partnership (RCEP), which is a trading union made up of fifteen nations (including ten AMS, Australia, China, Japan, New Zealand, and South Korea), could be of considerable steadiness, the bilateral economic dispute in the rising geopolitical rivalry between the US and China will negatively impact the ACRF's plan to boost ASEAN economic integration and its members' involvement in global trade and investment flows. The RCEP thus includes many least developing countries (LDCs) from which few countries will graduate in the coming years soon. The RCEP trade pact will provide a large market opportunity to these graduating countries [29].

Furthermore, the US government's sanctions against Chinese technological firms and China's initiatives to increase its technological independence are hastening the technological split in both local and global contexts. For instance, AMS are implementing various 5G technologies and standards, which will make it more difficult for them to realize its goal of a regionally connected digital economy. It will be difficult to harmonize technical standards across the area as long as Beijing and Washington vie for technological supremacy. Escalating the US-China competition may make it more difficult for the ACRF to deploy economic digitalization as part of ASEAN's post-pandemic recovery and economic integration initiatives.

The Russia's invasion of Ukraine in 2022 surprised the world, and particularly to many it signaled as the end of American predominance since it demonstrated that America could no longer thwart forces of revisionism and uphold the world system it had established [30]. Nevertheless, the Russia-Ukraine war had a minor influence on trade, economic growth, and the likelihood of more regional integration in Southeast Asia. Both Russia and Ukraine are minor economic and investment partners for AMS. However, there are worrying ramifications for both national and regional operations in Southeast Asia as a result of the conflict and the severe economic and financial sanctions the US and its allies have placed on Russia [4]. Price increases for agricultural products, energy supplies, and other commodities exported by Ukraine and Russia are one immediate and possibly long-term result. According to the Organization for Economic Cooperation and Development (OECD), Russia and Ukraine export approximately 10% of the world's natural gas, 20% of its grain, 30% of its wheat, and 1% of its oil. The war's disruption of Russian and Ukrainian shipments of these items is causing price inflation for both food and energy supplies, which has a detrimental impact on both the public and private sectors of ASEAN members. Food and energy costs in particular account for more than 40% of the baskets of consumer prices for products and services purchased in the Philippines, Thailand, and Vietnam. As prices rise, ASEAN members may place a higher priority on aiding their local consumers and economies, including through subsidies, to mitigate the impact of inflation. Less funding for post-pandemic national and regional recovery and resilience programs, such as enhancing health systems, may result from such policies. Furthermore, Ukraine generates 50% of the world's supply of neon gas used in the manufacture of microchips. Exports of this commodity from Ukraine have been interrupted because of the conflict, which has affected worldwide supply chains for numerous businesses relying on microchips, such as robotics, electronics, and electrical appliances. By hampering the ACRF's ambition to increase economic digitization across ASEAN countries, this interruption jeopardizes the region's post-pandemic recovery and economic integration plans.

4.4.4 Opportunities and Possibilities for Growth in the Post-Pandemic

In the post-pandemic lifespan, the COVID-19 pandemic has also created chances and prospects for growth and development in the ASEAN region. These are some instances.

Rebuilding and rebounding from the crisis: According to the ADB, the ASEAN region's GDP will expand by 4.4% in 2021 and 5.1% in 2022, as domestic and external demand progressively recovers from the pandemic shock [5]. The Regional Comprehensive Economic Partnership (RCEP), which was signed in November 2020 by 15 countries, including all ASEAN members, would also improve trade and investment flows in the area and beyond. By 2030, the RCEP is predicted to boost ASEAN's GDP by 0.4% [29].

Diversifying and upgrading economic frameworks: The COVID-19 pandemic has highlighted the weaknesses and risks of relying on specific industries or markets for economic growth. Governments and stakeholders in ASEAN have the potential to diversify while strengthening the structure of their economies through stimulating new sources of growth such as green economy, digital economy, creative economy, circular economy, and social economy. These new sources of growth have the potential to increase job creation, productivity, environmental sustainability, social inclusion, and resilience.

Regional integration and collaboration must be strengthened: The COVID-19 pandemic has underlined the need of regional integration and cooperation in solving common challenges and promoting shared objectives. ASEAN governments and stakeholders now have a chance to strengthen the region's unity.

Regional cooperation and integration must be enhanced: The COVID-19 outbreak has highlighted the significance of regional integration and cooperation in addressing common difficulties and advancing shared goals. ASEAN countries and stakeholders now have an opportunity to fortify the region's solidarity. Regional integration and collaboration must be strengthened: The COVID-19 pandemic has highlighted the importance of regional integration and cooperation in tackling common challenges and achieving common goals. ASEAN countries and stakeholders now have a chance to strengthen the region's cohesiveness. These programs seek to gather resources, improve readiness and reaction, aid in recovery and resilience, and allow safe and gradual border reopening.

Efforts at digital transformation: ASEAN governments and stakeholders have increased their digital transformation activities in response to the pandemic's challenges and potential. Promoting digital connection and inclusion, improving digital literacy and skills, stimulating digital innovation and entrepreneurship, strengthening digital governance and security, and harnessing digital technology for social and economic development are all part of these activities. The ASEAN Digital Masterplan 2025 provides a strategic framework and action plan for accelerating the region's digital evolution. With the Possibilities and Prospects for Post-Pandemic Growth and

Development in the post-pandemic age, the COVID-19 pandemic has also created chances and prospects for growth and development in the ASEAN region.

4.5 Conclusion

The year 2022 is the second year following the global pandemic, in which the globe and particularly AMS are dealing with a major dilemma for health and economic development. The current chapter attempts to investigate the impact of the COVID-19 pandemic on the ASEAN economy from numerous aspects and how the AMS responded to the pandemic to recover their economy in the post-pandemic era. Additionally, the significant external challenges affecting ASEAN's post-pandemic strategy were addressed.

The COVID-19 pandemic has impacted AMS in numerous aspects, including food, healthcare, construction, manufacturing, trade and exports, tourist, and real estate sectors. It is believed that a return to normal economic activity is enabled by growing vaccination rates and a decline in hospitalization in many countries. Singapore had fast and high vaccination rates among AMS patients. Vietnam, Indonesia, and Malaysia were the most hit by COVID-19 infection, while Indonesia had the most COVID-19-related deaths among all AMS, followed by the Philippines and Vietnam.

Responding to the global pandemic, the AMS has taken collective efforts and programs to tackle its multifaceted repercussions and thereafter continue to accomplish the fallout from the crisis. The "ASEAN Comprehensive Recovery Framework (ACRF)" and "Implementation Plan" were approved and put into action by the AMS at the 2020 ASEAN summit by focusing on the following five broad strategies: (1) enhancing human security; (2) expanding intra-ASEAN economic integration; (3) speeding inclusive digital transformation; (4) boosting regional sustainability; and (5) boosting regional resilience.

The findings demonstrate that several challenges originating from the external world are likely to affect ASEAN's post-pandemic strategy for economic recovery, trade facilitation, and regional integration. Additionally, the uncertainties and underlying dynamics of US-China competition and the worldwide repercussions of the Russia-Ukraine war caused a delay and procrastination in the implementation processes of the ACRF. Effective measures can be worked out to develop a coordinated framework for the pandemic governance of COVID-19. Nevertheless, the analysis presented in the current chapter has some limitations. Due to time and resource constraints, however, we could not cover all other possible sources of relevant data for the current analysis. We hope future researchers may overcome the limitations and undertake more empirical studies on various dimensions of the work.

Acknowledgements The authors are grateful to the editors and anonymous referees for their incisive suggestions to improve the quality of this chapter. They would also like to thank Mr. Rashid Nizamani for his technical assistance.

Declaration of Conflicting Interests Regarding the research, writing, and/or publication of this paper, the authors have disclosed that they have no potential conflicts of interest.

References

1. ASEAN_Policy_Brief (2020) Economic impact of COVID-19 outbreak on ASEAN. In: ASEAN Integration Monitoring Directorate (AIMD) and Community Relations Division (CRD). Association of Southeast Asian Nations (ASEAN), pp 1–17
2. Suriyankietkaew S, Nimsai S (2021) COVID-19 impacts and sustainability strategies for regional recovery in southeast Asia: challenges and opportunities. Sustainability 13(16):8907
3. Law CC, Katekaew R (2022) COVID-19: ASEAN aviation policy and the significance of intra-regional connectivity. J Asian Econ Integr 4(1):1–23
4. Pitakdumrongkit K (2022) Southeast Asia's economic future after COVID-19: geopolitics and war threaten ASEAN's post-COVID plans for economic recovery, integration, and resilience. https://www.thinkglobalhealth.org/article/southeast-asias-economic-future-after-covid-19. Accessed April 28–August 12, 2022
5. ADB (2022) Southeast Asia rising from the pandemic. Asian Development Bank (ADB), Manila, Philippines
6. Djalante R et al (2020) COVID-19 and ASEAN responses: comparative policy analysis. Prog Disaster Sci 8:100129
7. Purnomo EP et al (2022) ASEAN policy responses to COVID-19 pandemic: adaptation and experimentation policy: a study of ASEAN countries policy volatility for COVID-19 pandemic. SAGE Open 12(1):21582440221082144
8. Chong TTL, Li X, Yip C (2021) The impact of COVID-19 on ASEAN. Econ Polit Stud 9(2):166–185
9. Donthu N, Gustafsson A (2020) Effects of COVID-19 on business and research. J Bus Res 117:284–289
10. ASEAN (2021) ASEAN development outlook 2021. Association of Southeast Asian Nations (ASEAN)
11. Beh L-S, Lin WL (2022) Impact of COVID-19 on ASEAN tourism industry. J Asian Public Policy 15(2):300–320
12. Riccardi L, Riccardi G (2021) Invest in ASEAN: countries analysis and treaties, 1 edn. Springer, Singapore
13. Lee YH, Lim SYR (2022) Efficacy in COVID-19 management: the case of ASEAN. Transform Govern: People, Process Policy 16(4):613–626
14. Kiyota K (2022) The COVID-19 pandemic and the world trade network. J Asian Econ 78:101419
15. Darmastuti S, Juned M, Widiastutie S (2021) Analysis on ASEAN and European union policies regarding Covid-19. Bp Int Res Crit Inst (BIRCI-J): Humlties Soc Sci 4(2):3220–3232
16. Chutiphongdech T, Zhao Y (2021) Market structure and its relationship to tourism revenue: industrial organization perspectives from ASEAN member countries. Available at SSRN 3992480
17. Mizik T, Szerletics Á, Jámbor A (2020) Agri-food export competitiveness of the ASEAN countries. Sustainability 12(23):9860
18. ASEAN (2021) ASEAN economic integration brief volume November 2021 Number 10. 2021, Association of Southeast Asian Nations (ASEAN)
19. OECD (2021) OECD science, technology and innovation outlook 2021: times of crisis and opportunity
20. Dwivedi YK et al (2021) Setting the future of digital and social media marketing research: perspectives and research propositions. Int J Inf Manag 59:102168

21. Shahriar S, et al (2021) Determinants of Bangladesh's leather exports to its major trade partners: a panel gravity model approach. Glob Bus Rev 09721509211036288
22. Goldstone JA, May JF (2023) The global economy's future depends on Africa: as others slow, a youthful continent can drive growth. Foreign Aff 1–2(3):1–8
23. Shahriar S (2022) Pandemic crisis and prospects of tourism along the BCIM economic corridor. In: Hassan A et al (eds) Tourism and hospitality in Asia: crisis, resilience and recovery. Springer Nature Singapore, pp 63–74
24. Huong LT (2023) How to survive a great-power competition: Southeast Asia's precarious balancing act. Foreign Aff 1(2):30–35
25. Fravel MT (2007) Securing borders: China's doctrine and force structure for frontier defense. J Strateg Stud 30(4–5):705–737. https://doi.org/10.1080/01402390701431790
26. Tham SY, Kam AJY, Abdul Aziz NI (2016) Moving up the value chain in ICT: ASEAN trade with China. J Contemp Asia 46(4):680–699
27. Yang Y, Li F (2020) Impact of COVID-19 on ASEAN-China cooperation and its prospects. East Asian Policy 12(03):19–32
28. Dollar D (2022) U.S.-China trade relations in an era of great power competition. China Econ J 1–13
29. Goswami GG, et al (2022) Should Bangladesh join regional comprehensive economic partnership (RCEP)? The gravity explanation of Bangladesh dilemma. Int J Emerg Mark (ahead-of-print)
30. Brooks SG, Wohlforth WC (2023) The myth of multi-polarity: American power's staying power. Foreign Aff 1–2(3):76–91

Part II
Impact of the COVID-19 Pandemic on Vulnerable Groups: Women and Migrants

Chapter 5
Women's Empowerment and Sustainable Development Goals in the Post-COVID-19 Era

Hebatallah Adam, Atiba Batul, and Firdous Ahmad Malik

Abstract The COVID-19 pandemic has had a disproportionate impact on women residing in the global south. Females residing in these geographical areas exhibit a higher probability of engaging in nonformal occupations, such as household labour, thereby rendering them more susceptible to experiencing unemployment and financial instability. Furthermore, the outbreak has exacerbated preexisting gender inequalities, including inequitable availability of essential resources such as health-care and education. Hence, it is imperative for nations across the globe to reassess the 17 Sustainable Development Goals (SDGs) defined in the 2030 Agenda for Sustainable Development, as they provide a comprehensive framework for advancing towards a sustainable future that ensures inclusivity. This theoretical study aims to analyse the impact of the economic downturn on the achievement of the Sustainable Development Goals (SDGs), with a particular focus on the empowerment of women. This study provides recommendations for addressing the health and economic obstacles that may hinder the attainment of sustainable development goals (SDGs). The authors assessed publicly available datasets encompassing a range of variables pertaining to healthcare services, the labour market, education, and community safety. The findings were visually represented by bar graphs, pie charts, and other similar methods. The results of the study indicate that the COVID-19 pandemic had differential impacts on individuals based on their gender. Specifically, it was found that disruptions to schooling were more pronounced for girls than boys. Additionally, instances of domestic violence increased, and women's unpaid workloads experienced a rise. Furthermore, women's income and labour force participation decreased because of the pandemic. Finally, it was observed that single rural women with children were the most severely affected demographic group. The present research

H. Adam (✉)
Jindal School of International Affairs, O.P. Jindal Global University, Haryana 131001, India
e-mail: dhadam@jgu.edu.in

A. Batul
Amity University—Kolkata Campus, Kolkata, India

F. A. Malik
University of People, Pasadena, CA, USA

H. Adam and R. Rena (eds.), *Political Economy of Development in the Global South Post-COVID-19 Pandemic*,
https://doi.org/10.1007/978-981-99-4074-5_5

advocates for the integration of evolutionary education in a more comprehensive manner, with the aim of fostering inclusivity and urging scholars and researchers to undertake significant efforts in this domain. Such endeavours are expected to advance equity and eradicate the marginalisation of entities from conventional perspectives. The present research serves as a valuable reference for scholars and professionals who are keen on exploring sustainability-related topics. It consolidates inputs from social scientists hailing from various regions across the globe.

Keywords Women empowerment · Sustainable development goals · Gender discrimination · Gender inequalities · COVID-19

5.1 Introduction

In 2015, global leaders officially approved the 2030 Agenda for Sustainable Development, comprising 17 Sustainable Development Goals (SDGs) aimed at promoting equitable progress towards a more favourable future for all individuals. The resolution, which was unanimously accepted by all UN Member States, serves as a call to action to eradicate extreme poverty and ensure environmental protection, with the goal of achieving universal peace and prosperity by 2030. The SDGs, which serve as a blueprint for a better future, cannot be accomplished without full participation. Achieving the SDGs depends on empowering women. Females play a pivotal role in providing care for their families, as they often assume the primary caregiver position. The political and economic empowerment of women can lead to a reduction in inequality and poverty, as well as the establishment of a more equitable and just society.

By 2030, these objectives aimed to create a global movement in favour of sustainable development for both the present and the future [43]. However, because of changes in government priorities, significant constraints, and spillover effects because of COVID-19 and because of the pandemic's long-lasting effects on massive health and economic calamities, goal accomplishment may be thwarted or postponed. The impact of COVID-19 on one or more SDGs is being increasingly highlighted in the literature [11]. For instance, studies have concentrated on the interdependencies of SDGs during COVID-19 [43], the policy aspects of governments towards SDGs in the post-COVID-19 era, and the difficulties SDGs face in low-income nations [30, 43]. The potential effects of COVID-19 on the energy sector, the economy and transportation, agriculture, the environment, and the energy sector were also discussed [31, 38].

The influence of COVID-19 on the SDGs has also been highlighted in recent publications and views [3, 19, 29, 34], which have similarly urged greater research. The primary objective of this paper is to present a comprehensive analysis of the short- and long-term effects of COVID-19 on the 17 Sustainable Development Goals (SDGs). This is crucial because, even before the outbreak, nations were having trouble achieving the SDGs. According to estimates from 28 countries, the majority of which are developing, nine of the SDGs (SDGs 1–4, 6, and 7) connected to human development will not be met by 2030 [28]. Prior to the COVID-19 pandemic, worldwide governments anticipated a $2.5 trillion gap [43]. It is reasonable to assume that COVID-19's unprecedented and persistent effects will have an international impact.

5.2 Literature Review

The WHO recorded over 9.4 million COVID-19 cases, including over 482,000 fatalities, in 213 countries by the end of June 2020 [48]. These numbers, despite their enormity, do not accurately reflect the pandemic's true scope. By limiting mobility, stopping travel, forcing businesses to close, and upsetting global supply networks, every aspect of human life has been impacted by COVID-19 [52]. According to the World Health Organisation, the total number of confirmed COVID-19 cases as of October 21, 2022, was 623,893,894, with 6,553,936 fatalities. The challenges that individuals may encounter upon entering poverty do not originate solely from the cessation of employment or other means of financial support. According to Mahler et al. [25], a projected 97 million individuals residing in the Global South are expected to experience poverty in 2020. The impact of the COVID-19 pandemic on women's health, society, and the economy is notably significant. As per the Organisation for Economic Co-operation and Development (2020), the medical workforce comprises approximately 70% of women, rendering them more vulnerable to infection. Bluedorn, Gopinath, and Sandri [4] have reported that the International Labour Organisation and the International Monetary Fund have projected a significant reduction in worldwide production for 2020. This is attributed to the current full or partial lockdown measures that affect 81% of the global workforce, which amounts to 2.7 billion workers. When it first began, the epidemic directly affected the number of working women. Only one in five men, in comparison, think of leaving their professions or changing occupations. The effects have affected all women. Women reported job losses at a higher rate than males between March 2020 and September 2021 (26% versus 20%, respectively), while more women than men reported quitting their occupations to care for family or friends (18% versus 12%, respectively). Women and girls reported dropping out of school 1.21 times more frequently than men and boys did, aside from school closings. According to Flor et al. [15], women were 23 times more likely than males to report an increase in gender-based violence during the epidemic. Even though women are anticipated to see faster job growth than males in 2021, this increase will not be enough to return women to their pre pandemic employment levels. In contrast to 68.6% of all men of working age, only 43.2% of women will be employed globally by 2021 [21].

In 2021, 47 million more women will fall below the international poverty line as a result of COVID-19. Due to the epidemic, women experienced less access to childcare, increased caring responsibilities, and reduced economic prospects (women are overrepresented in hard-hit industries, including tourism and informal professions) [44]. Women were more affected than men by the effects of food and water insecurity, such as concern over not having enough to eat and reduced food consumption. This is particularly problematic given that women's diets were not diverse. In many nations, water insecurity can range from mild to severe, and according to Alvi et al. [2], women are more likely than men to report it.

Women in India were seven times more likely than men to lose their employment during the lockdown in April 2020 if they had occupations previous to the outbreak, and they were eleven times more likely to never return to the workforce if they had lost their jobs during the lockdown. Women with advanced degrees are more susceptible to layoffs compared to men with comparable educational backgrounds. Most of the men who quit working ended up working for themselves or for pay on a daily basis in an industry such as construction, trading, or agriculture. However, according to Agarwal, Venkatachalam, and Cerniglia [1], women were unable to negotiate adequate substitute job arrangements.

The COVID-19 epidemic in Pakistan was more likely to afflict women than men (82% versus 74%). In Senegal, 46% of men and 56% of women reported having excessive worry on a regular basis. In Armenia, more women than men reported having extreme anxiety, with 43% of women doing so compared to 29% of men [17]. Women in China's rural migrant community, who made up 35% of the 290 million rural migrant population, were particularly vulnerable during the pandemic in terms of their economic and health status, but many urban women were shielded from the effects because they could work from home [1].

The closure of schools, daycare centres, and shelters in Brazil resulted in an increased burden of domestic work for women [1]. The gender-based disparity in remuneration within the healthcare profession is attributed to several factors, such as differences in working hours (6.9%), occupational distribution (9.0%), and a discrepancy of 11.2% for comparable jobs and working hours. Physicians exhibited a 13% hourly salary differential in contrast to nurses and midwives. This implies that a significant proportion of the pay gap within the industry can be attributed to occupational segregation. According to projections, the distribution of medical, nursing, and midwifery workforces is anticipated to undergo changes within the next two decades. These changes are expected to result in a reduction in the current occupational segregation-related gap from 9.9% to 7.0% [5]. According to the World Health Organisation [51], before the onset of the pandemic, the mortality rate due to pregnancy and childbirth complications was estimated to be 810 women per day on average. Most of these fatalities, approximately 94%, occurred in low- and lower-middle-income countries.

In 2020, preventable or treatable causes were responsible for 95% of deaths in children under the age of five. The regions of Sub-Saharan Africa and South Asia are accountable for the majority of global maternal, paediatric, and adolescent mortalities. The maternal mortality rate in sub-Saharan Africa is significantly higher than that of Europe or North America, with a woman facing a risk of death during pregnancy or childbirth that is over 130 times greater. The lack of adequate prenatal care, skilled labour attendants, and postpartum care in low- and middle-income countries increases the likelihood of mortality and disability among women, as reported in the Summary of Progress by the UN Secretary-General in 2022. The incidence of maternal mortality and morbidity, adolescent pregnancies, and the transmission of HIV and other sexually transmitted diseases have escalated in the aftermath of past pandemics. The 2019 Policy Brief of the United Nations Secretary-General [45] indicated that disparities arising from various factors, including geography, age, race, disability, ethnicity, socioeconomic class, and sexual orientation, may accumulate and exacerbate over time. The COVID-19 pandemic is anticipated to exacerbate the existing gender disparity in poverty, resulting in a projected impact on approximately 47 million additional women and girls. Empirical data collected from a sample of 16 nations indicate that women undertook a weekly childcare workload that was 29% greater than that of men during the pandemic. A survey conducted across 13 countries by UN Women's Facts and Figures revealed that approximately 50% of women have encountered instances of violence since the onset of the epidemic. Globally, an estimated 740 million women are engaged in the informal labour sector. In certain nations, females continue to receive compensation that is up to 35% lower than their male counterparts, despite the existence of a 16% worldwide wage disparity. According to a 2020 policy brief by the United Nations on the impact of COVID-19 on women, data from 2017 indicate that 72% of men and 65% of women possessed bank accounts.

More than 590 million people directly benefited from the introductions, expansions, and changes of COVID-related programmes, according to preliminary figures [16]. If current trends continue and no action is made to ameliorate the negative effects on women's economic involvement, the world's GDP may be $1 trillion lower in 2030 than it would be if female unemployment rates were equal to those of males. If we take action now to improve gender equality compared to the gender-regressive scenario, the global GDP might increase by $13 trillion in 2030. The potential would be reduced by more than $5 trillion in the middle if we waited until the crisis was over before acting. This latency is expensive Ie it may account for 75% of the possible COVID-19 GDP loss [24]. The primary objective of the study is to identify the various ways in which a slowing economy may jeopardise the Sustainable Development Goals. The second set of difficulties includes issues with women's empowerment, the economy, and health.

5.3 Methodology

This theoretical paper provides insights into various implications of economic slowdown on the achievement of SDGs, with a primary focus on women's empowerment. Issues are discussed under health and economic concerns, and suggestions are made to overcome those challenges in achieving SDGs. Datasets that were made accessible to the public and contained information on a number of indicators linked to health care services, economic and employment issues, education, home and community safety, etc., were examined, and the findings are shown in bar graphs, pie charts, etc. The findings of the study show that men and women were affected differently, girls' education was disrupted more than boys' education, domestic violence increased, women's unpaid work increased, their income and labour force participation declined, and single rural mothers were the most severely affected. Bringing together contributions from national and international social scientists, this paper is a resource for academics and practitioners interested in sustainability research and women's empowerment.

This paper follows a descriptive approach. The methodology employed in this study involves a reliance on secondary sources, specifically reports and exploratory analyses of various articles and research studies. These sources were accessed from reputable organisations such as the United Nations Women (UN Women) conference, the World Bank, the World Health Organisation (WHO), and the Organisation for Economic Co-operation and Development (OECD), among others. Descriptive statistics, including stacked bar graphs, pie charts, and percentage analysis, are commonly employed to present the data collected.

5.4 Discussion

5.4.1 Women Empowerment: Concept Definition

The 2030 Global Agenda prioritises the acknowledgement of the interconnection between gender equality, health, and education as a key objective. Undeniably, there has been progress in the healthcare industry. However, the healthcare system has not consistently acknowledged the determinants that impact the health status of women or efficiently addressed women's health concerns. Women globally encounter numerous challenges in accessing healthcare services. The persistent disparities between males and females, particularly in the regions of Asia and Africa, are among the most remarkable phenomena. According to Deshpande and Bhat [8], the eradication of gender inequality can facilitate the resolution of issues pertaining to women's health. Although the concept of women's empowerment has been widely discussed for a very long time, its importance has increased since countries committed to adopting and achieving SDGs [23]. The World Bank defines "empowerment" as the process of enhancing a person's or a group's ability to make choices and carry those choices in the desired ways. It is the process that addresses the capacity of women to make decisions about their life based on their preferences, priorities, and choices. It can occur in various aspects of life, including economic, social, and political aspects. True empowerment emerges from liberty in all these facets. Even though women are successful in a variety of sectors, including academia, athletics, medicine, entertainment, and politics, a large part of them remain victims of societal ills and conventional burdens and lack even the most basic substance of life. Women continue to endure discrimination in terms of birth, education, employment rights, and compensation, although they account for half of the population. Women have many opportunities to contribute directly to the progress of the economy, yet they are financially excluded [14, 20, 27]. From the experiences of the majority of Africa, Asia, and Latin America, it has been learned that a lack of economic autonomy increases the likelihood of violence against women. If they are more involved in paid jobs than in an abusive relationship, it will provide them with opportunities to build skills, knowledge, and self-confidence and make them more sociable [6]. As a result of their adherence to gender-specific norms, women in less developed and developing countries have a lower status and are disproportionately disempowered than men. The process of protecting women against all forms of abuse entails empowering them through access to education, work, and an altered social structure. Women's empowerment, then, is the phenomenon of raising women's economic, social, and political status in society [41]. Governments, civil groups, and other stakeholders have been promoting gender equality through SDGs on a worldwide scale. Commitment is required for the effective implementation of SDGs to stop violence against women and increase women's economic empowerment [9, 42].

Promoting gender equality will accelerate development since equal rights and opportunities are a question of social fairness and human rights [35]. Inequality in women's access to economic resources indicates their inferiority in any community, and programmes that do not adequately address women's participation have billion-dollar repercussions. Girls and women must everywhere have equal rights and opportunities to live in peace, free from discrimination and violence. Not only is the empowerment and equality of women one of the 17 SDGs, but it is also a cornerstone of all aspects of inclusive and sustainable development. In essence, the accomplishment of Goal 5 is a requirement for the other Sustainable Development Goals. To achieve gender equality by 2030, we must address the core causes of discrimination that continue to limit women's rights in the private and public realms. Only by safeguarding women's rights across all goals can a nation achieve justice and inclusiveness, an economy that works for all, and a sustainable environment for current and future generations [49].

5.4.2 COVID-19 Pandemic Impacts on Women

The pandemic has generated distinct experiences for men and women. According to Grown and Paramo [17], females have encountered greater setbacks in terms of income, safety, and employment because of the COVID-19 pandemic than their male counterparts. Table 5.1 illustrates that, in terms of health, men typically exhibit a higher mortality rate than women, except in the Middle East and North Africa. The tabulated nations exhibit the greatest count of verified female fatalities within the pertinent regions.

Table 5.1 Regional Proportion of Female & Male Deaths in Confirmed Cases. *Source* World Bank Gender Data Portal (retrieved on 03.04.2021)

Deaths in confirmed cases date	Region	Country	Cases where sex-disaggregated data is available	Deaths where sex-disaggregated data is available
17/02/2021	East Asia and Pacific	Australia	28,797	909
12/02/2021	North America	Canada	8,10,576	20,903
15/02/2021	Europe and Central Asia	Finland	51,047	726
06/04/2020	South Asia	India	28,77,791	3,711
17/02/2021	Middle East and North Africa	Iraq	6,49,982	13,192
27/09/2020	Sub-Saharan Africa	Uganda	4,904	31
07/02/2021	East Asia and Pacific	Vietnam	2,001	35
17/02/2021	Middle East and North Africa	Yemen	2,155	619

Increased mortality rates among males can exert a significant impact on the surviving family members, particularly on women who may be compelled to compensate for the absence of male income and may experience reduced earnings. The COVID-19 pandemic has posed a significant threat to the achievement of the Sustainable Development Goals (SDGs) related to gender equality by 2030. The progress achieved in various domains towards the promotion of gender equality and the empowerment of women since 2015 has been undermined by the present situation. In addition, the COVID-19 pandemic has had significant economic and social ramifications, particularly in underprivileged segments of society where poverty is rampant. These effects have further amplified preexisting disparities and biases against females. Furthermore, the allocation of funds away from the historical and present requirements of women has impeded gender-transformative initiatives and reforms [33]. It is imperative for policymakers to advocate for a substantial augmentation in spending to address the gender disparity, which has gained greater significance in light of the pandemic's impact, to attain the objectives outlined in the 2030 Agenda. According to the Organisation for Economic Co-operation and Development (OECD), impoverished nations allocate the third-lowest amount of funding towards SDG 5. Despite their current lack of urgency, the issue of how women's empowerment may impact the SDGs warrants a platform for discourse. The long-term ramifications of the pandemic on both the economy and individuals' mental well-being are expected to persist for several decades. It is imperative for humanity to expeditiously act and pledge to "build back better," as a preliminary measure towards formulating a novel development ideology for a resilient and sustainable future.

5.4.3 *Impacts of the Pandemic on the SDGs—Goal 5*

During the early outbreaks of contagious diseases such as Nipah and Ebola, only a handful of effective gender-based studies were turned into policy initiatives. During the Ebola outbreak in Africa, certain studies revealed that men and women were affected differently. These studies were published in Lancet and undertaken by the World Health Organisation (WHO). If nations do not embrace this reality and understand how to address it, they will be unable to implement policies that benefit women through timely intervention and treatment [36]. One should consider women as a specific target group who have campaigned for awareness, the specific vulnerabilities of those women who had high exposure yet still fought against the pandemic, as active agents in decision-making and to ensure that countries will learn to be gender-sensitive in the future during all such episodes and listen to the specific concerns of women in handling these crises [36]. According to the OECD report "Policy Responses to Coronavirus (COVID-19)", the pandemic will have a major impact on achieving SDG 5 [32]. A longer period is required for both developed and developing countries to achieve their gender equality goals due to the slower rate of advancement.

5.4.4 *The Pandemic and Violence Against Women*

According to the International Centre for Research on Women (2020), instances of gender-based violence tend to escalate during periods of hardship, thereby impeding the ability of women and girls to engage in economic activities. Since the onset of the COVID-19 pandemic, there has been a surge in incidents of violence against women, with domestic violence being particularly affected. As per the data presented in Fig. 5.1 of the Policy Brief by the Secretary-General of the United Nations in 2020, a total of 243 million females aged between 15 and 49 years were subjected to physical and/or sexual violence in the context of an intimate relationship before the outbreak of the pandemic. Prior to the outbreak of the pandemic, the proportion of women who sought treatment after experiencing violence was below 40%. According to UN Women (2020), there has been a surge in domestic abuse reports and emergency calls by as much as 25% in several countries following the adoption of social distancing measures.

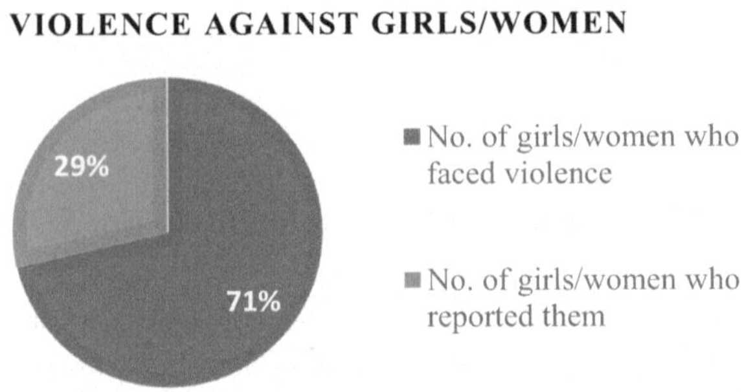

Fig. 5.1 Percentage of Girls/Women who faced violence and reported it. *Source* UN Women (2020)

5.4.5 *Health Impacts of the Pandemic on Women*

Dominguez and Spain [10] found that in the 104 countries examined, the proportion of women in the health industry workforce was 67%. Figure 5.2 illustrates that a significant number of males are employed in the medical field as physicians, dentists, and chemists across various nations, while a substantial number of females work as nurses and midwives, as depicted in Fig. 5.3.

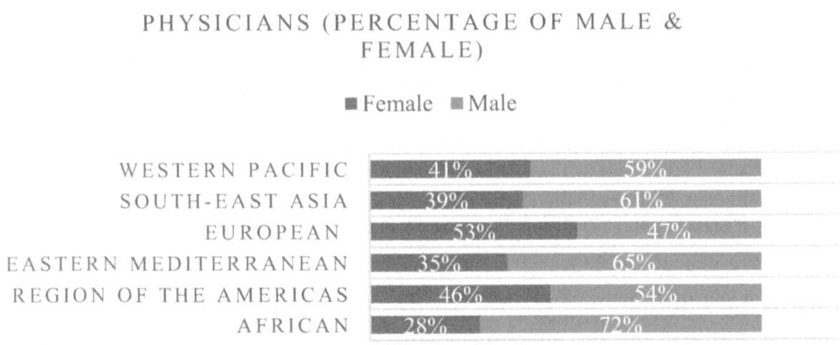

Fig. 5.2 Distribution of physicians. *Source* World Health Organisation (2019)

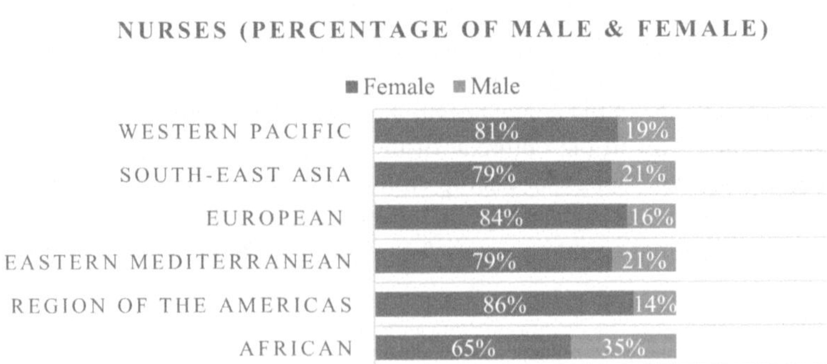

Fig. 5.3 Distribution of nurses by gender. *Source* World Health Organisation (2019)

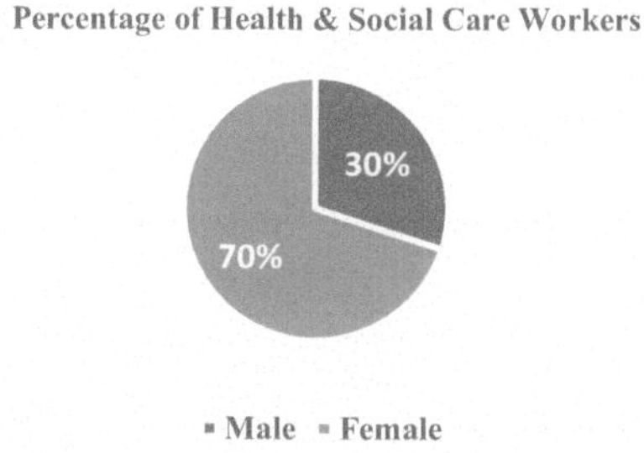

Fig. 5.4 Distribution of Health and Social Care Workers by Gender. *Source* Author's compilation based on data collected from the UN Secretary-General's Policy Brief (2019)

In all regions, however, there are still gender-based disparities in the occupation system [5]. The percentage of female physicians in OECD countries increased by 13% between 2000 and 2017 (an average of 0.58% per year). The statistics from 57 nations' Labour Force Surveys (LFS) confirm this tendency. In recent years, women have dominated higher-paying health professions (such as physicians, dentists, and pharmacists) among those under the age of 40 [5]. Seventy percent of the global health workforce comprises women working (Fig. 5.4) as nurses, midwives, community workers, etc., as well as service professions such as cleaners, launderers, caterers, etc. (UN Secretary- General's Policy Brief, 2019).

According to a preliminary study conducted by Wenham et al. [47], males are frequently more susceptible to COVID-19 than females. According to a clinical characteristics study conducted in China, 58% of patients were male [18]. As of mid-July 2020, it was found that only 37% of COVID-19 cases had been disaggregated by both gender and age, according to the UN Secretary-General's Policy Brief of 2019. Additionally, the World Health Organisation [50] reports that the fatality rates among male individuals who contract the virus are 65% higher than those among their female counterparts. According to the Organisation for Economic Co-operation and Development (OECD) in 2020, there exists a higher propensity for noncommunicable diseases to manifest in men than in women. These diseases are known to pose a risk to the mortality of COVID-19-infected individuals and may include conditions such as strokes, heart ailments, most types of malignancies, and diabetes. Historically, men have exhibited a higher mortality rate than women, although this trend is not universal and is notably reversed in the regions of the Middle East and North Africa. The following diagram, depicted in Fig. 5.5, presents a comparative analysis of mortality rates between the male and female populations.

Despite the apparent lower mortality rates for women, certain groups of women remained at elevated risk. Public Health England [39] has advised that pregnant women, along with the elderly and individuals with underlying health conditions, should take additional measures to protect themselves against infections, particularly in the United Kingdom [39]. The implementation of this preventive measure was prompted by the revelation that expectant mothers have been subject to a disproportionate impact from diverse respiratory infections in the past [13, 40]. The occurrence of pandemics poses a challenge to the accessibility of medical attention and treatment for women and girls. The situation is exacerbated by a range of potentially

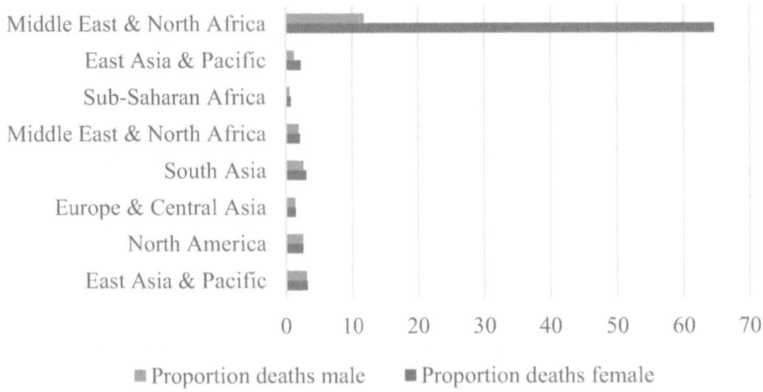

Fig. 5.5 Comparison of regional proportion of female and male deaths in confirmed cases. *Source* Author's compilation based on data collected from the World Bank Gender Data Portal (2021)

intersecting disadvantages, encompassing factors such as ethnicity, socioeconomic status, disability, age, race, geographical location, and sexual orientation. These factors impede decision-making and hinder access to crucial healthcare services and COVID-19-related information. Females residing in rural and underprivileged regions experience limited access to superior healthcare services, essential medications and immunisations, maternal and reproductive healthcare, and health insurance coverage for both anticipated and unanticipated medical expenditures. Apart from conforming to social expectations and gender-based preconceptions, women's ability to obtain healthcare is hindered by rigid social conventions. Each of these factors exhibits distinctive impacts in the context of a widespread health crisis. As a result of occupational segregation, women are susceptible to hazardous or unsafe conditions. In various geographical areas, the female population encountered limited availability of personal protection equipment that was tailored to their specific physical dimensions. Despite these findings, women's involvement in COVID-19 response decision-making at the national or international level is infrequent. The provision of sexual and reproductive health services, including but not limited to prenatal care and interventions aimed at mitigating gender-based violence, is of paramount importance for the promotion of the health, rights, and overall welfare of women and girls. The diversion of attention and necessary resources from these treatments may lead to adverse consequences such as elevated rates of maternal mortality and morbidity, adolescent pregnancies, HIV infections, and other sexually transmitted diseases, as reported by the United Nations forum in 2019.

5.4.6 Economic Impacts of the Pandemic on Women

The COVID-19 pandemic has had a significant impact on global trade, with women in developing nations bearing the brunt of this harm. Women in the developing world are more likely to work in precarious and informal jobs, such as housework, making them more susceptible to economic shocks. The epidemic has made this situation worse, as numerous woman have lost their jobs or had their hours reduced, which has reduced their income. There is still a substantial gender disparity in labour market participation, with women frequently encountering more impediments to entering and remaining in the workforce than males. Figure 5.6 illustrates that there are more men than women in the labour force who are between the ages of 25 and 54.

The gender wage gap is the leading source of gender disparity in labour force participation. Women are frequently paid less than men for the same work, which can reduce their likelihood of entering or remaining in the labour force. This is especially the case for mothers, who frequently cannot afford to take time off to care for their children. In addition, women frequently face discrimination in the job, which can result in their being overlooked for promotions or other chances. Inadequate access to education and training is the second driver of gender inequality in labour market participation. Women in developing countries are frequently less likely to have access to higher education or acquire training in specific domains, limiting their capacity to pursue specific professions. In addition, women are frequently expected to perform more unpaid labour, such as childcare and housework, which might hinder their participation in the labour market. Women spend three times as much time as males doing unpaid domestic and caregiving tasks, according to the United Nations' Policy Brief (2020), which restricts their ability to find adequate jobs. Finally, there is the question of cultural expectations and standards. In developing societies, women are frequently expected to assume more conventional duties, such as being a homemaker or a caretaker, which might hinder their capacity to participate in the work market.

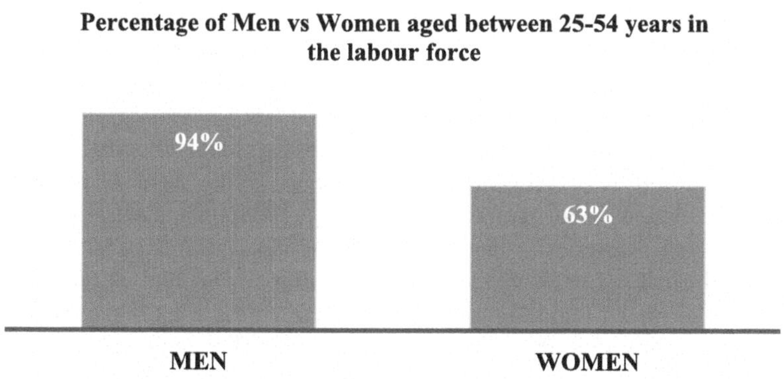

Fig. 5.6 Labour force participation of men and women aged between 25–54 years. *Source* Policy Brief: The Impact of COVID-19 on Women, United Nations (2020)

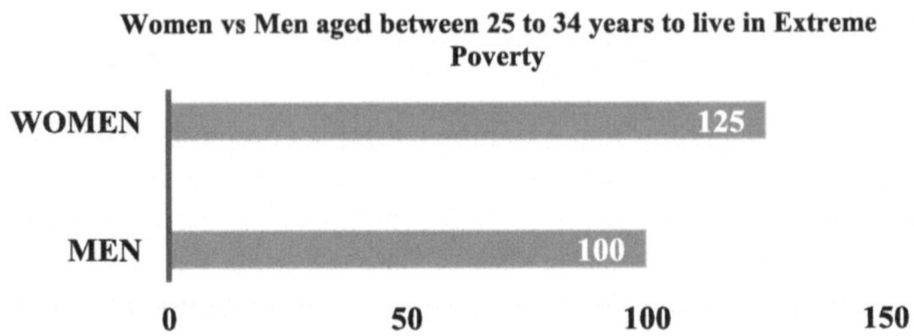

Fig. 5.7 Global proportion of genders aged between 25 and 34 years living in poverty. *Source* Policy Brief: The Impact of COVID-19 on Women, United Nations (2020)

In addition, women are frequently viewed as less capable than men, which can result in their exclusion from specific positions or promotions.

The COVID-19 pandemic has exacerbated the vulnerabilities of women who are already facing precarious situations. Females hailing from developing regions of the world exhibit a higher probability of engaging in sectors such as hospitality, retail, and tourism, which have experienced the most adverse effects due to the ongoing pandemic. The loss of employment opportunities decreased working hours, and reduced wages have resulted in a significant number of women living in poverty. According to the United Nations Policy Brief (2020), Fig. 5.7 depicts that globally, women aged 25 to 34 exhibit a 25% higher likelihood of residing in extreme poverty than men. The COVID-19 pandemic has had an adverse effect on women's access to financial services. The closure of banks and other financial institutions has resulted in a significant number of women being unable to secure the necessary funds for their sustenance. Consequently, their susceptibility to poverty has significantly increased.

In 2019, the International Labour Organisation (ILO) reported that a significant proportion of the global workforce, specifically 81%, which equates to over 2.7 billion individuals, was confined. The COVID-19 pandemic has triggered an unprecedented worldwide economic downturn. Empirical data indicated that women experienced unequal and disproportionate effects on their economic and productive activities. Globally, female demographic experiences have reduced earnings, decreased savings rates, heightened employment instability, and a greater prevalence of informal employment prospects, as per the UN Secretary-General's Policy Brief of 2019. As illustrated in Fig. 5.8, there exists a global disparity in the distribution of casual jobs between genders, with men occupying a greater proportion of such positions than women. Women are often engaged in precarious and low-wage occupations such as domestic labour, street vending, and small-scale agriculture within the informal sector. Female employees occupying such positions often lack the safeguard of labour regulations, rendering them vulnerable to mistreatment and exploitation. According to the data presented in Fig. 5.9, it can be observed that in low- and lower-middle-income countries, there exists a higher probability of women engaging in informal sector employment compared to men.

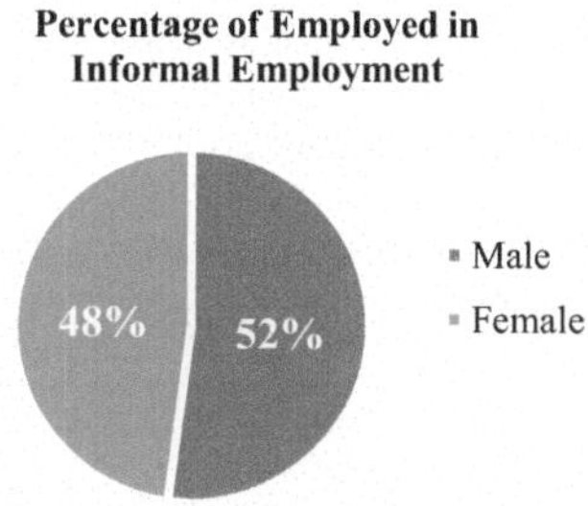

Fig. 5.8 Global distribution of employed in informal employment by gender. *Source* UN Secretary-General's Policy Brief [45]

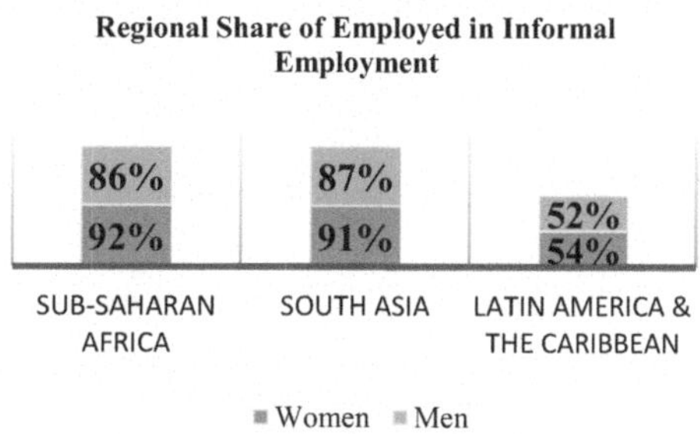

Fig. 5.9 Regional distribution of employed in informal employment. *Source* UN Secretary-General's Policy Brief [45]

The COVID-19 pandemic has rendered women in the informal economy increasingly vulnerable. The cessation of commercial operations and subsequent unemployment have resulted in a significant proportion of women being deprived of a source of sustenance. As per the findings of the United Nations research conducted in 2019 [37], a significant proportion of women's employment, amounting to 70%, is concentrated in the informal economy. This sector lacks safeguards against involuntary termination of employment, paid medical leave, and adequate access to social security benefits. Because of this situation, they are presently incapable of providing for their household and fulfilling their necessities. Moreover, the absence of social safety nets and healthcare services has rendered numerous women in developing countries' informal sectors susceptible to impoverishment and deteriorating health [38]. According to the United Nations forum in 2019, individuals who had managed to overcome extreme poverty due to recent economic growth were susceptible to relapsing into it prior to the outbreak of the epidemic.

Females constitute the predominant demographic in single-parent households and encounter restricted availability of social protections. Females exhibit a comparatively lower resilience to economic shocks than males. The career prospects of women became increasingly uncertain in a disproportionate manner as they assumed greater responsibility for domestic caregiving duties. The potential ramifications of these outcomes pose a threat to the tenuous advancements achieved by women in the workforce, potentially impeding their ability to provide for their families and themselves, particularly in households reliant on a sole income provider. In several nations, the initial round of workforce reductions was notably harsh within the service

Table 5.2 Comparative price increases for median product for June 2020–June 2021. *Source* New Statesman Analysis of ONS Data (2022)

Item	Women's item (%)	Men's item (%)
Shoe (formal)	75	14
Boots	32	−21
Electric hair appliance/ electric razor	30	−6
Blouse/formal shirt	29	−6
T-shirt	27	33
Trainers	15	0
Casual trousers	12	10
Tights/socks	11	±0
Jeans	7	11
Jumper	7	23
Haircut	5	3
Formal skirt/trousers	±0	±0
Pants/boxers	−32	±0

sector, encompassing retail, hospitality, and tourism, and exhibited a disproportionate representation of female employees.

Furthermore, the pandemic has had a disproportionate impact on women due to their comparatively lower income and increasing inflation. Prior to the onset of the inflation crisis, it was observed that women possessed comparatively lower levels of wealth than men on a global scale [26]. The Office for National Statistics (ONS) has reported that the products aimed at the female demographic have experienced a greater rise in price compared to those targeted at the male demographic, as indicated in Table 5.2 [12], for the period ending in June 2022.

Most healthcare workers are women, but an analysis of median wages based on LFS data from 21 countries reveals significant gender-related pay gaps, with female health workers earning 28% less than males on average. This is slightly higher than the worldwide numbers on the gender pay gap, which suggest that women earn approximately 22% less than males (Global Wage Report 2018–19). Women's purchasing power can be hampered by gender wage inequalities. The gender digital divide hindered women's capacity to access crucial services or adapt enterprises or jobs to social distance [22].

5.4.7 COVID-19 Pandemic and Girls' Education

The COVID-19 pandemic has had multiple impacts on the field of education, such as the closure of educational institutions, a reduction in the disposable incomes of households, and a decline in school budgets due to a decrease in tax revenues or developmental aid. Females are subject to a disproportionate impact from these perturbations and are vulnerable to experiencing a widening gender gap in comparison to males. Females residing in developing nations exhibit a higher probability of assuming responsibility for younger siblings, encountering limited access to scarce familial resources (such as technology for remote learning), exhibiting a greater likelihood of discontinuing their education due to early marriage, and displaying increased susceptibility to gender-based violence.

The COVID-19 pandemic has significantly disrupted the educational pursuits of women and girls. Based on a comprehensive analysis of 193 nations, it was found that females were 21 times more likely to discontinue their education than their male counterparts. Upon the conclusion of their formal education, a greater proportion of female students in West and Central Africa, specifically 60%, were unable to pursue further academic opportunities, in contrast to their male counterparts, of which 44% faced similar limitations (World Bank, 2022).

5.4.8 Gender Responsive Measures Adopted by Governments to the COVID-19 Pandemic

As of April 2019, a total of 106 countries had implemented or adjusted their social safety nets and employment initiatives as a reaction to the COVID-19 pandemic. According to the data presented in Fig. 5.10, the social assistance tool is the most widely used among the packages, followed by social insurance and supply-side labour market reforms. According to Gentilini et al. [16], cash transfers represent the predominant modality of social assistance.

The COVID-19 outbreak has prompted governments to prioritise gender policy as a key area of concern, given its disproportionate impact on women and girls. In response to the COVID-19 epidemic, various governmental measures have been implemented to ensure that women and girls are not marginalised. The implementation of these policies has played a pivotal role in guaranteeing equitable access to social services, healthcare, education, and employment opportunities for women and girls. As per the COVID-19 Global Gender Response Tracker [46], which monitors

Fig. 5.10 Number and Types of Programmes that have been Introduced/Adopted by Regions as COVID-19 Responses. [16] *Source* Gentilini et al.

Table 5.3 Number and types of gendered programmes that have been introduced/adopted by regions as COVID-19 responses. *Source* Data Futures Platform, UNDP [7]

Region	Gender sensitive	Unpaid care	Violence against women	Women's economic security
Africa	270	14	112	144
Americas	455	50	227	178
Asia	360	35	197	128
Europe	419	113	247	59
Oceania	101	14	70	17
Total	1,605	226	853	526

the actions taken by governments worldwide to address the pandemic and emphasises those that have integrated a gender perspective, approximately 226 countries and territories have implemented nearly 5,000 policy measures. The measurements encompassed dimensions of diverse magnitudes, as illustrated in Table 5.3.

According to the UN Policy Brief (2020), sectors with a largely female workforce and disrupted supply chains should have access to financing, loans, and grants to retain female workers. To make benefits available to women and girls, distribution methods must incorporate their care responsibilities and informal work status.

5.5 Findings and Conclusion

The COVID-19 pandemic had a disparate and negative impact on the economic and productive activities of women in comparison to men. Furthermore, the aftermath of the crisis had a prolonged impact on the economic security and livelihoods of women in comparison with men, whose economic activity swiftly returned to precrisis levels once preventive measures were lifted. The education of girls is more frequently disrupted by crises than that of boys, resulting in long-lasting consequences for their ability to acquire the skills and knowledge necessary to progress in the economy. The current economic crisis has resulted in a surge of unpaid work for women, rendering the restoration of precrisis conditions a formidable task. Furthermore, attaining a fair allocation of household chores and unpaid caregiving responsibilities between genders by 2030 may prove to be an arduous feat. The COVID-19 global recession has had a detrimental impact on women's income and labour force participation, further exacerbating the preexisting disadvantages faced by this demographic. Women are disproportionately represented as frontline healthcare workers in various regions of the world, which places them at a heightened risk. The issue concerning the prioritisation of health professionals, a crucial component of any government's strategy, has been insufficiently addressed. In households where men hold unilateral decision-making power and women are subjected to inequitable treatment, women assume the role of primary caregivers. Undertaking a transformation of the gendered division of household labour is crucial in improving the effectiveness of businesses for women. The coexistence of illiteracy, ignorance, and domestic violence can pose supplementary hindrances to attaining enduring success. To attain socioeconomic transformations, it is crucial for both genders to collaborate and contribute equitably.

5.6 Recommendations and Policy Implications

It is crucial to have a gender perspective integrated into policy responses in crisis-affected regions to achieve economic, social, and environmental objectives. This necessitates strong political dedication. It is crucial to acknowledge that global challenges cannot be effectively addressed through a one-size-fits-all approach. Civil society possesses the capacity to champion the reformation of childcare policies, heighten awareness concerning the matter, and provide aid to mothers in developing countries. The effective mitigation of political violence requires the imperative presence of women in civil service and professional roles. Facilitating climate-resilient and sustainable livelihoods, while ensuring fair access, control, and ownership of resources, can augment the resilience of women and girls to cope with the consequences of climate change, environmental hazards, and natural as well as human-made disasters.

5.7 Future Work

The present research recommends the integration of evolutionary education through a more comprehensive approach, urging all scholars and researchers to undertake significant efforts in this domain. Such endeavours would foster parity and eradicate the marginalisation of entities from conventional perspectives. This manuscript serves as a valuable reference for scholars and professionals who are keen on conducting research on sustainability, as it consolidates insights from social scientists across the globe. The challenges and opportunities associated with carrying out research that is pertinent to policymaking are crucial for the advancement of social science's role in the discourse on sustainability. The exigency for a meticulous contemplation of the methodological predicaments that ensue in policy-relevant research is imperative. Furthermore, it is essential to deliberate on how the latest methodological approaches in the realm of sustainability can potentially defy the conventional outlook of policymakers towards the execution of sustainability research.

References

1. Agarwal B, Venkatachalam R, Cerniglia F (2022) Women, Pandemics and the Global South: an introductory overview. Econ Polit 39:15–30. https://doi.org/10.1007/s40888-022-00257-9
2. Alvi FM, Gupta S, Barooah P, et al. (2022) Gendered impacts of COVID-19: Insights from 7 countries in Sub-Saharan Africa and South Asia. In: International Food Policy Research Institute (IFPRI)
3. Barbier EB, Burgess JC (2020) Sustainability and development after COVID-19. World Dev 135:105082
4. Bluedorn J, Gopinath G, Sandri D (2020) An Early View of the Economic Impact of the Pandemic in 5 Charts. Int Monetary Fund Blog
5. Boniol M, et al. (2019) Gender equity in the health workforce: Analysis of 104 countries. Health Workforce Working paper 1, World Health Organisation
6. Capraro C (2017) Rights and Realities: A Briefing on Women and the Economy. Womankind Worldwide
7. Data Futures Platform, UNDP. https://data.undp.org/gendertracker/
8. Deshpande A, Bhat R (2019) Women & sustainable development goals-agenda 2030 [Gender Inequality & Women Health Issues from Indian Perspective]. Sch Int J Bus Policy & GovAnce 06(4):30–42
9. Dhar S (2018) Gender and sustainable development goals (SDGs). Indian J Gend Stud 25(1):47–78. https://doi.org/10.1177/0971521517738451
10. Domínguez M, Sapiña L (2021) She-coronavirus: how cartoonists reflected women health workers during the Covid-19 pandemic. European J Women's Studies 2(29):282–297. https://doi.org/10.1177/13505068211048402
11. Fenner R, Cernev T (2021) The implications of the Covid-19 pandemic for delivering the Sustainable Development Goals. Futures 128:102726
12. Ferber A, Swindwells K, Merwe B (2022) Prices are rising faster for items aimed at women, who tend to be poorer already. How inflation is worse for women
13. FIGO (2020) COVID-19 (Coronavirus) Statement. https://www.figo.org/news/covid-19-coronavirus-statement1
14. Finnegan G (2015) Strategies for women's financial inclusion in the commonwealth. Discussion Paper, Commonwealth Secretariat (2015)
15. Flor L et al (2022) Quantifying the effects of the COVID-19 pandemic on gender equality on health, social, and economic indicators: a comprehensive review of data from March, 2020, to September, 2021. The Lancet 399(10344):2381–2397
16. Gentilini U, Almenfi M, Orton I (2020) Social protection and jobs responses to COVID-19: a real-time review of country measures. "Living paper" version 3
17. Grown C, Paramo S (2021) COVID-19 casts different shadows over the lives of men and women. Voices, World Bank Blogs
18. Guan W et al. (2020) Clinical characteristics of coronavirus disease 2019 in China. N Engl J Med NEJMoa2002032, http://dx.doi.org/https://doi.org/10.1056/NEJMoa2002032
19. Health TLG (2020) Mental health matters. Lancet Glob Health 8(11):e1352
20. Hendriks S (2019) The role of financial inclusion in driving women's economic empowerment. Dev Pract 29(8):1029–1038
21. ILO (2021) Gender equality: Fewer women than men will regain employment during the COVID-19 recovery says ILO. http://www.ilo.org/global/about-the-ilo/newsroom/news/WCMS_813449/lang--en/index.htm
22. International Center for Research on Women (2020) COVID-19 and Women's Economic Empowerment. OCHA
23. Lohani M, Aburaida L (2017) Women empowerment: a key to sustainable development. The Social Ion Print ISSN: 2319-358, Indexed in DRJI 6(2):26–29
24. Madgavkar A, White O, Krishnan M, Mahajan D, Azcue X (2020) COVID-19 and gender equality: Countering the regressive effects. McKinsey Global Institute

25. Mahler DG, Yonzan N, Lakner C, Aguilar AC, Wu H (2021) Updated estimates of the impact of COVID-19 on global poverty: Turning the corner on the pandemic in 2021? World Bank blogs (2021)
26. Mao B (2022) Gender inequality: inflation affects women more than men. World Economic Forum
27. Maurya P (2015) Financial inclusion and women empowerment in India. ABS Int J Manag
28. Moyer JD, Hedden S (2020) Are we on the right path to achieve the sustainable development goals? World Dev 127:104749
29. Naidoo R, Fisher B (2020) Reset sustainable development goals for a pandemic world. Nature 583(7815):198–201
30. Nhamo L, Mabhaudhi T, Mpandeli S, Dickens C, Nhemachena C, Senzanje A, Modi AT (2020) An integrative analytical model for the water-energy-food nexus: South Africa case study. Environ Sci Policy 109:15–24
31. Nundy S, Ghosh A, Mesloub A, Albaqawy GA, Alnaim MM (2021) Impact of COVID-19 pandemic on socioeconomic, energy-environment and transport sector globally and sustainable development goal (SDG). J Clean Prod 312:127705
32. OECD Policy Responses to COVID-19 (2019) Women at the core of the fight against COVID-19 crisis
33. OECD Policy Responses to Coronavirus (COVID-19) (2020) Women at the core of the fight against COVID-19 crisis. Version (01/04/2020)
34. Oldekop JA, Horner R, Hulme D, Adhikari R, Agarwal B, Alford M, Zhang YF (2020) COVID-19 and the case for global development. World Dev 134:105044
35. OSAGI (2001) Factsheet on "Important Concepts underlying Gender Mainstreaming".
36. Panicker L (2020) Involve Women in the Battle Against Covid-19. COLUMNS
37. Policy Brief (2019) The Impact of Covid-19 on Women. United Nations
38. Protect the Promise (2022) Bi-Annual Summary of Progress. World Health Summit, Berlin
39. Public Health England (2020) Guidance on Social Distancing for Everyone in the UK. https://www.gov.uk/government/publications/covid 19 guidance on social distancing-and-for-vulnerable-people/guidance-on-social-distancing-for-everyone-in the-uk-and-protecting-older-people-and-vulnerable-adults
40. RCOG (2020) Coronavirus Infection and Pregnancy, https://www.rcog.org.uk/en/guidelines-research-services/guidelines/coronavirus-pregnancy/covid-19-virus-infection-and-pregna ncy/
41. Shettar, R (2015) A study on issues and challenges of women empowerment in India. IOSR J Bus Manag (IOSR-JBM), 17(4) Ver. I. 13–19
42. Shetty SS, Hans BV (2018) Women Empowerment in India and Financial Inclusion Barriers. Int Res J Manag Sociol Humlties 9(3)
43. Shulla K, Voigt BF, Cibian S, Scandone G, Martinez E, Nelkovski F, Salehi P (2021) Effects of COVID-19 on the sustainable development goals (SDGs). Discov Sustain 2:1–19
44. Sverdlik A (2020) Addressing Gendered and Other Inequalities Will Be Central To COVID-19 Recovery. Int Inst Environ & Dev (IIED)
45. UN Secretary-General's policy brief: The impact of COVID-19 on women (2019) UN-Women. https://interactive.unwomen.org/multimedia/explainer/covid19/en/index.html
46. UN Women Calculations based on Oxford COVID-19 Government Response Tracker. Blavatnik School of Government, University of Oxford. https://www.bsg.ox.ac.uk/research/research-projects/oxford-covid-19-government-response-tracker
47. Wenham C, Smith J, Morgan R (2020) COVID-19: the gendered impacts of the outbreak. Lancet Publishing Group. https://doi.org/10.1016/S0140-6736(20)30526-2
48. WHO COVID-19 Dashboard (2020) Geneva: World Health Organisation. Available online: https://covid19.who.int/
49. Women and the Sustainable Development Goals (SDGs) (n.d.) UN Women – Headquarters. https://www.unwomen.org/en/news/in-focus/women-and-thesdgs
50. World Health Organisation (2020) Coronavirus Age, Sex, Demographics (COVID-19)- Worldometer. https://www.worldometers.info/coronavirus/coronavirus-age-sex-demograph ics/

51. World Health Organization (2021) Maternal mortality. https://www.who.int/news-room/fact-sheets/detail/maternal-mortality
52. Yount K, Hernandez W, Undie CC (2020) COVID-19 and Gender Based Violence in the Global South. Women's Empowerment in Development (WED) Lab

Chapter 6
Evaluating Public Policy Approaches to Women's Empowerment During the COVID-19 Pandemic: A Perspective from the Global South

Rubina Pradhan

Abstract Governments, mostly in the Global South, have faltered as policymakers to bring about systematic and concrete approaches to women's empowerment because of the intersection of various factors concerning gender disparities. As Wenham (2020) has rightly pointed out, the pandemic has affected and impacted gender differently, whether by infection by a pathogen or public health response policies (Wenham C in The gendered impact of the Covid-19 crisis and PostCrisis Period. Policy N, 2020). More than a virus, the gendered consequences are a result of policies introduced by governments to decrease the spread of the virus and introduce gender-neutral policies. The impact has been greater in regions such as the Asia–Pacific, the Middle East, Sub-Saharan Africa, and Latin America. This chapter aims to explain gender disparity in public policymaking. It highlights the effect of the COVID-19 pandemic on women, particularly in the Global South, among whom the degree of violence and vulnerability has substantially risen because of ineffective COVID-19 policy measures. The assessment of the impact has also been carried out in the regions of the Global South. The chapter explores and examines the public policy approaches undertaken by various governments in the Global South concerning providing protection, proper healthcare measures, social security, etc., for attaining a long-term goal of empowering women. It also highlights and analyses the economic policy responses as documented by the International Monetary Fund by the governments in the Global South to minimize the impact of the pandemic. Furthermore, the chapter brings to light the women-centric policy measures adopted by the countries in the Global South. The chapter will conclude by evaluating the women-centric government policies in the Global South and providing alternative policy approaches that could achieve women's empowerment in the post-COVID-19 world.

R. Pradhan (✉)
Centre for Research in Social Science and Education (CERSSE), JAIN (Deemed-to-be University), Bangalore, India
e-mail: rubina.pradhan@jainuniversity.ac.in; rubinap8@gmail.com

H. Adam and R. Rena (eds.), *Political Economy of Development in the Global South Post-COVID-19 Pandemic*,
https://doi.org/10.1007/978-981-99-4074-5_6

Keywords Public policy · COVID-19 pandemic · Women's empowerment · Global south · Inclusive policy

6.1 Introduction

The years 2019 and 2020 heralded a new beginning for policymakers. COVID-19, taking the form of a pandemic, has taken a toll on human lives in various social, economic, and political spheres. Although the effects of the pandemic are faced by all human beings, its effects have been compounded on women all over the world, particularly in the Global South. What is more troubling is the policy approaches of governments, which to a greater degree have been inadequate in addressing certain common challenges faced by women. Although governments' policies have to a certain extent focused on women's economic empowerment and intersecting inequalities in recent years, post-pandemic policy approaches fail to examine the 'public' aspect of the policy. The pandemic has mooted the working of public policy analyses.

The surge in gender-based violence during COVID-19 shows that the policy initiatives by governments to date have faltered in addressing the existing systemic/structural inequalities associated with gender. Gender-based violence is rooted in toxic masculinity, which is no less than another deadly pandemic witnessed in more severe forms during the COVID-19 pandemic [2]. Gender biases may be blanketed in policies, budgets, regulations, decision-making and procurement practices [3]. It has been observed that addressing such biases in policymaking would be pivotal in Gross Domestic Product (GDP) growth in the future [3]. As the impacts of the COVID-19 pandemic have been all-encompassing and touched on almost all policy areas, there is a need for governments with other stakeholders to respond with diverse policies, agreements, and institutions [4]. Dlamini (2020) suggests the necessity of more systematic and inclusive mechanisms to protect women, taking into consideration the intersection of discrimination and marginalization of certain sections of women who are prone to gender-based violence and the pandemic [2]. It has, therefore, been recommended to integrate existing gender inequality perspectives across all levels of government actions, which would help the government to make inclusive decisions on women's empowerment.

In recent years, women's empowerment has received special attention internationally with various measures undertaken by the UN. Goal 5 of the Sustainable Development Goals (SDGs) highlights the achievement of gender equality and empowerment of all women and girls [5]. Taking this as a reference, progress has been made in the last few years wherein a maximum number of girls are going to school, a decrease in child marriage has been witnessed, more women are in higher positions of leadership, and most countries have started to formulate policies for the advancement of gender equality [5]. The UN Secretary-General made a very interesting remark and said, "limited gains in gender equality and women's rights made over the decades are in danger of being rolled back due to the COVID-19 pandemic and urged governments to focus on women and girls for their recovery efforts" [6]. In his speech, he emphasizes that COVID-19 should be taken as a challenge to global human health mechanisms and as a test for all humankind. Talking about humans, he meant inclusive of all genders without discrimination. Many countries in the Global South used virtual tools such as hotlines and other online measures to address domestic violence for the first time, which increased exponentially during the quarantine phase of the pandemic [7]. However, the question that needs to be addressed is, are these policies effective in solving or preventing gender-based violence? Has every gender-based violence victim been able to access the measures provided by the government?

The pandemic has affected most of the countries in the Global South differently than the countries in the Global North in two of the most important aspects: economic growth and social well-being. It has been identified by Agarwal et al. (2022) in their article that governments in the Global South have failed to provide proper data on the crucial questions of 'health equity'—national data rarely focus on inequalities such as caste, ethnicity, geographical location, race, religion, occupation or class and their intersection with gender [8]. The unavailability of data in the first place would create significant gaps in understanding the effects of the gendered impact of the pandemic, which surfaces in policy formulation and implementation by governments.

6.2 Literature Review

Various academic writings have seen the issue of gender and the pandemic, but the policy approach towards women's empowerment during the COVID-19 pandemic and post-pandemic period has been largely missing. Adeola et al. (2022) highlighted the constraints primarily faced by female entrepreneurs and the repercussions they had on the business during the pandemic [9]. The authors also claim that women were found to be more disadvantaged than men and that the COVID-19 pandemic supposedly increased this inequality. The ineffectiveness of policymakers in mitigating this gap has been reflected, and post-pandemic strategies should be that of participation and parity for women [9]. Dotsey (2022), on the other hand, has recommended providing better nonfinancial services and the availability of microfinance at low and sustainable interest rates to women in Ghana [10]. A conceptual framework has been provided by Agarwal (2022), wherein she argues that women lack bargaining power at home in the first place—from their spouses, elder members in the house, etc., in terms of assets such as land, which are mostly held by men—which is the major reason for the disproportionate economic distribution [8]. Hence, COVID-19 has led to the worsening of distributional outcomes for women. It has also been argued that the existing feminist literature has not taken this aspect into account when highlighting the impact of COVID-19 and has focused primarily on domestic violence and care work, which buried very important aspects such as above [8]. Miranda and Alfredo (2022) have mostly focused on the aspect of socially just policies that would help in strengthening unity and constructing participatory democratic societies among generations, genders, and various social groups in the Global South [11].

Francis (2020) highlighted that it is essential for researchers and feminist writers to delve into framing policies that contribute to gender equality and women's empowerment as a post-pandemic recovery measure [12]. Francis (2020) also tried to build on the gendered economy in South Africa wherein the focus was made on the unpaid labour of women, job loss and the pandemic proliferating it even more [12]. Francis (2020) recommended working on policies that would create more jobs for women in South Africa [12]. McLaren, Wong, et al. (2020), in a similar fashion, have reflected on the additional burden endured by women and how it has escalated during the pandemic, and the post-pandemic phase has witnessed a worsening gender burden [13]. The dimension of intersectionality has been highlighted by Gaurilovic et al. (2022) in certain aspects such as race, ethnicity, disability and nationality but has not focused on how these factors have been linked to gendered policies during the COVID-19 pandemic and post-pandemic recovery period [14].

Grugel et al. (2022) criticize the policies made that failed to respond to gender inequality, and the argument has also been made that the poorest women and girls in the poorest region of the world suffer more because of violence, job, health, education, dignity, etc. [15]. There has been a gap between bridging the gaps between policies formulated and addressing gender inequalities. This observation has been made based on research conducted across Latin America and Sub-Saharan Africa. Global responses have been insufficient to respond to these kinds of outcomes revolving around gender, which has been aggravated due to the pandemic. The proposal has been made to formulate useful policies that focus on reducing gender inequalities that have been aggravated due to COVID-19 [15]. Clinging et al. (2021) and Al-Ali [26] have also highlighted that women failed to receive any additional support from the state authorities or that the state was unable to provide societal protection, particularly in West Asia [16].

Most of the academic literature has primarily highlighted the post-pandemic economic recovery programme with very little emphasis on socioeconomic perspectives. The existing academic literature focuses very little on the policy approaches by the government catering to women's empowerment in the post-COVID-19 pandemic, especially in the Global South. Perhaps, the available literature has ignored the causes underpinning the exclusion of women in policymaking during the pandemic and its impact on the post-pandemic recovery programme. Moreover, the policy perspective has not been given enough attention, particularly in the Global South and policies on women's empowerment at large. Therefore, this chapter tries to draw the attention of academics to fill this gap and develop a framework to address the issue of gender-inclusive policy.

6.3 Methodology

Adopting a qualitative analysis method, mostly using secondary data, the chapter aims to address the question related to health equity, the intersection of gender with caste, ethnicity, religion, race, etc. The method involves organizing the available data and systematically analyzing them for an effective conclusion. The existing data that have been analyzed included peer-reviewed journals, valid internet resources, e-textbooks, government archives and organizations' websites. The chapter also identifies the gap between the data available and gender-exclusive policies of the governments in the Global South despite their effort at economic recovery measures. Some suggestions have been provided, such as recognizing the need for gender-inclusive policies, education as a means of policy reform, capacity-building programmes, and integrating global agendas on gender equality and women's empowerment with domestic policies. The study has recommended that there should be an effort to prevent the widening of the gender gap in case of any crisis. The study does not provide a comparative study for analyzing the impact of the COVID-19 pandemic on women and does not provide a comparison between or among governments for examining their policy approaches. The study focuses on the wider implications of the pandemic on women in the Global South and a general analysis of policies adopted by governments in the Global South to draw the attention of policymakers in formulating inclusive policies for women's empowerment. The study, however, uses already existing data to back up the analysis and determine the specific region(s) in the Global South that experienced the brunt of COVID-19 concerning women and the effectiveness of the policies introduced for women's empowerment.

6.4 Gender Disparity in Public Policymaking

Bridging gender inequality as a goal of SDG Goal 5 has remained a distant dream and a critical issue across the globe. Goal 5 of the SDG focuses on "achieving equality and empowering all women and girls" [5]. The progress of any nation-state depends on the policy it implements that caters to solving societal problems. It is the government that can play an effective role in intensifying progress or in working towards gender parity through various institutions and processes, such as legislation, fiscal measures, public–private partnerships, and programmatic change [17]. One of the examples cited by Gupta et al. (2019), is the doubling of labor force participation among women in Singapore from 28% in 1970 to 58% in 2016 [17]. This reflects the plethora of policies by the government to help women achieve various aspects of life, such as work-life harmony, including paid maternity leave, increased tax relief, and infant care subsidies. However, this is not true for policymaking and implementation in every country in the Global South due to resource constraints and other factors. McKinsey and Company have reported that "North America and Western Europe had progressed in the case of gender parity with gender parity scores of 0.73 and 0.71, respectively" [17]. On the other hand, regions such as the Middle East, Asia–Pacific and sub-Saharan Africa have a long way to go in terms of gender parity, with values of 0.50, 0.56 and 0.57, respectively [17]. Therefore, it is imperative on the part of governments, mostly in the Global South, to redefine policymaking by partnering with civil society organizations and private-sector organizations.

Research has been conducted to analyze the policies of governments regarding gender inequalities. It shows the gap in the formulation and implementation of policy approaches. Llorens et al. (2021) analyzed 2895 records in Medicine, Web of Science and Scielo regarding policy approaches that were implemented or proposed for formulation [18]. However, out of those, 91 full articles were analyzed, and approximately 22 papers described the process of formulation of policies and implementation/evaluation of policies aimed at reducing gender inequalities in health: 6 highlighted recommendations and the other 5 focused on both issues [18]. What can be calculated from the above data is the inadequate measures and ineffectiveness of the policies designed and implemented.

The immediate requirement demands gender-sensitive policies, especially in the post-COVID world, where millions of women and girls are left unheard for their vulnerabilities at home as well as in public spaces. Incorporating gender into health policies would cater to achieving equity in health, which could be a step in working towards women's empowerment.

6.5 Impact of the COVID-19 Pandemic on Women of the Global South

National and international efforts toward gender equality and women's empowerment have been shattered due to the outbreak of the COVID-19 pandemic, and the response of the governments of the Global South has been inadequate to fill this gap. The United Nations Policy Brief [19] has highlighted that the existing gender inequalities in social, political, and economic spheres have been intensifying since the outbreak of the COVID-19 pandemic—particularly for women and girls just because of their sex [19]. Women and girls have felt the economic impacts that have doubled during the pandemic and after due to low pay, job insecurity, and finding most of them in poverty [19]. It has also been found that in countries of every other economic size with greater emphasis on the global south, numerous women have been seen losing income, and the freight of unpaid care work and domestic work has increased manifold [20]. Concerning the pay gap, women have not always been on par with their male counterparts, even though 70% of health workers are women [20]. It has been seen through our experiences that it is, most of the time, the responsibility of women to take care of the family when they are ill along with other household chores without pay. It is appalling to see such a burden when women are working outside with less pay or no pay as well as heading back home to more work without pay considering it to be the duty of a woman.

Apart from the increased risk of insecurity in the economic sphere, women faced the brunt of social exploitation in the form of domestic violence abuse or harassment when the crisis was at its peak, and they were under home quarantine. The COVID-19 pandemic took a toll on many vulnerable groups and will continue to have an adverse impact post-pandemic—women being the most vulnerable and heavily affected [21].

According to the OECD Development Centre's Social Institutions and Gender Index (SIGI), women carry out 10 times more care work than men [21]. It is certain that during the lockdown, almost all countries that experienced working women were expected to work from home with additional household chores. Despite such horrendous experiences, women's voices were ignored or left unheard by policymakers whose intervention and response to such crises might have protected women from being victimized.

The COVID-19 pandemic has also seen the likeliness of women and girls dropping out of school more than men/boys, mostly in regions such as Latin America, the Caribbean and Sub-Saharan Africa, for various reasons, one among which is gender-based violence, which rose during the pandemic. The study undertaken by Flor et al. (2022) found that the preexisting gender gaps and inequalities between men and women intensified during the COVID-19 pandemic [22]. The direct impact of the pandemic, mostly related to health, has been irreparable. However, the indirect impact of the pandemic, such as gender marginalization and women being the disadvantaged target, is more adverse than the health-related impacts.

6.5.1 Assessing the Impact of the COVID-19 Pandemic Regionally in the Global South

Gender inequalities cannot always be seen in terms of economic inequalities; rather, they are the intersection of multiple factors. Gender inequality deepens when they overlap with the 'intersectional deprivation' of caste and race [8]. Delving into the facets of gender inequality, it is essential to research on how caste, race and religion have impacted gender equality and women's empowerment to be specific. Women belonging to a particular race, caste or religion will have a probability of being marginalized and affected more than those belonging to the privileged category. Agarwal et al. (2022) have highlighted some of the critical points that have been ignored by the literature, such as the effects of care work and domestic violence in the Global South [8]. The back-breaking labor in 'poor countries in the Global South where women have to fetch water from outside sources due to a lack of piped water connection at homes or fetching firewood from the forest as it is the common fuel for cooking in most of South Asia and Sub-Saharan Africa. Apart from these types of ground reality, other forms of social subjugation occur—such as early marriage, selling of girls, etc., as a means of survival in the post-pandemic situation. This kind of situation demands appropriate policy measures to first identify such problems and formulate and adopt a gender-inclusive policy approach.

Globally, men and women both felt unsafe at home, but while looking at it regionally, women reported a higher rate of feeling unsafe at home, e.g., in Latin America and the Caribbean, central Europe, eastern Europe, Central Asia, southeast Asia, east Asia and Oceania [22]. However, the data varied according to the source from which the data were collected, viz., data from Gender Equality at Home found women to be the victim of gender-based violence more than men, and the data collected from the 'COVID-19 Rapid Gender Assessment Surveys' showed the opposite (e.g., in South Asia, men reported more gender-based violence than women) [22]. Therefore, while analyzing the data, one should be aware of the nuances contained in them as well as the validation of the data collecting source. According to the survey undertaken by Flor et al. (2022), women in sub-Saharan Africa, Latin America and the Caribbean reported disruption in sexual and reproductive healthcare at a higher level than men [22]. Gender gaps related to preventive care were seen in most regions, which eventually were reduced except in sub-Saharan Africa.

Dropout rates among girls and women have been found to increase due to COVID-19 pandemic-related measures, mostly in Sub-Saharan Africa. It has been reported that 90% of students, of whom 800 million are girls and women, have been affected by the pandemic [23]. It has been observed that most of these girls live in the Global South, where access to education has been a problem and the COVID-19 pandemic has worsened the existing inequalities. In Sub-Saharan Africa, the already existing sociocultural or systemic obstacles have affected empowerment opportunities, as COVID-19 has necessitated teenage girls and young women to drop out of school. According to UNICEF (2021), an estimated 69 million children have failed to attend school because of the COVID-19 pandemic and pre-pandemic factors such as an inability to pay school fees, poor transportation facilities, child labor due to poverty, forced marriage, an inability to afford sanitary napkins, and challenges for children with disabilities across Eastern and Southern Africa [24]. It was reported that out of 21 countries in Eastern and Southern Africa, only 5 governments have been allocating 20% of their national budget to education to fulfil the 'Education for All' target set before the crisis [24]. UNICEF (2021) also recommends that the governments in these countries frame policies that would address the urgent need for education and focus on formulating safe measures to open schools to compensate for the loss due to the pandemic [24].

It has also been recorded that the pandemic had a wide-ranging impact on women and girls in southern and eastern Africa with minimum or no access to menstrual health and hygiene. It has also been reported that more than 60% of women suffer from mental and emotional stress in Ethiopia and Kenya [25]. Data from UNFPA (2020) have shown that a "77% increase in calls to the national hotline pre/post-COVID-19 in Kenya was registered" [25]. Similarly, "in South Sudan, compared to January 2020, a 72% increase in cases of protection monitoring was reported in May 2020" [25]. Between 30 March and 30 May 2020, Zimbabwe recorded 90% of calls to national hotlines mostly related to violence by intimate partners [25]. On the other hand, South Africa recorded a 70% decrease in various forms of violent crime during lockdown compared to the same period in 2019, which has been ascribed to proper law enforcement and the prohibition of liquor. However, there was a 67% increase in gender-based violence in South Africa according to the data from a civil society between March and the beginning of April.

Regarding inequalities in employment, women live in the peripheral section of the African economy, such as small-scale farming, petty trading, small business, and low-wage domestic tasks [24]. Gender exclusion in the region is highly apparent, which also shows low socioeconomic welfare and questions the policy approaches of governments from the lower level of governance to the highest level.

The struggle in terms of economic inequalities, limited infrastructure, inadequate healthcare facilities, no access to clean water and electricity, growing unemployment and disparity in educational access have been witnessed in countries in the Global South. This situation has further been aggravated due to the COVID-19 pandemic leading to famine, poverty, ill health, and extreme hardship. Rogers (2020), cited in Al-Ali (2020), highlighted that COVID-19 has exacerbated food shortages, famine, and malnutrition in the Global South, leading to more casualties than the virus [26]. It has also been found that women in Central Asia, North Africa, and the Middle East, including women from central and eastern European countries, reported having more issues accessing medication than men [23]. According to the UN Women and Women Count, as reported by the Diplomat, 67% of parents in the Asia–Pacific region have reported an increase in the domestic work of their daughters compared to 57% of their sons [27]. Reports of cyberbullying and sexual exploitation have also been reported and have increased due to lockdowns and strict quarantine rules, leading to most of them spending time online. In Asia, thousands of girls have been put through forced early marriage, which was already prevalent in the region but has been deemed to have doubled in 2020. For example, in Indonesia, "33,000 child marriages were permitted in the first six months of 2020" [27]. The Philippines has also recorded approximately "280,000 cases of online sexual abuse against children" in approximately 3 months, i.e., 1 March to 24 May 2020, which is four times more than in 2019 [27]. These figures expose the vulnerability of girls and women in the Global South primarily concerning regions such as Sub-Saharan Africa and Asia.

Apart from the data collected by the 'COVID-19 Rapid Gender Assessment Surveys', all other data that have been used in the chapter show that the intensification of violence and subjugation against women, increasing rate of women/girls dropping out from school, and lack of healthcare facilities for women during the COVID-19 pandemic were beyond measure. Given the economic side of pandemic-led crises, the crisis of gender-based violence has deepened the already existing gender inequalities.

6.5.2 COVID-19 Pandemic and Policy Responses to Women's Empowerment

Given the complexities that women faced since the outbreak of the pandemic, the policy approaches by the government must take immediate heed so that women's concerns are heard, and proper policies are formulated and implemented for their emancipation. In addition to the Global South, the policy responses in developed nations, viz. in Europe and the US about women's empowerment faltered drastically. The policy Department for Citizens' Rights and Constitutional Affairs has recorded that 76% of 49 million healthcare workers are women, and they have been at the forefront of combating the COVID-19 pandemic, including other broad sectors [28]. However, the policies implemented by the government do not fulfil the gendered nature of inequality that exists in society, particularly among women.

The vulnerability is much more evident among women refugees in the global south. The UN Women (2020) recorded an interview with a Rohingya women volunteer in a Bangladesh refugee camp who communicated her sorrow and fear of missing essential ingress to resources, no proper medical facilities and hygiene, and lack of availability of doctors and nurses [20]. It is visible how government policies work in places such as refugee camps where a large number of people stay without basic health and hygiene facilities.

The lockdown was enforced by the state as an emergency that created stricter rules, arrests, and crackdowns on common citizens. Jordanian and Nigerian governments were two of many countries that imposed the strictest lockdowns in the world [16]. Scholars have witnessed that the impact of lockdowns has been greater among vulnerable populations, such as internally displaced people or people involved in the informal economy, affecting the livelihood of thousands. As has been highlighted in the above section, the vulnerability of women during the COVID-19 pandemic and the impact that the pandemic had on women's economic empowerment has been recognized globally in the last few years.

The measures or policies taken up by the Jordanian government might have eased and benefitted certain sections of society, but women, mainly refugees and IDPs, had to face the brunt, as the national health provision introduced by the government did not include national protection mechanisms for refugee women [16]. Although the Jordanian women were assisted in cash by the National Aid Fund, the women who were not Jordanian or a refugee could not avail themselves of this assistance. Governments worldwide should realize that every refugee, migrant and IDP are human and need to be protected. The study conducted by Clingain et al. (2021) found that women did not receive any additional support, such as state or nonstate financial assistance, social protection, or any kind of remittances—be it displaced or the host community [16]. The only minimal support they received was informal help from family and friends. The responses of the governments in the West Asian region during the pandemic have been more repressive, especially to women. State responses to the pandemic in the region have been associated with repressive measures such as militarization and control over people's liberties, movements, and freedom of expression [26]. It does not stop there; the authorities refrained from providing any vital means of social protection or assistance to the people hit hardest by the pandemic [26]. Not only in the countries in the Global South but also the women in some countries in the Global North, most remarkably the US, have not been able to rely on state and state-led institutions, such as the police and the judiciary, to shield them from gender-based and sexual violence or even make resources available to them and provide support and security.

Many instances were reported where governments and militaries have been at the fore of worsening structural inequalities, forms of inequalities and violence [26]. In the Global South and some countries in the Global North (mostly the US), women could not rely on state institutions to protect themselves from gender-based violence either from the police or the judiciary. While, Al-Ali (2020) argues that these state-led institutions have tried to control women's bodies, mobility, sexuality, dangerous authoritarian politics, and patriarchal gender regimes [26]. Although the policies of the government in the Global South have intensified virtual policy measures such as extending hotline services and online services, government policy should extend beyond these measures to be accessible 24 × 7 for emergencies, have broader geographical coverage and invest more in infrastructure for shelter, emergency services, etc. [7]. Unless these basic provisions are implemented, discourse on women's empowerment post-COVID-19 pandemic remains a far-fetched dream. In addition, some questions need attention, i.e., how far is the advocacy of the feminists of the Global South successful in intervening in the state's policy formulation? How does their strategy criticize the gender-biased policies of the government? The feminist understanding of the situation faced by women during the pandemic would essentially help in building a theoretical framework to provide policymakers with options for women's empowerment post-COVID-19 pandemic.

The UN policy brief highlighted that 105 countries had passed fiscal response packages that amount to US$4.8 trillion by March 21, 2020, and almost 106 countries had introduced social protection measures responding to COVID-19 by April 13, 2020 [19]. The policy brief also highlighted that this kind of social intervention should also include data on sex disaggregation, a gender perspective, targeting of women, and education gaps based on gender [19]. What can be gathered from the report on the policy brief by the UN is that the social protection system, especially during the pandemic and after, is very narrow not only in the Global South but also in some countries in the Global North. The countries in the Global South, mainly in South Asia, Sub-Saharan Africa, and Latin America, have more women engaged in informal employment apart from agricultural work—80%, 74% and 54%, respectively [19]. This makes it more pertinent that the government should have provided enough social protection systems, such as paid sick and maternity leave, pensions and health insurance.

6.5.3 Economic Responses of the Governments in the Global South: IMF Policy Tracker

The International Monetary Fund Policy Tracker has briefed on the economic responses that the governments were undertaking to minimize the impact of the COVID-19 pandemic—both the economic and the human impact [29]. However, the data provided show that the policy responses of the various governments in the Global North, as well as the Global South, have addressed the economic aspects of the COVID-19 pandemic through huge budget allocation for Covid-related spending.

The policy measures taken by countries such as Algeria included postponement of income tax, cutting the policy rates, etc. Afghanistan responded by using contingency funds to respond to pandemic emergencies, providing free bread to poor people in

Kabul and elsewhere. Approximately 0.8% of GDP was allocated for social assistance under the REACH programme funded by the World Bank, and the government also extended the deadline for filing taxes by 45 days for the first quarter of 2020 [29]. Argentina also allocated more than 50% of its GDP to COVID-related measures, mostly health-related measures. The government of Bhutan has started initiatives to boost employment among youths, and the budget has also been allocated for an Economic Contingency Plan that aims to help various sectors. Given the healthcare system in Burundi, the government aims to strengthen the healthcare system and social safety. However, the Burundian authorities had managed to recruit at least one doctor and a nurse in every 116 municipalities apart from the capital Bujumbura and apart from the pandemic response plan, sectors such as transport and hotels are also being supported by forgiving taxes to those hotels that were unable to pay. Regarding the gender inequality index, most of the countries in South and Southeastern Asia as well as most countries in Africa are ranked the lowest. Asia's female labor participation rate declined by 13% compared to a 1% fall for males between December 2019 and June 2020 [30]. Concerning access to necessary products in countries such as Afghanistan, Bangladesh, Maldives, Nepal, the Philippines and Thailand, women faced difficulties more than men [30].

India was one of the hardest hit countries by the COVID-19 pandemic, and the government announced several relaxation measures, such as the interstate movement of the stranded people and the relaxation of economic activities in the orange and green zone areas [30]. The Indian government focused on 2 categories of support responses: (i) "above-the-line measures" that mainly focused on areas related to social protection and healthcare and (ii) "below-the-line measures" that aimed at supporting business sectors [30].

It is rather interesting to note that Lesotho (a small kingdom in South Africa) has allocated a minimum amount of LSL 5.2 million in support of gender-based violence survivors and sports, which is <0.1% of the GDP [30]. It is certain from the above records that the government authorities have allocated funds for healthcare during and after the COVID-19 pandemic (2020–2021) and have introduced several social and economic measures to cope with the damage caused by the pandemic, but no policy responses have been recorded specifically to gender aspects.

The above account of the policies introduced by the government also shows that the policy lacks a broad approach that involves women's empowerment, which is desirable and necessary for post-COVID recovery. Therefore, the need for the hour is for the governments in the Global South to develop comprehensive policies that would be inclusive and gender-neutral.

6.6 Women-Centric Policy Measures Adopted by Countries in the Global South

Most of the academic literature has focused on the economic aspect of the COVID-19 pandemic, including the policies of governments, which happen to be economic reforms at large. This being said, very little effort has been made to social reforms, particularly concerning women's empowerment. The studied policies by various governments remained largely exclusionary regarding measures adopted for women's empowerment during and after the pandemic. It is essential that for policies to be inclusive, reforms must be made that are inclusive.

What has been observed in various scholarly articles and op-ed articles is the pertinent patriarchal form of violence and the poisonous effect of masculinity. Empowerment is usually a long-term and additional process wherein conducive structural changes must be made for women's individual as well as collective empowerment [16]. For most of the regions in the Global South, the priority was mostly given to the health sector. However, the facilities and policies of governments concerning employment, poverty alleviation, etc., were often gender biased, and the pandemic has triggered biases. Gaurilovic et al. (2022) have highlighted that the socioeconomic fallout of the COVID-19 pandemic has remained gendered across the globe, and hardly one out of five global protection measures have been able to address gender-related violence and inequalities [14]. According to the data provided by the authors, the social measures undertaken by various governments show that sub-Saharan Africa has contributed the least of 2% for supporting unpaid care, followed by Northern Africa and Western Asia (4%), Central and South Asia (4%), Latin America and the Caribbean (4%), Eastern Asia, South Eastern Asia and Oceania (5%), and Europe, North America, Australia and New Zealand have contributed the highest of 15% [14]. Overall, out of 3099 measures, only 7% of the social policies were related to gender, including the Global North and the Global South [14]. The figure shows that the efforts of the governments in the Global South to address the gendered impact of the COVID-19 pandemic remain poor, especially in Sub-Saharan region of Africa.

UN Women and UNFPA (2021) have underlined some efforts to mitigate post-COVID recovery about gender-based violence [26]. The research conducted by UN Women and UNFPA (2021) specific to the East and Southern African regions found that there was no reliable data on gender-based violence, which is very problematic [26]. To bridge this gap, there must be more drivers to identify gender-based violence and develop specific policies; there must be a more efficient use of technology so that it can be used as a reporting mechanism for survivors of GVB; the police should be given general training that should aim at preventing police brutality across the region; and the training of law enforcement agencies should be carried out so that they will be educated on how to receive and manage complaints from survivors and victims of rape and sexual and gender-based violence [26]. In the report of the OECD (2020), highlights have been made on the government extending access to unemployment benefits to disadvantaged groups. To achieve this, emphasis was placed on ensuring support for women victims of violence trapped at home with abusers by ensuring that service providers worked together and exchanged information [22]. One of the most pivotal policy measures should be to embed and put enough effort into mainstream gender in government responses to the crisis. Applying a gender lens to policy measures during any kind of emergency should be taken into account so that in the future, the government would have a very well-structured and well-functioning system of gender mainstreaming. Government policies should also take into consideration the effect of their policies and adjustments on both men and women [22]. The report of the UN Women and UNFPA [26], as well as OECD [3], have extensively suggested gender-inclusive measures that show that governments faltered in formulating policies that focused on women's emancipation and safety [22]. Therefore, it can be said that the policy approaches of the governments during the pandemic in some of the countries in the Global South were exclusionary, which has been laid out clearly in the studies conducted by the organizations stated above. What comes as a surprise is that the policies have been exclusionary in terms of gender (women's security in particular) in OECD countries as well.

It is the responsibility of the governments in the Global South that they recognize the embedded gender biases in their policies and start conceptualizing gender-inclusive policy responses that would work towards women's empowerment. According to Hunt and Samman [31], one should recognize the long-term significance of empowerment and that it is a gradual process; for women, individual as well as collective empowerment requires the creation of conducive structural conditions backed by context and experience. The authors also highlighted that there is no 'one size fits all' approach, and therefore, a policy approach towards achieving empowerment can be fruitful if one can identify the building blocks that can be used pragmatically [16]. Different countries would require a unique and different policy approach to deal with post-pandemic recovery, especially concerning women's empowerment. Having said so, the utmost care and consideration need to be taken while considering the social, political, and economic aspects given the country's nature for policy making.

6.7 Policy Reforms: The Way Forwards

The countries in the Global South mostly focused on the unpaid work of women and social issues such as domestic violence, largely ignoring the policy perspectives, especially regarding policies for women's empowerment and protection. It has been highlighted by Paul (2013) that developing countries' participation in global policy-making has been evolving in recent years, and it has been shaping the global normative framework through international negotiations promoting a balance between national interest and overall development [32]. Given this backdrop, it is the responsibility of the countries in the Global South to include and involve women in decision-making so that they have an equal voice with men. Moreover, eliminating gender discrimination at the grassroots level would ensure inclusive policy approaches. This means that the actors involved in public policymaking should emphasize the gender-inclusive education system from the very start of children's education. However, the role of the family as a primary unit for education cannot also be ignored. This is possible if policymakers focus on substantive policymaking, which calls for a participatory policy-making approach.

Al-Ali (2020) highlighted that feminists in the West Asian region should respond to the post-pandemic health crisis in the context of their already existing struggles with authoritarian regimes against political suppression, corruption, war and conflict, displacement, and settler colonialism [26]. Highlighting policy reforms in authoritative regimes, feminist activists, as well as other civil society organizations (engaged with women's empowerment), must associate themselves with the government in helping formulate gender-neutral policy and demand gender-neutral human rights, universal healthcare and most importantly demand for ending state-led oppression and discrimination.

Since most of the Global South countries have colonial pasts and their policymaking involves development as a major policy focus, they must start by including gender and women's empowerment issues in their development-related policymaking. Some of the post-pandemic reforms that governments in the Global South can take in their 'public' policymaking are as follows:

(a) Recognising the gendered nature of the healthcare workforce is pivotal in the first place. Hence, identifying the problem is the very first step in formulating and implementing policies. In this case, the identified problem is the gendered societal structure and lack of policy approaches to women's empowerment.
(b) Capacity-building and awareness programmes in local-level governance should include gender sensitization in schools and communities, workshops for entrepreneurial skills, etc. Strengthening the engagement of women in any policy related to crisis management could be a measure to improve women's participation.
(c) Gender-inclusive education systems from pre-primary to higher education should be the topmost priority so that the future generation of policymakers can understand the significance of inclusive policymaking.
(d) Selecting partners from the domestic and international levels that will help focus on inclusive recovery. The role of the international organization could not be undermined when it comes to global crises [33]. The aspects of partnerships, such as cooperation and coordination between and among regional and international organizations along with the civil society organizations, would result in a positive outcome.
(e) Inclusion of various national and international women's rights organizations in policymaking.
(f) The intersection of the public policy approach with the Generation Equality Forum at the domestic level of policymaking would make a difference. In doing so, the government can work towards the Global Accelerating Plan for gender equality, which was also envisioned by the UN Decade of Action (2020–2030) to meet the Sustainable Development Goal [34].

Policymakers must realize that priority has been given to women's empowerment globally by the Convention on the Elimination of All Forms of Discrimination against (CEDAW) in 1979 [35]. The UN Security Council Resolution 1325 and the subsequent resolution have also highlighted that the attainment of positive peace is not possible without the meaningful involvement of all members of society and recognized the significant role of women and girls as partners in the peace process at every level [36]. Although the above convention and resolutions are not binding, countries must adhere to them as a moral responsibility and act at the local level to fulfil common global goals. The global recovery programme would falter if it excluded women's empowerment agenda or gender equality aspect. To recover faster in the post-pandemic world, it is mandatory to consider gender equality and women's right to build a better future and a better world. Therefore, any policy would require an inclusive approach to a long-run women's empowerment goal.

6.8 Conclusion

The pandemic has reinforced global social and economic inequalities, which has led to complex and integrated economic, social, political, environmental and health crises. Questions on inclusive social protection and change in social norms are essential prerequisites to address the stigma and discrimination faced by women since times immemorial, and the pandemic has only brought these discriminations to the fore. Tracing goal 5 of the SDG, very little has been done by the governments of the Global South that caters to women's empowerment. The rolling back of little achievement made on gender equality and women's empowerment due to COVID-19, as highlighted by Secretary-General Antonio Guterres, has been true, as we see from the data analyzed in the sections above and the hardships that women had to endure. The apparent increase in domestic violence, poor health equity, subjugation, and domination due to unplanned quarantine measures adopted by governments is proof that governments in the Global South need to rethink their public policy strategy.

What had been lacking during the pandemic and has been lacking post-pandemic recovery policies is the all-inclusive policymaking approach that should incorporate all the stakeholders—not only the bureaucracy or the politicians but the array of nongovernmental organizations and civil society organizations that represent women. Such inclusiveness would help identify problems properly, leading to the proper formulation and implementation of the policies achieving the public aspect of the policy. Public policy means, in simple words, the number of actions implemented to solve problems in society through various policy initiatives. COVID-19 and its aftermath have unfurled unplanned actions by the government and its inability to formulate and implement policies that in the true sense solved societal problems.

The global trends viz. climate change, terrorism, pandemic, human insecurity, etc., also impacts states equally at different rates. Hence, the policy prospects need to be all-encompassing, especially in the Global South, as most of the countries in the Global South tend to focus more on economic development rather than social development at large. Various theories, such as the neo-Marxist, neo-Weberian and rational choice theorists, have highlighted that public policy creates division among classes, usually satisfies the interest of the elite and depends on cost–benefit analysis. This theoretical analysis has been validated through various data and policy approaches adopted by governments in the Global South.

Women in the Global South were adversely affected by the pandemic, such as low pay, unequal pay, lack of job opportunities, or insufficient financial help from the government on the economic front. On the social front, domestic violence, harassment, emotional abuse, early marriage, school dropout, etc. were the stories that dominated the pandemic phase. There is also a need to ponder on issues such as religion, caste, race, and region concerning women, which also determines the provision of socioeconomic assistance and facilities provided by the governments in South Asia, Sub-Saharan Africa, Latin America, and West Asia. As Flor et al. [22] have highlighted the intensification of the gender gap during COVID-19, the post-pandemic policy approach should prioritize inclusive policy alternatives to prevent women and girls from bearing the brunt in any crisis/conflict situation. From a policy perspective, such rooted problems need to be identified first, and then proper problem identification and policy formulation can take place. The inability to identify problems hinders public policy prospects.

As a policy response to the COVID-19 pandemic, governments in the Global South failed to provide enough financial assistance to women, and most female refugees were worst affected by the pandemic, as the host government failed to include refugee women in their policy framework. There were instances where countries had introduced social protection measures in response to the COVID-19 pandemic, but it was narrow in terms of South Asia, Sub-Saharan Africa and Latin America. According to the IMF, in countries such as Algeria, Afghanistan, Argentina, Burundi, and India, the focus has been more on economic factors such as releasing budgets for the improved healthcare system and supporting business sectors. These were general economic policies adopted by the governments—the policies specific to women's empowerment and gender were missing. Interestingly, Lesotho had allocated a budget in support of survivors of gender-based violence. Regarding women-centric policies in the Global South, importance was given only to the health sector, which was gender biased.

The scope of the study is limited to cases from regions such as Latin America, Asia, the Middle East, and Africa as a whole because of the dearth of sufficient data. The data on GBV were collected by agencies and organizations such as UN FPA and UN Women, which highlighted that the data were not very reliable; hence, it is problematic to assess the real issues faced by women as well as assess the policy approaches. The available data are found to be limited to economic and health-related measures. The data also show the exclusionary nature of government policies in terms of gender and policies designed toward women's empowerment. However, the study has found Sub-Saharan Africa to be the most vulnerable among others regarding women and girls, and the COVID-19 pandemic has triggered the existing social stigma surrounding gender. The study attempts to further extend research on how inclusive government policies could be a steppingstone in bringing about gender sensitivity and preventing GBV, school dropouts, early marriages, etc. It could also be a means to achieve women's empowerment not only in the West but also in the most vulnerable regions, such as Sub-Saharan Africa. Only when the governments in the affected countries choose to adopt gender-inclusive policy approaches can women's empowerment truly be achieved in the long run. The studied in this chapter has multifaceted challenges that need systematic and in-depth research so that certain specific aspects can be studied for a better policy framework.

References

1. Wenham C (2020) The gendered impact of the Covid-19 crisis and post-crisis period. Policy N
2. Dlamini NJ (2020) Gender-based violence, twin pandemic to COVID-19. Crit Sociol 47(4–5)
3. OECD: Policy Framework for Gender-Sensitive Public Governance (2021) Meeting of the Council at Ministerial Level, 5–6 October 2021. C/MIN, 2. https://www.oecd.org/mcm/Policy-Framework-for-Gender-Sensitive-Public-Governance.pdf. Accessed 21 Nov 2022
4. Alcazar L, Bebapriya B, Estefania C, Tausi K, Desmond M, Andrea O (2021) COVID-19 in the global south: impacts and policy responses. Occasional Paper Series No. 69. Southern Voice (2021)
5. UN: Sustainable Development Goals: Goal 5: Achieve gender equality and empower all women and girls. https://www.un.org/sustainabledevelopment/gender-equality/. Accessed 30 Sept 2022
6. UN News (2020) Put women and girls at the centre of COVID-19 recovery: UN Secretary-General. https://news.un.org/en/story/2020/04/1061452. Accessed 20 Sept 2022
7. Blofield M, Khalifa A, Madera N, Pieper J (2021) The shadow pandemic: policy efforts on gender-based violence during COVID-19 in the global south. GIGA Focus Global, p 6
8. Agarwal B, Ragupathy V, Floriana C (2022) Women, pandemics and the global south: an introductory overview. Econ Politica 39:15–30
9. Adeola O, Paul AI, Olaniyi E (2021) Women economic empowerment and post pandemic recovery in Africa: normalising the "Un-Normal" outcome of Covid-19. In: Adeola O (eds) Gendered perspectives on Covid-19 recovery in Africa. Palgrave
10. Dotsey S (2022) COVID-19 and microcredit: dissecting an NGO's training, financial support, and women empowerment programmes. Soc Sci 11(9):402
11. Miranda A, Miguel AA (2022) Transitions in the post-pandemic COVID-19 context: building youth policies in the global south. J Appl Youth Stud 5:233–247
12. Francis G (2020) Unemployment and the gendered economy in South Africa after Covid-19. Transformation critical perspectives on southern Africa. Transformation 104:103–112
13. McLaren HJ, Karen RW, Kieu NN, Komalee NDM (2020) Covid-19 and women's triple burden: vignettes from Sri Lanka, Malaysia Vietnam and Australia. Soc Sci 9(5):87
14. Gavrilovic M, Monica R, Francesca B, Roupa H, Silke S, Ruth GG, Charlotte B, Ruby K, Amber P, Bobo D, Laura A, Aroa S, Zehra R, Rebecca H, Juan G, Jaramillo M, Constanza T (2022) Gender-responsive social protection post-COVID-19. Policy Forum 375(6585):1111–1113
15. Grugel J, Matt B, Tallulah L, Maria EG, Jessica O (2022) The gendered face of COVID-19 in the global south—the development, gender and health nexus. Bristol University Press Digital
16. Clingain C, Daphne J, with Abigail & Amanda GM (2021) Women's economic empowerment in the face of Covid-19 and displacement: restoring resilient futures. Humanitarian Policy Group Commissioned Report. ODI, London
17. Gupta V, Solveigh H, Mekala K, Anu M (2019) Accelerating gender parity: What can governments do? McKinsey & Company (2019). https://www.mckinsey.com/industries/public-and-social-sector/our-insights/accelerating-gender-paritywhat-can-governments-do. Accessed 7 Nov 2022

18. Llorens NC, Ildefonso HA, Elisa CR (2021) Have policies tackled gender inequalities in health? A scoping review. Int J Environ Res Pub Health 18(1):327, 1–12
19. UN Policy Brief (2020) The impact of Covid-19 on women. https://www.un.org/sexualviolenceinconflict/wp-content/uploads/2020/06/report/policy-brief-the-impact-of-covid-19-on-women/policy-brief-the-impact-of-covid-19-on-women-en-1.pdf. Accessed 8 Aug 2022
20. UN Women (2020) COVID-19 and its economic toll on women: the story behind the numbers. https://www.unwomen.org/en/news/stories/2020/9/feature-covid-19-economic-impacts-on-women. Accessed 8 Aug 2022
21. OECD: Women at the core of the fight against COVID-19 crisis. https://read.oecd-ilibrary.org/view/?ref=127_127000-awfnqj80me&title=Women-at-the-core-of-the-fight-against-COVID-19-crisis. Accessed 8 Aug 2022
22. Flor LS, Joseph F, Cory NS et al (2022) Quantifying the effects of the COVID-19 pandemic on gender equality on health, social, and economic indicators: a comprehensive review of data from March 2020 to September 2021. The Lancet
23. Ahinkorah BO, John EH Jr, Edward KA, Abdul-Aziz S, Thomas S (2021) COVID-19 pandemic worsening gender inequalities for women and girls in sub-Saharan Africa. Frontiers in Global Women's Health. Sex and Gender Differences in Diseases
24. UNICEF (2021) 40 per cent of children in Eastern and Southern Africa are not in school. Press Release. https://www.unicef.org/press-releases/40-cent-children-eastern-and-southern-africa-are-not-school. Accessed 20 Nov 2022
25. UN Women & UNFPA (2021) Impact of COVID-19 on gender equality and wome's empowerment in East and Southern Africa. East and Southern Africa Regional Offices, Nairobi
26. Al-Ali N (2020) Covid-19 and feminism in the global south: challenges, initiatives and dilemmas. Eur J Women's Stud 27(4):333–347
27. Babb J. In addition, Natalie B. COVID-19 leaves millions of girls at risk of school dropout in Asia-Pacific. The Diplomat. https://thediplomat.com/2020/11/covid-19-leaves-millions-of-girls-at-risk-of-school-dropout-in-asia-pacific/. Accessed 20 Nov 2022
28. European Parliament (2000) Department of Citizens' Rights and Constitutional Affairs, Directorate-General for Internal Policies, Brussels (ND)
29. International Monetary Fund (IMF): Policy responses to COVID-19. Policy Tracker. https://www.imf.org/en/Topics/imf-and-covid19/Policy-Responses-to-COVID-19#R. Accessed 30 Aug 2022
30. Elbehri A, Tugrul T, Fethiye BC, Surabhi M, Failin K, David D (2022) Covid-19 pandemic Impacts on Asia and the Pacific: a regional review of socioeconomic, agrifood and nutrition impacts and policy responses. Food and Agriculture Organisation of the United Nations, Bangkok
31. Hunt A, Samman E (2016) Women's economic empowerment: navigating enablers and constraints. Research Report, Development Progress. Overseas Development Institute, London
32. Paul I (2013) The rise of the global south: implications for the provisioning of the global public goods. Occasional Paper 2012/08. United Nations Development Programme, Human Development Report Office
33. Balfour R, Lizza B, Marta M (2022) Coronavirus and the widening global north–south gap. Working Paper. Carnegie Endowment for International Peace. Washington, DC
34. Generation Equality Forum. https://forum.generationequality.org/about. Accessed 26 Sept 2022
35. UN: Convention on the elimination of all forms of discrimination against women. Adopted and opened for signature, ratification, and accession by General Assembly resolution 34/180 of 18 December 1979
36. UN: S/RES/1325. Adopted by the Security Council at its 4213th meeting on 31 October 2000

Chapter 7
Governing Migrant Workers Post-COVID-19 in Southeast Asia: Vulnerability, Mitigation and Transformative Agenda

Andi Luhur Prianto, Aqmal Reza Amri, and Goran Ilik

Abstract The vulnerability faced by migrant workers during the COVID-19 pandemic is one of the crucial issues to be discussed and opens the agenda for discussing the political economy. Hence, this paper aims to investigate the role of Southeast Asian countries in governing migrant workers in the Southeast Asian region during the COVID-19 pandemic and to analyse Southeast Asian countries' cooperation to consolidate transnational mitigation strategies to ensure the rights of migrant workers during the COVID-19 pandemic era. This article considers primary literature as well as secondary sources, such as news articles, reports from international organizations, and scientific studies. This article shows that in the early days of the pandemic, Southeast Asian countries were cut off and failed to build solidarity in the south. Each country only focuses on mitigation at the domestic level, so it is not regionally integrated. The efforts of ASEAN member countries to overcome the impact of the pandemic on migrant workers can only be seen at the end of 2020 with the convening of the 13th ASEAN Forum on Migrant Labor (AFML) and the presence of the ASEAN Comprehensive Recovery Framework (ACRF). The AFML and ACRF guidelines serve as guidelines and frameworks for transnational mitigation strategies for the recovery of conditions in the Southeast Asian region in the post-COVID era.

Keywords Migrant workers · Pandemic COVID-19 · Mitigation strategies · Southeast Asia

A. L. Prianto (✉) · A. R. Amri
Department of Government Studies, Universitas Muhammadiyah Makassar, Makassar, Indonesia
e-mail: luhur@unismuh.ac.id

G. Ilik
Faculty of Law, University "St. Kliment Ohridski", Bitola, North Macedonia

H. Adam and R. Rena (eds.), *Political Economy of Development in the Global South Post-COVID-19 Pandemic*,
https://doi.org/10.1007/978-981-99-4074-5_7

7.1 Introduction

Migrant workers are one of the important issues to be discussed in the twenty-first century [32]. Migrant workers are closely related to globalization and are an unavoidable logical consequence of the globalization process [23, 49, 64, 66]. The growth of technology, science, and transportation has made it possible for employees to migrate from one country to another and even from one region to another. Moreover, economic issues such as poverty and a lack of opportunity push people to move to find employment [54]. Since the twentieth century, migration activities for economic reasons have continued to increase, thus becoming a global phenomenon [14]. More than 280 million people, or 3.6% of the worldwide population, choose to live abroad [71], of which approximately 169 million are migrant workers coming from the Asia and Pacific regions [38]. In recent years, since the incessant process of globalization in the mid-1980s, migration in pursuit of employment and financial resources has become a special issue in the study of political economy, especially on the issue of remittances supplied by migrant workers [20].

The state achieves financially from the remittances of migrant workers. The contribution of migrant workers' remittances stimulates national economic growth, so migrant workers are often referred to as "remittance heroes" [49]. In addition, migrant workers are necessary for developed countries to carry out national economic activities. In Southeast Asia, the phenomenon of worker migration forms an interdependent relationship between industrialized and developing countries in the region. Developed countries are considered capable of providing high life expectancy and security while developing countries have not been able to solve structural problems such as poverty, so migrating to developed countries is an option for some people in developing countries to improve economic conditions [57].

In the modern era, migrant workers make a huge contribution to the economic development of Southeast Asian countries [31]. For instance, Malaysia, one of Southeast Asia's most economically developed nations, is heavily dependent on migrant labour. Approximately 15% of Malaysia's workforce is made up of migrant workers, and currently, there are approximately 2.5 million registered migrant workers, or approximately 20% of all employment [63]. The advantages that the state receives from migrant workers' remittances, however, do not correspond to the vulnerability that migrant workers face. Even though they have figured prominently in strengthening a country's bargaining power, especially in the context of political economy, migrant workers still often experience neglect in the protection of their rights. Inequitable practices such as abrupt termination of employment contracts, lower wages, stigmatization, discrimination, and deportation are frequently experienced by migrant workers.

The arrival of the coronavirus pandemic wave at the end of 2019 made the injustice faced by migrant workers much worse [65]. The pandemic has affected many aspects of human life, particularly for community groups that have suffered a significant amount of discrimination. The pandemic has brought concern for migrant workers' matters in numerous nations. Considering the pandemic, migrant workers are among the most at risk due to their low wages, working conditions, and substandard living situations. Numerous workers were already living in fear of contracting contagious diseases, being imprisoned, and being unemployed [63].

The pandemic caused an economic reduction of $2 trillion worldwide, slowed global growth, and added 25 million impoverished people worldwide. The International Labor Organization (ILO) predicted that by the second quarter of 2020, approximately 265 million full-time jobs, or 15.2% of total lost hours in Asia and the Pacific, would be lost. Estimates place the drop in Arab nations at 16.9% or 10 million full-time jobs. Regarding the three 2020s, it is predicted that working hours will decline by 12.4% in Arab nations and 10.7% in Asia and the Pacific [37], and in Southeast Asia, the number of migrant workers will decrease by 75% [2]. According to these figures, the pandemic has become a crucial fact in the global crisis, with a direct impact on the migrant worker sector.

Southeast Asian countries have not been spared by the pandemic crisis. Almost every country has established extensive rules and mitigation measures in place [28]. However, the panic in restricting the virus's spread has a severe influence on vulnerable groups, which includes migrant workers. Thailand, for instance, as the most popular destination country for migrant workers in Southeast Asia, has placed many migrant workers in precarious situations. The bulk of migrant workers is isolated in inadequate dormitories with living conditions that exceed the shelter ratio, leading to disease spread among migrant workers [63, 65]. The effect of the coronavirus outbreak provides a possibility to analyse various responses related to employment in times of crisis [30]. The significant flow of migrant workers in Southeast Asia requires collaboration between governments of origin and destination countries to establish transnational solutions to protect and ensure migrant workers' circumstances, especially during the pandemic crisis. For instance, consider Indonesia [18], which experienced a decline in public consumption during the pandemic, increasing the number of unemployed. However, a lack of public consumption and unemployment have no significant impact on GDP. Remittances from Indonesian workers, on the other hand, have a significant effect on financial stability. This fact supports the thesis that cooperative communication focused on the issue of migrant workers as a transnational mitigation strategy is urgently needed, especially given how many member countries rely on labour migration.

Figure 7.1 shows how the pandemic crisis is related to the crisis and issues of migrant worker protection. Many studies have been conducted to investigate the connection between the COVID-19 pandemic and the circumstances of migrant workers. Bretones [14], Dewi et al. [24], Fassani and Mazza [27], Koh [46], Mishra [53], Reid et al. [59], Ullah et al. [72], as well as those limited to the regional scale of South Asia [29] and national scales such as in Italy [62], Ukraine [21], China [78], and India [12, 58, 67, 77]. There are also several studies on migrant workers in the pandemic era that specifically limit the object of research to one particular problem, such as the problem of the remittances of migrant workers [20], migrant workers' psychological conditions and health issues throughout the COVID-19 pandemic [17, 19, 47], human trafficking issues [15], and migrant workers' rights [13]. On the other hand, several studies discuss migrant worker circumstances and the migrant labour

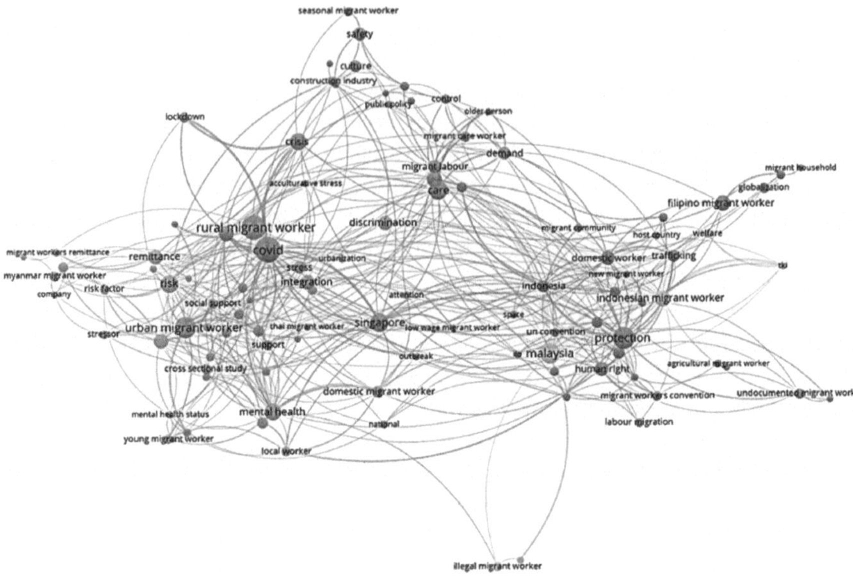

Fig. 7.1 Identification and analysis of research issues. *Source* Processed by Authors Using VosViewer

market on the Southeast Asian regional scale [30, 48] or specifically on the discussion of several Southeast Asian countries, such as Malaysia [51, 73], Singapore [50, 69], the Philippines [7], and Indonesia [10, 60]. Furthermore, some studies discuss the response of Southeast Asian countries to the COVID-19 pandemic crisis [9], however, the object of the research is not specific to the issue of migrant workers. Moreover, based on the literature exploration that has been carried out, there are no research articles that comprehensively examine the insecurity of migrant workers throughout Southeast Asian countries and analyse the attempts of regional countries in cooperating to establish mitigation strategies in the pandemic era. Therefore, this kind of research needs to be done because it reflects the weakness of intraregional regulations and policies that critically and comprehensively look at the vulnerability of migrant workers. Furthermore, the results of this study can be used as a basis for countries in the region to formulate integrated and effective policies in mitigating migrant workers' insecurity in times of crisis.

7.2 Research Method

The purpose of this research is to investigate the response of Southeast Asian countries in mitigating migrant workers' vulnerability in the COVID-19 pandemic era and analyse the ability of Southeast Asian countries to mobilize regional solidarity in mitigating the effect of the pandemic. This is qualitative research with a reach

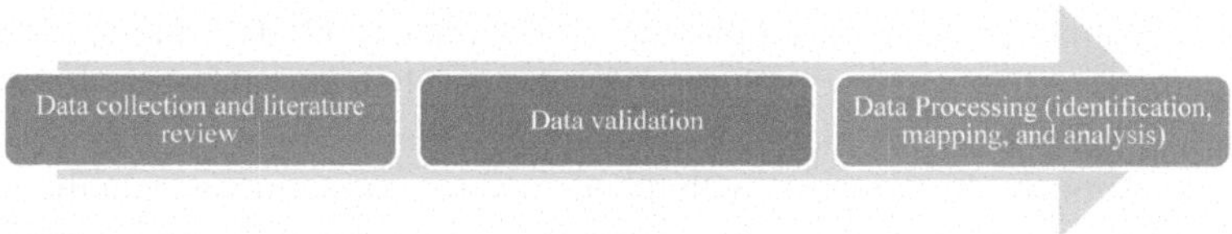

Fig. 7.2 Research stage. *Source* Processed by Authors

as an effort to elaborate on and understand a social problem [22, 45]. Data for this study were gathered from exploratory primary and secondary sources, including news articles, reports from international organizations, official government policies, and scientific articles relevant to the focus of research studies, namely, the response of South Asian countries to migrant workers' vulnerability issues. This study uses a phenomenological approach to determine the vulnerability of migrant workers in the pandemic era and the response of Southeast Asian countries to mitigating the vulnerability of migrant workers. The choice of a phenomenological approach in this study is based on an effort to explain in depth the phenomenon of vulnerability experienced by migrant workers in the Southeast Asian region during the COVID-19 pandemic. The research stage begins by examining various sources of literature that have been collected that are related to the focus of the research problem. Furthermore, validation and data processing is carried out, which includes the processes of identification, mapping and data analysis (Fig. 7.2).

7.3 Results and Discussion

7.3.1 The Vulnerability of Southeast Asian Migrant Workers During the Pandemic COVID-19 Crisis

The flow of migrant workers in Southeast Asia encourages regional interdependence between Southeast Asian countries. This is due to the employment sector's supply and demand process. Based on the ILO [37] report, workers from Indonesia, Myanmar, and the Philippines account for the majority of migrant workers from Southeast Asian countries.

Throughout 2019, there were approximately 220,972 Filipino migrant workers, 104,666 Indonesian migrant workers, and 317,330 Myanmar migrant workers [2]. This information demonstrates that labour demand in Southeast Asia persists quite considerably. A large percentage of migrant workers work in domestic and nursing jobs, construction, service sectors such as hotels, tourism, entertainment, stores, clerical/office services, cleaning and security services, manufacturing, and other industries such as agriculture, marine and fisheries, education, and health [37]. The absorption of labour in Southeast Asia is spread across several countries with relatively good economic stability, such as Singapore, Malaysia and Thailand. As of 2019, Thailand became a destination country, employing approximately 60,947 migrant workers from Southeast Asian countries. Figure 7.3 is higher than the other two destination countries, Singapore and Malaysia. The countries that become the destination of migrant workers are the countries with the highest per capita incomes in the Southeast Asia region, with the main economic resources engaged in the industrial and service sectors. The high supply chain turnover in these countries, of course, requires a large stock of labour as well, thus opening opportunities for regional cooperation among countries in Southeast Asia (Fig. 7.4).

However, at the beginning of 2020, Southeast Asia became a region affected by the coronavirus pandemic. This situation affects the national economies of each country.

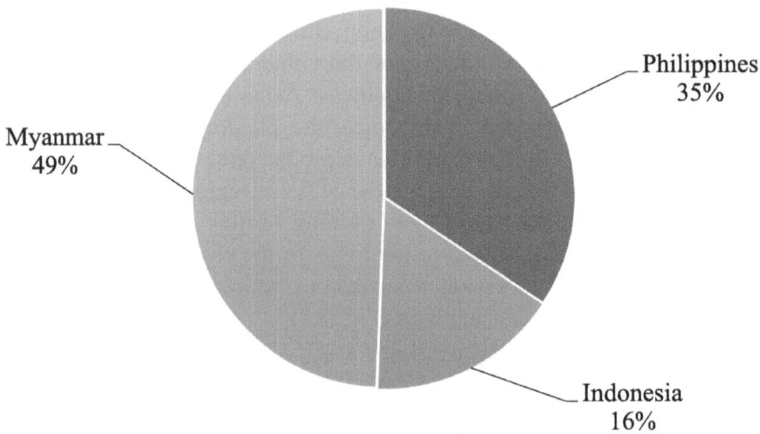

Fig. 7.3 Top three origins of migrant workers in Southeast Asia. *Source* ADBI et al. [2]

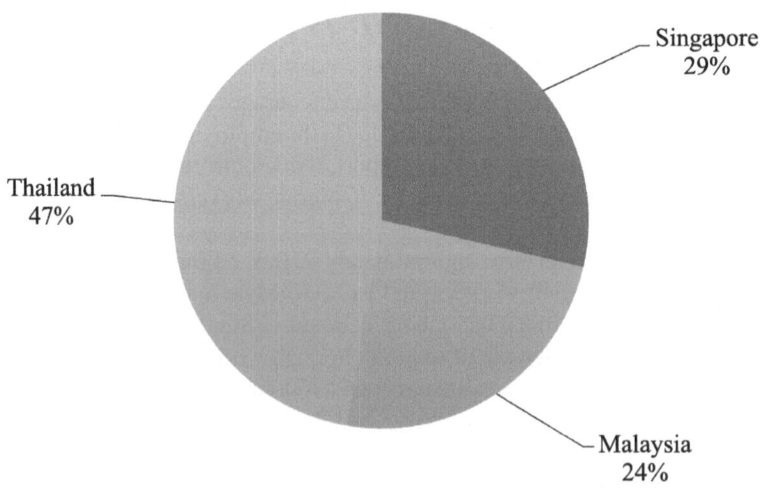

Fig. 7.4 Top three destinations of migrant workers in Southeast Asia. *Source* ILO [37]

The coronavirus pandemic has an impact on reducing employment, both in the formal and informal sectors, which will significantly increase the number of poor people in Southeast Asia. Based on a UNESCAP report, the coronavirus crisis disrupted the employment and income of 218 million informal workers, estimated to account for 51–90% of the subregion's nonagricultural national working population [65]. According to the data, Southeast Asian economies have been rattled by the pandemic, primarily on poverty indicators and welfare, particularly among vulnerable and informal workers. Intraregional migrant workers are among the toughest segments of society and face extreme socioeconomic pressures [53]. Migrant workers, as a vulnerable subgroup, frequently ignore protection under government decisions, they are assigned hard tasks with harmful working and living conditions [8]. The experience of migrant workers in Southeast Asian countries during the pandemic faced various difficult situations, such as termination of contracts, reduction of working days and wages, unemployed and unable to achieve benefits from social security [36].

During the pandemic, many workers in the main destination countries (Singapore, Thailand, and Malaysia) did not receive overtime pay. Overtime losses are primarily experienced by female workers in the domestic sector (Singapore), as well as migrant workers in the construction sector (Malaysia) and workers in the manufacturing sector (Thailand) [37]. The various wage cuts are intended to cover additional costs that employers have incurred during the COVID-19 pandemic. In Thailand, employers argue that the proceeds from wage deductions will be allocated to social security and workers' paperwork costs. In Malaysia, salary cuts for migrant workers are mentioned for the accommodation costs of workers and the cost of COVID-19 tests. This condition is further exacerbated by a decrease in monthly wages. In Thailand, the average wage for migrant workers fell from US$299 to US$253; US$420 to US$343 in Malaysia; and US$982 to US$750 in Singapore [37]. Reducing migrant workers' wages, of course, has a systemic impact on the families and countries of origin of migrant workers who rely on remittances to send workers abroad.

The coronavirus outbreak is resulting in more than just a public health emergency; moreover, it is causing a financial recession that negatively affects global economic activity [18, 60]. Several policies implemented during the COVID-19 pandemic, such as restricting community activities and closing borders, slowed the economy and disrupted regional activities. Although these policies help the government minimize the spread of the coronavirus, they have a significant effect on economic productivity, affecting business people, industry, companies, and migrant workers [77]. Due to each country's lockdown policies, the majority of migrant workers in Southeast Asia were laid off unilaterally and forced to accept lower wages during the coronavirus outbreak. It has been reported that by 2020, the number of migrant workers between Southeast Asian countries will have decreased by 75% [2]. Given the significant contribution that migrant workers made to maintaining national economic stability during the COVID-19 pandemic, worker mobility and safety were critical during the pandemic. The reduction in working hours and the lack of job opportunities are caused by restrictions on migrant workers' mobility and stigmatization as a group

Table 7.1 Flows of workers in Southeast Asian countries

	Philippines	Indonesia	Myanmar
Total 2019	220.972	104.666	317.330
Total 2020	42.943	20.306	69.364

Source ADBI et al. [2]

that can create new clusters of coronavirus spread, thereby causing fear among job providers.

Table 7.1 illustrates how the coronavirus pandemic unexpectedly disrupted the supply chain of migrant labourers in Southeast Asia. Three of the largest migrant worker distributors (the Philippines, Indonesia and Myanmar) saw a significant decline in stock in 2019–2020. However, the coronavirus disease outbreak possesses direct effects not only on the reduced supply of migrant workers and lower wages but also on work safety and access to health services, both of which are severely limited in destination countries. The pandemic situation has increased the health risks for migrant workers even further. In general, many migrant workers do not have employer-provided health insurance [39]. Additionally, they have limited opportunities to routinely wash their hands and receive safety equipment, including shields. Moreover, a workplace does not comply with the social distancing protocol [41]. A lack of access to preventive and responsive health services is a key factor leading to the rising rate of coronavirus infections in many migrant workers [1, 4, 43].

In Singapore, for example, the vulnerability of migrant workers' safety is caused by disproportionate policies that ignore the interests and rights of migrant workers. The Singapore government is still considered to exclude migrant workers. That case can be seen from the virus's outbreak in migrant worker dorms, which are overcrowded due to the lack of accommodation and protection for migrant workers [68]. Over the pandemic's early phase in Singapore, most workers (47%) were infected with the COVID-19 virus [43]. One of the reasons for the presence of migrant worker clusters in Singapore is the cramped conditions of migrant workers' dormitories [55]. The magnitude of the risk of disease transmission correlates with overcrowding in dormitories and the lack of sufficient infrastructure for migrant workers' health and well-being, such as ventilation, shared facilities and sleeping spaces [26, 66]. There were 200,000 migrant workers in 43 dormitories as of early April 2020 [25]. Singapore's failure to prevent COVID-19 transmission among migrant workers contributed to an increase in coronavirus infections at the earliest stages of the coronavirus pandemic wave.

COVID-19 virus spread in Singapore is classified into two groups based on the source of the virus's spread: imports and non-imports. Imported cases are transmissions that originate from groups who have travelled from abroad, whereas nonimported cases are transmissions that originate from groups of people living in the country who do not travel from abroad, such as Singaporeans, workers who do not live in dormitories, and workers who do live in dormitories. Figure 7.5 [46] illustrates that in the first wave of the pandemic, migrant labourers living in dormitories became a vulnerable group to coronavirus exposure. It is estimated that the virus

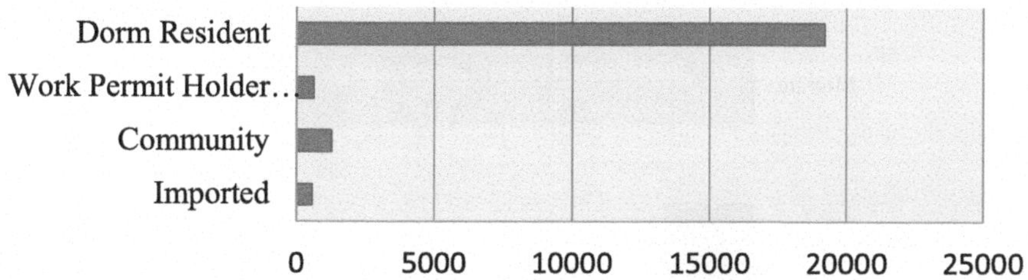

	Imported	Community	Work Permit Holder not Residing in Dorms	Dorm Resident
■ Number of Covid-19 Cases in Singapore During March-May	579	1272	624	19232

Fig. 7.5 Coronavirus cases in Singapore from March to May 2020. *Source* Koh [46]

has infected approximately 88% of workers in the dormitory. This figure is very high when compared to the other three groups, which are the general public (6%), imported cases (3%), and nondormitory workers (3%). The wide spread of the coronavirus among workers living in dormitories demonstrates that the conditions of migrant workers are frequently subordinated and escape the attention of the state, increasing migrant workers' vulnerability in the workplace.

During the early stages of the COVID-19 outbreak, employees in Singapore were quarantined (April–June), which may have been a negative experience for workers who live in dormitories, as well as disproportionate risk management by the Singapore government. Similarly, when the Thai government closed all land access in early 2020 to combat virus transmission, a large number of migrant workers were stranded at the border [33]. Border closures prevent migrant workers from entering Thailand as well as Thai workers from returning home. As a result of these conditions, over 90,000 people have been housed in nine shelters along the Thai-Myanmar border [65]. The vulnerability of migrant workers' safety and security in Thailand is exacerbated by the Thai government's "bubble" policy. The "bubble policy" is a method of preventing the spread of the coronavirus by detaining migrant workers in the workplace or worker's dormitory [75]. As of July 31, 2021, migrant workers accounted for approximately 24% of the disease's spread in Thailand. When compared to Thailand's indigenous population (7 per 1,000 people), the number of migrant workers exposed to COVID-19 is three times higher (24 per 1,000 people) [2, 76] (see Fig. 7.6).

The bubble and seal method is intended to limit migrant workers' mobility in Thailand. This approach is frequently used for migrant labourers in the industries of manufacturing and construction. The employer controls the various activities and needs of migrant workers so that they remain in the work location and dormitories, also known as "bubble areas" [70]. Simultaneously, the "bubble and seal" locking

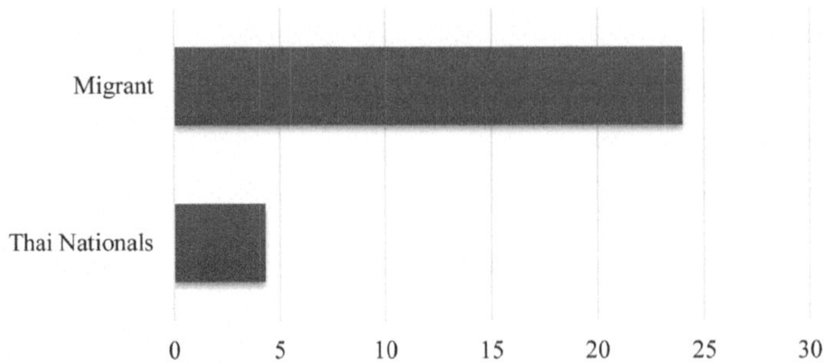

Fig. 7.6 Number of COVID-19 cases per thousand persons in Thailand, Juli 2021. *Source* ADBI et al. [2], WHO [76]

method was implemented in all factory locations and migrant worker dormitories in Thailand in August 2021. However, according to the Migrant Working Group [52], policies that use the "bubble and seal" method exacerbate migrant workers' conditions. Some migrant workers who live in bubble areas do not have enough food. Workers are not permitted to travel for groceries, receive medical treatment, or live in crowded conditions with inadequate hygiene [11, 74]. The government even installed barbed wire in the locking area to restrict worker movement [2]. The Thai government's lockdown has the potential to violate migrant workers' rights. Although the objective of restricting the transmission of the coronavirus and safeguarding the public's safety is admirable, it is not carried out well and has consequences for worker safety. Isolating workers without adequate support facilities puts them in perilous situations, increasing their risk of disease infection.

Malaysia, like Singapore and Thailand, as migrant worker destinations in Southeast Asia, has implemented restrictions on migrant worker mobility by sealing migrant worker dormitories. When it is discovered that a worker has been exposed to the virus or has tested positive for COVID-19, the workers' confinement will be extended until the dormitory is declared virus-free [2]. In the long term, the Malaysian government's implementation of the movement control order (MCO) policy is considered to have worsened the conditions of migrant workers (Fig. 7.7).

Malaysia's border-locking policy to stop the spread of coronavirus invasion raised questions about the welfare of migrant workers [16]. Malaysia's movement control

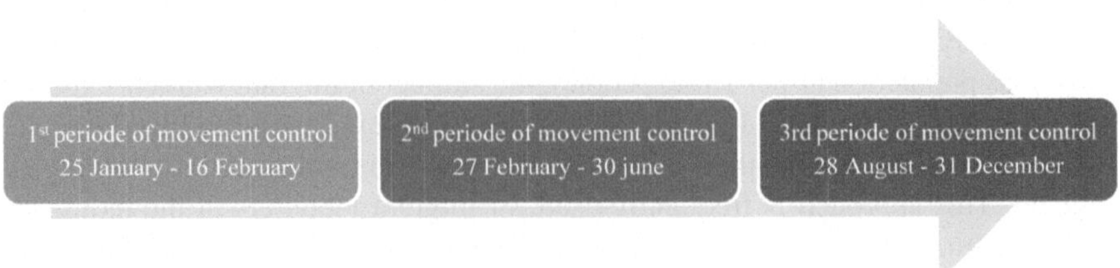

Fig. 7.7 Movement control order's timeline in 2020. *Source* Wahab [73]

policy confines migrant workers in dormitories with disproportionate accommodation, increasing the number of positive coronavirus infection cases among workers [73]. Many workers were denied permission to work during the MCO's implementation [51]. Some were granted work permits, but only for a few days per month. Such conditions, of course, have an impact on worker income, which has decreased dramatically, especially since the MCO is implemented in stages rather than all at once. The sealing and restrictions on worker movement in dormitories also make it difficult for workers to send money to families in their hometowns, which has implications for the condition of migrant workers' families who are fighting the COVID-19 pandemic without a main source of income. According to the IOM report, the COVID-19 pandemic has harmed developing countries, where the majority of citizens rely heavily on remittances from family members working abroad [65].

Furthermore, border closures and lockdowns in several Southeast Asian countries have resulted in mass deportations of migrant workers. Deportation represents the culmination of migrant labourers' vulnerability in the coronavirus pandemic era. Deportation is a systemic effect of destination countries imposing social restrictions without considering the presence of migrant workers. Several industrial sectors were forced to close or halt production due to restrictions and lockdowns. The closure of manufacturing plants forced migrant workers to remain at home, unsure when they would return to work. The main reasons for the mass repatriation of migrant labourers to their home country are a lack of job opportunities and the stigma that workers are the source of the virus's spread. Since the coronavirus pandemic, many migrant labourers in Southeast Asia have returned home due to border closures and lockdown policies. Cambodia, Lao People's Democratic Republic, Myanmar, and Indonesia are the supplying countries for nearly 500,000 workers who have returned from their destination countries. Many migrant workers return to their home countries due to deportation or job loss [41]. Furthermore, the repatriation of migrant workers or those who have been deported endangers the conditions of the workers, particularly those in temporary shelters or detention, as happened in Sabah, Malaysia.

The detention of migrant workers and their families in Malaysia's Sabah region is deemed a violation of migrant worker handling and safety standards. Both the Malaysian and Indonesian governments are accused of failing to accommodate migrant workers' interests at the border. Due to complicated deportation procedures, undocumented migrant workers face prolonged detention at the Temporary Detention Center, or Immigration Depot, in Sabah, Malaysia, rather than immediate repatriation to Indonesia. The Indonesian government's decision to inform the authorities in Sabah to postpone deportation due to a lack of funds to receive migrants by complying with COVID-19 handling procedures in the Nunukan border area also hampered immediate repatriation. The deportees were tortured for longer in the Temporary Detention Center, which had been a long-standing issue [44].

The detention of migrant workers in Sabah for an extended period increases the number of cases exposed to COVID-19 among migrant workers. Cases in Sabah have quadrupled since September 2020. As of the end of September, there were 1,386 migrant workers infected with COVID-19, which tripled to 5,493 people by mid-October, and the cumulative amount of coronavirus infection in Sabah reached

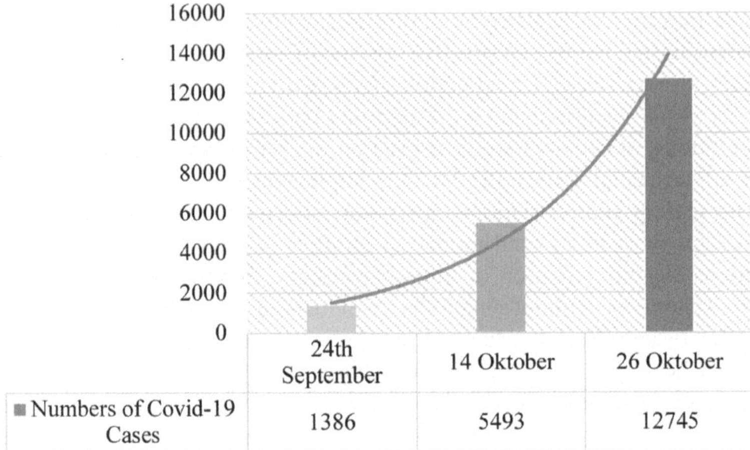

Fig. 7.8 Number of COVID-19 cases in Sabah 2020. *Source* Susilo [68]

12,745 at the end of October (see Fig. 7.8). Moreover, the conditions of detention facilities that are inappropriate for migrant workers have resulted in the emergence of acute skin disease, namely, Norwegian scabies (scabies), which is very easy to spread. Inadequate facilities in detention centres exacerbate deportees' physical and mental health conditions. Several detainees also reported becoming ill and dying without access to medical care [68].

7.3.2 Southeast Asian Countries' Transnational Mitigation Cooperation Mechanism on Migrant Worker Issues

Labour migration activities in the Southeast Asian region are important in opening up connectivity opportunities for regional member countries, in addition to contributing to economic development. This is a "soft" infrastructure that enables citizens to interact and form an international network, suggesting that the safeguards of migrant labourers through the establishment of transnational mitigation must be a primary concern for countries in the region. During COVID-19, countries in many regions or regions are more likely to implement unilateral policies and close their borders. Even the European Union, as one of the more established regions, is not completely integrated into attempting to address the pandemic problem [61]. Due to the significance of worker migration in the Southeast Asian region, the topic of migrant worker governance cannot be avoided in the study of regional political economy. To establish conducive conditions for migrant workers' movement and activities in the region, cooperative policymaking on the matter of migrant workers is needed. The IOM migration governance framework can be applied to determine the extent to which transnational mitigation has been established in Southeast Asian country

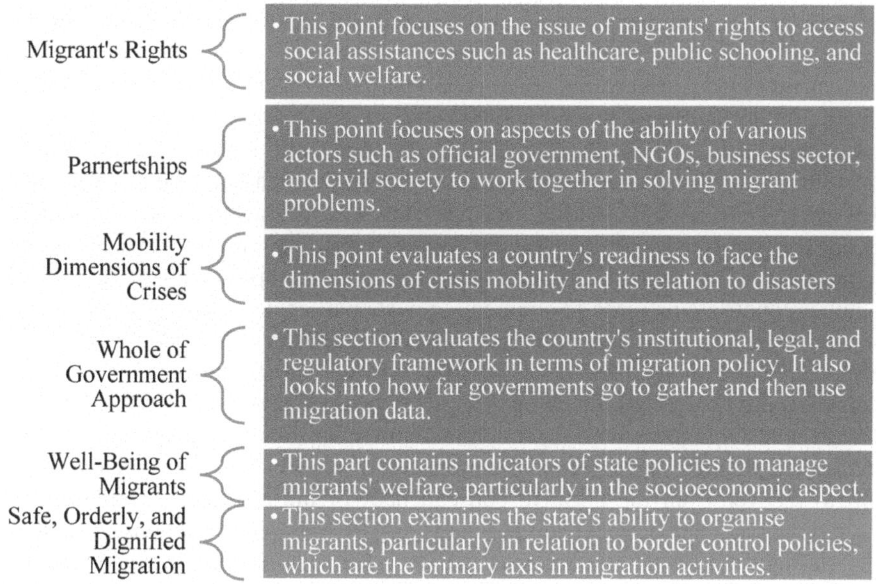

Fig. 7.9 Migration governance framework. *Source* IOM [42], Srinivas and Sivaraman [65]

relations, especially during the time of pandemic crisis. Migrants' rights; Partnerships; Mobility Dimensions of the Crisis; Whole-of-Government Approach; Migrant Well-Being; Safe, orderly, and dignified There are six important points in regulating migration activities [42, 65]. The framework focuses on the advancement of SDGs, which includes a call for improved migration management. The Migration Governance Framework is pertinent to the topic of standards for migrant worker protection in various countries and regions, and it can be used to examine the seriousness of a country or region in efforts to resolve migrant worker problems (Fig. 7.9).

ASEAN Forum on Migrant Labor (AFML): Institutions Integrating and Migrant Worker' Rights Protection. The magnitude of the coronavirus outbreak's impact on remittance income in Southeast Asian countries has encouraged member countries to work together to solve the problems of migrant workers. Workers' rights protection in the pandemic era is the starting point for all stakeholders (state, civil society, and private) to demonstrate their seriousness in paying attention to migrant workers' circumstances within the framework of migration governance. ASEAN member countries agreed to hold a "Declaration of the Special ASEAN Summit on Coronavirus Disease 2019" that will be issued in mid-2020 as part of an attempt to address issues raised by member nations throughout the coronavirus pandemic. However, the declaration does not fully address the consequences of the pandemic on the migrant workforce, which is the most vulnerable group [68]. Member countries focus more on technical issues and at least discuss issues of crisis and vulnerable groups in the pandemic era in an integrated manner.

During the pandemic's early stages (middle of 2020), there was fear in the region as the virus spread and had an impact on workers' rights. However, in the subsequent periods, there was some developing consensus among several stakeholders in the Southeast Asian region to voice concern for the circumstances and vulnerabilities of migrant labourers during the pandemic period. One of them is the 13th ASEAN Forum on Migrant Labor (AFML), which will take place in mid-November 2020. AFML focuses on improving migrant labourers' circumstances in the pandemic era and encouraging a more collective and attentive Southeast community. AFML provides a coordination forum for all representatives of ASEAN member countries' national governments, private parties, trade unions or organizations, civil society organizations (CSOs), ASEAN Employers' Confederation (AEC), ASEAN Trade Union Council (ATUC), ASEAN Services Employees Trade Union Council (ASETUC), Task Force on ASEAN Migrant Workers (TFAMW), International Labor Organization (ILO), International Organization for Migration (IOM), and United Nations. AFML emphasizes the significance of binding regulations that aim to recover from the negative consequences of the coronavirus outbreak on migrant workers and employment providers in ASEAN member nations. Additionally, during the COVID-19 pandemic, AFML prioritizes meeting the requirements of female migrant workers. Furthermore, AFML recommends a variety of actions that ASEAN member countries should take to reduce the effect of the pandemic on migrant workers.

There are several mitigation points among the twelve points set by AFML that target the issue or concentrate on protecting the rights of migrant workers, including the first point, which asks countries receiving and supplying migrant workers to guarantee that all migrant workers get access to medical care, such as coronavirus cure, screening, and urgent aid measures, as well as social security. Furthermore, the second point emphasizes that parties must improve salvation and sanity standards in the work area and housing offered by employers, including sanitation, welfare living conditions and personal safety equipment, as a safety precaution to decrease the risk of coronavirus infection involving migrant labourers. Moreover, in the third point, through an effective complaint system and support services, AFML emphasizes the economic fulfilment of workers' rights by setting adequate compensation for workers and sustaining their income during the pandemic. The 13th ASEAN Forum on Migrant Labor encourages Southeast Asian states, including origins and destination countries, to establish good, coordinated mitigation strategies.

The special conference of ASEAN ministers for the field and development emphasized ASEAN member nations' commitment to decreasing the pandemic's impact on migrant workers. The committee decided on seven important aspects to reduce the harmful effects of the pandemic and accelerate recovery for ASEAN's poorest and most vulnerable groups, including social protection facilities and social spending; protection of migrant workers' rights, security, and honour; and ensuring the health and safety of workers, particularly social workers. Development of a complete and integrated post-COVID rehabilitation program; ASEAN member countries are all-embracing technology and addressing digital issues [3].

Furthermore, the Joint Statement of the ASEAN Ministers of Manpower regarding the reaction to the consequence of the pandemic is also evidence of joint mitigation efforts between countries in the Southeast Asian region to reduce the impact of the pandemic on migrant workers. A joint statement by the ASEAN Ministers of Manpower promised support for migrant workers both in terms of economic support and health services. The ASEAN Ministers of Manpower Joint Statement document includes nine strategic steps, ASEAN [6]: Migrant workers encountered several challenges during the COVID-19 pandemic, including the loss of their primary source of income and the risk of workplace safety. Aid is required to assure remuneration and unemployment benefits from employment agencies or government social assistance. Give employees equal access to crucial medical services and assistance. Providing help and support to ASEAN migrant workers who are repatriated to their home countries; increasing the efficacy of labour market policy at the national and regional levels; using digital technology as a complaint medium for employees; improving public information and communication services about worker conditions in the pandemic era; increasing collaboration between stakeholders in carrying out post-pandemic recovery plans; and, finally, the establishment of a dialogue forum about ASEAN member countries' experiences in efforts to strengthen worker and job provider resilience.

The involvement of AFML, in addition to a joint statement by ASEAN Ministries, demonstrates that Southeast Asian countries are competent to organize regional cooperation to handle the negative consequences of the pandemic in the region. Although each country was not integrated and was busy with domestic concerns that tended to shut down in the early days of the pandemic, in the end, ASEAN member countries were able to work together to solve pandemic problems and even establish a recovery framework upon entering the post-pandemic era.

ASEAN Comprehensive Recovery Framework (ACRF). ASEAN, as a coordination forum for Southeast Asian countries, has established a collective and long-term recovery strategy for socioeconomic situations, known as the ASEAN Comprehensive Recovery Framework (ACRF). ACRF is present as a member country response to the necessity of recovering from post-COVID-19 regional circumstances, especially in strategic sectors and segmentation of the most impacted populations per the regional agenda. Through ACFR, Southeast Asian countries focus on five strategies: increasing the healthcare system's quality; enhancing human security; optimizing market opportunity in Southeast Asia and expanding economic cooperation; accelerating the aspect of inclusive digital transformation; and seeking a sustainable and resilient future [5].

ACRF provides five key elements for ASEAN member nations to consider as they attempt to restore the post-COVID Southeast Asia region's status. ACRF is a shared resource for ASEAN countries seeking to reduce the consequences of the COVID-19 epidemic. The elements in the ACRF are the primary precondition for launching regional recovery efforts and supporting the existence of coordinated policies among ASEAN member nations to help restore normal circumstances before the COVID-19 epidemic. The prevalence of ACRF in migrant workers' issues is likely to reduce the

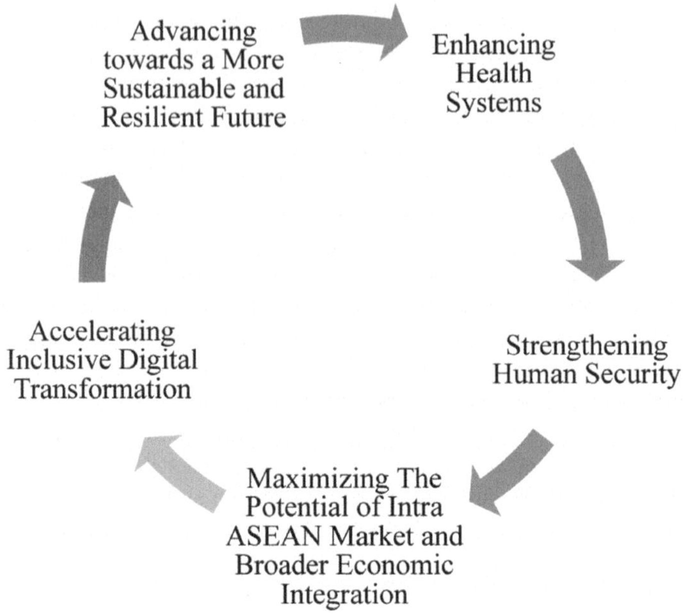

Fig. 7.10 ASEAN comprehensive recovery framework. *Source* ASEAN [5]

presence of migrant worker clusters while increasing unemployment owing to the COVID-19 pandemic (Fig. 7.10).

As a first step, enhancing the health system in the ASEAN Comprehensive Recovery Framework is a starting point for the region's recovery in the post-COVID era. Healthcare strengthening in the ACRF is a strategy component that prioritizes improving vital health services, including vaccination programs, strengthening health human resources, and sustaining nutrition in a crisis. The majority of the ACRF's health system strengthening is concentrated on infrastructural facilities. Meanwhile, important considerations such as strategic priorities to address mental health issues remain unresolved. Regional mental health concerns must be a priority for ASEAN member countries to return regional circumstances to normal. This is due to several issues during the pandemic that rendered mental health sensitive to stress.

The second strategic step is strengthening human security. Human security in the pandemic era is very important to discuss, particularly in the aspect of migrant labourers as the most disadvantaged group. Human security includes livelihood issues, which include job availability and work environment security. The magnitude of the consequences of the pandemic on labour in the Southeast Asia region has put migrant workers at risk of falling into poverty due to the declining demand for labour supply. In addition, the unpredictable spread of the virus poses a threat to workers in the work environment, so establishing workplace health and safety standards in the pandemic era needs to be formulated. It is at the point of strengthening human security that labour migration policies to protect migrant workers during pandemics and other crises are discussed. Strengthening human security is an important point to encourage the birth of a consensus at the ASEAN regional level on ensuring the welfare of migrant workers.

The third strategic step is optimizing market opportunity in Southeast Asia and expanding economic cooperation. Considering that post-pandemic recovery efforts require more trade, the third point is here to focus on increasing cross-ASEAN economic cooperation activities. This point is an effort to maximize the ASEAN Free Trade Area policy and the ASEAN Economic Community consensus that had previously been implemented before the pandemic era. However, the opening of a competitive market as a step to strengthen the region in the post-COVID era must be accompanied by policies that guarantee the condition of migrant workers as subjects in the market mechanism. This is done to minimize exploitative market mechanisms.

Efforts to increase economic power through regional markets are then continued with the digitization of market mechanisms. The opening of regional markets with digital media is the focus of discussion on the fourth point in the ACRF. The digital transformation that is inclusive of ASEAN member countries is considered capable of increasing the opportunities for economic recovery for regional communities in the post-COVID era [56]. This is because the use of digital technology has grown very rapidly in almost all regions of the ASEAN. The confidence of ASEAN member countries in the positive impact of digital economic transformation is manifested in the framework of regulating digital trade activities, such as the establishment of an ASEAN e-commerce coordination committee, which promotes an inclusive and integrative digital economy. If the governments of ASEAN member countries dare to accommodate digital skills training for workers, especially digital-based MSME management skills, this could be an alternative space for employees who were laid during the outbreak period.

Furthermore, the last strategy in the ASEAN Comprehensive Recovery Framework seeks to synergize the sustainable development model with increasing the resilience of ASEAN post-pandemic economic development. ASEAN member countries seek to encourage policy-making that represents the points in the concept of SDGs that include finance, industry, agriculture, infrastructure improvements, emergency management and long-term finance. The change in the development paradigm in the post-COVID era is expected to be able to encourage the improvement of the conditions of migrant workers who, historically, have often been excluded and even become victims of the development agenda. The ASEAN Comprehensive Recovery Framework is a symbol of the solidarity spirit of regional member countries in guarding the problems that arise due to the COVID-19 pandemic. In addition, as guidelines, the ACRFcano integrates the recovery of conditions in the post-COVID Southeast Asia region.

7.3.3 The Post-COVID Transformative Agenda and Future of Migrant Workers

Southeast Asia has gradually recovered from the coronavirus outbreak. For most migrant workers, post-pandemic and reconstruction have not promised a prosperous future. The COVID-19 pandemic has become one of the world's most serious humanitarian concerns. However, the crisis scenario presents an opportunity to begin the process of establishing a more effective and integrated worker migration governance framework among Southeast Asia countries. Due to the various vulnerabilities experienced by migrant workers leading up to and during the COVID-19 pandemic crisis, governments from relevant countries (origin and destination) in the region should strengthen intraregional cooperation to achieve stronger systemic protection for migrant workers, as well as effective implementation and strengthen the resilience of post-COVID-19 migrant workers. Better labour standards will result in a more resilient labour market, particularly during times of crisis [40]. To establish a transformative agenda and ensure the protection of post-COVID-19 migratory workers, it is crucial to reflect on the policies adopted by both host and home countries throughout the pandemic.

Connectivity between countries in the Southeast Asia region was tested during the COVID-19 pandemic. If we reflect on the policies implemented by Southeast Asian countries, there is a tendency for each country to focus only on domestic countermeasures without any policy synchronization on a regional scale. Attempting the rebuilding process, countries in the region need to carry out reforms in various sectors, including the labourer migration system and strengthening the safeguarding of migrant workers' interests. The resumption of migration will be a significant component in stimulating development provided mobility is secure and equitable and fundamental rights and international labour standards are respected. Several transformative agenda should be pushed and brought out through Southeast Asian nations in the post-COVID-19 transition period, including reforming the migration system, strengthening job security, protecting wages, improving work systems, and social dialogue (Fig. 7.11).

Migration System Reform. The recovery and strengthening of the position of migrant workers after COVID-19 need to be carried out comprehensively and fundamentally by improving the international migration system in the region. One of them is the region's efforts to decrease illegal migration, such as establishing official labour migration routes more accessible and affordable. The rebuilding effort requires increasing the effectiveness of official and legal channels to reduce the practice of illegal migration. Based on the ILO's 2020 report, it was found that among migrant workers in Thailand, especially those from Cambodia and Myanmar, only 3% migrated through regular routes [35]. Expensive labour migration processes, as well as onerous paperwork processing and delayed methods, lead migrant workers to prefer entering Thailand lawfully through brokers, who are perceived to be less expensive and more practical.

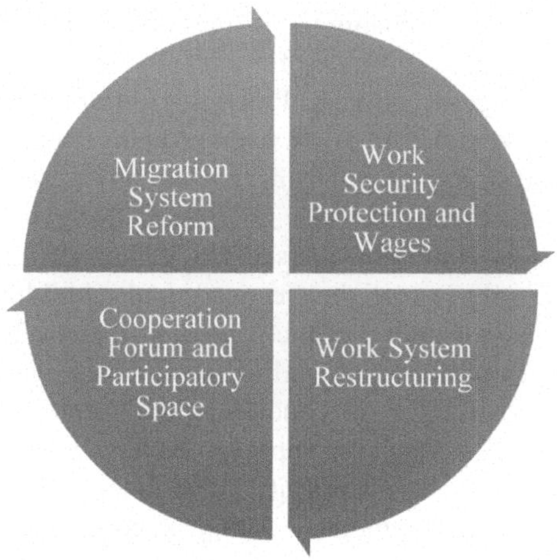

Fig. 7.11 Post-COVID transformative agenda. *Source* Processed by Authors

The general mechanism is thought to be complex, time-consuming, and costly when compared to the alternative of accessing Thailand illegally through a less stringent border. This is not only bad for the state but also has a direct and long-term impact on the safety of migrant workers. Migrant workers who enter the destination country illegally have lower wages and disadvantaged working circumstances and are significantly likely to be subjected to workplace abuses of basic principles and rights. Furthermore, migrant workers frequently spend more hours each week with no days off.

Worker migration can be encouraged per labour market demands, and governmental routes should be simplified to decrease the time and expenses borne by prospective migrant workers [1]. Migrant workers' interests must be protected without compromising states' authority in governing their borders. The International Labor Organization (ILO) Migrant Workers Agreement (Supplemental Provisions) 1975 (No. 143) outlined all essential steps to minimize the rate of unlawful migration, including punishment of labour service providers and renters. Furthermore, the migrant employee agreement has secured all migrant workers' rights to remuneration payments, social security and the ability to ask for compensation for income disputes [1].

Work Security Protection and Wages. Migrant workers have disproportionately experienced unemployment during the coronavirus pandemic. To guarantee that upcoming catastrophes will not have the same consequences as job loss without compensation, destination countries must implement legal and policy changes that guarantee migrant workers' fair treatment in terms of work security. According to ILO about worldwide worker protections, migrant workers should not face discrimination if measures to reduce the labour force are implemented. Migrant workers who are fired do not immediately lose their residency or work visas; however, they should be given enough time to seek job opportunities.

The establishment of rules and standard operating procedures in the workplace, especially in times of crisis, is also an important indicator in securing the future of migrant workers. Reflecting on the early days of the pandemic, when migrant workers had to work without being equipped with personal protective equipment and strict protocols, migrant workers were placed in conditions that were vulnerable to outbreaks.

In addition to job security guarantees, the right to wage protection is also a top priority in realizing recovery and rebuilding in the labour sector. Ratification and implementation of the Migrants' Income Safety Declaration 1949 (No. 95) should indeed be emphasized to strengthen wage protection for migrant workers. Agreement number 95 concerning bankruptcy, particularly in times of crisis, involves that if a company/employer declares bankruptcy, the payment of migrant workers' wages must take priority. Governments are indeed mandated to guarantee prompt and complete payment, including all compensation owed in the event of job termination. This is necessary to reduce the impact felt by migrant workers when they are laid off. The agreement also states that foreign employees have the right to salaries earned in legal cash at frequent intervals and that if they receive a portion of their earnings in kind, the products must be calculated reasonably and equitably so that the migrant workers benefit.

In Southeast Asia, only the Philippines and Singapore had already formally adopted agreement No. 95. The coronavirus outbreak crisis has become a culmination for other countries in the region to be encouraged to participate in ratifying the agreement. This pandemic also highlights the importance of effective complaint mechanisms to provide access to remedies for migrant workers who experience wage violations. All migrant workers, including those in vulnerable situations such as losing their jobs, especially in times of crisis, should enjoy equal treatment with respect to rights such as compensation, social protection (particularly in the case of work-related accidents), and other advantages. These interests are formalized in the International Labor Organization (ILO) Declaration No. 143 and Recommendation No. 151. However, only the Philippines, as an ASEAN member, has formally adopted declaration No. 143.

As stipulated in the ILO Salary Setting Agreement 1970, basic income is an important indicator for protecting migrant workers from underpaid wages and preventing employers from exploiting workers (No. 131). As one of the destination countries, Malaysia formally adopted agreement number 131 and implemented a min salary arrangement. In addition to Malaysia, Thailand already has a national minimum wage system [2]. However, it should be emphasized that certain workers, such as those in the domestic sector, are usually exempt from min salary arrangements [39]. The minimum wage system must be broadly enforced to encompass all industries that use migrant workers and to guarantee that it is applied equally, especially in moments of emergency, such as the coronavirus outbreak.

Work System Restructuring. Migrant workers often experience discrimination at almost every stage, starting from pre-departure, through the working period, and upon going to their home countries. During the employment period, migrant workers must receive the same treatment as domestic workers and be in line with the standards of treatment for migrant workers that have been set by International Labor Migrants. Improvements in the work system need to be integrated into attempts to restore migrant workers' circumstances after the pandemic given the many rights violations experienced by migrant workers during times of crisis. The experience of migrant workers during the pandemic shows the need for stricter regulations and enforcement in realizing the circumstances of workers in Southeast Asia. Migrant workers' vulnerability during COVID-19 has prompted the need to improve the work system. A proportional work system can reduce the vulnerability faced by migrant workers during a pandemic crisis. For example, before the coronavirus outbreak, most destination countries used a two-tier or bifurcated system as a working system [31]. In actuality, the bifurcated system solely considers the circumstances of professional employees and overlooks the low-income sector. The presence of low-wage employees is sometimes regarded as incapable of overcoming the receiving nation's skills issue; on the other hand, professional workers are seen to be capable of promoting and imparting their abilities to the recipient country. Low-wage labour is one of the reasons for domestic unemployment in nations that send migrant workers. This viewpoint reflects the impact of the implementation of a two-tier system in labour migration activities, which continues to confuse the roles of professional workers and low-wage workers, implying that restructuring the work system of migrant workers must be carried out as a transformative agenda post-COVID-19.

Furthermore, the pandemic era has led to new rules and limitations on migrant worker movement, which, if not effectively handled, can raise the expenses of migration and migrant worker recruitment [34]. Each Southeast Asian country must implement regional policies to control migration costs, particularly during the COVID-19 crisis. That complies with the International Labor Organization's Private Recruitment Companies Agreement (No. 181) and the ILO Legal Concepts and Institutional Standards for Equitable Employment and the Classification of Salaries and Associated Costs and is intended to ensure that migrant workers do not bear these costs. According to ILO agreement No. 181, recruiting companies may not charge migrant employees a fee. The International Labor Organization unequivocally states that no enrolment payments or related costs should be passed on to workers or job applicants. The expenditures in question include, among other things, medical expenses, insurance premiums, travel expenses and accommodation costs, which might plausibly be read to involve COVID-19 screening, vaccines, and isolation fees. To prevent the collection of fees that would affect migrant workers, the terms of these fees must be expressly regulated.

Through the Ministry of Manpower in July 2020, Indonesia, as one of Southeast Asia's primary labour suppliers, recognized and defined the necessity of labour migration for economic recovery by prioritizing workers' recruitment in the post-COVID phase. The provision says that prospective and migratory employees cannot be penalized as a consequence of the adoption of safety standards, including payments for COVID-19 testing and quarantines [40]. In addition to Indonesia, the Philippines is also a country in Southeast Asia that has issued temporary guidelines regarding the cost of coronavirus tests and isolates for migrant workers. According to the guides, employment agencies or companies of migrant workers have to establish coronavirus screening and subsidize the costs of isolation, such as nourishment, diagnostic testing, and healthcare. During the isolation period, employees end up leaving earnings cannot be utilized. Nevertheless, based on the rules, employment agencies as well as business owners are also not mandated to cover workers' wages while they are sequestered.

The International Labor Organization (ILO), an international organization that regulates the protection and rights of migrant workers, expressly states that the meaning of Allowances and Associated Expenses acknowledges that the appropriate government possesses adaptability to establish fee classification exclusions, however, after consulting with the main relevant worker and employer organizations. Whatever exclusions must serve the best interests of the worker in question, limited to specific categories of employees and services, and communicated to workers before employment acceptance. The 1948 Employment Services Agreement number 88 further states that governmental assistance in the workplace must serve without charge. Under agreement No. 181, governments are also obligated to make efforts to offer appropriate protection and avoid the exploitation of migrant workers by private hiring agencies [40].

Cooperation Forum and Participatory Space. A comprehensive and implementable post-COVID-19 recovery for migrant workers can be achieved by involving all elements of society and policymakers at both the national and regional levels. Policies taken by a country will be right on target if they go through a participatory and transparent process. Policy making must be two-way by considering the interests of many stakeholders, such as migrant worker groups. Therefore, all efforts and transformative agenda can be maximally achieved if they are through a dialogue process as part of democratic principles. Social dialogue needs to be carried out by involving employers as service providers, workers' organizations, and the government to overcome inadequacies for worker safeguards. Improved collaborations are required to safeguard migrant workers' interests and involvement in the workplace during the post-COVID-19 recovery agenda, especially in vulnerable sectors where migrant workers historically have difficulty accessing their rights. In this case, ASEAN, as a regional organization, then takes an important role in mediating various policies and national interests of each country to guarantee migrant workers' welfare.

7.4 Conclusions, Recommendations and Future Work

This research shows that in a pandemic situation, migratory workers are the most disadvantaged category. Migrant workers' vulnerability is exacerbated by the policies of Southeast Asian countries that are considered disproportionate to breaking the chain of the spread of the coronavirus and the absence of transnational mitigation between countries to safeguard migrant workers' circumstances, as one of the strategic sectors in the political economy of a country. Each country is busy with domestic affairs and is not integrated regionally, so it does not show seriousness in dealing with migrant workers' issues and seems unresponsive. The efforts of ASEAN member countries in resolving the pandemic's effects on new migrant workers will be visible at the end of 2020 when the 13th ASEAN Forum on Migrant Labor (AFML) is held. Through AFML, the receiving and sending countries of migrant workers formulate 12 strategic steps to solve the problems of migrant workers, which include focusing on fulfilling migrant workers' rights and interests, improving economic conditions, and accessing medical care. AFML triggered the birth of solidarity among member countries of the region. This is proven by the existence of the ASEAN Comprehensive Recovery Framework (ACRF) as a guide in efforts to restore conditions in the Southeast Asian region in the post-pandemic era. AFML and ACRF have transnational mitigation strategies among ASEAN member countries and show that ASEAN can solve existing problems collectively, even though in the early stages, they were not connected and failed to build solidarity in southern countries.

The ongoing and unpredictability of the pandemic phenomenon, as well as the poor experiences of Southeast Asian countries at the start of the pandemic, were not integrated into significantly reducing the implications of the coronavirus outbreak on migrant workers. Migrant workers' governance in the pandemic era through transnational mitigation strategies is an issue that must be considered by professionals and academics. Therefore, the authors recommend several recommendations to resolve the vulnerability of migrants in times of crisis, including the government being encouraged to be able to provide proper dormitories for migrant workers with adequate facilities, especially in crises; providing protection facilities in transit areas or at the entrance of the border for departure; maximizing diplomacy between destination countries and origin countries to simplify the repatriation mechanism of deported migrant workers; and ending the approach that restricts the mobility of migrant workers in dealing with COVID-19. Regional cooperation between Southeast Asian countries is needed, which is embodied in texts or guidelines on the protection of migrant workers in times of crisis. Furthermore, as a recommendation for future work, an extensive study is needed that focuses not only on regional cooperation at the national level but also on other actors in the region, such as private companies and community organizations.

References

1. ADBI, OECD, & ILO (2021). Labour migration in Asia: impacts of the COVID-19 crisis and the post-pandemic future
2. ADBI, OECD, & ILO (2022) Labor migration In Asia: Covid-19 impacts, challenges, and policy responses
3. ASEAN (2020c) Joint statement of the Asean ministerial meeting on social welfare and development mitigating impacts of COVID-19 on vulnerable groups In Asean
4. ASEAN Parliamentarians for Human Rights (APHR) (2021) Press release: to tackle COVID-19 outbreaks, ASEAN MPs call for more inclusive policies for migrant workers
5. ASEAN (2020a) ASEAN comprehensive recovery framework

6. ASEAN (2020b) Joint statement of ASEAN labour ministers on response to the impact of coronavirus disease 2019 (COVID-19) on labour and employment
7. Abd Aziz SN, Basir SM (2022) Position of ICMW in ASEAN and a glimpse into the philippine practise on migration. Jurnal Hukum Volkgeist 6(2):123–128
8. Alahmad B, Kurdi H, Colonna K, Gasana J, Agnew J, Fox MA (2020) COVID-19 stressors on migrant workers in Kuwait: cumulative risk considerations. BMJ Glob Health 5(7):e002995
9. Amul GG, Ang M, Kraybill D, Ong SE, Yoong J (2022) Responses to COVID-19 in Southeast Asia: diverse paths and ongoing challenges. Asian Econ Policy Rev 17(1):90–110
10. Anaf A, Ibnu F, Romdiati H, Noveria M (2022) Indonesian migrant workers: the migration process and vulnerability to COVID-19. J Environ Public Health
11. Apisitniran L (2021) Factories adopt harsher bubble, seal measure. Bangkok Post. Bangkok Post. https://www.bangkokpost.com/business/2139975/factories-adopt-harsher-bubble-seal-measure
12. Azeez EP, A., Negi DP, Rani A, & AP, SK (2021) The impact of COVID-19 on migrant women workers in India. Eurasian Geogr Econ 62(1), 93–112
13. Bangun BH (2022) ASEAN's role in protecting migrant workers' rights during the Covid-19 pandemic. Pandecta Res Law J 17(1):50–57
14. Bretones FD (2020) Migrant workers, hazards and vulnerability. In Health, safety and well-being of migrant workers: new hazards, new workers. Springer, pp 9–22
15. Buckley P, Pietropaoli L, Rosada A, Harguth B, Broom J (2022) How has COVID-19 affected migrant workers vulnerability to human trafficking for forced labour in Southeast Asia?—a narrative review. J Pub Heal, Emerg, p 6
16. Carruthers AM (2020) Movement control and migration in Sabah in the time of COVID-19
17. Chan LG, Kuan B (2020) Mental health and holistic care of migrant workers in Singapore during the COVID-19 pandemic. J Global Health 10(2)
18. Chong TTL, Li X, Yip C (2021) The impact of COVID-19 on ASEAN. Econ Polit Stud 9(2):166–185
19. Choudhari R (2020) COVID 19 pandemic: mental health challenges of internal migrant workers of India. Asian J Psychiatr 54:102254
20. Chowdhury MB, Chakraborty M (2021) The impact of COVID-19 on the migrant workers and remittances flow to Bangladesh. South Asian Surv 28(1):38–56
21. Churski P, Kroczak H, Łuczak M, Shelest-Szumilas O, Woźniak M (2021) Adaptation strategies of migrant workers from Ukraine during the COVID-19 pandemic. Sustainability 13(15):8337
22. Creswell JW, Creswell JD (2017) Research design: qualitative, quantitative, and mixed methods approaches. Sage
23. Dancygier RM, Walter S (2015) Globalization, labor market risks, and class cleavages, in: P. Beramendi et al. (eds.), The politics of advanced capitalism, Cambridge University Press: Cambridge. Mass pp. 133–156
24. Dewi MK, Puspasari N, Khotimah S (2022) The human resources management process: domestic migrant workers perspective. Sustain Compet Adv (SCA), 11(1)
25. Djalante R, Nurhidayah L, Van Minh H, Phuong NTN, Mahendradhata Y, Trias A, Lassa J, Miller MA (2020) COVID-19 and ASEAN responses: comparative policy analysis. Progr Disast Sci 8:100129
26. Dutta MJ (2021) Singapore's extreme neoliberalism and the COVID outbreak: culturally centering voices of low-wage migrant workers. Am Behav Sci 65(10):1302–1322
27. Fassani F, Mazza J (2020) A vulnerable workforce: migrant workers in the COVID-19 pandemic. Publications Office of the European Union Luxembourg
28. Fauzi MA, Paiman N (2020) COVID-19 pandemic in Southeast Asia: intervention and mitigation efforts. Asian Education and Development Studies
29. Ferdous J, Ullah AKM (2022) Covid-19 and the migrant population: the resilience of South Asians. Int J Asia-Pacif Stud 18(2)
30. Ford M, Ward K (2021) COVID-19 in Southeast Asia: implications for workers and unions. J Ind Relat 63(3):432–450

31. Gerard K, Bal CS (2020) Labour migration in Southeast Asia: the political economy of poor and uneven governance. In: The political economy of Southeast Asia. Springer, pp 249–270
32. Hewison K, Young K (2006) Introduction: globalization and migrant workers in Asia. In: Transnational migration and work in Asia. Routledge, pp 15–26
33. ILO (2020a) COVID-19: Impact on migrant workers and country response in Thailand
34. ILO (2020b) Ensuring fair recruitment during the COVID-19 pandemic
35. ILO (2020c) Recruitment fees and related costs: what migrant workers from cambodia, the Lao People's democratic republic and Myanmar pay to work in Thailand
36. ILO (2020d) The migrant pay gap: Understanding wage differences between migrants and nationals
37. ILO (2021a) Experiences of ASEAN migrant workers during COVID-19: rights at work, migration during the pandemic, and remigration plans (Second assessment)
38. ILO (2021b) ILO global estimates on international migrant workers: result and methodology
39. ILO (2021c) Making decent work a reality for domestic workers: progress and prospects ten years after the adoption of the domestic worker, 2011 (no 189) convention
40. ILO (2021d) Recovery and labour migration in the post-pandemic future. International Labour Organization
41. ILO (2021e) Supporting migrant workers during the pandemic for a cohesive and responsive ASEAN Community Thematic background paper for the 13th ASEAN Forum on Migrant Labour
42. IOM (2019) Migration governance indicators: a global perspective. IOM
43. Illmer A (2020) COVID-19: Singapore migrant workers infections were three times higher. BBC News
44. KBMB (2020) Laporan Tim Pencari Fakta Tentang Kondisi Migran Indonesia yang Dideportasi Selama Masa Covid-19 dai Sabah, Malaysia ke Indonesia (Juni 2019–September2020)
45. Kamal S (2019) Research paradigm and the philosophical foundations of a qualitative study. PEOPLE: Int J Soc Sci 4(3):1386–1394
46. Koh D (2020) Migrant workers and COVID-19. Occup Environ Med 77(9):634–636
47. Kumar K, Mehra A, Sahoo S, Nehra R, Grover S (2020) The psychological impact of COVID-19 pandemic and lockdown on the migrant workers: a cross-sectional survey. Asian J Psychiatr 53:102252
48. Li J, Lim B, Pazim KH, Furuoka F (2021) COVID-19 pandemic's impact on the labour market in ASEAN countries. AEI INSIGHTS 7(1):59–76
49. Maksum A (2021) Indonesian post-migrant workers: a challenging problem for human security. Soc Sci Human Open 4(1):100223
50. Mattar SAM, Kan JYL, Goh OQM, Tan Y, Kumaran SS, Shum KL, Lee G, Balakrishnan T, Zhu L, Chong CJ (2022) COVID-19 pandemic unmasking cardiovascular risk factors and non-communicable diseases among migrant workers: a cross-sectional study in Singapore. BMJ Open 12(5):e055903
51. Mia MT, Putul SJ (2020) Covid-19 in Malaysia: protection of migrant workers in this pandemic situation. J Asian Afric Soc Sci Human 6(3):21–32
52. Migrant Working Group (MWG) (2021) Report on the situation of migrant workers amidst the pandemic and COVID-19 restriction measures focusing on Samut Sakhon from 19 December 2020–31 March 2021
53. Mishra DK (2021) Migrant labour during the Pandemic: a political economy perspective. Indian Econ J 69(3):410–424
54. Misra N (2007) The push & pull of globalization: How the global economy makes migrant workers vulnerable to exploitation. Human Rights Brief 14(3):1
55. Muhibat SF (2020) COVID-19 in Southeast Asia: 10 countries, 10 responses. CSIS Indonesia
56. Nasution MS, Handoko T, Rahmanto F, & Mayarni M (2023) Post-COVID tourism recovery strategy for tourism villages: Multi-stakeholder participatory approaches. J Contemp Govern Public Policy 4(2):131–148
57. Paitoonpong S (2011) Managing International Labor Migration in ASEAN: Thailand (Immigration). Philippine J Dev 38(1/2):163

58. Pal SC, Saha A, Chowdhuri I, Roy P, Chakrabortty R, Shit M (2021) Threats of unplanned movement of migrant workers for sudden spurt of COVID-19 pandemic in India. Cities 109:103035
59. Reid A, Ronda-Perez E, Schenker MB (2021) Migrant workers, essential work, and COVID-19. Am J Ind Med 64(2):73–77
60. Rochmaedah D, Basrowi B, Suseno BD (2022) Strategy of former indonesian migrant workers from Qatar in the era of the Covid-19 outbreak. Int J Bus Manag Econ 3(2):185–195
61. Rother S (2021) ASEAN connectivity through labour migration? The role of migrant civil society for the decent work agenda
62. Sanfelici M (2021) The impact of the COVID-19 crisis on marginal migrant populations in Italy. Am Behav Sci 65(10):1323–1341
63. Saragih YM, Sabri AZSBA, Abu R (2021) COVID-19's impact on migrant workers in malaysia: a case study. In: The 2nd international conference and call paper, vol 1, no 1
64. Segal UA (2019) Globalization, migration, and ethnicity. Pub Health 172:135–142
65. Srinivas S, Sivaraman S (2021) Understanding relevant sustainable development goal targets related to labour migration in the association of Southeast Asian Nations during the Coronavirus disease pandemic
66. Suhardiman D, Rigg J, Bandur M, Marschke M, Miller MA, Pheuangsavanh N, Sayatham M, Taylor D (2021) On the Coattails of globalization: migration, migrants and COVID-19 in Asia. J Ethn Migr Stud 47(1):88–109
67. Suresh R, James J, RSJ B (2020) Migrant workers at crossroads—the COVID-19 pandemic and the migrant experience in India. Soc Work Pub Health 35(7):633–643
68. Susilo W (2020) ASEAN, Pekerja Migran dan Krisis COVID-19. DW. https://www.dw.com/id/asean-pekerja-migran-dan-krisis-covid-19/a-53728802
69. Tam WJ, Gobat N, Hemavathi D, Fisher D (2022) Risk communication and community engagement during the migrant worker COVID-19 outbreak in Singapore. Sci Commun 44(2):240–251
70. The Star (2020) Covid-19: foreign workers in Klang, Seremban to begin mandatory screening on December 1. https://www.thestar.com.my/news/nation/2020/11/28/covid-19-foreign-workers-in-klang-seremban-to-begin-mandatory-screening-on-dec-1-says-hr-minister
71. UN (2020) Migration data portal: the bigger picture. https://www.migrationdataportal.org/data?i=stock_workage_perc&t=2020&m=1
72. Ullah AKMA, Nawaz F, Chattoraj D (2021) Locked up under lockdown: the COVID-19 pandemic and the migrant population. Soc Sci Human Open 3(1):100126
73. Wahab A (2020) The outbreak of Covid-19 in Malaysia: pushing migrant workers at the margin. Soc Sci Human Open 2(1):100073
74. Wiriyapong N (2021) Don't leave migrant workers behind. Bangkok Post. https://www.bangkokpost.com/opinion/opinion/2154731/dont-leave-migrant-workers-behind
75. Wongsamuth N (2021) Migrant workers face tough quarantine in Thailand as COVID-19 cases surge. Reuters. https://www.reuters.com/article/us-health-coronavirus-thailand-migrants-idUSKCN2D9217
76. World Health Organization (WHO) (2021) Brief COVID-situation and response in Thailand
77. Yadav S, Priya KR (2021) Migrant workers and COVID-19: listening to the unheard voices of invisible India. J Anthropol Surv India 70(1):62–71
78. Yueping S, Hantao W, Xiao-yuan D, Zhili W (2021) To return or stay? The gendered impact of the COVID-19 pandemic on migrant workers in China. Fem Econ 27(1–2):236–253. https://doi.org/10.1080/13545701.2020.1845391

Part III
Markets, Finance and Development Challenges in the Global South Post-COVID-19 Pandemic

Chapter 8
Identifying the Factors Affecting International Financial Institutions Lending to Pakistan in the Context of Political Economy

Muhammad Hassam Shahid, Ravinder Rena, Sadaf Mubeen, and Iftikhar Yasin

Abstract This article studies the drivers of multilateral aid from international financial institutions (IFIs) to Pakistan, concentrating on the world's largest international financial institutions, the World Bank, the International Monetary Fund, and the Asian Development Bank. International aid allocation decisions may be influenced by political and economic issues, including bureaucratic interests, recipient need, recipient merit, bilateral donor interests, and the financial interests of significant shareholders. This study utilized the pooled Tobit methodology and random effect methodology to capture the impact of different factors on international financial institutions' decision-making regarding loans to Pakistan. Gross official transfers to Pakistan compared to overall official flows to developing nations were taken from the OECD database as a dependent variable. The pooled Tobit methodology results support that GDP per capita negatively influences international financial decisions regarding lending. Political instability has a positive and significant impact on international financial institutions' lending decisions. Moreover, bureaucratic interests are considerable factors in allocating funds, as the Pakistani executives' directors' voting authority increased the funds' allocation by these international financial institutions.

M. H. Shahid (✉)
Department of Economics, Virtual University of Pakistan, Lahore, Pakistan
e-mail: hassam.shahid@vu.edu.pk

R. Rena
Durban University of Technology, ML Sultan Campus, PO Box: 1334, Durban 4001, Republic of South Africa
e-mail: RavinderR@dut.ac.za

S. Mubeen
Ilma University, Karachi, Pakistan
e-mail: sadaf.mubeengcu@yahoo.com

I. Yasin
Department of Economics, The University of Lahore, Lahore, Pakistan
e-mail: Iftikhar.yasin@econ.uol.edu.pk

H. Adam and R. Rena (eds.), *Political Economy of Development in the Global South Post-COVID-19 Pandemic*,
https://doi.org/10.1007/978-981-99-4074-5_8

Although recipient needs are another significant predictor of financing, bureaucratic considerations rank higher. The results obtained by the random effects model also suggest that bilateral donor interest remains insignificant in this study. Moreover, the impact of the COVID-19 pandemic on international financial institutions' lending to Pakistan has been significant. In 2020, the World Bank approved a $1 billion loan for Pakistan, and the IMF also approved a $6 billion loan to support its efforts to respond to the COVID-19 pandemic.

Keywords Financial lending · IMF · World bank · Political economy · Tobit

8.1 Introduction

According to political economics research, choices about multilateral financing are made based on political and economic issues, where donor interest takes precedence over recipient necessity. It is widely believed that international bureaucracy and its utility-maximizing behaviour have a significant effect [1–7]. Internal career hierarchies and opportunities for higher employment in their governments incentivize bureaucrats in global financial organizations to transfer funds to their own countries. Additionally, the monetary and governmental interests of the main shareholders, as well as their influence at IFIs, are believed to be the primary factors in loaning to underdeveloped countries [8, 9].

The current study examines the loan-offering processes of the major IFIs in Pakistan via a political and economic lens. Since 1960, Pakistan's three major IFIs have been the World Bank (WB), International Monetary Fund (IMF), and Asian Development Bank (ADB). These IFIs offered Pakistan financial funding and policy guidance throughout the latter half of the twentieth century. Pakistan came in second place among International Development Agency (IDA) commitment recipients in 2002. In addition, after India, Pakistan remained the main beneficiary of ADB grants in 2002, obtaining $1.15 billion. Pakistan has received 723 loans, grants, and technical support from the ADB, totalling $37 billion. The cumulative amount of loans and grants disbursed to Pakistan is $28.27 billion. These were financed by normal and concessional resources, the Asian Development Fund, and other special funds. The current ADB sovereign portfolio in Pakistan consists of 48 loans and three grants totalling $8.42 billion. The WB explains its substantial economic assistance to the Pakistani government by claiming that "it reflects Pakistan's success in several critical reform areas."

According to Hashmi (2017), IMF funding choices have no connection to Pakistan's poor macroeconomic stability. In addition, it has been repeatedly observed that despite Pakistan's failure to fulfil IMF conditions and World Bank objectives, new agreements were nonetheless reached [10, 11].

Moreover, Pakistan was among the top five developing nations with the most professional personnel at the IMF. There are also indications that Pakistanis who worked for the IMF or other IFIs eventually attained positions of importance inside their home government. This raises some issues regarding the true aims of IFIs' loan decisions and should be investigated further: Why have IFIs extended Pakistan loans during the past six decades? Was the loan of IFIs to Pakistan based on necessity, its prior economic performance, or bureaucratic interests? A more significant proportion of voting power within IFIs can affect their decision-making processes.

The current research analyses the data of the ADB, WB, and IMF lending to Pakistan to address these issues and others of a similar nature. Regarding the World Bank, we differentiate between IDA and the "International Bank for Reconstruction and Development (IBRD)" since the respective shareholder nations' influence on the two organizations' executive boards is distinct.

Previous research, such as that of Barro and Lee [57], employs a study for an organization, notably the IMF, to explore similar problems. When a developing state has a larger ratio and qualified IMF staff, it is more likely to obtain large and numerous loans or when it has closer political and economic ties to the significant owning countries of the IMF. This study will conduct a cross-institutional analysis of a particular recipient nation. This technique offers the benefit of examining possible disparities in the incentive structures of various donor entities. In addition, focusing on a single country enables us to track the country's progress in greater depth.

Considering the above-given debate, this study aims to analyse the IFI's lending decisions to Pakistan. This study will also explore the determinants of an IFI's lending decisions. Additionally, the current research examines voting power percentages' role in lending decisions in these institutions.

The research is organized into four sections. The second part provides a summary of IFI lending practices in Pakistan. In part III, concepts on political decision-making will be offered, along with regression findings for likelihood and grant size. We will also give the donor-specific data and compare their differences in this part. In section IV, the conclusions are provided.

8.2 Literature Review

Since the 1990s, much material has been written about the variables that affect an IFI's loan choices. Bird [12] provides a summary of prior studies on the issue. An overview of the studies conducted since the mid-1990s is given by [13, 14]. They discover a lack of consensus about the criteria governing IMF participation and conflicting data regarding the role of political factors in IMF funding. Youssef and Zaki [15] determine which of the numerous political and economic factors from past studies are reliable predictors of an IFI's financing choices. Additionally, Copelovitch [16] discover that the bulk of political factors put out in prior studies are not substantially correlated with the two dependent variables, signing an IMF agreement and using IMF credit. For example, an IFI's loan tends to be mostly tied to economic issues, even while political circumstances, such as changes in the programs country's administration, impact the signing of an IFI agreement [17–21].

The temporary UNSC membership association with IMF programs is examined [22]. Temporary UNSC representatives could be ready to exchange their UNSC voting ballots for easier access to IMF grants, which they regard more highly than their UNSC voting authority. Thus, the UNSC voting record is a reliable indicator of US geopolitical goals. Clark and Dolan [23] also discover evidence that UNSC representation lessens conditionality in IMF programs and a strong positive association between UNSC membership and participation in IMF programs. Other studies also find that the chance of an IFI's agreement being signed in a certain year and the magnitude of loans are associated with voting for or against the US [7, 24–26].

Later studies by Potrafke [27], Lang [28], and Andresen [29] concluded that a variety of noneconomic factors are shown to have strong relationships with the dependent variables in an updated extension of the study by Sturm et al. [13]. Using information from January 2008 to June 2010, Presbitero and Zazzaro [30] analyse a more recent set of IMF lending decisions made during the GFC. They discover that political resemblance to the G7 increases the chance of authorization an IMF grants in a particular year.

Breen and Doak [21] discover that the economic exposure of a group of the biggest IMF shareholders, the G5 nations, which include the US, the UK, France, Germany, and Japan, is a factor in the observed variance in conditionality in a dataset of 87 IMF programs from 1997 to 2016. However, economic considerations are weak predictors of conditionality variance. Another paper by Ray, Gallagher [24] makes the case that the G5 collaborate to lessen requirements in an IMF program when their exporters and banks are exposed to the requesting nation and would suffer loss if IMF payments were suspended for failing to satisfy the criteria set.

8.3 International Financial Institutions Lending to Pakistan: Evidence

IFIs have significantly supplied Pakistan with substantial loans in the past 60 years. Pakistan received $41 billion from the IMF, according to figures released by the "Development Assistance Committee (DAC)" of the OECD on total official flows. In contrast, Pakistan received US$ 40 billion from the World Bank between 1960 and 2021. More than 80% of these official multilateral flows originated from the WB, the ADB, and the IMF.

Since 1950, Pakistan has been associated with the WB. Since 1950, the WB has provided a support contribution of forty billion dollars. The "Country Partnership Strategy" for FY2015-2020 governs the WB's operation, which has four key engagement areas: power, private enterprise expansion, inclusion, and service sector. There are 58 projects and a total commitment of $13.8 billion in the current portfolio. Pakistan is one of the top 10 receivers of World Bank loans.

Meanwhile, funding by the World Bank to Pakistan has changed over time. In 2000, Pakistan received the lowest amount from the World Bank since 1990 ($300.8

million). In 2001, the World Bank significantly raised its credit to Pakistan to $669.17 million. Moreover, Pakistan ranked second among the top 10 receivers of significant IDA pledges in 2002. In 2002, with disbursements exceeding obligations by even more (961.1 million US dollars), Pakistan became the largest beneficiary of World Bank credit. Pakistan took a loan from the World Bank on different occasions. Recently, Pakistan and the World Bank agreed on a loan totalling over $1.3 billion, including $600 million for budget support, lubricating the government's external financial channels following the resurrection of the bailout package.

In 1966, Pakistan became a founding member of the ADB. Pakistan has received 723 loans, grants, and technical support from the ADB, totalling $37 billion. The cumulative amount of loans and grants disbursed to Pakistan is $28.27 billion. These were financed by normal and concessional capital resources, the Asian Development Fund, and other special funds. The current sovereign portfolio of the ADB in Pakistan consists of 48 loans and three grants totalling $8.42 billion.

Most loans from these institutions, notably in the last two decades, have been used to finance structural adjustment and social action programs. Structural adjustment loans stipulated developments in the financial sector, tax system, and government expenditures to shrink trade and budgetary shortfalls. Birdsall, Malik [31] notes that World Bank financing rose during the 1990s, despite macroeconomic imbalances being well beyond agreed-upon targets and showing few indications of adjustment. In addition, a substantial percentage of this credit was policy lending, which was released more swiftly than loans for individual projects. Foreign funders, led by the World Bank, spent $8 billion on the Social Action Programs initiative, yet evidence suggests that the SAPP has been unsuccessful [11, 32–34].

After 1988, the IMF, the third international financing source, signed several agreements with Pakistan. Since then, Pakistan has continuously utilized IMF financing. Lending from the IMF was intended to cover a balance of payment deficit under various facilities. However, it fulfilled nearly the same commitments as the ADB and the World Bank.

Although Pakistan's ties with the IMF have not been easy, it remains the IMF's largest borrower among developing nations. From 1988 to 2000, Pakistan received just 51.5% of the total 4.07 billion dollars in IMF loans. From 2000 to 2019, the IMF agreed to provide a loan of Rupees 18,068 million, and only Rupees 13,031 million were issued. This was a result of Pakistan's history of ineffective policy execution. Despite this, previous IMF agreements were replaced by new ones, and the same unfulfilled conditions were continually repeated.

According to the IMF's independent review office, Pakistan is a prime illustration of how politics have influenced the IMF's decision-making process since the 1980s. Personal relationships also appear to have a significant effect. Conversations continued, and agreements were struck with the IMF and WB at various periods when Pakistani administrations involved representatives from these organizations. Former World Bank Director Mahbub-ul-Haq served as Pakistan's Finance Minister in 1988, and Moeen Qureshi remained the Senior Vice-President of the WB and performed duties as Pakistan's Caretaker Prime Minister in 1993. Shahid Javed Burki also held the position of Vice President and served as Pakistan's Finance Minister in 1994 and

1996. This occurred in 1988, 1993, and 1996 at the same time as new loan arrangements. In the recent past, Dr. Nadeem-ul-Haque also held the position of Resident Representative of the IMF in various countries and served as the Deputy Chairman of the Planning Commission of Pakistan.

It shows that development or economic concerns are not the only factors influencing Pakistan's main IFI financing. In the past two decades, IFI financing through SAP, economic transformation, and sectoral loans has cast doubt on the applicability of publicly specified loaning policies, prioritizing economic necessity and policy success. In light of this, the following section will explore IFI lending to Pakistan in further detail, considering the benefits of the various agents in these organizations.

8.4 The Political Economy of International Financial Institutions Lending to Pakistan

Prior studies have acknowledged that a suitable model for explaining loan choices should be comprehensive and take into consideration both the lender's and the beneficiary's interests and qualifications. The current section discusses this "hybrid" approach, in which multilateral institutions' bureaucratic inertia and political interest may account for the multilateral contributors' objectives. IFIs' bureaucratic interests might impact loan choices to Pakistan, as detailed in Section II. Reinsberg, Kern [10], Analysing IMF funding for many nations, discover some support for this notion. This strategy is founded on the economic principles of bureaucracy, in which officials allocate funds to maximize their utility [5, 35, 36]. In addition, donor states inside IFIs have different interests and frequently seek to exploit IFIs to achieve their agenda [37–39]. With this in mind, we regard IFIs as bureaucratic and political entities that increase the satisfaction of their participants, i.e., officials and large investor nations, when analysing their loans to Pakistan.

8.4.1 Determinant of International Financial Institutions Lending Decision: Hypothesis

Two distinct sets of variables may be used to characterize the lending reasons directly correlating to IFIs' publicly stated goals. The first identifies the requirements of beneficiaries, while the second assesses their "merits," or earlier efforts to promote a solid economic policy framework [40–46].

With an income per capita of only $1798, Pakistan is a low-income nation (Pakistan Economic Survey, 2022). According to statistics, approximately 21.5% of the population lives in absolute poverty (PIDE, 2021). The poverty rate declined in the late 1980s and early 1990s but began to climb again by the late 1990s. Moreover, Pakistan's economy has been plagued by major internal and foreign economic issues during the past few decades. Thus, according to our first testable hypothesis, Pakistan ought to have received more substantial assistance from foreign agencies during those periods of extreme economic crisis.

Hypothesis 1: International financial institutions' lending is positively linked to Pakistan's financial requirements

Now, we will discuss "merit," which is often discussed in relation to "excellent governance." Good governance is a multidimensional notion, and the financial and broader political dimensions are significant in this context. Let us begin by considering economic governance. According to stated development policy financing plans, executing growth-promoting policies is another fundamental factor for IFI loan distribution. According to the WB and IMF's joint strategy documents, development policy funding is often restricted to countries with a sufficient macroeconomic framework. Therefore, lending should involve positive incentives, and IFIs should reward successful performance with more special financing [47, 48]. Despite Pakistan being a developing nation, its economic success in the late 1980s was remarkable.

In contrast, economic progress in the 1970s was quite dismal, and it also dropped significantly in the late 1990s owing to naive policies, resulting in a somewhat erratic growth pattern. These variances should be reflected in the lending practices of IFIs. Consequently, we develop our next hypothesis:

Hypothesis 2: IFI Lending is positively correlated with enhanced progress in Pakistan's Economy

The second proposition addresses financial governance; we will examine political governance and the added necessity for IFI funding based on merit. There are compelling claims that strong political governance indirectly affects economic growth and reduces poverty [49–51]. If this is the case, we might anticipate IFIs considering economic and political governance when making loan choices. However, prior research on IMF and World Bank financing has not shown substantial proof of a connection between political governance and loan choices [52–54]. Pakistan, which has undergone a variety of regimes, poor political institutions, and several periods of ineffective government, provides an intriguing new testing ground for determining if political governance has influenced IFIs' loan agreements. This brings us to our third supposition:

Hypothesis 3: International Financial Institutions' loaning is positively associated with political governance

Thus far, we have only discussed the rationale for need- and merit-based IFI financing. Let us examine the political and economic motivations for IFI loans to Pakistan. Regarding loan choices to developing nations, we suggest that IFIs must be considered bureaucratic and political entities. It is assumed that bureaucrats serving in these organizations would campaign for policies and lending that benefit their home countries to obtain better posts. Any favourable decision, such as more loans to their nation, will increase their utility. Thus, multilateral officials are interested in transferring funds to their home nations, even if those nations have not met earlier objectives and conditions [23, 55]. Despite receiving fresh funds, Pakistan has not complied with IFI requirements, as shown in section I. Concurrently, we find considerable shifts in Pakistan's participation in the primary bodies of IFIs. Every post held by bureaucrats in international organizations may be anticipated to secure more loans for their country and ultimately maximize their utility, according to those stated in the previous political and economic study. Consequently, we propose our fourth hypothesis:

Hypothesis 4: The likelihood that Pakistan will obtain more and larger loans increases with the number and influence of Pakistani citizens working for IFIs

8.4.2 Impact of the COVID-19 Pandemic on International Financial Institutions Lending to Pakistan

The COVID-19 pandemic has had a profound impact on the global economy, and international financial institutions' lending to Pakistan is no exception. The pandemic has resulted in significant economic disruption, leading to a slowdown in economic growth and a reduction in government revenues. In response, the government of Pakistan has sought support from international financial institutions such as the World Bank and the International Monetary Fund (IMF).

In 2020, the World Bank approved a $1 billion loan for Pakistan to support its efforts to respond to the COVID-19 pandemic. This loan was designed to help the government address the immediate health and economic impacts of the pandemic, as well as support its efforts to rebuild the economy in the aftermath of the crisis. The World Bank loan was intended to help cover the costs of emergency health interventions, support the government's efforts to protect the most vulnerable members of society, and provide support for businesses and workers affected by the pandemic.

The IMF also approved a $6 billion loan for Pakistan in July 2020 as part of its Rapid Financing Instrument (RFI). The RFI is a flexible, fast-disbursing loan designed to help countries respond to sudden and exceptional economic shocks, such as those caused by the COVID-19 pandemic. The loan was intended to help Pakistan address the immediate economic impacts of the pandemic, support its efforts to maintain financial stability, and help restore economic growth over the longer term.

The impact of the COVID-19 pandemic on international financial institutions' lending to Pakistan has been significant. On the one hand, the support provided by these institutions has been crucial in helping the government respond to the immediate health and economic impacts of the pandemic. Without this support, the economic and social consequences of the pandemic would likely have been even more severe.

On the other hand, the increased reliance on international financial institutions' lending has also had some negative consequences. First, the terms and conditions of these loans can be restrictive, requiring the government to implement structural reforms and fiscal austerity measures. These reforms can be politically challenging and can lead to public discontent, particularly if they result in cuts to public spending or reductions in social welfare programs.

Second, the increase in borrowing from international financial institutions also increased the government's debt burden, which can have long-term implications for the economy. In particular, the government's debt service obligations can increase, reducing its ability to invest in infrastructure and other long-term development projects. This can have a negative impact on economic growth and hinder the country's ability to achieve its long-term development goals.

In conclusion, the impact of the COVID-19 pandemic on international financial institutions' lending to Pakistan has been significant. While the support provided by these institutions has been crucial in helping the government respond to the immediate health and economic impacts of the pandemic, the increased reliance on their lending has also had some negative consequences.

8.4.3 Data and Methodology

We employ the Tobit approach, adopted by most aid allocation research, to examine these assumptions empirically. This method allows us to account for the total official flows to Pakistan from IFIs. This technique predicts aid in a single step. It is suitable if the exogenous factors are anticipated to have the same influence on the likelihood of obtaining help and the quantity of aid given after that [56–59].

Gross official transfers to Pakistan compared to overall official flows to developing nations (ToFDev) were taken from the OECD database as a dependent variable. Using disbursements instead of pledges indicates the real expenditure of funds. Considering gross rather than net flows solves the problem of debt repayments being managed by the recipient nation instead of the donor nation. Given the purpose of our research, the proportion of Pakistan's aid relative to that of other developing countries is a more appropriate dependent variable than aid amount or assistance per capita. It illustrates the nation's importance in comparison to other beneficiaries. Other studies that contain middle-income and high-income countries used just the proportion of aid relative to total financing to developing nations [60–63]. Since this study examines Pakistan, a low-income country's proportion of aid payments to other low-income countries may be a reliable alternative measure. Considering both options might be crucial, mainly if we presume that there may be predetermined total amounts for some nation categories, such as low-income countries. The panel considers each institution, beginning with the year it is lending to developing nations was formed.

We need information on economic needs and performance measures to investigate Pakistan's economic merit in connection to IFIs' loan choices, as covered in hypotheses 1 through 3. GDP per capita is the direct measure of a country's need for international assistance. Brissimis, Hondroyiannis [64] argue that domestic and global economic pressures may be seen as current account and government budget deficits. Therefore, to evaluate Pakistan's financial needs, this study analysed the data on per capita GDP (GDPPC), current account deficit as a ratio of GDP (CAD), and budgetary deficit as a proportion of GDP (BD).

The annual GDP growth rate was chosen as an indicator variable for Pakistan's economic performance. Higher GDP growth signals a more robust economy. The GDP growth rate and all other economic factors were utilized with a one-period lag to determine IFIs' financing to Pakistan, as completely up-to-date information is often unavailable for decision-making, even for international institutions.

Previous studies have employed the rule of law and democracy to measure political governance [57]. However, Harrigan, Mosley [65] suggest that political stability, mainly the frequency of government change, maybe a superior indication of political governance. This might be true when complete democracy and rule-of-law indicators were unavailable in the early years. Governance indicators were calculated for the first time in 1996, although the Freedom House index on freedoms and political rights was created in the early 1970s [66]. Therefore, we attempt to represent political governance by including political instability (PI), which enables us to construct the necessary time series beginning in 1960.

8.5 Results and Discussion

This section presents the key findings and insightful analysis regarding the factors affecting international financial institutions (IFIs) lending to Pakistan in the context of political economy. Through an in-depth examination of political and economic indicators, this study sheds light on the intricate dynamics that shape lending decisions in this critical context. The analysis unveils a range of influential factors, highlighting the significant role of recipient need, recipient merit, bureaucratic interest and bilateral donor interest, economic performance and political considerations. Furthermore, this section explores the policy reforms and structural adjustments demanded by IFIs and assesses their implications for Pakistan's borrowing prospects. By dissecting these factors, this chapter aims to provide a comprehensive understanding of the multifaceted landscape surrounding IFIs lending to Pakistan and offers recommendations for policymakers, international financial institutions, and other stakeholders to enhance lending opportunities and navigate potential challenges.

As assessed by the frequency of government transitions, political instability is well suited to Pakistan, as the country's governments have frequently been replaced before their mandates have expired. In our estimations, each change in the Pakistani government is represented by a 1, while a 0 indicates that no changes occurred. A closer value to 1 suggests a more significant number of government transitions or political instability. Polity IV provided the statistics of changes in government.

To measure the influence of bureaucracy and lobbying on IFI loans to Pakistan, our research would have benefited from data on the Pakistani managers and professionals employed at each organization. Unfortunately, such data are unavailable from IFIs and are only available for highly brief periods when they are accessible, such as the IMF Diversity Office. Therefore, we utilized the Pakistani executive director's voting authority (PEDV) as a % of the voting power. The number of senior Pakistani officials (PSO) was calculated as a ratio to the total number of officers at each organization. Unoccupied positions were not included while collecting the information.

Several dummy variables were introduced to represent the political lending interests of the IFIs' largest owners, including a dummy for 1985, when the US Senate passed the "Pressler Amendment." This study added a dummy for the Pakistan nuclear blasts in 1998 and a dummy (dummy01-02) for 2001 and 2002 to quantify the consequence of September 11 on Pakistan's aid distribution. We also include bilateral assistance from large shareholder nations as supplementary factors. We add dummy variables for the early 1980s, late 1990s, and 2007 to examine how international financial institutions (IFIs) have dealt with global crises such as those in Latin America and Asia and how they have affected IFI financing to Pakistan. Our regression findings are presented in Table 8.1. We deploy a pooled Tobit model and a random effects IFI-specific Tobit model.

The results of the analysis reveal intriguing insights into the factors affecting gross official transfers to Pakistan compared to overall official flows to developing nations. Notably, our findings indicate a positive relationship between the number of Pakistani executives' voting authority and the current account deficit with the dependent variable, suggesting their significance in determining the allocation of financial resources to Pakistan. As predicted, the per capita GDP has a strong negative effect on both regressions. The computed coefficient suggests that all else being equal, a low per capita GDP in Pakistan will increase the likelihood and amount of IFI financing to Pakistan. The analysis of the results reveals a noteworthy finding regarding the

Table 8.1 Regression Results of Lending to Pakistan

	Tobit		Random effect	
	ToFDev		ToFDev	
	Coefficient	P value	Coefficient	P value
Recipient need				
GDP per capita	−0.05	0.04	−0.04	0.03
Current account deficit	0.23	0.36	0.28	0.35
Budget deficit	−0.21	0.60	−0.22	0.58
Recipient merit				
GDP growth	−0.04	0.93	−0.06	0.69
Political instability			5.40	0.09
Bureaucratic interest				
Pakistani executive director's voting authority	1.47	0.00	0.59	0.04
Pakistani senior officials	−0.10	0.75	−0.49	0.16
Bilateral donor interest				
Dummy			1.46	0.54
Constant	9.45	0.06	12.58	0.00

Source Authors' calculations based on the OECD database

negative relationship between per capita GDP and gross official transfers to Pakistan compared to overall official flows to developing nations. This finding suggests that as Pakistan's income level per person increases, there is a decrease in the proportion of financial assistance received from international financial institutions and donor countries.

The negative relationship between per capita GDP and gross official transfers may be explained by several factors. Firstly, higher per capita GDP indicates a relatively stronger economic position and potentially greater capacity for self-financing. International financial institutions and donor countries may perceive countries with higher per capita GDP as having a reduced need for external financial assistance, as they may have a higher ability to generate domestic resources to meet their developmental and financial requirements.

In contrast, current account and budget deficits are insignificant and presented in Table 01 regressions. The positive relationship observed between the current account deficit and the dependent variable suggests that a higher deficit is associated with an increased allocation of financial assistance. This result indicates that international financial institutions and donor countries may be more inclined to provide financial support to help mitigate Pakistan's external imbalances and address its trade-related challenges.

Notably, evaluating the impact of the current account deficit might be inaccurate. Increased deficits imply an important resource requirement but may also result from poor economic policies. If IFIs respond in part, the sign of the overall coefficients is ambiguous. It is only necessary to estimate the coefficients if one element predominates. This uncertainty also exists to some extent concerning interpreting the GDP growth coefficient. In this case, the goals of responding to needs and acknowledging extraordinary economic achievement are easier to distinguish due to the inclusion of GDP per capita separately.

Although the projected coefficient of GDP growth has a negative indication in both regressions, it does not appear statistically significant. This suggests that our data do not confirm hypothesis 2, which argued that aid from IFIs favoured Pakistan's economy. If we read this coefficient's sign, it would suggest that vigorous economic development may reduce IFI lending. In addition, the outcomes for governance measured by political stability do not support our theory. The analysis of the results uncovers a significant finding regarding the positive relationship between political instability and gross official transfers to Pakistan compared to overall official flows to developing nations. This finding suggests that higher levels of political instability within Pakistan are associated with an increase in the proportion of financial assistance received from international financial institutions and donor countries. This indicates that frequent changes in administration, and consequently more political insecurity, appear to be compensated rather than punished by IFIs.

The positive relationship between political instability and gross official transfers may be attributed to several factors. Firstly, countries experiencing political instability often face significant economic challenges and uncertainties. In such circumstances, international financial institutions and donor countries may provide greater financial assistance to support the country's stability and mitigate potential economic downturns. This assistance can help alleviate the negative impacts of political instability on the country's economy. Moreover, heightened political instability may lead to increased attention and international engagement. The international community, recognizing the need for stability, may allocate a larger share of financial resources to countries experiencing political turbulence. This support aims to promote stability, foster economic development, and address the underlying causes of political instability.

However, it is crucial to note that the positive relationship between political instability and gross official transfers does not imply a desirable or sustainable situation. Political instability can have detrimental effects on governance, economic growth, and the overall welfare of a nation. While increased financial assistance may provide temporary relief, addressing the root causes of political instability and implementing effective governance reforms remain essential for long-term stability and sustainable development. The positive relationship observed between political instability and gross official transfers highlights the importance of addressing political challenges to secure financial assistance. While financial support can provide short-term relief, sustainable development necessitates long-term stability and effective governance reforms.

In our regression results, the IFI interest and shareholder interest variables appear to be more significant than the need and merit variables. The Pakistani executive voting power at each organization reveals that the bureaucratic interests of Pakistan are all significant. Thus, we uncover evidence of a substantial relationship between the influence bureaucrats wield and loans to their home nations. The positive relationship between the number of Pakistani executives' voting authority and the dependent variable suggests that a higher representation and influence of Pakistani executives within international financial institutions may lead to a greater allocation of financial resources to the country. This outcome can be attributed to the ability of Pakistani executives to advocate for Pakistan's specific financial needs and interests within the decision-making processes of these institutions. In our models, the additional variable of senior Pakistani officials indicating the politicization of officials at IFIs in favour of increased loans to Pakistan is insignificant. This may be because, unlike the political team, i.e., the managerial team does not ponder the relative status of their nation while advocating for increased financing for their country, regardless of the situation in other countries.

However, staff employees do not make loan choices directly but rather indirectly by lobbying the executive board when there is a greater probability of obtaining decisions that are advantageous to their nation. In addition, the professional staff under their control frequently creates pertinent policy documents and meeting materials, allowing them authority to define the agenda. Our regression estimates of the overall effect may be inaccurate because we have no information on the overall number of administrative officials. However, we do have information on senior officials.

The outcomes support the hypothesis that bureaucratic concerns are significant as beneficiaries' requirements or merit in deciding IFIs' financing to Pakistan. There are insufficient data to support hypothesis 2, which proposes a link between financial aid and economic growth. Regarding country merit and political stability, it is possible to reject hypothesis 3. Thus, the bureaucratic interest of IFIs appears to be the most significant factor in IFI loan decisions to Pakistan.

8.6 Conclusions and Recommendations

This study analyses the factors influencing the loan choices of the top IFIs in Pakistan. Regression indicates that the IFIs' bureaucratic interest may be more influential in loan choices than the goals of responding to recipients' needs and rewarding excellent economic policies. Each IFI's executive board is dominated by international bureaucrats who support lending to their home economies and defence funding to any nation with large default risk. Another group of economic and political variables partially explains the economic interests of the largest owners of IFIs. This article uses Tobit estimates and some factors to examine the WB, IMF, and ADB support of Pakistan and draw conclusions on the country's political and economic factors of international lending. IFIs, particularly the ADB and IDA, apparently stray from their initially intended monetary financing goals. Consequently, investigating how international donor organizations make financial decisions for other countries remains a possible future research objective.

8.7 Future Work

This study offers evidence for the political economic factors that influence multilateral financing by utilizing Tobit estimates and a variety of specifications based on the example of loans from the World Bank, IMF, and ADB to Pakistan. IFIs, in particular the ADB and the IDA, tend to stray from their initially stated goals for economic financing. Exploring how international donor institutions act in relation to lending choices to other nations thus remains a viable area of research for the future.

References

1. McLean EV (2015) Multilateral aid and domestic economic interests. Int Organ 69(1):97–130
2. Schneider CJ, Tobin JL (2013) Interest coalitions and multilateral aid allocation in the European Union. Int Stud Quart 57(1):103–114
3. Michaelowa K, Borrmann A (2006) Evaluation bias and incentive structures in bi-and multilateral aid agencies. Rev Dev Econ 10(2):313–329

4. Boone P, Faguet J-P (1998) Multilateral aid, politics and poverty: Past failures and future challenges
5. Anwar M (2006) The political economy of international financial institutions' lending to Pakistan. Pak Econ Soc Rev 155–180
6. Kilby C (2011) Informal influence in the Asian development bank. Rev Int Organ 6(3):223–257
7. Andresen LL (2021) Essays on lending by the International Monetary Fund, ETH Zurich
8. Fleck RK, Kilby C (2006) How do political changes influence US bilateral aid allocations? Evidence from panel data. Rev Dev Econ 10(2):210–223
9. Kaya A, Kilby C, Kay J (2021) Asian Infrastructure Investment Bank as an instrument for Chinese influence? Supplementary versus remedial multilateralism. World Develop 145:105531
10. Reinsberg B, Kern A, Rau-Göhring M (2021) The political economy of IMF conditionality and central bank independence. Eur J Polit Econ 68:101987
11. Analytica O (2019) Pakistan will face accusations of subservience to IMF. Emerald Expert Briefings, 2019(oxan-es)
12. Bird G (1996) Borrowing from the IMF: the policy implications of recent empirical research. World Dev 24(11):1753–1760
13. Sturm JE, Berger H, De Haan J (2005) Which variables explain decisions on IMF credit? An extreme bounds analysis. Econ Politics 17(2):177–213
14. Knight M, Santaella JA (1997) Economic determinants of IMF financial arrangements. J Dev Econ 54(2):405–436
15. Youssef J, Zaki C (2021) On the determinants and outcomes of IMF loans: a political economy approach. 2021. Economic Research Forum (ERF)
16. Copelovitch MS (2010) Master or servant? Common agency and the political economy of IMF lending. Int Stud Quart 54(1):49–77
17. Deniz A, Angin M, Angin P (2022) Understanding IMF Decision-Making with Sentiment Analysis. In 2022 30th Signal Processing and Communications Applications Conference (SIU). 2022. IEEE
18. Forster T, Stubbs TH, Kentikelenis AE (2022) The politics of the International Monetary Fund. In Handbook on the Politics of International Development 2022, Edward Elgar Publishing. pp. 376–391
19. Moon C, Woo B (2022) Curse of friendship: IMF programme, friendship with the United States and foreign direct investment. World Econ 45(7):2188–2221
20. Copelovitch M, Powers R (2021) Do we really know what we think we know about the politics of IMF lending? Measuring and Reassessing US Influence in Global Financial Governance
21. Breen M, Doak E (2021) The IMF as a global monitor: surveillance, information, and financial markets. Rev Int Polit Econ 1–25
22. Dreher A, Sturm J-E, Vreeland JR (2009) Development aid and international politics: does membership on the UN Security Council influence World Bank decisions? J Dev Econ 88(1):1–18
23. Clark R, Dolan LR (2021) Pleasing the principal: US influence in World Bank policymaking. Am J Polit Sci 65(1):36–51
24. Ray R, Gallagher KP, Kring W (2022) "Keep the Receipts:" The political economy of IMF austerity during and after the crisis years of 2009 and 2020. J Glob Dev 13(1):31–59
25. Dreher A et al (2022) Bilateral or multilateral? International financial flows and the dirty-work hypothesis. J Politics 84(4):1932–1946
26. Ray R, Gallagher K, Kring W (2020) IMF austerity since the global financial crisis: new data, same trend, and similar determinants. 2020 Global Development Policy Center Boston, MA
27. Potrafke N (2015) The evidence on globalisation. World Econ 38(3):509–552
28. Lang V (2021) The economics of the democratic deficit: The effect of IMF programs on inequality. Rev Int Organ 16(3):599–623
29. Andresen LL (2022) The influence of financial corporations on IMF lending: Has it changed with the global financial crisis?

30. Presbitero AF, Zazzaro A (2012) IMF lending in times of crisis: Political influences and crisis prevention. World Dev 40(10):1944–1969
31. Birdsall N, Malik A, Vaishnav M (2005) Poverty and the Social Sectors: The World Bank in Pakistan 1990–2003
32. Azizi SL (1999) An Analysis of the social action program and education of women in Pakistan. Virginia Tech
33. Khan SR (1999) An overview of basic education under the social action plan in Pakistan. 1999: Sustainable Development Policy Institute
34. Easterly W (2003) Can foreign aid buy growth? J Econ Perspect 17(3):23–48
35. Dreher A, Simon J, Valasek J (2021) Optimal decision rules in multilateral aid funds. Rev Int Organ 16(3):689–719
36. Gulrajani N (2016) Bilateral versus multilateral aid channels. Strategic choices for donors. London: Overseas Development Institute
37. Fraser A (2005) Poverty reduction strategy papers: Now who calls the shots? Rev Afr Polit Econ 32(104–105):317–340
38. Tangri R, Mwenda AM (2008) Elite corruption and politics in Uganda. Commonw & Comp Polit 46(2):177–194
39. Heinzel M et al (2021) Birds of a feather? The determinants of impartiality perceptions of the IMF and the World Bank. Rev Int Polit Econ 28(5):1249–1273
40. Usman W (2009) Determinants of foreign aid with the use of IMF compliance conditionality index: case study of Pakistan (1973–2006). Available at SSRN 1725986
41. Javed F, Sarwar S An Evil in Policy Making for Developing Nations: Bureaucracy or Uncertainty. Entrepreneurship: A Case Study of Light Engineering Units Operating in Gujranwala District: p. 31
42. Cashel-Cordo P, Craig SG (1990) The public sector impact of international resource transfers. J Dev Econ 32(1):17–42
43. Isenman P (1976) Biases in aid allocations against poorer and larger countries. World Dev 4(8):631–641
44. Buntaine MT (2016) Giving aid effectively: The politics of environmental performance and selectivity at multilateral development banks. 2016: Oxford University Press
45. Mamoon M (2015) Does political instability in developing countries attract more foreign aid. Int J Econ Financ 8(1):208–216
46. Nilsen BE (2016) Struggle for Sway: Chinese aid as determinant of World Bank aid allocations in sub-Saharan Africa. NTNU
47. Easterly W (2003) IMF and World Bank structural adjustment programs and poverty. Managing currency crises in emerging markets. University of Chicago Press, pp 361–392
48. Marchesi S, Sirtori E (2011) Is two better than one? The effects of IMF and World Bank interaction on growth. Rev Int Organ 6(3):287–306
49. Azam M (2022) Governance and economic growth: evidence from 14 Latin America and Caribbean countries. J Knowl Econ 13(2):1470–1495
50. Sharma SD (2007) Democracy, good governance, and economic development. Taiwan J Democr 3(1):29–62
51. Rivera-Batiz FL (2002) Democracy, governance, and economic growth: theory and evidence. Rev Dev Econ 6(2):225–247
52. Easterly W (2005) What did structural adjustment adjust?: The association of policies and growth with repeated IMF and World Bank adjustment loans. J Dev Econ 76(1):1–22
53. Leuz C, Oberholzer-Gee F (2006) Political relationships, global financing, and corporate transparency: Evidence from Indonesia. J Financ Econ 81(2):411–439
54. Liedong TA, Rajwani T (2018) The impact of managerial political ties on corporate governance and debt financing: Evidence from Ghana. Long Range Plan 51(5):666–679
55. Grindle MS (2004) Good enough governance: poverty reduction and reform in developing countries. Governance 17(4):525–548
56. Chletsos M, Sintos A (2020) The effects of IMF conditional programs on the unemployment rate. Available at SSRN 3515996

57. Barro RJ, Lee J-W (2005) IMF programs: Who is chosen and what are the effects? J Monet Econ 52(7):1245–1269
58. Grigorian DA, Manole V (2002) IMF working paper
59. Stubbs T et al (2020) How to evaluate the effects of IMF conditionality. Rev Int Organ 15(1):29–73
60. Hansen H, Tarp F (2001) Aid and growth regressions. J Dev Econ 64(2):547–570
61. Dalgaard CJ, Hansen H, Tarp F (2004) On the empirics of foreign aid and growth. Econ J 114(496):F191–F216
62. Fink G, Redaelli S (2011) Determinants of international emergency aid—humanitarian need only? World Dev 39(5):741–757
63. Amusa K, Monkam N, Viegi N (2016) The political and economic dynamics of foreign aid: A case study of United States and Chinese aid to sub-Sahara Africa. ERSA-Econ Res South Afr 21(5):363–373
64. Brissimis SN et al (2012) Current account determinants and external sustainability in periods of structural change. Econ Chang Restruct 45(1):71–95
65. Harrigan J, Mosley P, Toye J (2013) Aid and Power-Vol 1: The World Bank and Policy Based Lending. Routledge
66. Kaufmann D, Kraay A, Mastruzzi M (2005) Governance matters IV: governance indicators for 1996–2004. World bank policy research working paper series, 2005(3630)

Chapter 9
The Changing Dynamics of Commodity Markets Volatility: Evidence from Major Commodity Indices

Jatin Trivedi, Mohd Merajuddin Inamdar, Rachana Baid, and Narsimhulu Siddula

Abstract Common observations on historical time series of asset returns are typically heavy-tailed, heteroskedastic, and serially dependent, particularly for financial markets. We consider random samples of commodity indices to test interdependency, the presence of the leverage effect, and associated value at risk (VaR) models. The sample of daily closing ten commodity indices obtained from Bloomberg and work covers observations from 2000-01-03 to 2022-01-07, on which we performed quantile estimations and VaR models. To capture the changes in volatility, we partitioned the data into three phases: before the COVID-19 movement, during the COVID-19 movement, and after the COVID-19 movement. We find that volatility is persistent, volatility shocks retain a long timeline, and exponential changes in volatility occur during a global pandemic.

Keywords Commodity markets · Volatility · COVID-19

9.1 Introduction

Global markets were affected for a very long time by the novel coronavirus. The financial market meltdown that affected the country's economic stability caused a significant fall throughout much of the nation. Additionally, the worldwide lockdown

J. Trivedi · M. M. Inamdar (✉) · R. Baid · N. Siddula
National Institute of Securities Markets, Mumbai, India
e-mail: Meraj.inamdar@nism.ac.in

J. Trivedi
e-mail: jatin.trivedi@nism.ac.in

R. Baid
e-mail: rachana.baid@nism.ac.in

N. Siddula
e-mail: narsimhulu.siddula@nism.ac.in

H. Adam and R. Rena (eds.), *Political Economy of Development in the Global South Post-COVID-19 Pandemic*,
https://doi.org/10.1007/978-981-99-4074-5_9

intensified the concern among investors and the corporate community. Commodities are essential commodities that are traded from one nation to another following past agreements. Globally traded commodities, including crude oil, metals, and grains, saw unanticipated swings. However, the effect was also felt by commodity instruments used as steady price hedges, such as gold and silver. As the majority of investors worldwide chose to hedge their investments in stable assets, one of the standard parameters, Value at Risk, increased by more than ten times for crude oil and by two times for Gold and Silver.

The unpredictable behavior of the pricing of a variety of commodities products has been drastically altered as a result of the occurrence, which has brought about a significant transformation. In contrast to the past, however, commodities such as feedlot cattle, energy, and livestock all reacted to value at risk in the same way. In the past, things were not like this at all. The financial markets have a well-deserved reputation for being highly volatile due to the high level of price speculation and index movement that is characteristic of these sectors. The recent occurrence of a global phenomenon known as COVID led to an increase in volatility that was more than 15 times higher than the norm, which caused similar fluctuations in the values of commodities assets. We look at a sample of 10 distinct commodities indices and assess changes in the Value at Risk, daily volatility, and annualized volatility to see how this event influenced investor behavior prior to, during, and after the COVID-19 pandemic. This is done in order to provide a comprehensive record of this event for future reference. Prokopczuk et al. [34] Examines the possibility that the unpredictable behavior of the commodity markets and the unpredictability of the economy are related to one another in some way. Our investigation revealed that volatility in the commodity market is closely associated with economic and financial unpredictability. This association is especially robust during periods of economic deceleration. It is now much simpler to arrive at an accurate estimate of the volatility of the commodities market as a result of the existence of variables related to credit risk, stress in financial markets, and changes in business circumstances. The predictability of commodities markets is particularly noticeable from the year 2004, and it reaches its maximum peak during the global financial crisis that happened between 2008 and 2009. Ding et al. [18] demonstrates the dramatically different liquidity implications on market volatility and correlation with the stock market following the commercialization of the gold, sugar, and wheat markets. These findings represent a considerable departure from the time before the financialization of these markets.

Prices of commodities are notoriously unstable due to the fact that they react quickly to a wide variety of uncontrolled events, such as labor disputes and demonstrations, changes in the state of the weather, fluctuations in the value of various currencies, speculations, and inflation [22]. Since 2020, market disruptions caused by the COVID-19 outbreak have resulted in significant price adjustments across numerous commodity markets [46]. These price swings have highlighted the necessity of risk management and commodity market volatility. According to Gorton and Rouwenhorst [23], the commodity markets have witnessed a significant increase in the number of investments over the course of the last few decades. One of the reasons for the growth of commodities investment is that it has a low correlation to equity markets, which is one of the reasons that investors are drawn to it for hedging purposes and portfolio diversity. According to Gorton and Rouwenhorst [23] and Erb and Harvey [20], the lack of a correlation between the two variables can be explained by the fact that the prices of commodities are affected by a wide range of factors, such as the climate, the outcomes of geopolitical events, and the relationship between demand and supply. According to Larson et al. [28], one of the most important considerations in derivative valuations, inventory management, and hedging is price volatility. According to Shiller [36], one of the most important factors to take into account while making financial decisions and managing risks is volatility. It is generally accepted that the volatility of financial markets has increased over the course of the past four decades as a direct result of the convergence of markets on a global scale [1, 6]. As a direct consequence of this, ever since the beginning of modern securities markets, crisis events have presented market regulators with a difficult issue. Examples of these types of crises include political unrest, pandemics, wars, terrorist attacks, and global financial and economic crises [11, 12, 16, 47]. Other types of crises include natural catastrophes and disasters caused by humans. According to Schwert [38], the quantity and direction of volatility spillover can change depending on the magnitude of the shock as well as the amount of time that has passed.

The demand-supply equilibrium of commodity prices was severely impacted by COVID-19 shocks [29]. Crude oil shows a leverage effect of negative shocks (Costola and Lorusso, 2022). Crude oil touched a historical low, and the largest one-month drop was observed at the end of April 2020. The crude oil futures contract traded at a discount to the spot price, a market condition known as backwardation, which is relatively uncommon in the futures market. The fall served as a contagion to other nonenergy commodities as well: as cotton and copper prices fell, manufacturers were forced to choose between making margin calls or liquidating their positions through price fixing. Producers overwhelmingly preferred the latter option, causing the market to fall even further [41]. Due to the slowing economy, agricultural goods have also seen a drop in demand [8]. Industrial commodity production was also hindered by the COVID-19 lockdown, resulting in a low supply [46]. The majority of commodities are used as direct or indirect inputs in industrial processes. The travel limitations and lockdown imposed by COVID-19, however, have resulted in a major decline in the demand for nonrenewable fuel, which accounts for two-thirds of global oil use [46]. The food price crisis of 2008 had a spillover effect on the crude oil and farm commodities markets [32].

Kang et al. examines the effects of global stock market volatility and global commodity price shocks on the output of various nations and finds that the impact of global stock market volatility on the output of the United States is exacerbated by the endogenous reactions of commodity prices. In addition, there is a reciprocal relationship between the volatility of the stock market and the shocks in the prices of commodities, which has an effect on the economy through a process of gradual and endogenous adjustment. In addition, the consequences of shocks caused by volatility in global stock markets on national economies might vary widely from country to country. Fang and Shao develop a brand new index that is able to accurately quantify the level of intensity of the conflict that is now continuing between Russia and Ukraine. This index will be used to investigate the degree of volatility risk in commodities markets, as well as the amount to which and the means by which this conflict has an effect on that level. Urom et al. investigates the connection between real economic activity and the financial and commodity markets from two quite different vantage points. They begin by employing the discrete wavelet approach in order to investigate the lead-lag relationship that exists between actual economic activity and the marketplaces that were previously discussed. And use the Time-Varying Parameter VAR (TVP-VAR) model to measure the degree of short-term and long-term integration among these variables. This model takes into account stochastic volatility. According to the findings of wavelet analysis, during times of economic slowdown, such as the COVID-19 pandemic, the real economic activity shock had a tendency to follow the lead of the chosen markets. This was the case even if it was not always the case. According to the findings of the TVP-VAR research, the interdependence between economic activity and the chosen markets is at its highest level when examined over a longer period of time or when the economy is undergoing a period of recession. Several scholarly articles exhibit the changes in commodity prices, financial market volatility, changes in the degree of value at risk, and investment hedge into precious metals such as gold and silver [2, 4, 5, 18, 19, 25, 34, 38].

This research is different from the current early literature on the COVID-19 pandemic, which focused on the link between COVID-19 and the crash in oil prices [3], the study of wheat markets during the early period of the COVID-19 pandemic [42], and predictions of the COVID-19 pandemic's impact on country-specific commodity trades [9]. Covid-19's impact on crude oil and agricultural futures nexuses [44] and a look at how the COVID-19 pandemic has affected major items from a socioeconomic aspect Nicola et al. [33] have also been explored in the past. These studies can be found in the references section of this article. The long-term dynamics of commodity market volatility both during the COVID-19 crisis era and in the post-COVID-19 recovery phase are the primary focus of the research that is being conducted at the present time.

9.2 Data and Methodology

This study considered daily observations from 10 randomly selected commodity indices, including the aggregate Commodity Index as well as the Crude Oil Future Index, MSCI World Metals and Minerals Index, Grain Sub Index, BBG Gold Index, Silver Sub Index, Feeder Cattle Sub Index, Energy Sub Index, Commodity Ex-Agri Livestock Index, and Commodity Agri Index. We obtained daily closing returns from 3rd January 2000 to 7th January 2022 using Bloomberg data. We hoped to uncover the relationship between the aggregate commodity index that absorbs the price behavior of commodity assets and nine selected commodity indices to check volatility and volatility clusters and to ascertain whether a volatility model can predict the commodity market and whether commodity price behavior captures past volatility to future prices. To obtain these objectives, we employed quantile estimation; hence we converted the data using logarithms to find log differences considered to deal with the unit root. Volatility is an important parameter for decisions such as trade and investments and is widely used for portfolio optimization, risk mitigation, and forecasting asset pricing.

First, data have been converted daily returns into log returns, and we consider the first difference of log returns using the log conversion process given below

$$r_t = \ln\left(\frac{p_t}{p_{t-1}}\right) = \ln(p_t) - \ln(p_{t-1}) \tag{9.1}$$

where p_t represents the current commodity prices of the selected sample indices divided by the immediate previous price, p_{t-1}. Furthermore, to test whether returns converted to stationary or not, we used an augmented Dickey-Fuller (ADF) regression process

$$\Delta y_t = c + \beta \cdot t + \delta \cdot y_{t-1} + \sum_{i-1}^{p} \gamma_i \Delta y_{t-1} + \varepsilon_t \tag{9.2}$$

$$(1 - L)yt = \beta 0 + (\alpha - 1)yt - 1 + \varepsilon i \tag{9.3}$$

where $y(t - 1)$ indicates the first lag of the returns and $\Delta y(t - 1)$ represents the first difference of the selected sample series at time $(t - 1)$ and follows the following process:

$$(1 - L)y_t = \beta_0 + (\alpha - 1)y_t - 1 + \varepsilon_i. \tag{9.4}$$

To minimize the mean square error (MSE), the following formula was utilized:

$$MSE = \frac{1}{n}\sum\nolimits_{i=1}^{n} (\mathrm{yi} - \beta 0 + \beta 1\mathrm{xi}1 + \cdots + \beta \mathrm{pxip})^2 \tag{9.5}$$

A lower MSE produces a better forecast, and therefore, we consider the summation ($\sum$), which represents the sum of a sequence of numbers from (I = 1 to I = n), considering (yi) as the coordinating value, which represents the intercept.

For the quantile regression model, the equation for the τth quantile is

$$Q_\tau(yi) = \beta_0(\tau) + \beta_t(\tau)xi1 + \cdots + \beta_t(\tau)xip \tag{9.6}$$

where p represents the number of features in the equation with the number of data points. Applying the quantile regression model with MSE allows one to compute any degree of quantile. Rather than remaining constant, the β coefficient can function with dependency on the quantile. This model considers the p value that provides asymmetric weight to the error terms that depend on the quantile and represents the overall sign of the error term.

Quantile regression, as introduced by Koenker and Basset, allows researchers to convert results to percentiles of the responses. The quantile process starts with a linear regression model, where n indicates the number of daily commodity returns and p provides the same number of features. The next process was to minimize the mean square errors for linear regression. Quantile regression (QR) models have achieved increasing interest in economic and financial studies, as they precisely capture the information in the data that conventional regression models likely do not. Most studies measured previously with traditional regression models initially found relationships between the expectancy of the dependent and explanatory variables. QR performs well in exploring the relationship and dependency of independent variables. To test the dependency and associated relationship of selected samples over the Commodity Index, we employed the following QR models with a 0.5 percentile matrix.

Regarding record changes in volatility during the global pandemic impact of COVID-19, we partitioned the data to compute value at risk (VaR), which supplies strong information about changes in daily volatility. To understand the associated degree of risk, we partitioned the data into the following three phases:

- Phase I Before the COVID-19 impact movement: In this phase, we considered data from 01-01-2019 to 31-12-2019, counting a total of 261 daily observations for all selected samples.
- Phase II During the COVID-19 impact movement: Data ranging from 01-01-2020 to 31-12-2020 were selected, counting 262 daily observations for all selected samples.
- Phase III After the COVID-19 impact movement: This phase includes data from 01-01-2021 to 31-12-2021, counting a total of 253 daily observations for all selected samples.

We consider the log difference of selected samples of commodity indices and apply the following Value at Risk (VaR) model:

$$VaR(\alpha) = \mu + Z(\alpha)\sigma \tag{9.7}$$

where μ represents the return of the assets, Z indicates the value of the 5% level of confidence considering a single tail test, σ represents the standard deviation of the daily asset returns, and α provides the value of the portfolio. Furthermore, we computed the possible risk factor beyond the VaR considering conditional VaR (CVaR), which is

$$CVaR(\alpha) = \frac{1}{\alpha}\int_0^\alpha VaR(x)dx \tag{9.8}$$

The conditional factor, which is noted in the above equation (C), accurately computes the extreme impact. Here, we consider the conditional expectation by using an inverse Mills ratio:

$$CVaR(\alpha) = \mu - \sigma \frac{\varphi\left(\frac{VaR(\alpha)-\mu}{\sigma}\right)}{\Phi\left(\frac{VaR(\alpha)-\mu}{\sigma}\right)} \quad (9.9)$$

CVaR provides tolerable risk that is reflected in samples of daily returns (commodity indices) or the computation of an expected shortfall. For instance, in the VaR, $(VaR(\alpha)X)$ is a noncurved and intermittent function of the confidence level (α) for discrete distributions. Therefore, as it is difficult to capture nonnormal distributions, CVaR alters the same for $(\alpha) =$ CVaR $\frac{1}{\alpha}\int_0^\alpha VaR(x)dx$, which confirms that X exceeds VaR and the results express mean excess loss.

VAR analysis provides the probability measures for loss potentials. Considering the minimum loss during the COVID-19 period, we partitioned the data into three subunits:

(1) VAR before COVID-19 (daily observations from 01-01-2019 to 31-12-2019)
(2) VAR during COVID-19 (daily observations from 01-01-2020 to 31-12-2020)
(3) VAR after COVID-19 (daily observations from 01-01-2021 to 31-12-2022).

9.3 Results and Discussion

The Commodity Index is a fixed-weighted index that takes into account an average of prices for all of the different asset classes that are classified as commodities. As a result, it is essential to make a note of how the remainder of the connected commodities assets perceives changes in conjunction with changes in the variable that is being reliant upon. Estimates provided by QR demonstrate a number of indices for commodities based on the quantile of 0.5%, which corresponds very closely to a level of 1%. This indicates that the relevance of the nine other linked indices of the commodities market may be depicted by looking at the Commodities Index, which is assumed to be constant. The indices with the lowest coefficients are the Silver Subindex, the MSCI World Metal Mining Index, and the Feeder Cattle Index. Each of these indices has a coefficient that is less than 0.08 in comparison to the constant. This further exemplifies the dependency that exists between the constant index and the commodities index. The quantile regression estimator found that the prices of commodity agri, energy, grain, and oil all have a substantial significant and positive effect with positive changes in the commodity index. This is in contrast to the BBG Gold index, which is just a sample of returns that have opposite correlations.

This demonstrates that the statistics at the middle quantile indicate clear differences with the rhythm of movement for the rest of the sample commodity price returns. Specifically, we are talking about Ex-Agri Livestock, Feeder Cattle, MSCI Silver, and the Silver Sub Index, all of which have a positive correlation and have the fewest characteristics to adopt changes in the Commodity Index.

A graphical representation of the movement of the chosen commodity indexes is provided in Fig. 9.1. In spite of the many various types of commodity assets that were chosen over the same time period, a very consistent pattern of behavior was seen. This was especially true for the Commodity Index, as well as the Grain, BBG Gold, Silver, Feeder, and Energy Indices. This reveals that current trade prices are at least more than 50% below what was anticipated when compared to trade prices in 2005, 2008, 2011, and 2014 for commodities, energy, agricultural livestock, silver, and food. The information presented in Fig. 9.2 pertains to shocks that were evident at various periods. In addition, when looking at the daily closing prices of gold, a persistent rise in price shows, which suggests the positioning of hedging, as well as somewhat unstable movement in the prices of silver as well. The shock from COVID-19 is absorbed by the prices of other commodities, but the most significant price shifts are reflected in the prices of crude oil assets.

The observed oscillations in the movement of several commodities indices revealed variable levels of disparity, despite the fact that they were selected for the same time intervals and featured a comparable number of daily data. According to the findings of the study, the movement pattern demonstrated by the selected indices is consistent with a random walk model and demonstrates anomalous distributions. During the process of analysis, it is essential to transform an aberrant distribution into a stationary (normal) distribution because the former does not offer any unique insights. When contrasted with the price swings that can be seen in the stock market, the price variations seen in the commodity market are often characterized by lower levels of volatility. During the COVID period, however, it was discovered that the price of crude oil exhibited greater volatility than the price of other commodities during acute panic events such as the appearance of a new coronavirus. This was the case regardless of whether or not the event was related to COVID. The volatility shocks that are being captured are depicted in Fig. 9.2, and they are derived from

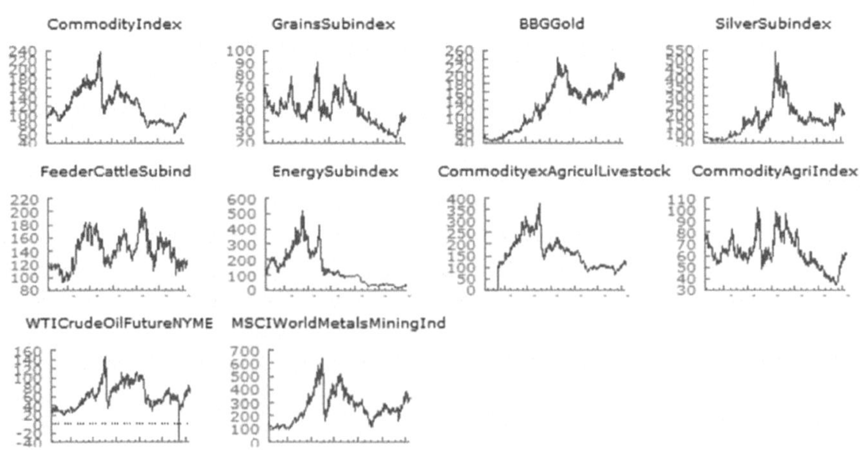

Fig. 9.1 Commodity Indices Price Movement [03-01-2000 to 07-01-2022]

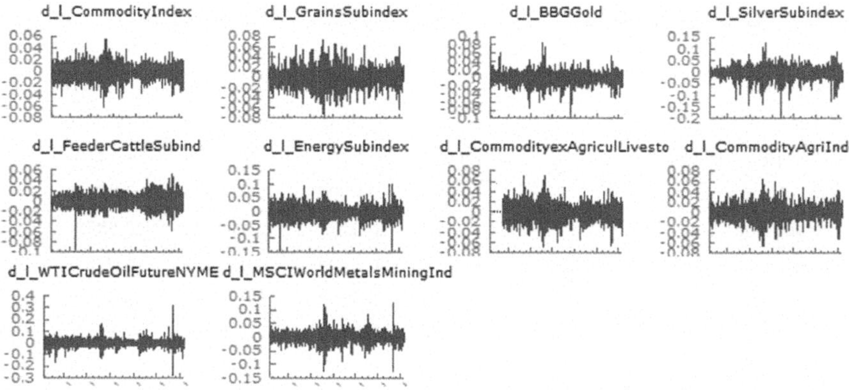

Fig. 9.2 Commodity indices price movement—first log difference [03-01-2000 to 07-01-2022]

the first log difference of the daily adjusted closing prices. During the course of the COVID period, it was noticed that the price of crude oil exhibited a greater degree of volatility in contrast to the price of other commodities at times of acute panic events, such as the appearance of a new coronavirus. The captured volatility shocks are illustrated in Fig. 9.2, and they are calculated by first finding the logarithmic difference between the daily adjusted closing prices.

According to Fama (1990), the volatility clustering phenomenon can be seen in the natural inclination of stock returns to vary in a manner that exhibits the phenomenon. According to this, it appears that high gains are frequently resentful of low returns. Figure 9.2 shows how a huge number of lesser shocks followed larger shocks, especially while the system was functioning poorly. These more minor tremors occurred after the more significant tremors. Figure 9.2 demonstrates further that all returns are depicted as percentages, which are continuously compounded, and that these percentages do not exhibit independent and identical distributions. All returns are expressed as a proportion of the initial investment. The fact that all returns are expressed as percentages is supported by this further data. The international financial crisis that was taking place at the time was visible in the form of volatility clustering, which occurred frequently between 2008 and 2009. This was one of the ways that the crisis manifested its impact. The significant number of volatility clusters that appeared in the year 2020 is one piece of evidence that points to COVID-19 having an effect on the pandemic spread of the virus over the planet. The WTI Crude Oil Futures on the New York Mercantile Exchange appear to have a significant degree of volatility when measured against the volatility of other commodity assets. The magnitude of the volatility shocks is larger than 0.3, which is a significant difference when compared to the rest of the commodity markets, which have a volatility magnitude of less than 0.0105. Table 9.1 contains the descriptive statistical information that may be discovered regarding the commodity return indexes.

With the exception of the Ex-Agricultural Livestock and Agricultural Index, all of the commodity samples exhibited negative skewness and a leptokurtic effect. It has

Table 9.1 Descriptive Statistics : Summary statistics, using observations 2000-01-03 to 2022-01-07

Variable	Mean	Std. Dev	Skewness	Ex. kurtosis
WTI crude oil future NYME	0.0003	0.0258	−0.0039	18.0860
MSCI world metals mining Ind	0.0001	0.0165	−0.4074	8.1410
Commodity index	0.0000	0.0099	−0.2959	2.8731
Grains subindex	−0.0001	0.0137	−0.0338	2.5832
BBG gold	0.0002	0.0109	−0.2332	6.0969
Silver subindex	0.0001	0.0193	−0.9025	8.0239
Feeder cattle subindex	0.0000	0.0098	−0.2582	3.5842
Energy subindex	−0.0002	0.0193	−0.2944	3.5936
Commodity ex-AgricultureLivestock	0.0000	0.0127	−0.2023	2.3129
Commodity agri index	0.0000	0.0112	−0.1198	2.8842

Source Author's computation using first differences of daily closing returns

been observed that the average returns for Grains and Energy assets exhibit a negative value. The standard deviation of Feeder Cattle and Crude Oil Futures exhibited the smallest values, falling within the range of 9–25%. The evidence presented indicates that bovine commodity values exhibit greater consistency and lower levels of volatility in comparison to futures contracts for petroleum, which are subject to significant price oscillations stemming from substantial agreements, thereby contributing to persistent fluctuations in returns. Distributions exhibiting a negative skewness and exhibiting an excess of kurtosis are indicative of a peaked distribution with a longer left tail. The leptokurtic behavior is frequently observed in the returns of stock prices among commodity assets, and such conditions are generally infrequent.

The statistical significance of the conditional variance equations for all sample commodities indices, except for the BBG Gold Index, has been observed at a level of 1% as indicated in Appendix Tables A9.1 and A9.2. The BBG Gold Index, on the other hand, has been found to be significant at a level of 5%. The study found that for MSCI World Metals and Minerals and BBG Gold, the conditional mean variances were deemed statistically significant at the 1% and 5% percentiles, respectively. However, beyond these percentiles, the variances were deemed insignificant. The reception of diverse responses led to the discovery of coefficients that were both positive and negative in nature. The markets for grains, silver, and the Agri Index exhibited negative returns. The MSCI Metals and Minerals index demonstrates that the Crude Oil index yields the most substantial positive returns, thereby signifying a significant positive gain for investors with a long-term investment horizon. The MSCI Metals and Minerals index has yielded favorable returns.

All of the sample indices for commodities, except for the BBG Gold Index, exhibit statistically significant conditional variance equations at the 1% level, as shown in Appendix Tables A9.1 and A9.2. The BBG Gold Index's significance threshold is set at a level of 5%. The study revealed that for MSCI World Metals and Minerals and

BBG Gold, the conditional mean variances were deemed statistically significant at the 1% and 5% percentiles, respectively. Nonetheless, it was established that beyond those percentiles, the said variances were deemed insignificant. The diversity of responses revealed both favorable and unfavorable coefficients. The cereals, silver, and Agri Index markets demonstrated a decline in returns during the latter part of the observed period. Long-term investors can expect significant positive gains from the Crude Oil index, which is closely monitored by the MSCI Metals and Minerals index, as it exhibits the highest positive returns.

The MSCI Metals and Minerals index currently holds the second position in its ranking. The MSCI Metals and Minerals index has demonstrated favorable returns, according to available data. The study found that all commodity samples, except for the Ex-Agricultural Livestock and Agricultural Index, exhibited a negatively skewed distribution and a leptokurtic effect. It has been discovered that the mean return on grains and energy assets exhibits a negative trend. The market exhibited relatively low degrees of standard deviation for Feeder Cattle and Crude Oil Futures with a range of 9–25%. This finding indicates that the price fluctuations of cattle exhibit greater stability and lower volatility in comparison to the price fluctuations of crude oil futures. The volatility of crude oil futures prices can be attributed to the substantial contracts involved, resulting in persistent fluctuations in returns. Distributions that display a negative skewness and an excessive kurtosis are suggestive of having attained their maximum point, leading to a prolonged left tail. The prevalence of leptokurtic behavior is observed to be higher in stock price returns as compared to commodity asset returns. However, such circumstances are typically infrequent (Tables 9.2).

The aforementioned quality provides a method that makes it possible to more precisely evaluate the outcomes of value at risk and conditional VaR models, both of which are founded on Mills' approach in order to gain an understanding of the differences that exist between regular commodities sample markets. This is done in order to gain an appreciation for the fact that regular commodities sample markets are not the same. Column 1 contains the sample indices for the commodities, and column 2 has the degrees of confidence interval parameters (1% and 5%, respectively). Figures for the typical VaR and CVaR are presented in Columns 3, 4, and 5, respectively. These columns contain data before, during, and after the installation of COVID-19. In order to arrive at this conclusion, the daily closing observations from a selection of sample markets over the course of a year were analyzed. When the extent of the risk is taken into consideration, a more realistic picture of the movements in the value at risk components is displayed. As can be seen from the data presented for VaR, crude oil still maintains its dominant position as having the largest amount of volatility in comparison to any of the other samples that were chosen. In crude oil, total volatility increased to 0.12% after COVID-19 trading, however, the period before COVID-19 saw a crude oil CVaR increase of more than ten times, reaching -58.30. This occurred despite the fact that total volatility increased to 0.12% after COVID-19 trading.

This is demonstrated by the fact that total volatility rose to 0.12% throughout this time period. Other commodity instruments that are utilized in international trade,

Table 9.2 Value at Risk and Conditional Value at Risk (CVaR) mills approach

1	2	3		4		5	
		Before COVID		During COVID		After COVID	
	C/I* (%)	VaR (%)	CVaR (%)	VaR (%)	CVaR (%)	VaR (%)	CVaR (%)
Crude oil	1.00	−4.78	−5.49	−51.06	−58.30	−4.87	−5.61
	5.00	−3.34	−4.22	−36.50	−45.42	−3.39	−4.30
Metals and mining	1.00	−2.11	−2.43	−4.76	−5.46	−3.47	−3.99
	5.00	−1.47	−1.86	−3.33	−4.21	−2.44	−3.08
Commodity index	1.00	−1.51	−1.73	−2.40	−2.75	−2.14	−2.47
	5.00	−1.06	−1.33	−1.70	−2.13	−1.48	−1.89
Grains subindex	1.00	−2.53	−2.90	−2.29	−2.63	−3.51	−4.04
	5.00	−1.79	−2.25	−1.60	−2.02	−2.46	−3.11
BBG gold	1.00	−1.61	−1.85	−3.02	−3.47	−2.17	−2.48
	5.00	−1.12	−1.42	−2.11	−2.67	−1.54	−1.92
Silver subindex	1.00	−2.78	−3.19	−6.48	−7.45	−4.48	−5.13
	5.00	−1.95	−2.46	−4.53	−5.73	−3.18	−3.98
Feeder cattle	1.00	−2.51	−2.87	−3.59	−4.11	−2.46	−2.82
	5.00	−1.78	−2.23	−2.55	−3.19	−1.73	−2.18
Energy	1.00	−3.66	−4.20	−6.72	−7.67	−3.86%	−4.45
	5.00	−2.58	−3.24	−4.80	−5.98	−2.68	−3.40
Livestock	1.00	−1.93	−2.21	−3.20	−3.67	−2.57	−2.96
	5.00	−1.35	−1.70	−2.28	−2.84	−1.79	−2.27
Commodity agri	1.00	−1.91	−2.19	−2.03	−2.33	−2.87	−3.31
	5.00	−1.35	−1.69	−1.42	−1.79	−2.00	−2.54

* C/I = Confidence interval

Source Author's computation using daily closing returns from sample commodity indices

such as metals and mining, grains, energy, and animals, do not experience an exponentially larger influence than crude oil does. When compared to the other commodity instruments, crude oil is in the best position to achieve this goal. For example, during the Phase I era, the investor's value at risk remained at 2.11% before the COVID-19 period, and then it climbed to 4.76%, which is only a 1.4-fold rise. This happened before and after COVID-19 pandemic. This would imply that, in comparison to other markets, the international commodities goods market has undergone the fastest rate of change in recent history. On the other hand, the change in the commodities index relatively implies a value at risk parameter of 2.4%, which indicates that the prices of metals continued to be higher in comparison to index beta levels. Because of the calculation of the value at risk parameter, it is possible to arrive at this conclusion. In addition to this, the variations in the value at risk component for the metal and mining businesses have remained higher than those found in any of the other commodity markets over the years in which they have been traversed. This is because the metal and mining sectors are more dependent on the price of the underlying resource.

As a result of the value at risk measure's confirmation that volatility across sample commodity indices increased greatly following COVID-19, even the least volatile commodities, such as cattle, energy, and silver, have begun to exhibit trading behaviors that deviate significantly from the norm. These behaviors include trading behaviors that have begun to exhibit significant variations from the norm. Even the trading of commodities that had been regarded to be rather stable up to this time was impacted as a result of the tactics that were being used. We discovered that the market for feeder cattle was the only market that saw less volatility than it did before the COVID-19 era. According to this conclusion, it would appear that investors have switched their interests in commodities from traditional commodity markets to alternative commodity markets in order to limit the amount of risk that they are exposed to.

In order to analyze fluctuations in volatility in the periods preceding, during, and following the global pandemic event, we have taken into account all three phases mentioned above and have employed the Computation of Volatility model for the calculation of volatility.

$$\sigma_t^2 = \frac{1}{m} + \sum_{i=1}^{m} u_{n-i}2 \tag{9.10}$$

where σ indicates the standard deviation derived from the daily log returns (assumed merely zero), where $\sum_{i=1}^{m} u_{n-i}2$ represents the squared daily returns. The average daily variance is considered to compute daily volatility and annual volatility using the SQRT_252 parameters (Tables 9.3).

Table 9.3 Daily volatility and volatility for the selected period

Impact	Before COVID		During COVID		After COVID	
Variable	DV (%)	VFP (%)	DV (%)	VFP (%)	DV (%)	VFP (%)
Crude oil	2.09	33.10	2.97	47.11	2.21	35.01
Metals and mining	0.93	14.75	2.10	33.13	1.51	24.01
Commodity index	0.66	10.36	1.03	16.32	0.97	15.34
Grains subindex	1.08	17.12	1.01	15.98	1.55	24.53
BBG gold	0.72	11.32	1.33	21.08	0.93	14.75
Silver	1.21	19.17	2.88	45.58	1.93	30.57
Feeder cattle	1.07	16.89	1.52	24.08	1.06	16.84
Energy	1.59	25.10	2.84	44.97	1.74	27.64
Livestock	0.84	13.33	1.37	21.67	1.15	18.30
Agri index	0.82	12.95	0.90	14.17	1.28	20.33

* DV indicates daily volatility.
** VFP indicates volatility for the selected period
Source Author's computation using daily closing returns from the sample commodity indices

Changes in commodity trading activity changed the pattern of volatility. We note that the daily volatility of selected samples increased for all selected indices during the pandemic phase except Grains, which surprisingly decreased but appeared to increase after the pandemic phase. Annual volatility increased exponentially during phase II, particularly for silver, metals, and energy. Unlike financial market indices, commodity markets are supposed to be less volatile because they are driven by demand rather than investment. Although the paper's findings are robust in terms of risk involvement, short-term investments are equally risky. We found that daily volatility in commodity markets increased after the COVID-19 fall and recovered during the samples from Jan 2020 to Dec 2020, except for the Feeder Cattle, where volatility seems to react otherwise. This indicates that commodities that are more interested in higher volatility criteria might have attracted investors and traders from Feeder Cattle markets.

9.4 Conclusion

This study examines the volatility patterns of nine commodity indices by analyzing various aspects such as volatility, volatility clusters, the leverage effect of volatility, and the potential risk of losses. The research findings indicate that crude oil exhibited the greatest degree of volatility amidst the COVID-19 pandemic. Amidst the COVID-19 pandemic, the conduct of crude oil volatility demonstrated the adverse impact of the leverage effect. The Value at Risk (VaR) metric indicated that crude oil exhibited greater volatility compared to the other selected samples. The findings of the study indicate that there is a significant and positive impact of changes in the Commodity Index on prices of Commodity Agri, Energy, Grain, and Oil, as revealed by the quantile regression estimator. These results are consistent with the literature reviewed by Hung (2021). The standard deviation of Feeder Cattle exhibited the smallest range, falling between 9 and 25%. The present study reveals that the volatility of gold prices during the COVID-19 pandemic was comparatively lower than that of other commodities. However, it was observed to be higher than the gold price volatility observed before and after the pandemic period. Amidst the COVID-19 pandemic, the gold commodity has demonstrated favorable hedging capabilities with minimal volatility, which aligns with the conclusions drawn by Yousef et al. [43].

The study identified daily volatility and annual volatility for three selected parameters. The results indicated that daily volatility exhibited a relative increase during the COVID-19 period, leading to the establishment of new-normal volatility parameters for the post-COVID-19 period (Jan 2021 to Dec 2021). The aforementioned statement suggests the employment of assertive commercial strategies aimed at recuperating losses and achieving profits in the context of markets characterized by significant fluctuations in prices. Differential performance of the Agri Index was observed among the various samples. Remarkably, the level of volatility following the COVID-19 pandemic surpasses that observed during and prior to the pandemic, thus exhibiting exceptional performance. This suggests that in the upcoming year, the Agri Index is expected to exhibit even greater volatility. The study's outcomes will offer comprehensive and enduring perspectives to investors, stakeholders in the commodity market, and policymakers. There exist certain lacunae in our comprehension of the fluctuations in commodity market volatility in times of crisis. During the composition of this manuscript, it has been observed that geopolitical risks have emerged as a significant determinant of commodity market volatility subsequent to the pandemic. A comprehensive analysis is required to examine the impact of geopolitical risks on commodity market volatility and draw parallels with the outcomes of the COVID-19 pandemic.

Appendix

See Tables A9.1, A9.2, and A9.3.

Table A9.1 Quantile estimates, using observations 2000-01-03:2022-01-07 ($T = 5745$)

	Coefficient	Std. Error	*t*-Ratio	*p* Value
Const	12.4907	0.51368	24.32	<0.0001
WTI Crude Oil Future NYME	0.17142	0.00359	47.8	<0.0001
MSCI World Metals Mining Index	0.07264	0.00073	99.48	<0.0001
Grains Sub Index	0.30582	0.0153	19.99	<0.0001
BBG Gold	−0.111986	0.00289	−38.70	<0.0001
Silver Sub Index	0.06235	0.00189	32.99	<0.0001
Feeder Cattle Sub Index	0.07979	0.00212	37.66	<0.0001
Energy Sub Index	0.15236	0.00099	154.5	<0.0001
Commodity ex-Agricul Livestock	0.06252	0.00126	49.47	<0.0001
Commodity Agri Index	0.39872	0.0168	23.74	<0.0001
Dependent variable				
Median depend. var	117.612	S.D	34.821	
Sum absolute residuals	15,115	SSR	76,843.5	
Log-likelihood	−15,284.60	AIC	30,589.2	
Schwarz criterion	30,655.8	HQ	30,612.4	

* Dependent variable: Commodity Index, tau = 0.5, where asymptotic standard errors assuming IID errors

Table A9.2 GARCH and EGARCH statistics for Commodity Index, Crude Oil, MSCI World, Grains and BBG Gold

Model	Variable	Commodity Index	WTI CrudeOil Future NYME	MSCI World Metals Mining Ind	Grains Sub Index	BBG Gold
GARCH (1, 1) Normal distribution	const	2.2E−05	0.0006	0.0004	−0.0001	0.0001
	omega	6.3E−07	9.21E−06	0.0000	1.8E−06	0.0000
	alpha	0.0414	0.0878	0.0621	0.0524	0.0320
	beta	0.9523	0.8990	0.9276	0.9376	0.9581
	p value	E − 1%	E − 1%	1−1%	E − 1%	E − 1%
GARCH (1, 1) Skewed t distribution	const	2.4E−05	0.0004	0.0002	−9.4E−05	0.0002
	omega	4.6E−07	6.5E−06	0.0000	1.7E−06	0.0000
	alpha	0.0443	0.0725	0.0553	0.0508	0.0361
	beta	0.9520	0.9174	0.9365	0.9413	0.9605
	p value	E − 1%	E − 1%	10−1%	E − 1%	5−1%
EGARCH (1, 1) Normal distribution	const	−6.8E−05	−0.0001	0.0001	−6.7E−05	0.0002
	omega	−0.1428	−1.9E−01	−0.1841	−0.1671	−0.1515
	alpha	0.0895	0.1223	0.1142	0.1104	0.0784
	gamma	−0.0138	−0.0759	−0.0448	0.0191	0.0126
	beta	0.9919	0.9868	0.9888	0.9903	0.9896
	p value	E−1%	E−1%	E−1%	E−1%	5−1%
EGARCH (1, 1) Skewed t distribution	const	1.7E−05	–	0.0001	−0.0001	0.0003
	omega	−0.1263	–	−0.1575	−0.1569	−0.1130
	alpha	0.0939	–	0.1077	0.1067	0.0878
	gamma	−0.0116	–	−0.0371	0.0195	0.0279
	beta	0.9940	–	0.9912	0.9912	0.9943
	p value	E−1%	–	E−1%	E−1%	5-1%

Source Author's computation using daily closing returns from sample commodity indices

Table A9.3 GARCH and EGARCH statistics for Silver, Feeder, Energy, Ex-Agri Live and Agri Index

Model	Variable	SilverSub Index	Feeder Cattle Sub Index	Energy Sub Index	Commodity ExAgricul Livestock	Commodity Agri Index
GARCH (1, 1) Normal distribution	const	-0.0001	0.0001	0.0000	0.0001	-0.0001
	omega	0.0000	0.0000	0.0000	0.0000	0.0000
	alpha	0.0451	0.0490	0.0565	0.0467	0.0492
	beta	0.9525	0.9458	0.9374	0.9473	0.9424
	p value	E−1%	E−1%	E−1%	E−1%	E−1%
GARCH (1, 1) Skewed t distribution	const	−0.0001	0.0001	0.0000	0.0001	−0.0001
	omega	0.0000	0.0000	0.0000	0.0000	0.0000
	alpha	0.0410	0.0583	0.0504	0.0483	0.0472
	beta	0.9609	0.9360	0.9468	0.9502	0.9454
	p value	E−1%	E−1%	E−1%	E−1%	E−1%
EGARCH (1, 1) Normal distribution	const	−0.0001	0.0000	−0.0002	0.0001	−0.0001
	omega	−0.1440	−0.1648	−0.1860	−0.1612	−0.1601
	alpha	0.1144	0.0972	0.1192	0.0996	0.1100
	gamma	0.0160	−0.0398	−0.0266	0.0169	0.0108
	beta	0.9923	0.9902	0.9880	0.9903	0.9915
	p value	E−1%	E−1%	E−1%	E−1%	E−1%
EGARCH (1, 1) Skewed t distribution	const	−0.0001	0.0000	−0.0001	0.0001	−0.0001
	omega	−0.1069	−0.2016	−0.1422	−0.1291	−0.1505
	alpha	0.1010	0.1156	0.1081	0.1032	0.1037
	gamma	0.0243	−0.0475	−0.0226	0.0144	0.0123
	beta	0.9951	0.9877	0.9924	0.9942	0.9920
	p value	E−1%	E−1%	E−1%	E−1%	E−1%

Source Author's computation using daily closing returns from sample commodity indices.

References

1. Abou-Zaid AS (2011) Volatility spillover effects in emerging MENA stock markets. Rev Appl Econ 7(1076-2016-87178):107–127
2. Ahmed MY, Sarkodie SA (2021) COVID-19 pandemic and economic policy uncertainty regimes affect commodity market volatility. Resources Policy, 74s. https://doi.org/10.1016/j.resourpol.2021.102303
3. Albulescu C (2020) Coronavirus and Oil Price Crash, Politehnica University of Timisoara. https://papers.ssrn.com/sol3/papers.cfm?abstract_id=3553452
4. Alfeus M, Sklibosios Nikitopoulos C (2020) Forecasting commodity markets volatility: HAR or rough? SSRN Electron J. https://doi.org/10.2139/ssrn.3520500
5. Aziz T, Sadhwani R, Habibah U, Al Janabi MAM (2020) Volatility spillover among equity and commodity markets. SAGE Open, 10(2). https://doi.org/10.1177/2158244020924418
6. Baele L (2005) Volatility spillover effects in European equity markets. J Financ Quant Anal 373–401

7. Baele L (2005) Volatility spillover effects in European equity markets. J Financ Quant Anal 373–401
8. Baffes J, Kabundi A, Nagle P (2020) The role of income and substitution in commodity demand
9. Barichello R (2020) The COVID-19 pandemic: anticipating its effects on Canada's Agricultural Trade. Can J Agric Econ
10. Bhuyan R, Lin EC, Ricci PF (2010) Asian stock markets and the severe acute respiratory syndrome (SARS) epidemic: implications for health risk management. Int J Environ Health 4(1):40–56
11. Bussière M, Fratzscher M (2008) Low probability, high impact: policymaking and extreme events. J Policy Model 30(1):111–121
12. Chesney M, Reshetar G, Karaman M (2011) The impact of terrorism on financial markets: an empirical study. J Bank Finance 35(2):253–267
13. Choudhry T, Jayasekera R (2014) Returns and volatility spillover in the European banking industry during global financial crisis: flight to perceived quality or contagion? Int Rev Financ Anal 36:36–45
14. Citigold (2020) COVID-19: a review of global economic impact. Monthly Market Outlook (March) 1–11
15. Corbet S, Larkin CJ, Lucey BM (2020) The contagion effects of the COVID-19 pandemic: evidence from gold and cryptocurrencies. Financ Res Lett May 2020
16. Cummins DJ (2007) Reinsurance for natural and man-made catastrophes in the United States: Current State of the market and regulatory reforms. Risk Manag Insur Rev 10(2):179–220
17. De Vijlder W (2020) The Covid-19 pandemic: economic consequences pervasive uncertainty, delayed recovery. BNP Paribas Economic Research Department (March) 1–51
18. Ding S, Cui T, Zheng D, Du M (2021) The effects of commodity financialization on commodity market volatility. Resour Policy 73. https://doi.org/10.1016/j.resourpol.2021.102220
19. Dutta A, Bouri E, Das D, Roubaud D (2020) Assessment and optimization of clean energy equity risks and commodity price volatility indexes: Implications for sustainability. J Clean Prod 243. https://doi.org/10.1016/j.jclepro.2019.118669
20. Erb CB, Harvey CR (2006) The strategic and tactical value of commodity futures. Financ Anal J 62(2):69–97
21. Frank N, Hesse H (2009) Financial spillovers to emerging markets during the global financial crisis (No. 9–104). International Monetary Fund
22. Goldman Sachs (2020) SARS-Coronavirus-2/COVID-19: An Update on Testing, Therapies, Vaccines, and the Healthcare System. The Investment Strategy Group (ISG) in the Consumer and Investment Management Division of Goldman Sachs., (Fifth in a Series), 1–36. Available at https://www.goldmansachs.com/insights/talks-at-gs/sharmin-mossavarrahmani-f/deck.pdf
23. Gorton G, Rouwenhorst KG (2006) Facts and fantasies about commodity futures. Financ Anal J 62(2):47–68
24. Hung NT (2021) Oil prices and agricultural commodity markets: evidence from pre and during COVID-19 outbreak. Resour Policy 73:102236
25. Hollstein F, Prokopczuk M, Würsig C (2020) Volatility term structures in commodity markets. J Futur Mark 40(4). https://doi.org/10.1002/fut.22083
26. IEA (International Energy Agency) (2020) Oil Market Report. International Energy Agency, Paris
27. King M, Sentana E, Wadhwani S (1990) Volatility and links between national stock markets (No. w3357)
28. Larson DF, Varangis P, Yabuki N (1998) Commodity risk management and development. Available at SSRN 597214
29. Kingsly KM, Henri K (2020) COVID-19 and oil prices. Retrieved from Available at SSRN: https://ssrn.com/abstract=3555880
30. Mensi W, Beljid M, Boubaker A, Managi S (2013) Correlations and volatility spillovers across commodity and stock markets: linking energies, food, and gold. Econ Model 32:15–22
31. Naidenova I, Parshakov P, & Shakina E (2020) Idiosyncratic and systematic shocks of COVID-19 pandemic on financial markets. International Laboratory of Intangible Driven Economy

32. Nazlioglu S, Erdem C, Soytas U (2013) Volatility spillover between oil and agricultural commodity markets. Energy Econ 36:658–665
33. Nicola M, Alsafi Z, Sohrabi C, Kerwan A, Al-Jabir A, Iosifidis C, Agha M, Agha R (2020) The socio-economic implications of the coronavirus and COVID-19 pandemic: a reviews. Int J Surg 78(June):185–193
34. Prokopczuk M, Stancu A, Symeonidis L (2019) The economic drivers of commodity market volatility. J Int Money Financ 98. https://doi.org/10.1016/j.jimonfin.2019.102063
35. Schwert GW (1989) Why does stock market volatility change over time? J Financ 44(5):1115–1153
36. Shiller RJ (1992) Market volatility. MIT Press
37. Shusong B, Min Y (2009) The dynamic relationships between stock price and exchange rate——an empirical analysis based on Chinese market. Nankai Econ Stud 2:46–60
38. Smales LA (2017) Commodity market volatility in the presence of U.S. and Chinese macroeconomic news. J Commod Mark 7. https://doi.org/10.1016/j.jcomm.2017.06.002
39. Tamakoshi G, Hamori S (2013) Volatility and mean spillovers between sovereign and banking sector CDS markets: a note on the European sovereign debt crisis. Appl Econ Lett 20(3):262–266
40. Theodossiou P, Lee U (1993) Mean and volatility spillovers across major national stock markets: Further empirical evidence. J Financ Res 16(4):337–350
41. United States Department of Agriculture (USDA) (2020) Weekly Cotton Market Review. Wkly Cotton Mark Rev 101(35):1–11
42. Vercammen J (2020) Information-rich wheat markets in the early days of COVID-19. Can J Agric Econ. https://doi.org/10.1111/cjag.12229
43. Yousef I, Shehadeh E (2020) The impact of COVID-19 on gold price volatility. Int J Econ Bus Adm 8(4):353–364
44. Wang J, Shao W, Kim J (2020) Analysis of the impact of COVID-19 on the correlations between crude oil and agricultural futures. Chaos, Solitons Fractals 136(July):109896
45. World Bank. (2019). The role of substitution in commodity demand. World Bank
46. World Bank. (2020). A Shock Like No Other:The Impact of COVID-19 on Commodity Markets . World Bank
47. Worthington AC (2008) The impact of natural events and disasters on the Australian stock market: A GARCH-M analysis of storms, floods, cyclones, earthquakes and bushfires. Glob Bus Econ Rev 10(1):1–10

Chapter 10
Unpacking Financial Literacy: A Critical Conceptual Model for the Global South

Firdaus Khan and Srinivas Surisetti

Abstract The COVID-19 pandemic has provided several insights into financial fragility, financial literacy and financial well-being. The financial literacy agenda elicits massive, pan-global and multistakeholder cooperation to bridge the disparity in inclusion and development parameters caused by historical power imbalances. In the post-pandemic, digitalized era, this endeavour will find impetus in two-way communication and experience sharing between the Global North and South. In the context of new realities, there is a need to trace financial literacy's historical development and fitment to the needs and challenges of developing countries. Published work between 1992 and 2022 was critically evaluated through a hybrid narrative that synthesized key aspects of conceptualization and measurement, evaluated financial literacy profiling and outcomes of financial literacy education, and probed for tacit assumptions and missing aspects in the popular view. The review found that financial literacy was birthed in the urgency of the 401-k launch in the USA, moving through two forks—financial literacy in the workplace and higher education—pushed to the Global South through deep-rooted global cooperation. The critical review found that postulations of micropositioning, homoeconomicus and efficient capital market theorizing are embedded in the financial literacy agenda, but these do not hold for developing countries. Furthermore, missing pieces critical to the development agenda were retrieved, and a transdisciplinary, conceptual model has been offered as a fresh lens for research and practice in the Global South.

Keywords Financial literacy · Financial literacy education · Financial inclusion · Development · Capital markets

F. Khan (✉)
S.P. Jain School of Global Management, Mumbai, India
e-mail: firdaus.khan@spjain.org

S. Surisetti
Tata Institute of Social Sciences, (Hyderabad off-campus), Mumbai, India
e-mail: srinivas.surisetti@tiss.edu

H. Adam and R. Rena (eds.), *Political Economy of Development in the Global South Post-COVID-19 Pandemic*,
https://doi.org/10.1007/978-981-99-4074-5_10

10.1 Introduction

Regulated financial markets are the cornerstone of economic development [137]. However, their increasing complexity has become a cause for concern [87, 216]. In this context, financial literacy (FL) has risen as a countervailing factor, a tenet of human capital development and a poverty alleviation tool [69]. Due to policy initiatives in this direction, lower- and middle-income households have entered capital markets, small businesses are no longer confined to bank loans, and women and youth have become active do-it-yourself investors, especially in the COVID lockdown period [19, 80, 97]. However, FL remains elusive: barely one-third of the global population is financially literate, half of the world's credit card users are ignorant about its features, and women less than 25 years are the most financially illiterate [79, 124, 182]. FL is similarly low to moderate across the globe [120]. In addition, the COVID-19 pandemic revealed that large sections of American and European citizens were just as financially fragile as those in developing countries [79, 148]. This begs the question: What have been the nature and outcomes of the FL agenda, as recorded in academic research for several decades?

Goyal and Kumar [90] found that 62% of published FL studies since 2000 were located in developed countries, while only 23% emerged from the Global South. Furthermore, 86% were empirical, 10% were conceptual and 3% were review papers. Desirable FL outcomes are increased retirement savings, solid credit scores or consistent investment in capital markets [99, 141, 149]. Given such evidence of an arbitrary understanding of *financially responsible behaviour*, the authors intuitively believe that the body of work may fall short of capturing the needs, aspirations and challenges of the developing world. It is imperative to consider the possibility that FL, despite being a popular construct, may yet be underexplored.

Calcagno et al. [44] recommended focusing on FL in the context of the Global South to render development outcomes rather than financialization objectives. The Global South is perceived as a repository of cheap natural and human resources, an untapped and underserved market and sometimes even as an experimental pool to further the sociopolitical and business agendas of the North. However, the digital era has resulted in healthy two-way communication and experience-sharing between the North and South to collaboratively deal with issues relating to sustainability, diversity, ethics, and historical power imbalances. Furthermore, the COVID-19 pandemic revealed that the financial resilience and financial capability of citizens are essential for any Govt's economic and social stability goals, whether in the North or South [127, 186].

10.2 Review of Literature

Financial literacy has found the full support of governments, central banks, global financial institutions, think tanks, nonprofit institutions, financial service providers and academia, each with their own agenda. It is therefore not surprising that it may have evolved over its history and undergone considerable iterations in conceptualization. Rashid and Surisetti [197] noted several alternative definitions of FL, namely, money management, being free from debt burden, avoiding misinformation and recognizing fraud and the capacity to confidently make long-term and short-term budgeting and investing decisions. Hogarth [102] has expanded FL into multiple, complex dimensions such as *knowledge, dispositions, skill set and experiences—all of which could be gender-related and may alter across the individual's progressive life stages.* Early disagreement notwithstanding, most FL research largely alludes to some cognitive ability related to financial concepts and behaviour related to debt and investing. Furthermore, measurement approaches converge over a few popular instruments and theoretical models.

The OECD/INFE questionnaire provides an FL score through financial awareness, financial attitude, financial knowledge, financial skill and financial behaviour, while the Big Three questionnaire tests cognition related to compounding, inflation and diversification [15, 146]. Few researchers have innovatively added new dimensions such as subjective perception bias, real and nominal interest rates, etc., for thematic surveys, thereby providing a nuanced empirical understanding of FL as credit literacy [210], debt literacy [144], portfolio diversification [94] and mutual funds literacy [181]. Other approaches include FL mapping for differences in economic development, FL scales with psychometric testing and FL scales with separate foundational FL and higher-order FL [39, 53, 56, 124, 128, 200, 213]. Béres and Huzdik [42] hypothesize that low cash dependency and greater digital financial transactions will lead to increasingly formalized financial experiences and greater opportunities for market participation.

High FL has several personal, firm-level, community-level and country-level outcomes, such as lower work-related anxiety, reduced absenteeism, improved credit ratings, higher employee retention, higher efficiency and greater financial stability [26, 32, 85, 107, 126, 228]. Studies also report that adverse micro-level outcomes such as increased vulnerability to informal debt, personal hardships and broader economic risks, poor stock market returns, stress, isolation, low self-esteem, mental illness, substance abuse and even a higher incidence of divorce may emerge from low FL [61, 147, 204]. In the recent pandemic, FL has played the crucial role of maintaining financial positivity, decreasing financial fragility and avoiding over indebtedness [10, 49, 133].

At the crux of the FL agenda is the shared understanding that FL is directly and positively correlated to financial well-being [3, 50, 145]. However, Brüggen et al. [38] have observed that several published studies reported financial well-being (FWB) levels and outcomes without providing any formal definition. Well-being has been conceptualized in earlier studies as *attitude* [191], *perception* [113], a *measure of overall life satisfaction* [11] and *quality of life* [33]. In the 1990s, cognitive, economic and psychological aspects formed important aspects in defining FWB, as researchers tried to anchor it to lived experiences and changing life circumstances [24, 27, 29]. However, at the turn of the century, increasing computing skills and national databases made it convenient to conceptualize FWB as a retirement corpus or financialized wealth at the individual level.

High FL is positively associated with age, professional and business occupations, and higher levels of education, while attributes of unemployment, lower educational qualifications, migrant status in the country of study, female gender and deficient proficiency in the English language have repeatedly been reported as markers of low FL across the globe [162, 164, 185, 232]. However, such positivist framing based on arbitrary FL outcomes fails to capture aspects of agency, social norms, historical cultural understanding of indebtedness, and moral obligation towards the next generation or personal goals of altruism. Hence, applying popular scales without testing for cultural fitment may lead to spurious profiling and homogenizing. Additionally, investors within sophisticated markets may fail to exhibit sound portfolio selection [12, 135]. Engels et al. [70] have attempted to answer the question "Who is better at detecting fraud?" The study found that Flees have a negligible effect on fraud detection, especially since fraudsters tend to use complex and sophisticated tactics to prey on the victim's subjective well-being. Huston [108] asserts that the dominant FL models are flawed, as they ignore behavioural biases, impulsive tendencies, idiosyncratic preferences or even systemic factors such as fraud or corruption, which could cause outcomes to deviate from predicted values.

In conclusion, FL studies seem to have a positivist preference, apply arbitrary financialized outcomes and extensively indulge in profiling financially illiterate individuals. There is adequate evidence to suggest that not all groups of people are sufficiently captured through the dominant positivist framing of financial behaviour, and there may be some tacit assumptions within the FL framework. Although meta-analyses and systematic literature reviews have been conducted, one major blind spot in the literature is the absence of a historical narrative regarding the evolution of FL—from the original policy thrust that birthed it to what it represents today and the challenges around this dominant FL agenda. This critical review, therefore, attempts to fill these gaps in the literature and address the following research objectives:

- What are the key aspects of the historical evolution of the FL narrative?
- Are there any tacit assumptions within the dominant FL models? Do these assumptions, if any, hold true in the context of the Global South?
- Are there some key missing aspects in FL theorizing that could be critical to research and practice in the Global South?

10.3 Methodology

For this review of the literature, 225 research objects in the form of published book chapters, journal articles, working papers, review notes, reports, review articles, dissertations and full abstracts of published journal articles or book chapters were reviewed for the past four decades, from 1992 to 2022. Since the authors sought to trace the entire evolutionary trajectory of the theme, studies emerged from several fields—financial markets and services, development studies, psychology and family studies, sociology and gender studies; although the primary scope was published research in Economics and Finance, using Econlit, JSTOR, Elsevier, and Proquest databases. Search words used were "financial literacy", "financial well-being", "financial knowledge" and "financial behaviour." Dixon-Woods et al. [63] selection criteria were applied for selecting papers for this review, focusing on papers with clearly articulated objectives and methodology along with conclusions that were adequately supported by data. Since the selected databases may inadvertently contain some exclusion criteria, the authors have additionally undertaken a selective country-wise search on Google Scholar to populate the list with research studies reporting from the Global South. This ensured that the review was representative and meaningful. Although financial inclusion was not a search word, it entered the empirical framework of several studies, as FL has stayed largely intertwined with financial inclusion due to state-mandated programs and policies in the Global South. This review work has been created in the form of a hybrid narrative, which, according to Dabić et al. [58], seeks to create an innovative framework for the continuity of the research agenda.

The review was conducted by applying the tools of synthesis and conceptual modelling as specified in Van Wee and Banister [229]. The first section of the review, found in Sect. 10.4 of the chapter, provides a narration of the key aspects of the historical trajectory of FL and presents its antecedents. A synthesis is performed to compare countries and regions to extract aspects of divergence in the literature. Next, in Sect. 10.5, three tacit assumptions have been excavated from the literature, namely, micropositioning, homoeconomicus and efficient capital market theorizing. In light of these tacit assumptions, the relevance of the dominant FL models to the realities of the Global South is evaluated. The third part of the review, contained in Sect. 10.6, attempts to retrieve some key dimensions of the FL phenomenon from the prior sections and attempts to respecify the relationship between FL and FWB through an alternative, transdisciplinary conceptual model offering a more meaningful theorization and implementation of FL in the Global South. The chapter closes with key insights and contributions of this review, some suggestions to redirect FL research and a few limitations of this review work.

10.4 Key Aspects of the Financial Literacy Narrative

Financial literacy studies are probably one of the most visible bodies of work in research. With greater digitization, fintech applications and concerns of financial resilience tested by pandemics or geo-political strife, this theme has gained a further spurt of intrigue; hence, the historical evolution of this popular construct can be meaningful.

10.4.1 The Germination of Financial Literacy

The intent and agenda of financial literacy (FL) germinated in the USA in the early 1990s as the government planned a shift to tax-qualified, defined contributions towards a pension (401-K), away from the prior defined benefit pension [24, 28]. Being concerned that generally Americans save less, borrow substantially and invest unwisely, often falling prey to fraudulent activities and financial scams, the Govt. offered financial education to an increasing number of individuals at educational institutions and the workplace, anticipating that this education about possible economic vulnerabilities could have a powerful effect on financial behaviour [26, 29]. Two early surveys of this period were Bernheim and Garrett [25, 28], examining whether a mandated financial curriculum in high school had any impact on adult financial decisions, and [22, 28], testing the effect of financial education at the workplace on the utilization rate of retirement plans. The former used a household survey fielded by Merrill Lynch, while the latter researched a panel of 1100 employers fielded by KPMG. The KPMG study concluded that non-highly compensated employees showed the highest response with greater retirement participation rates and higher contribution rates.

Following the KPMG survey, the impact of financial literacy education (FLE) at the workplace became a consistent topic of interest, especially tracking FL outcomes of saving and investment behaviour, goal setting, asset allocation, worker productivity and earnings [52, 66, 86]. Concurrently, several studies were conducted to evaluate the effect of the State-mandated High School Financial Planning Program or HSFPP. The impact was found to be very encouraging, as a higher savings rate, better money management, improved self-reported knowledge and a significant increase in wealth were reported by several studies [26, 105]. Furthermore, Danes [59] quantified that the efficacy of a short ten-hour FLE training on financial behaviour and understanding could last up to three months. However, it is important to note here that the long-term impact of the FLE has remained suspect, and Lusardi [140] concluded it to be weak or nonexistent.

Mandell [158] reported a poor impact of FLEs received in high school on post-high school behaviour after one to five years, showing no improvement with age and experience. Similarly, when Cole and Shastry [55] attempted to replicate the HSFPP study using census data rather than using a questionnaire, they did not find any significant impact of state-mandated FLEs on the savings behaviour of young adults. Amidst this impasse, a key breakthrough was Peng et al. [188] observation that when information is relevant to life-cycle needs, FLEs in college have a greater impact. Soon the insight of FLE's timeliness morphed into several elaborate programs to reach the financially illiterate or unskilled at "teachable moments" across their life cycle namely, credit counselling in early youth or when applying for education loans or a mortgage loan as an early professional; when seeking risk protection (insurance products) or wealth solutions (retirement plans) in mid-life [51, 101, 149]. A few researchers, however, were sceptical while interpreting results from such studies.

Mandell [159] raised concerns about peer effects, while Clark and d'Ambrosio [52] objected to one-time training programs being called 'interventions.' Overall, despite the Govt. backing and positive outcomes in early empirical studies, FLE seems to have consistently fallen short. A small number of studies continued to, concurrently, report people's poor objective and perceived understanding of core financial concepts, their inability to improve their actionable financial knowledge or their low volition to access information pertinent to their financial situation [55, 94]. This reticence in people, surprisingly, persisted even in the face of plummeting savings and rising indebtedness across America during the subprime crisis of 2008–11 [106, 150, 187, 199]. Furthermore, Allgood and Walstad [8] as well as West [230] showcased that the financially literate does not necessarily exhibit solid financial behaviour and that education about their own behavioural biases was more important than education about financial markets and products. Despite the few voices of caution, US-HSFPP research continued to inspire several other studies across the globe, and FL was inextricably linked with retirement planning and the financial behaviour of citizens.

10.4.2 Nationwide Strategies to Promote Financial Education

Emulating American policy initiatives, Australia, Japan, the UK & Netherlands also conducted large household surveys and found similar results. Financial behaviour was diverse, and the average household exhibited inefficient financial management (Rooij 2008, [14, 183, 200]. As a result, a government-backed FLE was launched targeting working professionals and emerging adults across several high-income and developed countries, reporting favourable results [73, 103]. Furthermore, recognizing FL as a key life skill in increasingly complex financial markets and uncertain labour markets, the Central Banks of several countries launched FLE programs targeting those in low-income Govt. jobs, youth and the poor [17, 194]. At this juncture, the research literature was forked into school-mandated FLEs for "emerging adults" in the Global North and FLEs linked to microcredit and financial inclusion in the Global South. Nonprofit organizations took on an active role in delivering a central bank-sponsored FLE program about banking, microcredit and insurance products to the hitherto financially excluded. However, FLEs were usually enmeshed within a range of other development training modules as diverse as health and nutrition, veterinary services, legal rights, government schemes, livelihood opportunities, etc. (as evident on the website www.grameenkoota.org). At the next stage, the microcredit data from such endeavours were consolidated nationally and regionally under OECD-specific initiatives. Nationwide strategies for augmenting financial inclusion and boosting financial education (NSFI and NSFE) are streamlined, and countries strive to improve their financial stability metrics.

OECD/INFE has led several research efforts focusing on policy analysis, industry good practices and curating a global database across 270 public institutions, including participating central banks, in 107 countries [182]. Augmenting FL is noteworthy as perhaps one of the rare areas of a unified global collaboration across the North–South divide, covering approximately five billion people and sixty non-OECD countries [118]. Of the participating countries under OECD/INFE, students and youth have been targeted by Indonesia, Israel, Japan, Korea, Lebanon, Malaysia and Singapore—the latter also target elderly individuals; women are the interest group for Indonesia, Malaysia, Lebanon, Pakistan and Saudi Arabia. Migrants are another category of interest in China, India, Indonesia and the Philippines, while Malaysia, Pakistan and Indonesia have targeted medium, small and micro enterprises [169, 218]. Low-income and marginalized groups, school children, senior citizens and military personnel have been named targets of India's FL and inclusion strategies.

Financial inclusion has led to numerous positive outcomes, such as choosing an appropriate livelihood, accessing loans, buying or selling assets, etc. [115]. Women were observed to improve in several realms of agentic decision-making, such as participating in their offspring's education, seeking help in cases of domestic violence, enjoying more visits to the natal family, better reproductive rights and increased self-confidence [34, 138, 177, 179, 190, 219, 235]. However, a few research studies have reported that FLE delivery misses the mark because such interventions are periodic and time-constrained, often disjointed from other topics and do not address grassroots realities such as innumeracy and a paucity of real opportunities to apply FL lessons within patriarchal households [131, 192]. Bose and Sadana [31] reported that FLE content applied in India was devoid of analytical principles, delivered without baseline metrics, led by semiskilled trainers and riddled with stereotypes such as the poor being ignorant. The researchers pointed out that from this prejudiced standpoint, moral lessons on savings and credit were doled out to the disadvantaged. Mader [156] vehemently cautioned that "high expectations of financial inclusion serving as a core pro-poor private sector-led development intervention lack justification."

For a considerable period, policy reports stayed over focused on the demand side, while supply-side issues such as fraud and mis-selling in financial services stayed overlooked [6, 154]. The FLE fork of the Global North also attracted critique. Researchers observed only short-term effects but rejected other claims due to missing robust practices such as random selection of participants, baseline measures, longitudinal studies and triangulation with related indices [75]. The long-term efficacy of school-mandated FLEs has been reported only recently as robust by applying the methodology of meta-analysis [118, 119]. However, the first longitudinal study of FLE intervention was finally conducted in the Global South, and it revealed positive long-run effects. Bruhn et al. [36] used administrative data regarding 16,000 former students of 892 public high schools under an FLE intervention conducted in Brazil by Bruhn et al. [35]. Among several positive effects, one unusual outcome was that the experimental group had taken high-cost credit card debt in their early high school days, but over the subsequent nine years, credit card debt was low, if not nil. The opposite was true of the control group.

Instead of longitudinal studies with robust baselines, comparison among countries at varying levels of economic development has been a more popular approach found in the literature. The OECD database has enabled the association of FL levels with national income levels, categorizing participants as high-, medium- and low-income countries.[1] The constraints holding back the South have been identified as a greater cultural preference for real assets, underdeveloped financial markets, trust and governance deficits in regulatory mechanisms, cultural diversity and the dominance of the informal sector (OECD 2015). Essentially, it is popularly believed that the sophistication and efficiency of a country's financial and legal systems influence the population's FL. NSFE for the Global South, therefore, is entrusted to play a pivotal role. This is where Faulkner [74] provides some startling insights. Faulkner conducted a study of NSFE documents of OECD and found that five of the eight highest-ranked, financially literate OECD countries did not have any NSFE, despite OECD itself having garnered more than 60 countries to commit to this long-term agenda. The OECD/INFE Adult Financial Literacy Competencies Test [182] shows a dismal score of 12.7 on average out of a possible total score of 21; OECD member nations averaged 13.0. Furthermore, of the countries having a formal NSFE, Faulkner reported that FLE goals were directly linked to national consumer protection policies. However, this was often not the case with non-OECD signatories.

This, undoubtedly, is the crux of the North and South divide—rights are guaranteed to citizens in the Global North as they interface with complex, sophisticated and powerful arrangements within modern financial systems and markets. However, citizens of the Global South are coerced into such arrangements without adequate safeguards or legal recourse.

10.4.3 Financial Literacy Profiling

Education is reported as the most dominant factor of FL, and several dimensions of education are significant, including the number of years of education, recency of education, level of education (school or college or university), subjects of study (math, economics, business studies), parent's education, and especially the mother's education [9, 55, 68, 94, 140, 141, 159]. Seeming like a carte blanche, it is necessary to remember that this is merely a correlation between formal education and FL, not causality. The reverse is also not true; an uneducated person is not necessarily

[1] Low-income countries under the OECD/INFE framework are those with gross national income per capita below $1,045 as per 2015 report.

financially illiterate. Formal education is assumed to increase financial awareness and financial knowledge and invoke rational decision-making and self-discipline, such as financial goal setting and planned personal finance [9, 114].

Income is reported to correlate highly with FL [141, 225]. Interestingly, Artavanis and Kara [13] have reported an FL wage gap, observing that students and young professionals with low FL invariably draw lower salaries and exacerbate their exposure to adverse income shocks, primarily because their beginning salary expectations are significantly lower than those with high FL. Although low-income levels correlate with low FL, is it due to a correlation between income and education (dropout rates) or income and savings? Wealth is another antecedent of FL [94, 232]. However, few studies have explored FL as a critical factor of wealth accumulation measured by income, savings, and asset ownership [144, 222]. Thus, there is some evidence that the core tenet of FL research seems marred by circular reasoning and probable bidirectional causality. To explicate the endogeneity between wealth and FL, Calcagno and Monticone [43] articulated a novel variable, namely, '*an underlying interest in finance*', which may influence both variables. Similarly, the number of dependents is another case of bidirectional causality in FL studies [127].

Employment status, membership in a unionized workforce, belonging to the knowledge economy and key aspects of one's employment profile (skilled, semiskilled or unskilled; full-time or part-time; steady income or freelance gigs)—all these aspects influence FL [48, 116, 125]. Interestingly, Surendar and Sarma [217] have observed that a niche investor community, namely, teachers in higher education, has high FL, especially in the dimensions of financial planning, retirement planning and tax planning. Furthermore, high financial knowledge was observed across the board, not limited to teachers facilitating math, economics, or business studies.

Age correlates highly with FL, but studies reveal an unusual nonlinear pattern such that FL peaks around mid-life, broadly between 35–50 years and drops with advancing age beyond that [143]. Interestingly, declining FL is not matched with lower confidence in financial decision-making skills, which makes senior citizens more vulnerable to financial scams and fraudulent activity [77, 84, 116]. However, FL outcomes of well-being can be extracted through a timely intervention based on life-cycle needs. Pre-workforce entry, early-life financial education by parents or school or college, pre-loan orientation and timely credit counselling in relation to the billing cycle are all potent entry points [23, 98, 110]. Since behavioural interventions generally have lower efficacy in mature candidates, western, industrialized cultures have focused on FLE in 'emerging adulthood' (teenage to early twenties), representing the exploratory-formative social process of independence from parents and family, formation of a self-identity and the embracing of financial responsibility [189, 211].

Self-efficacy was named as an antecedent of FL in early studies by Bernheim in the 1990s; however, surprisingly, it has found scant support in the plethora of empirical studies. Instead, researchers tend to diagnose socialization agents such as parents and peers. Socialization agents shape FL through dimensions such as attitudes and beliefs regarding money, savings, wealth, retirement and risk and the style of communication as well as conformity or autonomy issues between socializers and the recipient individual [83, 109, 122, 236]. Nanziri and Leibbrandt [175] reported that more than 63% of their sample in South Africa turned to their family and friends for financial information rather than financial newspapers, financial advisers, schools, churches, communities, etc. Joo and Grable [113] observed that some parents had socialized their wards towards responsible credit card behaviour and practical knowledge of its best use. Studies in India and China have posited the negative effects of parental socialization and attitudes towards financial planning and education as likely causes for low FL, despite exemplary financial behaviour [112, 157, 180, 196].

In recent studies, social capital has emerged as a factor of FL and is conceptualized as goodwill, collaboration, association and consideration between individuals and their extended families, neighbours and community members [174, 195, 234]. Social capital can be very potent in the Global South, as it was found to mediate FL's relationship with the savings behaviour of small and medium enterprise owners in Uganda, it mediated FL and financial inclusion of Indonesian students, and it was reported to liberate working women from sociohistorical dependencies by augmenting self-efficacy and FL [57, 121, 173]. Khan and Surisetti [123] have reported that social capital has further evolved in the internet era such that cashless transactions and self-socialization through digital financial experiences are reported to actively shape people's perceptions and financial behaviour.

FL studies have also explored several sociopsychological aspects of people's meaning-making and choice-making processes. In a Japanese study, Yeh and Ling's [233] study found that confidence was a significant mediating factor between FL and behaviour; its valence was equivalent if not greater than FL. Ahyan (2019), Davutyan and Öztürkkal [60] and Sevim et al. [208] have reported on several cultural subjectivities, such as migrant status and religious beliefs, among others, impacting the savings and borrowing behaviour of Turkish households. Collins and Urban [165] have reported that the social construction of safety, duty, self-preservation, independence and such related constructs (which are often pivotal in culturally rich or more traditional systems of patriarchy and feudal order, as found in the Global South) could lead to varied outcomes even if socioeconomic indicators are common.

10.4.4 Theoretical Underpinnings of Financial Literacy

The Life Cycle Hypothesis [167, 168], the Theory of Consumer Socialization [171, 227] and the Theory of Planned Behaviour [4] are dominant theories in FL studies. Researchers postulate an inverted U-shape for FL and FWB [111, 151, 152]. The rational, discerning person is able to accumulate savings in the high-earning phase of her youth and tighten purse strings during the low or no earnings phase of old age, having invested in a retirement product to end with greater terminal wealth [10, 45]. As observed in Sect. 4.2, a North–South divide exists in the orientation of national strategies for financial education. FLE goals in the Global North are linked to national consumer protection policies, and therefore, theorizing based on the consumer behaviour paradigm may be appropriate for developed countries. However, countries of the Global South have committed NSFE to the development agenda. Hence, the authors believe that Amartya Sen's theorizing would be appropriate to postulate FL and FWB constructs.

In Amartya Sen's capability approach, well-being is the "freedom of choice" that a person exercises to achieve what she considers most valuable to her and has reason to value [206]. According to Sen, freedoms are opportunities for "doings" and "beings" technically termed '*functionings*' [7]. '*Capabilities*' depict the real freedom that people enjoy or the true spectrum of choices available to them in terms of the meaning they assign to the functioning. For example, an individual could understand FWB as personal wealth by amassing physical assets such as land, gold, bank balance, etc. However, for another, it could mean safeguarding loved ones from the sudden loss of income or property or loss of health or life. Sen [206] proposes that an individual's well-being should be assessed based on who they are and what they do ('beings' and 'doings'), not based on the means to those ends (wealth, income, cash flow, etc.). Sen also insists that the evaluation must weigh both actual achievements (functioning) and effective freedom (capability). This means-ends distinction, according to Sen, is a vital yardstick to understand the true measure of 'quality of life' and its requisite connection with social justice and policy change.

Through Sen's lens, some persistent weaknesses of the FL rhetoric emerge. Mader [155, 156] and West [230] have raised the question of Governmentalism, observing that choices are made on behalf of vulnerable groups of people through FL training, but the onus of these choices is laid entirely on the individuals. Marron [161] has expressed the need to look beyond the obvious and has warned of neo-liberal Governmentalism, which invariably leads to less-than-optimal outcomes in the Global South. Undoubtedly, both the push for 401-K savings in the North and the microcredit phenomenon in the South can be aptly described in Williams' [231] perspective as a state-mandated, normative preference scale of responsible behaviour. The FL agenda seems committed towards financial inclusion, but FL is not matched with an equivalent and determined focus on 'cleaning up' financial services and strengthening the financial system. In conclusion, the effective freedom or capability spectrum is ignored in the dominant FL models, which is problematic for application to the Global South. To recap the evolutionary FL narrative contained in this section, a visual overview is provided in Fig. 10.1.

10.5 Unpacking Assumptions of the Financial Literacy Model

Section 10.4 revealed that key aspects of the FL agenda, when observed through an evolutionary, development lens, seem to be based on some tacit assumptions. This section unpacks the three tacit assumptions of micropositioning, efficient capital markets and homoeconomicus and checks for their fitment with the realities of developing countries.

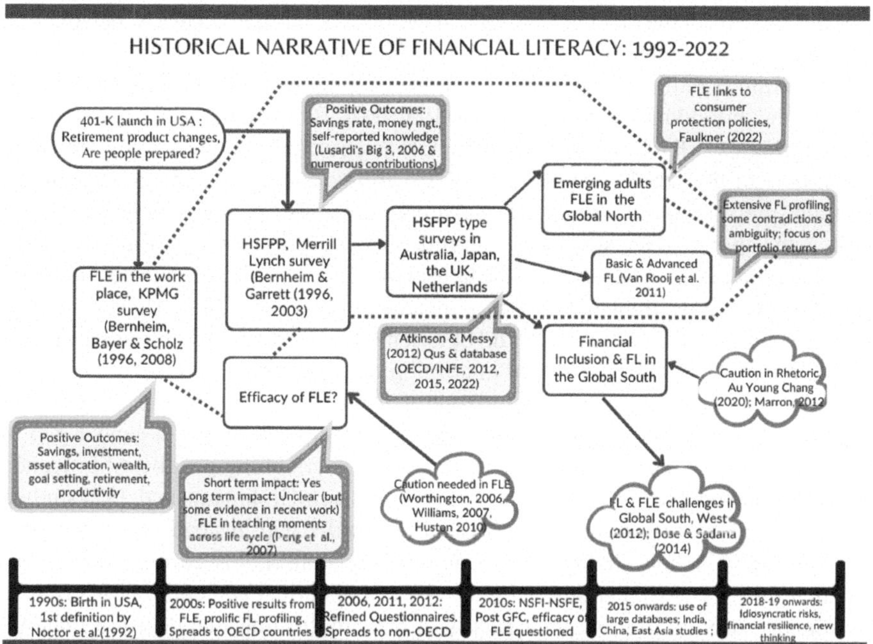

Fig. 10.1 Historical narrative of financial literacy (*source* Authors' own)

10.5.1 Micropositioning

Many FL studies of the Global North micro position financial decision-making upon the emerging adult, considered as a unit of economic identity and financial independence. The decision-maker in the dominant FL models acts with autonomy, self-efficacy and tacit accountability for his own life choices. Historically, micropositioning has been linked to the launch of the 401-K social policy initiative and subsequent targeting of college students for education loans and credit card business. This may seem appropriate in the absence of a culture of sociomoral obligations or parental interference, as found in the Global South. Although emerging adults are largely absent within patriarchal and feudal societies, interestingly, a considerable number of studies have unraveled this construct to be a myth even in developed nations [106, 187, 199, 202].

Jorgensen et al. [114] and Mandell and Klein [160] have reported that emerging adults have deficient financial knowledge, do not necessarily break free from their parents and often depend on parental financial resources even late into mid-adulthood. Additionally, financially independent young people may intermittently revert to their family on a need basis to tide over liquidity problems; for example, almost 33% of American adults between 18–34 years turned to their parents during the financial crisis of 2008 [71, 82, 117, 207]. Reducing financial choices to the age dimension robs the analysis of the other psychological factors that build FL, namely, personality, self-identity, impulsiveness, emotions, and self-efficacy [1, 72, 96, 134].

Furthermore, bidirectional causality has been reported between the financial capability of the individual and the household [93, 100]. Barrafrem et al. [21] found that stress during COVID-19 lockdowns in the UK and Sweden was due to the immediate uncertainty of household income and one's feeling of being financially ignorant. In addition, the household's financial decisions may cause personal financial strain, such as the spouse's decision to pursue full-time education, or sometimes the individual may cause financial stress to the household, for example, through accumulated gambling debt or the financial impact of incarceration [41, 65, 209]. Thus, instead of micropositioning, the household could be a richer level of financial decision-making. A research practice largely adopted in developing countries.

Moreover, the micropositioning assumption breaks down when observed from a gender lens. The authors believe that the persistent reporting of a gender gap in FL may be one of the worst consequences of the overarching positivist FL agenda such that empirical results get stripped of their context. Grohmann et al. [92] studied Thailand's middle-income class and found no gender gap; instead, women played an active role in household finance, particularly households earning mandatory minimum wages. Social stratification has been a historical and cultural inheritance of women, severely limiting their access to meaningful financial decision-making. Consequently, women's lived experiences in the Global South require nuanced reporting [124]. Traditional, seemingly antiquated, and regressive gender practices such as wife battering can remain strongly entrenched and can even shockingly coexist with other empowerment indicators. For example, the state of Karnataka in India recorded the highest rate of spousal violence at 44.4% in NFHS-5[2] despite having topped in several empowerment indicators for women, namely, the highest proportion of women owning and using a bank account, the highest proportion using a personal mobile phone and second highest land or house ownership by women (singularly or jointly) in the country.

Studies also report that women with lower levels of FL are less likely to take retirement plans and are more dependent on their family and friends for their saving and investment planning [146, 196]. This raises the question—is there a tacit assumption in the literature that the individual should only fend for herself and that the family unit plays no role in her later life; especially given that female labour force participation rates are low to very low across the Global South? Interestingly, Santos [202] has unpacked a devious neo-liberal agenda as she reports a reconstruction of the self-reliant individual—one who is essentially cut off from collective resources and counsel, commodified and reshaped in the material culture of financialization.

The lack of evidence of a financialized product does not signify an absence of an old-age safety net. India's demonetization exercise, conducted on 8th November 2016 without much planning, unearthed the phenomenon of unaccounted household petty cash savings by homemakers, amounting to thousands and lakhs of rupees in most households, effected through several years of careful budgeting [179]. A considerable

[2] More than doubling from 20.6% recorded in NFHS-4.

percentage of these women hoarders were literate and from stable homes (though there was a higher percentage of women from the lower-income group). Hard cash serves as a lifeline for women in general, a much-needed safety net for victims of abuse contemplating a safe exit and a survival strategy for women entrepreneurs [203, 223, 224]. However, not all women are alike, nor are their circumstances. Studies in Kenya and Malawi disclosed an antipodal tendency such that women prefer to lock away their savings in illiquid financial products to keep them safe from unexpected intrahousehold and interhousehold demands [37, 67]. Additionally, women faced with issues such as access to their earnings, bargaining power related to intrahousehold resources, mobility and safety issues often rely on group savings [179, 224]. Thus, micropositioning and homogenizing human circumstances without explicating the meaning-making of well-being is a grave fallacy in the FL agenda [123, 124].

In conclusion, the assumption of micropositioning breaks down in the Global South and is not well established in the Global North.

10.5.2 Efficient Capital Market Theorizing

The dominant FL models assume free and easy access to capital markets, and the financial system is assumed to be efficient. The decision-makers in such a model can easily access financial products and services, acquire all relevant information and based on an aggregation of their choices, be able to influence market pricing. Such capital market theorizing is highly problematic. Although approximately 60% of Americans are reported to own company stocks (most in ETF portfolios), high levels of market participants are not observed worldwide. Barely 13% of the UK population, 6% of Japan, 4% of China and less than 3% of India, Sweden, France, Germany and Australia own company stocks [142, 215]. Additionally, insurance penetration for most of the global population has stayed low [215]. Although the financial inclusion policy has improved bank penetration in the Global South, other sophisticated products are not commonly held [91]. Therefore, Moore [170] has argued for financial experience to be added as a dimension of FL, representing lived experiences within diverse socioeconomic systems [170].

Financial experiences are mediated by socialization factors, and the market structure of information is very different in the Global South than in the largely efficient markets of the North. Although most researchers have applied concepts of consumer experience or investor experience, a handful of researchers have tried to inject nuance by focusing on financial experience through instrumental variables such as status of permanent residency [81], financial situation of eldest sibling [9] and economic knowledge [12]. Financial experiences of Chinese and Indian investors have been reported through meaningful proxies such as perception about the capital market regulator, hassle factor in investing and social interaction or experience-sharing among investor communities or the affluent [104, 212]. Breaking down financial behaviour itself, savings behaviour is often found to be strong in Asian countries, but investing behaviour is deficient. This could be attributed to an opaque financial system with investors/customers finding it difficult to determine the fees behind financial products or feeling timid to counter question relationship managers who may be pushing complex products or who may have fallen victim to fraud but face poor avenues of legal redressal. To avoid all these stressors, people may just decide to entirely skip or stay at the periphery of capital markets [99]. Nguyen [178] observed the presence of "uncertainty avoidance" in the social fabric of Vietnam and recommended trustworthy financial guidance to weed out the status quo of the system.

Pushing the vulnerable populace of the Global South to embrace financialized assets without offering adequate systemic checks and balances can cause idiosyncratic risk. In part, it also perpetuates the continued dominance of informal credit markets, accessed especially by agricultural households, small business owners, urban slum dwellers and women without property holding [20, 132]. For example, the NSSO 70th round results in India in 2013 disclosed that 40% of all loans generated were in informal markets, and petty money lenders formed 26% of this activity. Despite improving regulation and deepening financial markets, several developing countries struggle with formalization, transparency, and ethical challenges due to predatory mis-selling of financial products and framing of financial returns. Studies have reported on financial scams in the Middle East and Africa [214], Indonesia [78] and Latin America [40]. Since capital markets in most countries are not as sophisticated or deep as those in the USA and marketing communication for financial products is inadequate, narrowing the focus of FL outcomes to efficient portfolios or to market-linked retirement and credit products is counterproductive [230].

Historical memory regarding scams and corruption, cultural perceptions and gaps in technical knowledge, underdeveloped capital markets and incomplete or inadequate grievance redressal systems continue to cause a distrust of financial markets such that improved FL does not necessarily lead to greater market participation. Hence, the context of financial decisions within underdeveloped capital markets is vital, and efficient market theorizing cannot be blindly generalized across vast regions of the world.

10.5.3 Homoeconomicus

Homoeconomicus [166] is another tacit assumption in the dominant FL models. It refers to a parsimonious economic model that approximates people's decision-making as rational, driven by self-interest, calculated, systematic and consistent [47]. Theoretically, the subject of FL studies is a rational and calculative decision-maker driven by self-interest. However, this is hardly the case. In most cases, this decision-maker operates in the shadow of other powerful economic actors, such as the government machinery, regulatory structure and idiosyncratic practices of financial service providers. Rashid [209], Al-Shami et al. [6], Boateng et al. [30] and Haldar and Stiglist [95] have reported predatory practices in the microfinance industry, such as unjustified interest rates, poaching of clients and even abandonment of borrower suicides due to coercive debt recovery. Furthermore, profit-seeking investors seemed to have connived with promoters in pursuit of high business valuations. What form of agency and self-interest can the vulnerable sections exercise in such systems of power and privilege?

Some researchers have further unmasked the neo-liberal rhetoric of the naïve "financial subject" crafted through the careful construction and overuse of ideas such as "*financial irresponsibility, irrationality and illiteracy.*" A few examples are Au-Yeung and Chan's [16] qualitative study on young workers in Hong Kong; [161] case study on the roots of the UK's government-backed financial capability agenda; Ayhan's [18] ethnographic study of FLEs in Turkey; and Kling's [129] comparative study to evaluate the application of Western financial inclusion models to Asia. Mill [166] may have created the hypothetical "economic human" to ruthlessly restrict the decision-making range in social science and render an effective methodology of economic thought. Unfortunately, neo-liberal policies turned it around such that the economic human came alive in the profit-seeking economic actors who insidiously abstracted rationality and responsible behaviour to create a system of over-selection of credit products, to the detriment of other inclusive financial services.

Self-interest as the main motivator in financial decision-making is a fallacious assumption. Honor, duty, community feeling, religious fervour, social good, altruism, generosity and many such anchors are known to guide long-term goals and FWB [60, 130, 165]. In the early 1990s, cognitive, economic, and psychological aspects informed the construct of financial well-being as studies probed lived experiences and changing life circumstances [24, 27, 29]. Furthermore, studies in related fields showcase a variety of well-being goals, namely, house property, stable income, savings and charity) [88, 114, 220, 226]. Essentially, FWB is a proxy for experiential happiness or relative life satisfaction and is impacted by personal traits, the decision-making context, social capital and behavioural biases [62, 89, 104, 174, 178]. However, a disproportionate number of published studies have narrowly defined FWB as the maximization of financialized wealth.

The main opposition to an assumption of Homoeconomicus lies in the fact that decision-making in the real world is neither systematic nor optimizing but rather satisficing in nature. Cojanu [54] articulated it as "*assessing and acting according to the given, actual, and imminent opportunity of choice; it is not about freedom of choice, but about the degree of freedom a person is willing and is able to take advantage of*". For example, Nanzini and Leibbrandt (2018) found that for a large sample in South Africa, poverty seemed to cause an aversion to risk. What the economic human seeks and how outcomes are prioritized or abandoned—these are grossly neglected aspects in FL theorizing and public policy.

10.5.4 Contextualizing Financial Literacy for the Global South

The FLE agenda has been built on the hypothesis that financially literate households, upon accumulating financial experience, will get more discerning and settle only for good quality financial products and services—thus unleashing the competitive spirit of transparency and efficiency within the financial services industry. It is theorized that this self-feeding cycle of increasing the financial sophistication of households and improving the quality of financial services can catapult the economy to a stable path of economic growth and development ([139, p. 14]). Not only is the unsuspecting individual supposed to carry the onus of his own FWB, but the system posits great faith in her ability to stay on track and even unleash a propensity to accumulate "*sound financial practices*." While doing good for himself, the individual is assumed to set in motion a domino effect for larger macroeconomic gains. By coupling Homoeconomicus with Micro positioning, the capitalist agenda cumulatively and dexterously delivers grand outcomes of financial development, which unfortunately are missing at ground zero [46].

The rational decision-maker with knowledge about financial markets and exhibiting '*responsible financial behaviour*' essentially belongs to a small subset of a very diverse global population. Such a model assumes a very specific financial decision-making milieu, namely, capitalist, neo-liberal and set within highly efficient capital markets and having strong consumer protection infrastructure. It is surprising to find that under OECD-backed national strategies for financial education (NSFE), the same standardized approach is prescribed and implemented across large swathes of the population despite the diversity in their legal-political structures, labour-market dynamics, school enrollment levels, poverty levels or even cultural interactions. This rich diversity was observed by Messy and Monticone [163] in their scoping study of 21 African countries. The problems of the Middle East and North African states are different from those in East Asia, South Africa or Latin America. Currently, Middle Eastern and North African countries are in dire need of financial inclusion and robust financial infrastructure, as they lag behind most countries of the world due to years of prolonged political and ethnic conflicts, unstable labour markets and high indebtedness [64, 153].

Different groups of people within different countries cannot have the same decision-making model or the same constraints; therefore, standardized solutions cannot usher in change. The authors postulate that financial decision-making takes place at the intersection of external factors such as the financial system, labour markets, politico-legal systems and the internal factors of confidence, self-efficacy, discipline, etc. For example, Douissa [64] reveals that the FL needs of Emirati youth are mediated by personal lifestyle choices and a misconstrued perception of government-mandated financial support offered to citizens. Thus, the subjective or internal factors of behavioural biases interact with the objective or external factors of easy bank credit and periodic waivers of bank liabilities by the UAE justice system. The researcher observed that breaking this vicious cycle will require copious doses of FL training. FL solutions also need to address other challenges such as high levels of internet fraud and money swindling faced by affluent families and the systemic vulnerability in retirement planning of expatriate workers in the volatile Middle Eastern labour markets.

The Global South has several cases of innovative solutions to deal with specific idiosyncratic risks. For example, instead of accepting the rhetoric of a gender gap in FL, the Financial Sector Deepening Network (FSDN), Kenya, has curated a comprehensive solution for *gendered financial products*. Instead of summarily bringing individuals into the inclusive realm, FSDN resolves to iterate and improve the financial system to make it inclusive of the needs of African people. Another example is the creative experiential solution offered by Abel et al. [2] to mitigate overindebtedness in South Africa. The participants were instructed to first roll one die until they obtained a six, followed by two dies until they rolled two sixes and so on. Participants were then informed that the probability of winning the lottery jackpot was equivalent to rolling all sixes with nine dies. The authors observed that individuals who arrived at two sixes through several arduous attempts seemed turned off by the lure of the lottery when compared to those in the control group.

Furthermore, there already exists a praxis of FL within the culture of the Global South, even if mired in some misrecognition and biases. Unfortunately, these sociopsychological processes that shape everyday financial decisions have remained underexplored, and research needs to probe outside the 30% of the world that comprises the Global North [93]. While the OECD and Consumer Financial Protection Bureau (CFPB) databases are well known and often referenced in research, other meaningful databases such as FinScope Consumer and MSME surveys for African countries have remained relatively unknown. The Finscope surveys are qualitative and have especially been bringing in voices from the informal markets of South Africa since 2002 (FSD Network n.d.). There is a dire need to remove the imbalance caused by the positivist paradigm dominant in the literature. Constructivist and interpretive paradigms for studies in the Global South can help respecify financial experiences and offer inputs to validate the existing models. There is a legitimate need for a more expansive FL model that incorporates the realities of the Global South.

10.6 Conceptual Financial Literacy Model for the Global South

The dominant FL models, built on tacit assumptions of micropositioning, capital market theorizing and homoeconomicus, may have served their purpose if Western countries were the focus; however, they are a misfit for the Global South. There are several psychosocial, economic and cultural-historical motivators and barriers in the financial decision-making process that are more meaningful when modelling FL in the Global South. The discussions above reveal several missing factors, such as parental socialization and social capital; self-efficacy and self-confidence; public memory of systemic fraud and the praxis of financial survival; cultural framing of honor, safety, and duty; economic agency and the power dynamics of the larger socioeconomic-legal system within which individuals operate. The positivist, aggregative agenda that dominates public policy is unable to capture the lived experiences of people, especially women, in developing countries. Consequently, FL needs to be reclaimed under the development agenda.

The authors propose an alternative, expansive FL-FWB model based on the development tenets of Sen's capability approach and the constructivist postulations of Pierre Bourdieu's theory of practice. This model represents the dynamic nature of agentic choice-making as it is exercised within institutionalized societies. For this expansive model, Hogarth's [102] definition of FL was further developed and defined as *the cumulative of financial awareness, financial knowledge, and financial behaviour, inclusive of the psychosocial elements of lived experience and a dynamic self-belief as individuals attempt to build, sustain and enhance their long-term financial well-being.* Empirically, it comprises five components—financial awareness, financial knowledge, financial self-efficacy, financial behaviour, and financial experience. Financial experience includes the experience of asset ownership, making cashless payments and daily experiences of budgeting, saving, bargaining, and prioritizing as well as confidence/anxiety related to financial decisions.

Financial well-being is defined as *the psychological and economic appraisal of the quality of one's life in terms of short-term financial stability as well as the steady progress towards or achievement of long-term financial goals.* It includes day-to-day financial capability as well as the larger "*meaning to life*" that financial resources can afford an individual. It is a subjective life position guided by an overarching orientation. Financial well-being is conceptualized as Sen's "doings" and "beings" that cause a person happiness and financial security. Based on the conceptualization of Khan and Surisetti [124], FWB has six goal orientations, namely:

- Retirement income (maintaining lifestyle in old age)
- Personal wealth (asset ownership)
- Personal financial independence (self-reliance and liquidity)
- Risk reduction (protection from uncertainty)
- Family responsibilities (parental/dependent care, meeting family goals)
- Wider lifestyle choices (vacations, philanthropy, hobbies, etc.).

This model is built on the premise that FL germinates at the interface of the objective (external) structure and the subjective (internal) structure. Financial decision-making unfolds within the individual's context, and the household itself forms a part of the individual's social world. Socialization factors always work on the individual, and there are two main sources of socialization in this proposed model—community (including parents and peers) and information (formal/informal and face-to-face or digital). Socialization by community and socialization by information are constantly occurring within the individual's social world. The individual decision-maker's social world has several fields—the household, livelihood/work/labour market, field of education, training and competencies, religious community, politico-legal system, financial system, etc. This is the external, objective structure of the decision-making model. On the other hand, there also exists a psycho-socio subjective structure made up of attributes such as interest, confidence, self-efficacy and commitment.

The expansive model further postulates that internal and external factors are essentially incorporated into FL through a practical reflexive sense or the *Habitus*, which enables the individual to know and recognize society's economic game—participating in generating and accumulating capital by adopting financial strategies. Through reflexivity or critical consciousness, the individual can recognize areas of improvement, progressively self-socialize, and improve FL, which will further augment FWB. Additionally, reflexivity may allow the individual to recognize his or her own behavioural biases or framing or possible fraudulent activity by the supplier/seller of financial products and services. Depending on the socialization levers and social learning by the individual, agency expands, and the person can be all that is within her realm of possibilities, the "beings and doings" residing in the FWB orientation. This transdisciplinary conceptual model applies Bourdieu's theoretical concepts of capital, field and habitus from sociology, Sen's theoretical concepts of agency and capability from developmental economics and Robert Bandura's social learning and self-efficacy from psychology. See Fig. 10.2 for a diagrammatic representation of the FL-FWB conceptual model for the Global South.

By theorizing the alternative FL-FWB model at the meso level, between the objective and subjective structures, the authors believe that this model meets the recommendation made by Bose and Sadana [31] exhorting that FL is approached from a wider theoretical lens "*to become a tool to raise critical consciousness and equip*

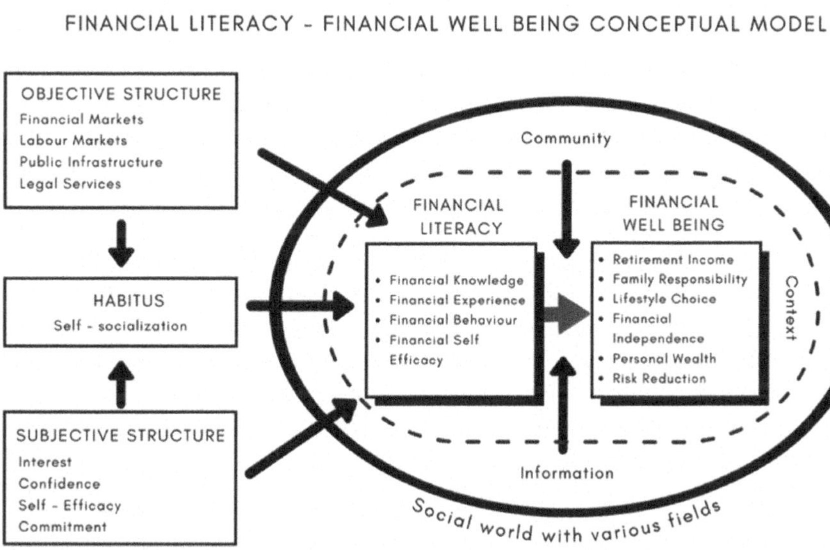

Fig. 10.2 Financial literacy—financial well-being conceptual model for the global south (*source* Authors' own)

people to respond to the challenges posed by the financial sector." Additionally, by incorporating self-socialization and effective freedom or competencies, this model seeks to realign the derailed FLE agenda, a recommendation made by Williams [231]. In her study, Williams provided evidence from the original Financial Services and Markets Bill, 1999, characterizing FLE "*as a resource that enables financial consumers to achieve whatever they choose as their goals*." Adopting the same approach, this proposed expansive model eschews financialized outcomes, makes no positivist claims as to what exactly FWB is and asserts that true empowerment is the freedom to be and do whatever one chooses.

10.7 Conclusion

Financial literacy is an essential tool of human capital development and empowerment that has been extensively studied for antecedents, outcomes, beneficiaries and laggards. However, the authors make a counterintuitive claim that FL is yet under-explored. The historical evolution of FL between 1992 and 2022 reveals two forks moving north and south. The FL agenda has changed its narrative with increasing financialization, and what it represents today may be insufficient for the realities of the Global South.

10.7.1 Key Insights and Contributions

The historical evolution of FL has been unusual. Birthed in concerns of retirement preparedness, two key paths emerged: one focusing on workplace interventions and the other on FLEs in high schools. Workplace research design has led to further studies on savings and investment behaviour, asset allocation, financial advice, and productivity in the context of financial resilience and financial capability. HSFPP research design has opened a focus on the savings rate, money management, self-reported knowledge, basic and advanced financial knowledge and planned wealth outcomes. In the Global North, HSFPP, FLE and the construct of emerging adults received ready acceptance across several countries during the second phase. Financial inclusion—financial literacy education has been the other fork moving into the Global South. The key differentiator between the North and South has been the presence or absence of a direct linkage between FLE and national consumer protection policy. The review reported key narratives such as the long-term efficacy of FLEs, their developmental claims and the rampant use of people-to-people and nation-to-nation FL profiling, despite overt differences.

The review extracted three tacit assumptions within the dominant FL models, namely, micropositioning, capital market theorizing and homoeconomicus. The construct of independent, self-reliant financial decision-makers was found to be missing; instead, collective resources and household counsel were found to be more appropriate. Underlying efficient capital market theorizing was found to be a fallacy. Large disparities in capital market deepening exist, and financial experiences are mediated by socialization factors and by the market structure of information. Homoeconomicus was found to be an abstraction that has essentially robbed the literature on the rich context within which financial decision-making truly resides. The review found evidence that differences in the meaning-making of FWB and the social construction of safety, duty, independence, and such related constructs could lead to varied outcomes even if socioeconomic indicators of the samples are common.

The review excavated some missing dimensions. Although FWB sits centre-stage in the FL model, it stays unspecified and stymied as a retirement product or a capital market portfolio. The model overlooks psych-socio indicators of well-being and financial experiences outside financialized interactions. Standardized implementation of national strategies tends to ignore cultural-historical fitment. Beneath the positivist agenda lies a vibrant community of contrarians who have reported Governmentalism; weak design, haphazard delivery, and monitoring of FLEs; poor efficacy of predictive FL models and insidious framing of 'responsible financial behaviour.'

An expansive FL model was proposed comprising an objective structure and a subjective structure, each of which feeds the social world within which financial decision-making resides. The decision-maker is an active, self-reflexive agent within the meso space. Socialization from the community and informational sources shape the perception, financial attitude and meaning-making of FWB. FL embodies itself as the amalgamation of financial awareness, knowledge, experience, behaviour, and self-efficacy. It impacts FWB, which is conceptualized as an orientation towards outcomes directed at oneself or others or a combination of both.

10.7.2 Future Financial Literacy Agenda

In the post-COVID-19 era, FL research needs to expand and explore the lived experiences of people in the Global South, capture the praxis of FL outside financialized decisions, articulate the value metrics of social capital and explore possible models for market information and financial advice. The internal psycho-socio structure and socialization factors differ between the North and the South; these could be fertile grounds for academic probing. There is an urgent need to enrich FL research through alternative databases built on nonpositivist paradigms, recording the power and privilege (if any) of economic agents in capital markets and social structures such as households and informal credit markets. Policy initiatives are required for redesigning FLEs on robust andragogy and a theory of change, increasing capital market compliance, mitigating hassle in capital market transactions, enforcing norms of mandatory skillset and ethical orientation in the financial services industry and strengthening consumer protection laws.

This review essentially attempted to broaden the theoretical lens of the FL agenda by putting the spotlight on agentic financial socialization and the effective freedom to exercise it. The critical review is limited by the published inputs it attempted to appraise and by the authors' development orientation. Operationalizing the model in the post-COVID-19 world will be the next step.

References

1. Aarts H, Bijleveld E (2014) The psychological science of money
2. Abel M, Cole S, Zia B (2021) Changing gambling behaviour through experiential learning. The World Bank Econ Rev 35(3):745–763. https://doi.org/10.1093/wber/lhaa016
3. Adam AM, Frimpong S, Boadu MO (2017) Financial literacy and financial planning: implication for financial well-being of retirees. Bus Econ. Horizon 13(2):224–236. https://doi.org/10.15208/beh.2017.17
4. Ajzen I (1985) From intentions to actions: a theory of planned behavior. In: Kuhl J (ed) Action control: from cognition to behavior. Springer Berlin Heidelberg, Berlin, Heidelberg, pp 11–39
5. Ajzen I, Kuhl J, Beckmann J (1985) Action control. In: SSSP springer series in social psychology. Springer, Berlin, Heidelberg
6. Al-Shami SSA, Razali MM, Majid I, Rozelan A, Rashid N (2016) The effect of microfinance on women's empowerment: evidence from Malaysia. Asian J Women's Stud 22(3):318–337
7. Alkire S, Kelly A (2012) Sen and the art of educational maintenance: evidencing a capability, as opposed to an effectiveness, approach to schooling. Camb J Educ 42(3):283–296. 0305764x.2012.706255
8. Allgood S, Walstad WB (2016) The effects of perceived and actual financial literacy on financial behaviors. Econ Inq 54(1):675–697. https://doi.org/10.1111/ecin.12255
9. Almenberg J, Säve-Söderbergh J (2011) Financial literacy and retirement planning in Sweden. J Pension Econ Finance 10(4):585–598
10. Anand S, Mishra K, Verma V, Taruna T (2020) Financial literacy as a mediator of personal financial health during COVID-19: a structural equation modelling approach. Emerald Open Res 2
11. Ardelt M (1997) Wisdom and life satisfaction in old age. J Gerontol Ser B: Psychol Sci Soc Sci 52(1):15–P27
12. Arrondel L, Debbich M, Savignac F (2015) Stockholding in France: the role of financial literacy and information. Appl Econ Lett 22(16):1315–1319
13. Artavanis N, Kara S (2020) Financial literacy and student debt. Eur J Financ 26(4–5):382–401. https://doi.org/10.1080/1351847X.2020.1717569
14. Atkinson A, McKay S, Collard S, Kempson E (2007) Levels of financial capability in the UK. Public Money Manage 27(1):29–36
15. Atkinson A, Messy F (2012) Measuring financial literacy: results of the OECD/International Network on Financial Education (INFE) pilot study. Papers on Finance, Insurance and Private Pensions
16. Au-Yeung TC, Chan KK (2020) Crafting the financial-subject: a qualitative study of young workers' experiences in financialised pension investment in Hong Kong. J Soc Policy 49(2):323–341
17. Australian Securities and Investment Commission (2013) Review of the national financial literacy strategy. Background report. Australian Securities and Investments Commission, Sydney
18. Ayhan B (2019) Constituting financialized subjectivities: cultural political economy of financial literacy in Turkey. Turk Stud 20(5):680–707
19. Baghai P, Howard O, Prakash L, Zucker J (2020) Women as the next wave of growth in US wealth management. McKinsey & Company report, downloaded
20. Balasubramanian SA, Kuppusamy T (2020) Does female labour force participation contribute to better financial inclusion? evidence from cross-country analysis. J Econ Adm Sci

21. Barrafrem K, Västfjäll D, Tinghög G (2020) Financial well-being, COVID-19, and the financial better-than-average-effect. J Behav Exp Financ 28:100410
22. Bayer PJ, Bernheim BD, Scholz JK (2009) The effects of financial education in the workplace: evidence from a survey of employers. Econ Inq 47(4):605–624
23. Behrman JR, Mitchell OS, Soo C, Bravo D (2010) Financial literacy, schooling, and wealth accumulation. NBER working paper no. 16452. National Bureau of Economic Research
24. Bernheim D (1995) Do households appreciate their financial vulnerabilities? an analysis of actions, perceptions, and public policy. Tax policy and economic growth 3:11–13
25. Bernheim BD, Garrett DM (2003) The effects of financial education in the workplace: evidence from a survey of households. J Public Econ 87(7–8):1487–1519
26. Bernheim BD, Garrett DM, Maki DM (2001) Education and saving: the long-term effects of high school financial curriculum mandates. J Public Econ 80(3):435–465
27. Bernheim D (1998) Financial Illiteracy, education, and retirement saving. In: Mitchell OS, Schieber S (eds) Living with Defined Contribution Pensions University of Pennsylvania Press, Philadelphia, pp 38–68
28. Bernheim BD (1996) Financial illiteracy, education, and retirement saving
29. Bernheim BD, Scholz JK (1993) Private saving and public policy. In: Poterba J (ed) Tax policy and the economy, vol 7. MIT Press, pp 73–110
30. Boateng AA, Boateng GO, Acquah H (2014) A literature review of fraud risk management in micro finance institutions in Ghana. Res J Finance Account 5(11)
31. Bose S, Sardana A (2014) Financial literacy in rural banking: proposal for an alternative approach. Econ Polit Weekly 49(26–27):80–85
32. Brennan R, Vos L (2013) Effects of participation in a simulation game on marketing students' numeracy and financial skills. J Mark Educ 35(3):259–270
33. Brod M, Stewart AL, Sands L, Walton P (1999) Conceptualization and measurement of quality of life in dementia: the dementia quality of life instrument (DQoL). Gerontologist 39(1):25–36
34. Brody C, Hoop TD, Vojtkova M, Warnock R, Dunbar M, Murthy P, Dworkin SL (2017) Can self-help group programs improve women's empowerment? a systematic review. J Dev Eff 9(1):15–40
35. Bruhn M, Leão LDS, Legovini A, Marchetti R, Zia B (2016) The impact of high school financial education: evidence from a large-scale evaluation in Brazil. Am Econ J Appl Econ 8(4):256–295
36. Bruhn M, Garber G, Koyama S, Zia B (2022) The long-term impact of high school financial education
37. Brune L, Giné X, Goldberg J, Yang D (2016) Facilitating savings for agriculture: field experimental evidence from Malawi. Econ Dev Cult Change 64(2):187–220
38. Brüggen EC, Hogreve J, Holmlund M, Kabadayi S, Löfgren M (2017) Financial well-being: a conceptualization and research agenda. J Bus Res 79:228–237
39. Bumcrot C, Lin J, Lusardi A (2011) The geography of financial literacy. Rand Working paper N. WR-893-SS
40. Butcher W, Galbraith JK (2015) Microfinance control fraud: poverty and profiteering in Latin America. In: Butcher W, Galbraith J (eds) Microfinance control fraud in Latin America, forum for social economics, vol 10, no 07360932, p 1056203
41. Button M, Lewis C, Tapley J (2014) Not a victimless crime: the impact of fraud on individual victims and their families. Secur J 27(1):36–54
42. Béres D, Huzdik K (2012) Financial literacy and macroeconomics. Public Finance Q 57(3):298
43. Calcagno R, Monticone C (2015) Financial literacy and the demand for financial advice. J Bank Finance 50:363–380
44. Calcagno R, Alperovych Y, Quas A (2020) Financial literacy and entrepreneurship. New Front Entrep Finance Res 271–297
45. Calvet LE, Campbell JY, Sodini P (2009) Measuring the financial sophistication of households. Am Econ Rev 99(2):393–398
46. Carroll T (2015) Access to finance and the death of development in the Asia-Pacific. J Contemp Asia 45(1):139–166

47. Cartwright P (2015) Understanding and protecting vulnerable financial consumers. J Consum Policy 38(2):119–138
48. Chen H, Volpe RP (1998) An analysis of personal financial literacy among college students. Financ Serv Rev 7(2):107–128
49. Chhatwani M, Mishra SK (2021) Financial fragility and financial optimism linkage during COVID-19: Does financial literacy matter? J Behav Exp Econ 94:101751
50. Chu Z, Wang Z, Xiao JJ, Zhang W (2017) Financial literacy, portfolio choice and financial well-being. Soc Indic Res 132(2):799–820
51. Clark RL, Morrill MS, Allen SG (2012) The role of financial literacy in determining retirement plans. Econ Inq 50(4):851–866
52. Clark R, d'Ambrosio M (2008) Adjusting retirement goals and saving behavior: The role of financial education. Overcoming the saving slump: how to increase the effectiveness of financial education and saving programs, pp 237–256
53. de Clercq B (2019) A comparative analysis of the OECD/INFE financial knowledge assessment using the rasch model. Empir Res Vocat Educ Train 11(1):1–29
54. Cojanu V (2017) Self-interest and the modernity of homo economicus. Int J Soc Econ. https://doi.org/10.1108/IJSE-07-2015-0192
55. Cole SA, Shastry GK (2009) Smart money: The effect of education, cognitive ability, and financial literacy on financial market participation. Harvard Business School, Boston, MA, pp 09–071
56. Cui X, Xiao JJ, Yi J (2019) Employment type, residential status and consumer financial capability: evidence from China household finance survey. Singap Econ Rev 64(01):57–81. https://doi.org/10.1142/S0217590817430032
57. Cwynar A, Świecka B, Filipek K, Porzak R (2022) Consumers' knowledge of cashless payments: Development, validation, and usability of a measurement scale. J Consum Aff 56(2):640–665
58. Dabić M, Vlačić B, Paul J, Dana LP, Sahasranamam S, Glinka B (2020) Immigrant entrepreneurship: a review and research agenda. J Bus Res 113:25–38. https://doi.org/10.1016/j.jbusres.2020.03.013
59. Danes SM (2004) Evaluation of the national endowment for financial education high school financial planning program. Family Social Science Department, University of Minnesota, St. Paul, MN
60. Davutyan N, Öztürkkal B (2016) Determinants of saving-borrowing decisions and financial inclusion in a high middle income country: the Turkish case. Emerg Mark Financ Trade 52(11):2512–2529
61. Demirgüç-Kunt A, Klapper LF (2012) Measuring financial inclusion: the global findex database. World bank policy research working paper (6025)
62. Diener E, Biswas-Diener R (2002) Will money increase subjective well-being? Soc Indic Res 57(2):119–169
63. Dixon-Woods M, Bonas S, Booth A, Jones DR, Miller T, Sutton AJ, Young B (2006) How can systematic reviews incorporate qualitative research? a critical perspective. Qual Res 6(1):27–44
64. Douissa IB (2020) Factors affecting College students' multidimensional financial literacy in the Middle East. Int Rev Econ Educ 35:100173
65. Downs C, Woolrych R (2010) Gambling and debt: the hidden impacts on family and work life. Commun Work Fam 13(3):311–328
66. Duflo E, Saez E (2003) The role of information and social interactions in retirement plan decisions: evidence from a randomized experiment. Q J Econ 118(3):815–842
67. Dupas P, Robinson J (2013) Savings constraints and microenterprise development: evidence from a field experiment in Kenya. Am Econ J Appl Econ 5(1):163–192
68. Education Commission (2019) Best practices for financial literacy and education at institutions of higher education
69. Engelbrecht L (2008) The scope of financial literacy education: a poverty alleviation tool in social work? Soc Work/Maatskaplike Werk 44(3)

70. Engels C, Kumar K, Philip D (2020) Financial literacy and fraud detection. Eur J Finance 26(4–5):420–442
71. FINRA Investor Education Foundation (2013) Financial capability in the United States: report of findings from the 2012 national financial capability study. FINRA Investor Education Foundation, Washington, DC
72. Farrell L, Fry TR, Risse L (2016) The significance of financial self-efficacy in explaining women's personal finance behaviour. J Econ Psychol 54:85–99
73. Fatoki O, Oni O (2014) Financial literacy studies in South Africa: Current literature and research opportunities. Mediterr J Soc Sci 5(20):409
74. Faulkner A (2022) Financial literacy around the world: what we can learn from the national strategies and contexts of the top ten most financially literate nations. Ref Libr 63(1–2):1–28
75. Fernandes D, Lynch JG Jr, Netemeyer RG (2014) Financial literacy, financial education, and downstream financial behaviors. Manage Sci 60(8):1861–1883
76. Financial resilience. Mind Soc 20:181–187
77. Finke MS, Howe JS, Huston SJ (2017) Old age and the decline in financial literacy. Manage Sci 63(1):213–230
78. Fitri FA, Syukur M, Justisa G (2019) Do the fraud triangle components motivate fraud in Indonesia? Australas Account Bus Finance J 13(4):63–72
79. Fornero E, Prete AL, Oggero N (2021) Now more than ever: why financial literacy is a key element of post-COVID-19 recovery. In: The Routledge handbook of financial literacy. Routledge, pp 137–152
80. Frame WS, Wall L, White LJ (2019) Technological change and financial innovation in banking: some implications for fintech. In: Berger A, Molyneux P, Wilson JOS (eds) Oxford handbook of banking, 3rd edn. Oxford University Press, Oxford, pp 262–284
81. Frijns B, Gilbert A, Tourani-Rad A (2014) Learning by doing: the role of financial experience in financial literacy. J Publ Policy 34(1):123–154
82. Fry-McKibbin R, Hsiao CYL, Tang C (2014) Contagion and global financial crises: lessons from nine crisis episodes. Open Econ Rev 25(3):521–570
83. Gaigalienė A, Legenzova R (2019) Insights on financial autonomy of Lithuanian high school students. In: Ribeiro H, Costa M, Cerovic L (eds) Economic and social development: 43rd international scientific conference. Rethinking management in the digital era: challenges from industry 4.0 to retail management, Aveiro, 15–16 July 2019. Varazdin: Varazdin Development and Entrepreneurship Agency, [no 43]. Varazdin: Varazdin Development and Entrepreneurship Agency
84. Gamble KJ, Boyle PA, Yu L, Bennett DA (2015) Aging and financial decision making. Manage Sci 61(11):2603–2610
85. Garman ET, Kim J, Kratzer CY, Brunson BH, Joo SH (1999) Workplace financial education improves personal financial wellness. Financ Couns Plan 10(1):79–88
86. Garman ET, Leech IE, Grable JE (1996) The negative impact of employee poor personal financial behaviors on employers. Finan Couns Plan 7:157–168
87. Gatto A, Sadik-Zada ER (2021) Revisiting the East Asian financial crises: lessons from ethics and development patterns. In: Economic growth and financial development. Springer, Cham, pp 23–31
88. Gibson-Davis CM, Edin K, McLanahan S (2005) High hopes but even higher expectations: the retreat from marriage among low-income couples. J Marriage Fam 67(5):1301–1312
89. Goldfayn-Frank O (2018) Personality traits and financial decisions of the households. Available at SSRN 2764175
90. Goyal K, Kumar S (2021) Financial literacy: a systematic review and bibliometric analysis. Int J Consum Stud 45(1):80–105
91. Grohmann A (2018) Financial literacy and financial behavior: evidence from the emerging Asian middle class. Pac Basin Financ J 48:129–143
92. Grohmann A, Hübler O, Kouwenberg R, Menkhoff L (2021) Financial literacy: Thai middle-class women do not lag behind. J Behav Exp Financ 31:100537

93. Gudmunson CG, Danes SM (2011) Family financial socialization: theory and critical review. J Fam Econ Issues 32(4):644–667. https://doi.org/10.1007/s10834-011-9275-y
94. Guiso L, Jappelli T (2008) The role of intuition and reasoning in driving aversion to risk, aversion to ambiguity and regret. Mimeo
95. Haldar A, Stiglitz JE (2014) The Indian microfinance crisis: the role of social capital, the shift to for-profit lending and implications for microfinance theory and practice. Columbia University, New York, NY
96. Hasler A, Lusardi A, Oggero N (2018) Financial fragility in the US: evidence and implications. Global Financial Literacy Excellence Center, The George Washington University School of Business, Washington, DC
97. Hastings J, Mitchell OS (2020) How financial literacy and impatience shape retirement wealth and investment behaviors. J Pension Econo Finance 19(1):1–20
98. Herd P, Holden K (2010) Early-life schooling and cognition and late-life financial literacy in the Wisconsin longitudinal study. Center Financ Secur WP 10:1
99. Hilgert MA, Hogarth JM, Beverly SG (2003) Household financial management: the connection between knowledge and behavior. Fed Res Bull 89:309
100. Himmelweit S, Santos C, Sevilla A, Sofer C (2013) Sharing of resources within the family and the economics of household decision making. J Marriage Fam 75(3):625–639
101. Hirad A, Zorn P (2002) Prepurchase homeownership counselling: a little knowledge is a good thing. Low-income homeownership: examining the unexamined goal, pp 146–174
102. Hogarth JM (2006) Financial education and economic development. In: G8 international conference on improving financial literacy
103. Holzmann R (2010) Bringing financial literacy and education to low and middle income countries: the need to review, adjust, and extend current wisdom
104. Huang H, Yuan J, Lin G, Chi J (2020) Underestimation of financial literacy and financial market participation. J Asia Pac Econ 1–26
105. Huddleston-Casas CA, Danes SM, Boyce LM (1999) Impact evaluation of a financial literacy program: evidence for needed educational policy changes. Consum Interes Annu 45:109–114
106. Hung AA, Yoong JK (2010) Federal financial and economic literacy education programs, 2009. RAND Corporation
107. Hussain J, Salia S, Karim A (2018) Is knowledge that powerful? Financial literacy and access to finance: an analysis of enterprises in the UK. J Small Bus Enterp Dev
108. Huston S (2010) Measuring financial literacy. J Consum Aff 44(2):296316
109. Jamal Mohammed EA, Madya Salniza Bt MS, Sanuri S, Bin MM (2018) The effect of family, peer, behavior, saving and spending behavior on financial literacy among young generations. Int J Organ Leadersh 7(3):309–323
110. Jappelli T, Padula M (2011) Investment in financial knowledge and saving decisions. CSEF Working Paper 272, University of Salerno
111. Jere B, Mitchell Olivia S, Cindy S, David B (2010) Financial literacy, schooling, and wealth accumulation. Am Econ Rev 102(3):300–304
112. Johan I, Rowlingson K, Appleyard L (2021) The effect of personal finance education on the financial knowledge, attitudes and behaviour of university students in Indonesia. J Fam Econ Issues 42(2):351–367
113. Joo S, Grable J (2004) An exploratory framework of the determinants of financial satisfaction. J Family Econ Issues 25(1):25–50
114. Jorgensen BL, Allsop DB, Runyan SD, Wheeler BE, Evans DA, Marks LD (2019) Forming financial vision: how parents prepare young adults for financial success. J Fam Econ Issues 40(3):553–563. https://doi.org/10.1007/s10834-019-09624-4
115. Kabeer N (2005) Is microfinance a 'magic bullet' for women's empowerment? analysis of findings from South Asia. Econ Political Wkly 4709–4718
116. Kadoya Y, Khan MSR (2020) What determines financial literacy in Japan? J Pension Econ Finance 19(3):353–371
117. Kahn JA, Kay BS (2019) The impact of credit risk mispricing on mortgage lending during the subprime boom. Available at SSRN 3363772

118. Kaiser T, Lusardi A, Menkhoff L, Urban C (2022) Financial education affects financial knowledge and downstream behaviors. J Financ Econ 145(2):255–272
119. Kaiser T, Menkhoff L (2020) Financial education in schools: a meta-analysis of experimental studies. Econ Educ Rev 78:101930
120. Karakurum-Ozdemir K, Kokkizil M, Uysal G (2019) Financial literacy in developing countries. Soc Indic Res 143(1):325–353
121. Khairani L, Pulungan DR, Pulungan DA (2019) The role of social capital as a mediator of relationship between financial literacy and financial inclusion of student. In: ICASI 2019: proceedings of the 2nd international conference on advance and scientific innovation, ICASI 2019, 18 July, Banda Aceh, Indonesia, p 8
122. Khan R, Khurshid A (2018) Parents as socialization agent in creating financial literacy among Pakistani young consumers. J Bus Econ 10(1):64–82
123. Khan F, Surisetti S (2021) Financial well-being of working women mediating effect of cashless financial experience and digital financial self-socialization. MDIM Bus Rev I(II):51–68
124. Khan F, Surisetti S (2022) Is woman a homogeneous category? understanding latent factors of financial literacy and financial well-being. In: Mahajan V, Chowdhury A, Kaushal U, Jariwala N, Bong SA (eds) Gender equity: challenges and opportunities. Springer, Singapore. https://doi.org/10.1007/978-981-19-0460-8_23
125. Kim M, Choi S, Lee J (2017) Economic system and financial literacy: evidence from North Korean refugees. Emerg Mark Financ Trade 53(11):2505–2527
126. Kimball M, Shumway T (2007) Investor sophistication and the home bias, diversification, and employer stock puzzles. University of Michigan, Mimeo
127. Klapper L, Lusardi A (2020) Financial literacy and financial resilience: evidence from around the world. Financ Manage 49(3):589–614
128. Klapper L, Panos GA (2011) Financial literacy and retirement planning: the Russian case. J Pension Econ Finance 10(4):599–618
129. Kling G (2020) Measuring financial exclusion of firms. Financ Res Lett. https://doi.org/10.1016/j.frl.2020.101568
130. Konow J, Earley J (2008) The hedonistic paradox: is homo economicus happier? J Public Econ 92(1–2):1–33
131. Kukreja R, Kumar P (2013) Tied in a knot: cross-region marriages in Haryana and Rajasthan: implications for gender rights and gender relations. Tamarind Tree Films, Kingston and New Delhi
132. Kumar A, Das R, Aditya KS, Bathla S, Jha GK (2020) Examining institutional credit access among agricultural households in Eastern India: trends, patterns and determinants. Agric Finance Rev
133. Kurowski Ł (2021) Household's over indebtedness during the COVID-19 crisis: the role of debt and financial literacy. Risks 9(4):62
134. Lea SE, Webley P (2006) Money as tool, money as drug: the biological psychology of a strong incentive. Behav Brain Sci 29(2):161–176
135. Lechman E, Marszk A (2019) ICT-driven economic and financial development: analyses of European countries. Academic Press
136. Legenzova R, Gaigalienė A, Leckė G (2019) Impact of parental financial socialization factors on financial literacy of Lithuanian high school students. Acta Prosper 10:41–60
137. Levine R (2005) Finance and growth: theory and evidence. In: Aghion P, Durlauf SN (eds) Handbook of economic growth, vol 1A. Elsevier, Amsterdam, pp 865–934
138. Littlefield E, Morduch J, Hashemi S (2003) Is microfinance an effective strategy to reach the Millennium development goals. Focus note 24(2003):1–11
139. Litvack K (2013) OECD Russia corporate governance roundtable. In: May 2013 technical seminar background paper
140. Lusardi A (2019) Financial literacy and the need for financial education: evidence and implications. Swiss J Econ Stat 155(1):1–8
141. Lusardi A, Mitchell OS (2008) Planning and financial literacy: how do women fare? Am Econ Rev 98(2):413–417

142. Lusardi A, Mitchell OS (2011) Financial literacy around the world: an overview. J Pension Econ Finance 10(04):497–508. https://doi.org/10.1017/S1474747211000448
143. Lusardi A, Mitchell OS (2011) Financial literacy and retirement planning in the United States. J Pension Econ Finance 10(4):509–525. https://doi.org/10.1017/S147474721100045X
144. Lusardi A, Tufano P (2009) Teach workers about the perils of debt. Harv Bus Rev 87(11):22–24
145. Lusardi A, Tufano P (2015) Debt literacy, financial experiences, and over indebtedness. J Pension Econ Finance 14(4):332–368
146. Lusardi A (2006) Financial literacy and financial education: review and policy implications. NFI Policy Brief (2006-PB) 11
147. Lusardi A, Hasler A, Yakoboski PJ (2020) Building up financial literacy and financial resilience. Mind Soc 1–7. https://doi.org/10.1007/s11299-020-00246-0
148. Lusardi A, Hasler A, Yakoboski PJ (2021) Building up financial literacy
149. Lusardi A, Keller P, Keller A (2008) New ways to make people save: a social marketing approach (No. w14715). Natl Bur Econ Res
150. Lusardi A, Michaud PC, Mitchell OS (2011) Optimal financial literacy and saving for retirement (September 3, 2011). RAND working paper series no. WR-905-SSA
151. Lusardi A, Mitchell OS (2007a) Baby boomer retirement security: the roles of planning, financial literacy, and housing wealth. J Monetary Econ 54(1):205–224
152. Lusardi A, Mitchell OS (2007b) Financial literacy and retirement planning: new evidence from the Rand American life panel. Mich Retirement Res Center Res Paper No WP 157
153. Lyons AC, Kass-Hanna J (2021) A multidimensional approach to defining and measuring financial literacy in the digital age. In: The Routledge handbook of financial literacy. Routledge, pp 61–76
154. Mackenzie C, Louth J (2020) The neoliberal production of deserving and undeserving poor: a critique of the Australian experience of microfinance. Soc Policy Soc 19(1):19–35
155. Mader P (2014) Financialisation through microfinance: civil society and market-building in India. Asian Stud Rev 38(4):601–619
156. Mader P (2018) Contesting financial inclusion. Dev Chang 49(2):461–483. https://doi.org/10.1111/dech.12368
157. Mahapatra MS, Alok S, Raveendran J (2017) Financial literacy of Indian youth: a study on the twin cities of hyderabad-secunderabad. IIM Kozhikode Soc Manage Rev 6(2):132–147
158. Mandell L (2006) Teaching young dogs old tricks: the effectiveness of financial literacy intervention in prehigh school grades. In: Academy of financial services 2006 annual conference, Salt Lake City, UT
159. Mandell L (2008) Financial literacy of high school students. In: Handbook of consumer finance research. Springer, New York, NY, pp 163–183
160. Mandell L, Klein LS (2009) The impact of financial literacy education on subsequent financial behavior. J Financ Couns Plan 20(1)
161. Marron D (2014) Informed, educated and more confident: financial capability and the problematization of personal finance consumption. Consum Mark Cult 17(5):491–511
162. Mathavathani V, Velumani M (2014) A study on financial literacy among rural women in Tamil Nadu. Ind J Appl Res 4(12):556–557
163. Messy FA, Monticone C (2012) The status of financial education in Africa
164. Messy FA, Monticone C (2016) Financial education policies in Asia and the Pacific. OECD. Working Papers on Finance, Insurance and Private Pensions No 40. OECD Publishing, Paris
165. Michael Collins J, Urban C (2020) Measuring financial well-being over the lifecourse. Eur J Finance 26(4–5):341–359
166. Mill JS (1967) On the definition of political economy; and on the method of investigation proper to it, London and Westminster Review, October 1836. Reprint, Mill, essays on some unsettled questions of political economy. 1844. Reprint, Collected works, vol 4. University of Toronto Press, Toronto, pp 120–164
167. Modigliani F, Ando AK (1957) Tests of the life cycle hypothesis of savings: comments and suggestions 1. Bull Oxf Univ Inst Econ Stat 19(2):99–124

168. Modigliani F, Brumberg R (1954) Utility analysis and the consumption function: an interpretation of cross-section data. Franco Modigliani 1(1):388–436
169. Monticone C (2015) Gender and financial literacy. OECD
170. Moore D (2003) Survey of financial literacy in Washington State: knowledge, behavior, attitudes and experiences. Technical Report No 03–39. Washington, D.C.: Social and Economic Sciences Research Center Washington State University
171. Moschis GP, Churchill GA Jr (1978) Consumer socialization: a theoretical and empirical analysis. J Mark Res 15(4):599–609
172. Mottola GR (2013) In our best interest: Women, financial literacy, and credit card behavior. Numeracy 6(2):4
173. Mpaata E, Koskei N, Saina E (2020) Financial literacy and saving behavior among micro and small enterprise owners in Kampala, Uganda: the moderating role of social influence. J Econ Finance Account Stud 2(1):22–34
174. Muir T (2017) Financial crises and risk premia. Q J Econ 132(2):765–809
175. Nanziri EL, Leibbrandt M (2018) Measuring and profiling financial literacy in South Africa. S Afr J Econ Manag Sci 21(1):1–17
176. National Family Health Survey, India (2006) https://dhsprogram.com/pubs/pdf/frind3/frind3-vol1andvol2.pdf
177. National Family Health Survey, India (2016). http://rchiips.org/nfhs/factsheet_nfhs-4.shtml
178. Van Nguyen H, Ha GH, Nguyen DN, Doan AH, Phan HT (2022) Understanding financial literacy and associated factors among adult population in a low-middle income country. Heliyon 8(6):e09638
179. Nikore M (2016) Assessing the impact of demonetization through the gender lens. South Asia@ London School of Economics
180. Niu G, Zhou Y, Gan H (2020) Financial literacy and retirement preparation in China. Pac Basin Financ J 59:101262
181. Nöth M, Puhan TX (2009) How to hide mutual fund fees-experimental evidence. Working paper, University of Hanburg
182. OECD (2022) OECD/INFE toolkit for measuring financial literacy and financial inclusion 2022. www.oecd.org/financial/education/2022-INFE-Toolkit-Measuring-Finlit-Financial-Inclusion.pdf
183. OECD (2005) Improving financial literacy: Analysis of issues and policies. OECD, Paris
184. OECD (2013) Financial literacy framework. In: PISA 2012 assessment and analytical framework: mathematics, reading, science, problem solving and financial literacy. OECD Publishing, Paris
185. OECD (2020) OECD/INFE 2020 international survey of adult financial literacy. https://www.oecd.org/financial/education/oecd-infe-2020-international-survey-of-adult-financial-literacy.pdf
186. Okumu M, Ansong D, Koomson I, Chen DG (2021) How financial resilience shapes social and public health policy choices in sub-Saharan Africa: empirical insights from the COVID-19 pandemic. J Soc Soc Work Res
187. Parker AM, De Bruin WB, Yoong J, Willis R (2012) Inappropriate confidence and retirement planning: four studies with a national sample. J Behav Decis Mak 25(4):382–389
188. Peng T-C, Bartholomae S, Fox JJ, Cravener G (2007) The impact of personal finance education delivered in high school and college courses. J Fam Econ Issues 28(2):265–284
189. Petrogiannis K (2011) Conceptions of the transition to adulthood in a sample of Greek higher education students. Int J Psychol Psychol Ther 11(1):121–137
190. Pitt MM, Khandker SR (1998) The impact of group-based credit programs on poor households in Bangladesh: does the gender of participants matter? J Polit Econ 106(5):958–996
191. Porter NM (1990) Testing a model of financial well-being. Virginia Polytechnic Institute and State University
192. Prabhakar K, Latha KL, Rao AP (2010) Empowerment of women through self-help groups (SHGs): a case study of Viswa Santhi Balananda Kendram (VSBK). Stud Home Community Sci 4(3):133–136

193. Prawitz A, Garman ET, Sorhaindo B, O'Neill B, Kim J, Drentea P (2006) InCharge financial distress/financial well-being scale: development, administration, and score interpretation. J Financ Couns Plan 17(1)
194. RBI (2012) National strategy for financial education. Reserve Bank of India. http://rbidocs.rbi.org.in/rdocs/PublicationReport/Pdfs/NSFE016072012.pdf
195. Rahardjo K (2021) The effect of social capital on financial literacy of small businesses in Malang, East Java. In: 3rd annual international conference on public and business administration (AICoBPA 2020). Atlantis Press, pp 30–33
196. Rai K, Dua S, Yadav M (2019) Association of financial attitude, financial behaviour and financial knowledge towards financial literacy: a structural equation modelling approach. FIIB Bus Rev 8(1):51–60. https://doi.org/10.1177/2319714519826651
197. Rashid KFM, Surisetti S (2018) Financial literacy of women in Hyderabad: an exploratory study. ASCI J Manage 47
198. Rashid KFM (2016) Risk concerns of Indian microfinance industry. Fraudulent Financial Practices in Indian capital market—issues and concerns, vol II, pp 1–14. ISBN: 978-93-85518-05-8
199. Reed M, Cochrane D (2012) Student debt and the class of 2011. The Institute of College Access & Success
200. Van Rooij MC, Lusardi A, Alessie RJ (2011) Financial literacy and retirement planning in the Netherlands. J Econ Psychol 32(4):593–608
201. Van Rooij M, Lusardi A, Alessie R (2011) Financial literacy and stock market participation. J Financ Econ 101(2):449–472
202. Santos AC (2017) Cultivating the self-reliant and responsible individual: the material culture of financial literacy. New Polit Econ 22(4):410–422
203. Saravanan S (2010) Violence against women in India: a literature review. Institute of Social Studies Trust
204. Seccombe K (2000) Families in poverty in the 1990s: Trends, causes, consequences, and lessons learned. J Marriage Fam 62(4):1094–1113
205. Sen A (1983) Development: which way now? Econ J 93(372):745–762
206. Sen A (1983) Liberty and social choice. J Philos 80(1):5–28
207. Settersten RA (2012) The contemporary context of young adulthood in the USA: from demography to development, from private troubles to public issues. In: Early adulthood in a family context. Springer, New York, NY, pp 3–26
208. Sevim N, Temizel F, Sayılır Ö (2012) The effects of financial literacy on the borrowing behaviour of Turkish financial consumers. Int J Consum Stud 36(5):573–579
209. Sexton TL (2016) Incarceration as a family affair: thinking beyond the individual. Couple Fam Psychol Res Pract 5(2):61
210. Shim S, Xiao JJ, Barber BL, Lyons AC (2009) Pathways to life success: a conceptual model of financial well-being for young adults. J Appl Dev Psychol 30(6):708–723
211. Sirsch U, Dreher E, Mayr E, Willinger U (2009) What does it take to be an adult in Austria? views of adulthood in Austrian adolescents, emerging adults, and adults. J Adolesc Res 24(3):275–292
212. Sivaramakrishnan S, Srivastava M, Rastogi A (2017) Attitudinal factors, financial literacy, and stock market participation. Int J Bank Market 35(5):818–841. https://doi.org/10.1108/IJBM-01-2016-0012
213. Sohn SH, Joo SH, Grable JE, Lee S, Kim M (2012) Adolescents' financial literacy: the role of financial socialization agents, financial experiences, and money attitudes in shaping financial literacy among South Korean youth. J Adolesc 35(4):969980
214. Sood P, Bhushan P (2020) A structured review and theme analysis of financial frauds in the banking industry. Asian J Bus Ethics 9(2):305–321
215. Statista (2022) Financial Markets: statistics and facts. Statista.com. https://www.statista.com/topics/1165/financial-markets/#topicOverview
216. Storm S (2018) Financialization and economic development: a debate on the social efficiency of modern finance. Dev Chang 49(2):302–329

217. Surendar G, Sarma S (2018) Financial literacy and financial planning among teachers of higher education a study of critical factors of select variables. Int J Pure Appl Mathem 118(18):1627–1649
218. Tambunan T (2015). Financial inclusion, financial education, and financial regulation: a story from Indonesia.
219. Todd H (2001) 'Paths out of poverty: the impacts of SHARE Microfin Ltd. in Andhra Pradesh', Imp-Act report
220. Townsend RM (2003) Microcredit and mechanism design. J Europ Econ Assoc 1(2–3):468–477
221. Van Rooij M, Lusardi A, Alessie R (2007) Financial literacy and stock market participation, NBER Working Paper No. 13565. National Bureau of Economic Research, Cambridge, MA
222. Van Rooij MC, Lusardi A, Alessie RJ (2012) Financial literacy, retirement planning and household wealth. Econ J 122(560):449–478
223. Vatuk VP, Vatuk S (1971) On a system of private savings among North Indian village women. J Asian Afr Stud 6(3):179
224. Verhoef G (2001) Informal financial service institutions for survival: African women and stokvels in urban South Africa, 1930–1998. Enterp Soc 2(2):259–296
225. Wagner J (2019) Financial education and financial literacy by income and education groups. J Financ Couns Plann 30(1):132–141
226. Waite L, Gallagher M (2001) The case for marriage: why married people are happier, healthier and better off financially. Crown
227. Ward S (1974) Consumer socialization. J Consum Res 1(2):1–14
228. Watkins KE, Marsick VJ (2009) Trends in lifelong learning in the US workplace. In The Routledge international handbook of lifelong learning. Routledge, pp. 129–138
229. Wee BV, Banister D (2016) How to write a literature review paper? Transp Rev 36(2):278–288. https://doi.org/10.1080/01441647.2015.1065456
230. West J (2012) Financial literacy education and behaviour unhinged: combating bias and poor product design. Int J Consum Stud 36(5):523–530. https://doi.org/10.1111/j.1470-6431.2012.01118.x
231. Williams T (2007) Empowerment of whom and for what? Financial literacy education and the new regulation of consumer financial services. Law & Policy 29(2):226–256
232. Worthington AC (2013) Financial literacy and financial literacy programmes in Australia. J Financ Serv Market 18(3):227–240
233. Yeh TM, Ling Y (2022) Confidence in financial literacy, stock market participation, and retirement planning. J Fam Econ Issues 43(1):169–186
234. Yeo J, Lee YG (2019) Understanding the association between perceived financial well-being and life satisfaction among older adults: does social capital play a role? J Fam Econ Issues 40(4):592–608
235. Zaman H (1999) 'Assessing the impact of microcredit on poverty and vulnerability in Bangladesh', policy research working paper 2145. World Bank, Washington
236. Zhu AYF (2020) Financial literacy types and financial behaviors among adolescents: role of financial education. J Financ Couns Plan

The manufacturer's authorised representative in the EU is Springer Nature Customer Service Centre GmbH, Europaplatz 3, 69115 Heidelberg, Germany. If you have any concerns regarding our products, please contact ProductSafety@springernature.com

Printed and bound by CPI Group (UK) Ltd, Croydon, CR0 4YY
01/10/2026
02226215-0002